H. Butterworth,

from

Cis.

April '98.

THE POETICAL
WORKS OF

JOHN *

* MILTON

Lemerciergravure Printed in Paris

John Milton

After the portrait by Pieter Van der Plaas

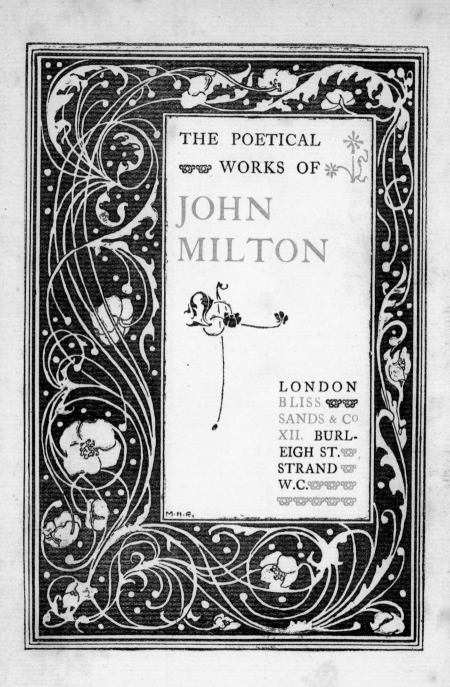

THE POETICAL
WORKS OF
JOHN
MILTON

LONDON
BLISS
SANDS & Co
XII. BURL-
EIGH ST.
STRAND
W.C.

M.H.R.

PREFACE.

More than two centuries and a quarter have passed away since the first edition of "Paradise Lost" was issued from the press of Samuel Simmons, next door to the "Golden Lion" in Aldersgate Street; and from that time to the present there has never been a period of any length when new editions of Milton's works were not passing through the press.

At least nine editions of "Paradise Lost" alone had been published before the famous review of the poem by Addison, which ran through the "Spectator" between January the 5th and May the 3rd, 1712—forty-five years after the poem's first appearance—gave a fresh impetus to the sale, and this in spite of a political bias, which more than all other prejudices affects Englishmen's views of men and matters. This bias lasted even to the time of that master of prejudice, Doctor Johnson, of whom Boswell writes: "His just abhorrence of Milton's political notions was ever strong. But this did not prevent his warm admiration of Milton's great poetical merit, to which he has done illustrious justice, beyond all who have written upon the subject."

Whether he be read or only admired, the demand for his works marches with the growth of population, despite the change of thought which renders the whole basis of his great epic poem, which to him and to his contemporaries was so real, to the modern reader almost as legendary as the "History of King Arthur and his Knights," which Milton first proposed to take for his subject and afterwards rejected.

PREFACE

But above and beyond all changes in human ideas the delight in the

"—— *voice whose sound was like the sea:*
Pure as the naked heavens, majestic, free,"

lives on, fulfilling that devout hope of the author, that "by labour and intent study (which I take to be my portion in this life), joined with the strong propensity of nature, I might perhaps leave something so written to after times, as they should not willingly let it die."

CONTENTS.

CONTENTS

BIOGRAPHICAL NOTE.

Comus, Arcades, Lycidas, L'Allegro, and *Il Penseroso*, and, with the exception of the Sonnets and Translations, nearly all Milton's Minor Poems, were written before he was thirty. It was probably in 1658, when he was in the fiftieth year of his life, and had been for six years totally blind, that he commenced his great Poem, *Paradise Lost;* and it was in 1665, within nine years of his death, that it was ready for the press. *Paradise Lost* was followed by *Paradise Regained* and *Samson Agonistes.* For twenty years in the middle of his life, save for an occasional sonnet, he did not compose a line of poetry.

Milton's life, then, seems to separate itself into three distinct parts, each complete in itself; but such apparent divisions in men's lives are nearly always deceptive. The parts are so interlinked with one another, the whole is so dependent on the parts, that there is no room for dividing lines.

By the time he had left Cambridge Milton had made up his mind that poetry was to be the vocation of his life, and very soon *Paradise Lost* had taken a prominent place in his mind as the subject of his great work, though he confesses that "industrious and select reading, steady observation, insight into all seemly and generous arts and affairs," are necessary conditions before he should be fit to carry out his undertaking.

The serious manner in which Milton speaks of his life-work is but a reflection of the tone of mind of a growing number of his countrymen. "The age of the Renascence," says J. R. Green, "was passing into the age of Puritanism. A sterner Protestantism was invigorating and ennobling life by its morality, its seriousness, its intense conviction of God. But it was at the same time hardening and narrowing it. The Bible was superseding Plutarch. The 'obstinate questionings' which haunted the finer souls of the Renascence were being stereotyped into the theological formula of the Puritans. The sense of a divine omnipotence was annihilating man. The daring which turned England into a people of 'adventurers,' the sense of inexhaustible resources, the buoyant freshness of youth, the intoxicating sense of beauty and joy, which created Sydney, and Marlow, and Drake, were passing away before the consciousness of evil, and the craving to order man's life aright before God."

Milton was not only the greatest of the Puritans, he was also the last of the Elizabethans.

On December the 9th, 1608, when he was born at his father's house in Bread Street, Cheapside, Shakespeare was about retiring from London to his old home at Stratford-on-Avon, leaving the sovereignty of the Wits at the "Mermaid Tavern" to his friend, Ben Jonson. *Coriolanus, The Winter's Tale, Cymbeline,* and *The Tempest* were probably still unwritten. Beaumont and Fletcher, Massinger and Ford, were still left to share with Ben Jonson the traditions of the Elizabethan writers.

But the younger generation of men, Pym, Hampden, and Cromwell, were cast in different mould, and at the "Spread Eagle" in Bread Street, as the house was distinguished in days before education rendered a name-plate a sufficient guide, the household was more in sympathy with the Reformers than the Wits. Here Milton's father, descended from a family of Oxfordshire yeomen, and cast off by his father for becoming a Protestant, carried on very successfully the business of scrivener.

The scrivener in the intervals of his business loved to exercise his talent for music. He was a composer of no mean order, and he taught his son both to sing and to play the organ. He spared neither pains nor expense in the education of his children. He engaged, as private tutor, Thomas Young, who became afterwards so prominent as an Anti-Episcopal controversialist; and, under his guidance and that of the two Gills of St. Paul's School, young John Milton became an enthusiastic scholar. "When he was very young," says Aubrey, "he studied very hard, and sate up very late, commonly till twelve or one o'clock at night; and his father ordered the maid to sit up for him."

In 1625, at the age of sixteen, he went up to Christ's College, Cambridge, where after some little trouble with his tutor, which led to a temporary absence in 1627, he took his degree of B.A. in 1628, and M.A. in 1632.

Milton was sent by his father to Cambridge to qualify for the Church, but he left the University in 1632 with a resolution almost formed not to take Orders. "The Church," he said afterwards, "to whose service by the intention of my parents and friends I was destined of a child, and in mine own resolutions, till coming to some maturity of years, and perceiving what tyranny had invaded in the Church, that he who would take orders must subscribe slave, and take an oath withal. . . . . I thought it better to prefer a blameless silence before the sacred office of speaking bought and begun with servitude and forswearing."

Milton's father had by this time retired from business with a sufficient fortune, and was living at Horton, a small village in Buckinghamshire, about four miles from Eton and Windsor. Whatever disappointment he may have felt at his son's decision with regard to the profession he had chosen for him, he behaved towards him in a sufficiently generous manner.

Poetry was Milton's deliberately chosen occupation, and his life at Horton was spent in meditation and reading with this object in view. "You make many inquiries as to what I am about," he wrote to Diodati. "What am I thinking of? Why, with God's help, of immortality! Forgive the word, I only whisper it in your ear! Yes, I am pluming my wings for a flight."

The five years that Milton lived at Horton were not years of preparation only. *L'Allegro, Il Penseroso, Lycidas*, and *Comus*, were all composed at this period. *Comus* was written at the request of Henry Lawes, the most popular composer of the day. Lawes had been applied to by the Earl of Bridgewater to provide an entertainment on the occasion of his entry upon the office of Lord President of Wales. The most fashionable form of entertainment of the time was the masque, and accordingly Lawes applied to Milton to write a masque. The performance was a magnificent one, and so great was the interest excited that Lawes was overwhelmed with requests for copies of the words, and, with Milton's consent, he had them printed in 1637.

Milton's mother died in 1637, and in the following year his father provided him with a sum sufficient for a visit to Italy—no inconsiderable amount in those days.

Returning to England at the end of 1639, he settled first in St. Bride's Church-yard, and afterwards in "a pretty garden-house in Aldersgate," where he undertook the charge of a few pupils, including his nephews, the sons of his sister, Anne Phillips. He was also preparing for publication a volume of poems.

This volume, which bore the title *Poems of Mr. John Milton, both English and Latin, compos'd at several times,* was published by Humphry Mosely, of St. Paul's Churchyard, in 1645, and with one or two exceptions contained all the poems written by Milton to that date.

In 1643, in the thirty-fifth year of his age, Milton married Mary, daughter of Richard Powell, a gentleman of the Royalist party living at Forest Hill, near Oxford. How he came to form so unpromising a union is unknown. Mary Powell was only seventeen, and possibly the Puritan strictness of Aldersgate Street, after the freedom of the Cavalier household, was distasteful to her. However it be, within a month of the marriage she left her husband and returned to her father's house. Milton sent a messenger to fetch her, but he was sent back with a contemptuous reply. The bitterness of Milton's feelings took the form of a pamphlet on *The Doctrine and Discipline of Divorce.* It was not until 1645, when the Royalist cause was declining, and the Powells were in financial difficulties, that they sought a reconciliation with Milton. Mary, by the connivance of friends of both parties, was secretly introduced to a house where he was visiting, and throwing herself at his feet begged for forgiveness. He not only freely forgave her, but took her whole family into his house. She bore him four children, and died in 1652, at the age of twenty-six.

England was now engaged in a pamphlet war, and into this battle, on the side of the Puritans, Milton threw himself with all the command he possessed over the resources of language. The great object of his life, the great poem that the world would not willingly let die, must wait. The assistance of his pen was required in the struggle for the liberty which was his creed, and he used it ungrudgingly, whether rising to the height of a prose style unequalled in the language, or descending to the lowest depths of scurrilous personal abuse.

On January the 30th, 1649, the King was beheaded at Whitehall; but the fall of the Monarchy did not release Milton from public affairs to the more congenial seclusion of his study. Six weeks after the King's death, the Council of State was formed to carry on the government. Of this Council a Committee of six were charged with the conduct of Foreign Affairs. The Committee required a Latin Secretary, and Milton was invited to accept the post.

It would have been well if he had made up his mind to decline the position. His eyes were already giving warning of the danger of over-use, and since his father's death in 1646 his circumstances had improved sufficiently to render him independent of the salary attached to the office. But the connection with the new Government of the country, even in that minor sphere, had some attraction for him, and he unhesitatingly accepted the offer, removing from Lincoln's Inn to Whitehall, and afterwards to a house in Petty France, overlooking St. James's Park.

His duties included, besides the translation of documents from foreign languages into English, and the conversion of the Council's correspondence with other nations into Latin, the task of replying to writers displeasing to the Government. In 1649 he was ordered to draw up a reply to *Eikon Basilike,* and he prepared his *Eikonoklastes.* In the following year he was directed to reply to Salmasius' *Defensio regia,* and accordingly he published his *Pro Populo Anglicano Defensio.*

He paid dearly for his industry. In 1650 he lost the use of the left eye, and, continuing his labour in spite of the warnings of the doctors, two years later, at the age of forty-three, he became totally blind.

Nothing daunted, however, the blind Secretary remained at his post, translating and pamphleteering, until the landing of Charles II. in May, 1660, and the restoration of the Monarchy sent him in hasty flight from his home in Petty France to the concealment of a friend's garret in Bartholomew Close.

The Royalists certainly had reason to dislike the man who had been put forward to justify the execution of the King, but with what vigour they pursued him is uncertain. His book was burnt by the executioner, but he himself seems to have escaped with a short imprisonment. In December, 1660, he was officially pardoned.

Thus at last the Poet was free to resume the vocation of his life after an interruption of fifteen years. His eyesight had gone in the service of the Commonwealth, and the greater part of his fortune was lost at the Restoration. Poor, solitary, blind,

> " . . . though fall'n on evil days,
> On evil days though fall'n, and evil tongues ;
> In darkness and with dangers compassed round
> And solitude,"

he was free to begin again in his fifty-third year—for though the work may have been commenced in the last year or two of his Secretaryship, the amount accomplished can have been but little—the task which he had set himself on leaving college.

For reading he was dependent on the kindness of friends. "He had daily about him," says his nephew Phillips, "one or other to read to him ; some persons of man's estate, who of their own accord greedily catch'd at the opportunity of being his reader, that they might as well reap the benefit of what they read to him as oblige him by the benefit of their reading ; others of younger years sent by their parents to the same end." Among these readers were Samuel Barrow, Cyriack Skinner, Phillips himself, and Ellwood the Quaker.

He was now living in a house in Jewin Street, near Aldersgate, with his three daughters, Mary, Deborah, and Anne, children of his first wife. Four years after their mother's death he had married a second wife, Catharine Woodcock, who, however, died within fifteen months of the marriage. In February, 1663, he was married again. His third wife was Elizabeth Minshull, of a respectable Cheshire family.

In 1665 the Plague broke out in London, and Milton wrote to his friend Ellwood, asking him to find him some convenient house in the country to which he might remove his family. Ellwood took for him a cottage in the village of Chalfont St. Giles, in the county of Buckingham, and here Milton remained until the Plague was abated.

At the time when Milton came to the village Ellwood had the misfortune to be in Aylesbury Gaol, whither he, with other Quakers, had been committed by some zealous magistrate. As soon as he was released he hastened to visit the Poet in his cottage. "After some common discourses," says Ellwood, "had past between us, he called for a manuscript of his, which, being brought, he delivered to me, bidding me take it home with me and read it at my leisure, and when I had so done, return it to him with my judgment thereupon. When I came home and set myself to read it, I found it was that excellent poem, which he entitled *Paradise Lost.*

The great poem, then, was completed in 1665. It was begun, says Aubrey, "about two years before the King came in"; that is in 1658, the fiftieth year of his life. According to Phillips it was dictated in small quantities, "ten, twenty, or thirty verses at a time," to whoever was at hand to act as amanuensis.

The Plague over, Milton returned to his house in Artillery Row, Bunhill Fields, whither he had removed after his marriage, and the manuscript was forwarded to the Archbishop of Canterbury to receive the necessary license for its publication. This, after some hesitation on the part of the Rev. Thomas Tomkyns, the Archbishop's Chaplain, who fancied he scented treason, having been granted, the manuscript was sent to the printer.

The agreement with the publisher, Simmons, was for five pounds down, five pounds after the sale of the first edition of thirteen hundred copies, and a further five pounds after the sale of each of two other editions of the same number.

The first edition was all sold within two years of publication, and on this Dr. Johnson remarks: "The call for books was not, in Milton's age, what it is at present; the nation had been satisfied from 1623 to 1664, that is forty-one years, with only two editions of the works of Shakespeare, which probably did not together make one thousand copies. The sale of thirteen hundred copies in two years, in opposition to so much recent enmity, and to a style of versification new to all and disgusting to many, was an uncommon example of the prevalence of genius."

Ellwood, having described how the manuscript of *Paradise Lost* was handed to him by Milton, proceeds as follows:—"After I had, with the best attention, read it through, I made him another visit, and returned him his book, with due acknowledgment of the favour he had done me in communicating it to me. He asked how I liked it, and what I thought of it; which I modestly but freely told him; and, after some further discourse about it, I pleasantly said to him, 'Thou hast said much here of *Paradise Lost*, but what hast thou to say of *Paradise Found?*' He made me no answer, but sate some time in a muse, then brake off that discourse and fell upon another subject. After the sickness was over, and the city well cleaned and become habitable again, he returned thither. And when afterwards I went to wait on him there (which I seldom failed of doing, whenever any occasion drew me to London), he shewed me his second poem, called *Paradise Regained*, and in a pleasant tone said to me, 'This is owing to you, for you put it into my head by the question you put to me at Chalfont, which before I had not thought of.'"

Paradise Regained was published in a volume with *Samson Agonistes* in 1671. Two years later, in 1673, appeared a second edition of the Minor Poems, containing all that was printed in the first edition twenty-eight years before, together with additional poems written since that date.

Of Milton's appearance in his last years we have the following description :—
"An ancient clergyman of Dorsetshire, Dr. Wright, found John Milton in a small chamber hung with rusty green, sitting in an elbow chair, and dressed neatly in black, pale but not cadaverous, his hands and fingers gouty, and with chalk stones.—He used also to sit in a gray coarse cloth coat at the door of his house near Bunhill Fields, in warm sunny weather, to enjoy the fresh air; and so, as well as in his room, received the visits of people of distinguished parts as well as quality."

"His domestic habits were those of a sober and temperate student. Of wine or of any strong liquors he drank little. In his diet he was rarely influenced by delicacy of choice. He once delighted in walking and every exercise, and appears to have amused himself in botanical pursuits; but after he was confined by age and blindness he had a machine to swing in for the preservation of his health. In summer he then rested in bed from nine to four, in winter to five. If at these hours he was not disposed to rise, he had a person by his bedside to read to him. When he first rose he heard a chapter in the Hebrew Bible, and commonly studied till twelve; then used some exercise for an hour, then dined; afterwards played on the organ or bass-viol, and either sung himself or made his wife sing, who, he said, had a good voice but no ear. After his regular indulgence in musical relaxation, he studied till six; then entertained his visitors till eight; then enjoyed a light supper; and after a pipe of tobacco and a glass of water, retired to bed."

In July, 1674, knowing that his life was drawing to a close, Milton sent for his brother Christopher, and dictated his will to the following effect :—"The portion due to me from Mr. Powell, my former wife's father, I leave to the unkind children I had by her, having received no parte of it; but my meaning is, they shall have no other benefit of my estate than the said portion, and what I have beside done for them, they having been very undutifull to me. All the residue of my estate I leave to the disposall of Elizabeth, my loving wife."

The cause of the disagreement between Milton and his daughters seems to have been that though he considered it unnecessary that they should learn any language but their own, saying that one tongue was enough for a woman, he yet expected them constantly to read to him in Italian, Spanish, French, Hebrew, Greek, and Latin, of which they understood not a word. The result was that they at last rebelled, and left his house.

On Sunday, the 8th of November, 1674, Milton died. He was buried next his father in the chancel of St. Giles', Cripplegate, being followed to the grave by "all his learned and great friends in London, not without a friendly concourse of the vulgar."

PARADISE LOST:

A POEM IN TWELVE BOOKS.

THE AUTHOR
JOHN MILTON.

THE VERSE.

THE measure is English heroic verse without rime, as that of Homer in Greek, and of Virgil in Latin—rime being no necessary adjunct or true ornament of poem or good verse, in longer works especially, but the invention of a barbarous age, to set off wretched matter and lame metre; graced indeed since by the use of some famous modern poets, carried away by custom, but much to their own vexation, hindrance, and constraint to express many things otherwise, and for the most part worse, than else they would have expressed them. Not without cause therefore some both Italian and Spanish poets of prime note have rejected rime both in longer and shorter works, as have also long since our best English tragedies, as a thing of itself, to all judicious ears, trivial and of no true musical delight; which consists only in apt numbers, fit quantity of syllables, and the sense variously drawn out from one verse into another, not in the jingling sound of like endings—a fault avoided by the learned ancients both in poetry and all good oratory. This neglect then of rime so little is to be taken for a defect, though it may seem so perhaps to vulgar readers, that it rather is to be esteemed an example set, the first in English, of ancient liberty recovered to heroic poem from the troublesome and modern bondage of riming.

THE POETICAL WORKS

OF

JOHN · MILTON.

PARADISE LOST.

BOOK I.

THE ARGUMENT.

THIS First Book proposes, first in brief, the whole subject—Man's disobedience, and the loss thereupon of Paradise, wherein he was placed: then touches the prime cause of his fall—the Serpent, or rather Satan in the Serpent; who, revolting from God, and drawing to his side many legions of Angels, was, by the command of God, driven out of Heaven, with all his crew, into the great Deep. Which action passed over, the Poem hastens into the midst of things; presenting Satan, with his Angels, now fallen into Hell—described here not in the Centre (for heaven and earth may be supposed as yet not made, certainly not yet accursed), but in a place of utter darkness, fitliest called Chaos. Here Satan, with his Angels lying on the burning lake, thunderstruck and astonished, after a certain space recovers, as from confusion; calls up him who, next in order and dignity, lay by him: they confer of their miserable fall. Satan awakens all his legions, who lay till then in the same manner confounded. They rise: their numbers; array of battle; their chief leaders named, according to the idols known afterwards in Canaan and the countries adjoining. To these Satan directs his speech; comforts them with hope yet of regaining Heaven; but tells them, lastly, of a new world and new kind of creature to be created, according to an ancient prophecy, or report, in Heaven—for that Angels were long before this visible creation was the opinion of many ancient Fathers. To find out the truth of this prophecy, and what to determine thereon, he refers to a full council. What his associates thence attempt. Pandemonium, the palace of Satan, rises, suddenly built out of the Deep: the infernal Peers there sit in council.

Of Man's first disobedience, and the fruit
Of that forbidden tree whose mortal taste
Brought death into the World, and all our woe,
With loss of Eden, till one greater Man
Restore us, and regain the blissful seat,
Sing, Heavenly Muse, that, on the secret top
Of Oreb, or of Sinai, didst inspire
That shepherd who first taught the chosen seed
In the beginning how the heavens and earth
Rose out of Chaos: or, if Sion hill
Delight thee more, and Siloa's brook that flowed
Fast by the oracle of God, I thence
Invoke thy aid to my adventrous song,
That with no middle flight intends to soar
Above the Aonian mount, while it pursues
Things unattempted yet in prose or rhyme.
And chiefly Thou, O Spirit, that dost prefer
Before all temples the upright heart and pure,
Instruct me, for Thou know'st; Thou from the first
Wast present, and, with mighty wings outspread,
Dove-like sat'st brooding on the vast Abyss,
And mad'st it pregnant: what in me is dark
Illumine, what is low raise and support;
That, to the highth of this great argument,
I may assert Eternal Providence,
And justify the ways of God to men.
　　Say first—for Heaven hides nothing from thy view,
Nor the deep tract of Hell—say first what cause
Moved our grand Parents, in that happy state,
Favoured of Heaven so highly, to fall off
From their Creator, and transgress His will
For one restraint, lords of the World besides.
Who first seduced them to that foul revolt?
　　The infernal Serpent; he it was whose guile,
Stirred up with envy and revenge, deceived
The mother of mankind, what time his pride
Had cast him out from Heaven, with all his host
Of rebel Angels, by whose aid, aspiring
To set himself in glory above his peers,
He trusted to have equalled the Most High,
If he opposed, and, with ambitious aim
Against the throne and monarchy of God,

6

Raised impious war in Heaven and battle proud,
With vain attempt. Him the Almighty Power
Hurled headlong flaming from the ethereal sky,
With hideous ruin and combustion, down
To bottomless perdition, there to dwell
In adamantine chains and penal fire,
Who durst defy the Omnipotent to arms.
　　Nine times the space that measures day and night
To mortal men, he, with his horrid crew,
Lay vanquished, rolling in the fiery gulf,
Confounded, though immortal. But his doom
Reserved him to more wrath; for now the thought
Both of lost happiness and lasting pain
Torments him: round he throws his baleful eyes,
That witnessed huge affliction and dismay,
Mixed with obdurate pride and steadfast hate.
At once, as far as Angel's ken, he views
The dismal situation waste and wild.
A dungeon horrible, on all sides round,
As one great furnace flamed; yet from those flames
No light; but rather darkness visible
Served only to discover sights of woe,
Regions of sorrow, doleful shades, where peace
And rest can never dwell, hope never comes
That comes to all, but torture without end
Still urges, and a fiery deluge, fed
With ever-burning sulphur unconsumed.
Such place Eternal Justice had prepared
For those rebellious; here their prison ordained
In utter darkness, and their portion set,
As far removed from God and light of Heaven
As from the centre thrice to the utmost pole.
Oh how unlike the place from whence they fell!
There the companions of his fall, o'erwhelmed
With floods and whirlwinds of tempestuous fire,
He soon discerns; and, weltering by his side,
One next himself in power, and next in crime,
Long after known in Palestine, and named
BEËLZEBUB. To whom the Arch-Enemy,
And thence in Heaven called SATAN, with bold words
Breaking the horrid silence, thus began :—
　　" If thou beest he—but Oh how fallen ! how changed
From him!—who, in the happy realms of light,
Clothed with transcendent brightness, didst outshine
Myriads, though bright—if he whom mutual league,
United thoughts and counsels, equal hope,
And hazard in the glorious enterprise,
Joined with me once, now misery hath joined
In equal ruin ; into what pit thou seest
From what highth fallen : so much the stronger proved
He with His thunder: and till then who knew
The force of those dire arms ? Yet not for those,
Nor what the potent Victor in His rage
Can else inflict, do I repent, or change,

Though changed in outward lustre, that fixed mind,
And high disdain from sense of injured merit,
That with the Mightiest raised me to contend,
And to the fierce contention brought along
Innumerable force of Spirits armed,
That durst dislike his reign, and, me preferring,
His utmost power with adverse power opposed
In dubious battle on the plains of Heaven,
And shook His throne.   What though the field be lost?
All is not lost—the unconquerable will,
And study of revenge, immortal hate,
And courage never to submit or yield :
And what is else not to be overcome.
That glory never shall His wrath or might
Extort from me.   To bow and sue for grace
With suppliant knee, and deify His power
Who, from the terror of this arm, so late
Doubted His empire—that were low indeed ;
That were an ignominy and shame beneath
This downfall ; since, by fate, the strength of Gods,
And this empyreal substance, cannot fail ;
Since, through experience of this great event,
In arms not worse, in foresight much advanced,
We may with more successful hope resolve
To wage by force or guile eternal war,
Irreconcilable to our grand Foe,
Who now triumphs, and in the excess of joy
Sole reigning holds the tyranny of heaven."

    So spake the apostate Angel, though in pain,
Vaunting aloud, but racked with deep despair ;
And him thus answered soon his bold compeer :—
    "O Prince, O Chief of many thronèd Powers
That led the embattled Seraphim to war
Under thy conduct, and, in dreadful deeds
Fearless, endangered Heaven's perpetual King,
And put to proof His high supremacy,
Whether upheld by strength, or chance, or fate !
Too well I see and rue the dire event
That, with sad overthrow and foul defeat,
Hath lost us Heaven, and all this mighty host
In horrible destruction laid thus low,
As far as Gods and Heavenly Essences
Can perish : for the mind and spirit remains
Invincible, and vigour soon returns,
Though all our glory extinct, and happy state
Here swallowed up in endless misery.
But what if He our Conqueror (whom I now
Of force believe almighty, since no less
Than such could have o'erpowered such force as ours)
Have left us this our spirit and strength entire,
Strongly to suffer and support our pains,
That we may so suffice His vengeful ire,
Or do Him mightier service as His thralls
By right of war, whate'er His business be,

8

Here in the heart of Hell to work in fire,
Or do His errands in the gloomy Deep?
What can it then avail though yet we feel
Strength undiminished, or eternal being
To undergo eternal punishment?"
    Whereto with speedy words the Arch-Fiend replied:—
"Fallen Cherub, to be weak is miserable,
Doing or suffering: but of this be sure—
To do aught good never will be our task,
But ever to do ill our sole delight,
As being the contrary to His high will
Whom we resist. If then His providence
Out of our evil seek to bring forth good,
Our labour must be to pervert that end,
And out of good still to find means of evil;
Which ofttimes may succeed so as perhaps
Shall grieve Him, if I fail not, and disturb
His inmost counsels from their destined aim.
But see! the angry Victor hath recalled
His ministers of vengeance and pursuit
Back to the gates of Heaven: the sulphurous hail,
Shot after us in storm, o'erblown hath laid
The fiery surge that from the precipice
Of Heaven received us falling; and the thunder,
Winged with red lightning and impetuous rage,
Perhaps hath spent his shafts, and ceases now
To bellow through the vast and boundless Deep.
Let us not slip the occasion, whether scorn
Or satiate fury yield it from our Foe.
Seest thou yon dreary plain, forlorn and wild,
The seat of desolation, void of light,
Save what the glimmering of these livid flames
Casts pale and dreadful? Thither let us tend
From off the tossing of these fiery waves;
There rest, if any rest can harbour there;
And, re-assembling our afflicted powers,
Consult how we may henceforth most offend
Our enemy, our own loss how repair,
How overcome this dire calamity,
What reinforcement we may gain from hope,
If not what resolution from despair."
    Thus Satan, talking to his nearest mate,
With head uplift above the wave, and eyes
That sparkling blazed; his other parts besides
Prone on the flood, extended long and large,
Lay floating many a rood, in bulk as huge
As whom the fables name of monstrous size,
Titanian or Earth-born, that warred on Jove,
Briareos or Typhon, whom the den
By ancient Tarsus held, or that sea-beast
Leviathan, which God of all His works
Created hugest that swim the ocean-stream.
Him, haply slumbering on the Norway foam,
The pilot of some small night-foundered skiff,

9

Deeming some island, oft, as seamen tell,
With fixèd anchor in his scaly rind,
Moors by his side under the lee, while night
Invests the sea, and wishèd morn delays.
So stretched out huge in length the Arch-Fiend lay,
Chained on the burning lake; nor ever thence
Had risen, or heaved his head, but that the will
And high permission of all-ruling Heaven
Left him at large to his own dark designs,
That with reiterated crimes he might
Heap on himself damnation, while he sought
Evil to others, and enraged might see
How all his malice served but to bring forth
Infinite goodness, grace, and mercy, shewn
On Man by him seduced, but on himself
Treble confusion, wrath, and vengeance poured.
    Forthwith upright he rears from off the pool
His mighty stature; on each hand the flames
Driven backward slope their pointing spires, and, rolled
In billows, leave i' the midst a horrid vale.
Then with expanded wings he steers his flight
Aloft, incumbent on the dusky air,
That felt unusual weight; till on dry land
He lights—if it were land that ever burned
With solid, as the lake with liquid fire,
And such appeared in hue as when the force
Of subterranean wind transports a hill
Torn from Pelorus, or the shattered side
Of thundering Ætna, whose combustible
And fuelled entrails, thence conceiving fire,
Sublimed with mineral fury, aid the winds,
And leave a singèd bottom all involved
With stench and smoke.   Such resting found the sole
Of unblest feet.   Him followed his next mate;
Both glorying to have scaped the Stygian flood
As gods, and by their own recovered strength,
Not by the sufferance of supernal power.
    "Is this the region, this the soil, the clime,"
Said then the lost Archangel, "this the seat
That we must change for Heaven?—this mournful gloom
For that celestial light?   Be it so, since He
Who now is sovran can dispose and bid
What shall be right: farthest from Him is best,
Whom reason hath equalled, force hath made supreme
Above His equals.   Farewell, happy fields,
Where joy for ever dwells!   Hail, horrors! hail,
Infernal World! and thou, profoundest Hell,
Receive thy new possessor—one who brings
A mind not to be changed by place or time.
The mind is its own place, and in itself
Can make a Heaven of Hell, a Hell of Heaven.
What matter where, if I be still the same,
And what I should be, all but less than He
Whom thunder hath made greater?   Here at least

We shall be free; the Almighty hath not built
Here for His envy, will not drive us hence:
Here we may reign secure; and, in my choice,
To reign is worth ambition, though in Hell:
Better to reign in Hell than serve in Heaven.
But wherefore let we then our faithful friends,
The associates and co-partners of our loss,
Lie thus astonished on the oblivious pool,
And call them not to share with us their part
In this unhappy mansion, or once more
With rallied arms to try what may be yet
Regained in Heaven, or what more lost in Hell?"
  So Satan spake; and him Beëlzebub
Thus answered:—"Leader of those armies bright
Which, but the Omnipotent, none could have foiled!
If once they hear that voice, their liveliest pledge
Of hope in fears and dangers—heard so oft
In worst extremes, and on the perilous edge
Of battle, when it raged, in all assaults
Their surest signal—they will soon resume
New courage and revive, though now they lie
Grovelling and prostrate on yon lake of fire,
As we erewhile, astounded and amazed;
No wonder, fallen such a pernicious highth!"
  He scarce had ceased when the superior Fiend
Was moving toward the shore; his ponderous shield,
Ethereal temper, massy, large, and round,
Behind him cast. The broad circumference
Hung on his shoulders like the moon, whose orb
Through optic glass the Tuscan artist views
At evening, from the top of Fesolè,
Or in Valdarno, to descry new lands,
Rivers, or mountains, in her spotty globe.
His spear—to equal which the tallest pine
Hewn on Norwegian hills, to be the mast
Of some great ammiral, were but a wand—
He walked with, to support uneasy steps
Over the burning marle, not like those steps
On Heaven's azure; and the torrid clime
Smote on him sore besides, vaulted with fire.
Nathless he so endured, till on the beach
Of that inflamèd sea he stood, and called
His legions—Angel Forms, who lay entranced
Thick as autumnal leaves that strow the brooks
In Vallombrosa, where the Etrurian shades
High over-arched embower; or scattered sedge
Afloat, when with fierce winds Orion armed
Hath vexed the Red-Sea coast, whose waves o'erthrew
Busiris and his Memphian chivalry,
While with perfidious hatred they pursued
The sojourners of Goshen, who beheld
From the safe shore their floating carcases
And broken chariot-wheels. So thick bestrown,
Abject and lost, lay these, covering the flood,

Under amazement of their hideous change.
He called so loud that all the hollow deep
Of Hell resounded:—"Princes, Potentates,
Warriors, the Flower of Heaven—once yours; now lost,
If such astonishment as this can seize
Eternal Spirits! Or have ye chosen this place
After the toil of battle to repose
Your wearied virtue, for the ease you find
To slumber here, as in the vales of Heaven?
Or in this abject posture have ye sworn
To adore the Conqueror, who now beholds
Cherub and Seraph rolling in the flood
With scattered arms and ensigns, till anon
His swift pursuers from Heaven-gates discern
The advantage, and, descending, tread us down
Thus drooping, or with linkèd thunderbolts
Transfix us to the bottom of this gulf?—
Awake, arise, or be for ever fallen!"
      They heard, and were abashed, and up they sprung
Upon the wing, as when men wont to watch,
On duty sleeping found by whom they dread,
Rouse and bestir themselves ere well awake.
Nor did they not perceive the evil plight
In which they were, or the fierce pains not feel;
Yet to their General's voice they soon obeyed
Innumerable. As when the potent rod
Of Amram's son, in Egypt's evil day,
Waved round the coast, up-called a pitchy cloud
Of locusts, warping on the eastern wind,
That o'er the realm of impious Pharaoh hung
Like Night, and darkened all the land of Nile;
So numberless were those bad Angels seen
Hovering on wing under the cope of Hell,
'Twixt upper, nether, and surrounding fires;
Till, as a signal given, the uplifted spear
Of their great Sultan waving to direct
Their course, in even balance down they light
On the firm brimstone, and fill all the plain:
A multitude like which the populous North
Poured never from her frozen loins to pass
Rhene or the Danaw, when her barbarous sons
Came like a deluge on the South, and spread
Beneath Gibraltar to the Libyan sands.
Forthwith, from every squadron and each band,
The heads and leaders thither haste where stood
Their great Commander—godlike Shapes, and Forms
Excelling human; princely Dignities;
And Powers that erst in Heaven sat on thrones,
Though of their names in Heavenly records now
Be no memorial, blotted out and rased
By their rebellion from the Books of Life.
Nor had they yet among the sons of Eve
Got them new names, till, wandering o'er the earth,
Through's God's high sufferance for the trial of man,

12

By falsities and lies the greatest part
Of mankind they corrupted to forsake
God their Creator, and the invisible
Glory of Him that made them to transform
Oft to the image of a brute, adorned
With gay religions full of pomp and gold,
And devils to adore for deities:
Then were they known to men by various names,
And various idols through the Heathen World.
  Say, Muse, their names then known, who first, who last,
Roused from the slumber on that fiery couch,
At their great Emperor's call, as next in worth
Came singly where he stood on the bare strand,
While the promiscuous crowd stood yet aloof.
  The chief were those who, from the pit of Hell
Roaming to seek their prey on Earth, durst fix
Their seats, long after, next the seat of God,
Their altars by His altar, gods adored
Among the nations round, and durst abide
Jehovah thundering out of Sion, throned
Between the Cherubim; yea, often placed
Within His sanctuary itself their shrines,
Abominations; and with cursed things
His holy rites and solemn feasts profaned,
And with their darkness durst affront His light.
First, *Moloch*, horrid king, besmeared with blood
Of human sacrifice, and parents' tears;
Though, for the noise of drums and timbrels loud,
Their children's cries unheard that passed through fire
To his grim idol. Him the Ammonite
Worshipped in Rabba and her watery plain,
In Argob and in Basan, to the stream
Of utmost Arnon. Nor content with such
Audacious neighbourhood, the wisest heart
Of Solomon he led by fraud to build
His temple right against the temple of God
On that opprobrious hill, and made his grove
The pleasant valley of Hinnom, Tophet thence
And black Gehenna called, the type of Hell.
Next *Chemos*, the obscene dread of Moab's sons,
From Aroer to Nebo and the wild
Of southmost Abarim; in Hesebon
And Horonaim, Seon's realm, beyond
The flowery dale of Sibma clad with vines,
And Elealè to the Asphaltic Pool:
Peor his other name, when he enticed
Israel in Sittim, on their march from Nile,
To do him wanton rites, which cost them woe.
Yet thence his lustful orgies he enlarged
Even to that hill of scandal, by the grove
Of Moloch homicide, lust hard by hate,
Till good Josiah drove them thence to Hell.
With these came they who, from the bordering flood
Of old Euphrates to the brook that parts

Egypt from Syrian ground, had general names
Of *Baalim* and *Ashtaroth*—those male,
These feminine.   For Spirits, when they please,
Can either sex assume, or both; so soft
And uncompounded is their essence pure,
Not tied or manacled with joint or limb,
Nor founded on the brittle strength of bones,
Like cumbrous flesh; but, in what shape they choose,
Dilated or condensed, bright or obscure,
Can execute their aery purposes,
And works of love or enmity fulfil.
For those the race of Israel oft forsook
Their Living Strength, and unfrequented left
His righteous altar, bowing lowly down
To bestial gods; for which their heads, as low
Bowed down in battle, sunk before the spear
Of despicable foes.   With these in troop
Came *Astoreth*, whom the Phœnicians called
Astarte, queen of heaven, with crescent horns;
To whose bright image nightly by the moon
Sidonian virgins paid their vows and songs;
In Sion also not unsung, where stood
Her temple on the offensive mountain, built
By that uxorious king whose heart, though large,
Beguiled by fair idolatresses, fell
To idols foul.   *Thammuz* came next behind,
Whose annual wound in Lebanon allured
The Syrian damsels to lament his fate
In amorous ditties all a summer's day,
While smooth Adonis from his native rock
Ran purple to the sea, supposed with blood
Of Thammuz yearly wounded: the love-tale
Infected Sion's daughters with like heat,
Whose wanton passions in the sacred porch
Ezekiel saw, when, by the vision led,
His eye surveyed the dark idolatries
Of alienated Judah.   Next came one
Who mourned in earnest, when the captive ark
Maimed his brute image, head and hands lopt off,
In his own temple, on the grunsel-edge,
Where he fell flat and shamed his worshippers;
Dagon his name, sea-monster, upward man
And downward fish; yet had his temple high
Reared in Azotus, dreaded through the coast
Of Palestine, in Gath and Ascalon,
And Accaron and Gaza's frontier bounds.
Him followed *Rimmon*, whose delightful seat
Was fair Damascus, on the fertile banks
Of Abbana and Pharphar, lucid streams.
He also against the house of God was bold:
A leper once he lost, and gained a king—
Ahaz, his sottish conqueror, whom he drew
God's altar to disparage and displace
For one of Syrian mode, whereon to burn

His odious offerings, and adore the gods
Whom he had vanquished.   After these appeared
A crew, who, under names of old renown—
Osiris, Isis, Orus, and their train—
With monstrous shapes and sorceries abused
Fanatic Egypt and her priests to seek
Their wandering gods disguised in brutish forms
Rather than human.   Nor did Israel scape
The infection, when their borrowed gold composed
The calf in Oreb; and the rebel king
Doubled that sin in Bethel and in Dan,
Likening his Maker to the grazèd ox—
Jehovah, who, in one night, when He passed
From Egypt marching, equalled with one stroke
Both her first-born and all her bleating gods.
Belial came last; than whom a Spirit more lewd
Fell not from Heaven, or more gross to love
Vice for itself.   To him no temple stood
Or altar smoked; yet who more oft than he
In temples and at altars, when the priest
Turns atheist, as did Eli's sons, who filled
With lust and violence the house of God?
In courts and palaces he also reigns,
And in luxurious cities, where the noise
Of riot ascends above their loftiest towers,
And injury and outrage; and, when night
Darkens the streets, then wander forth the sons
Of Belial, flown with insolence and wine.
Witness the streets of Sodom, and that night
In Gibeah, when the hospitable door
Exposed a matron, to avoid worse rape.
   These were the prime in order and in might:
The rest were long to tell; though far renowned
The Ionian gods—of Javan's issue held
Gods, yet confessed later than Heaven and Earth,
Their boasted parents;—*Titan,* Heaven's first-born,
With his enormous brood, and birthright seized
By younger *Saturn:* he from mightier Jove,
His own and Rhea's son, like measure found;
So *Jove* usurping reigned.   These, first in Crete
And Ida known, thence on the snowy top
Of cold Olympus ruled the middle air,
Their highest heaven; or on the Delphian cliff,
Or in Dodona, and through all the bounds
Of Doric land; or who with Saturn old
Fled over Adria to the Hesperian fields,
And o'er the Celtic roamed the utmost Isles.
   All these and more came flocking; but with looks
Downcast and damp; yet such wherein appeared
Obscure some glimpse of joy to have found their Chief
Not in despair, to have found themselves not lost
In loss itself; which on his countenance cast
Like doubtful hue.   But he, his wonted pride
Soon recollecting, with high words, that bore

Semblance of worth, not substance, gently raised
Their fainting courage, and dispelled their fears:
Then straight commands that, at the warlike sound
Of trumpets loud and clarions, be upreared
His mighty standard. That proud honour claimed
Azazel as his right, a Cherub tall:
Who forthwith from the glittering staff unfurled
The imperial ensign; which, full high advanced,
Shone like a meteor streaming to the wind,
With gems and golden lustre rich emblazed,
Seraphic arms and trophies; all the while
Sonorous metal blowing martial sounds:
At which the universal host up-sent
A shout that tore Hell's concave, and beyond
Frighted the reign of Chaos and old Night.
All in a moment through the gloom were seen
Ten thousand banners rise into the air,
With orient colours waving: with them rose
A forest huge of spears; and thronging helms
Appeared, and serried shields in thick array
Of depth immeasurable. Anon they move
In perfect phalanx to the Dorian mood
Of flutes and soft recorders—such as raised
To highth of noblest temper heroes old
Arming to battle, and instead of rage
Deliberate valour breathed, firm, and unmoved
With dread of death to flight or foul retreat;
Nor wanting power to mitigate and swage
With solemn touches troubled thoughts, and chase
Anguish and doubt and fear and sorrow and pain
From mortal or immortal minds. Thus they,
Breathing united force with fixèd thought,
Moved on in silence to soft pipes that charmed
Their painful steps o'er the burnt soil. And now
Advanced in view they stand—a horrid front
Of dreadful length and dazzling arms, in guise
Of warriors old, with ordered spear and shield,
Awaiting what command their mighty Chief
Had to impose. He through the armèd files
Darts his experienced eye, and soon traverse
The whole battalion views—their order due,
Their visages and stature as of gods;
Their number last he sums. And now his heart
Distends with pride, and, hardening in his strength,
Glories: for never, since created Man,
Met such embodied force as, named with these,
Could merit more than that small infantry
Warred on by cranes—though all the giant brood
Of Phlegra with the heroic race were joined
That fought at Thebes and Ilium, on each side
Mixed with auxiliar gods; and what resounds
In fable or romance of Uther's son,
Begirt with British and Armoric knights;
And all who since, baptized or infidel,

16

Jousted in Aspramont, or Montalban,
Damasco, or Marocco, or Trebisond,
Or whom Biserta sent from Afric shore
When Charlemain with all his peerage fell
By Fontarabbia.   Thus far these beyond
Compare of mortal prowess, yet observed
Their dread Commander.   He, above the rest
In shape and gesture proudly eminent,
Stood like a tower.   His form had yet not lost
All her original brightness, nor appeared
Less than Archangel ruined, and the excess
Of glory obscured: as when the sun new-risen
Looks through the horizontal misty air
Shorn of his beams, or, from behind the moon,
In dim eclipse, disastrous twilight sheds
On half the nations, and with fear of change
Perplexes monarchs.   Darkened so, yet shone
Above them all the Archangel: but his face
Deep scars of thunder had intrenched, and care
Sat on his faded cheek, but under brows
Of dauntless courage, and considerate pride
Waiting revenge.   Cruel his eye, but cast
Signs of remorse and passion, to behold
The fellows of his crime, the followers rather
(Far other once beheld in bliss), condemned
For ever now to have their lot in pain—
Millions of Spirits for his fault amerced
Of Heaven, and from eternal splendours flung
For his revolt—yet faithful how they stood,
Their glory withered: as, when Heaven's fire
Hath scathed the forest oaks or mountain pines,
With singèd top their stately growth, though bare,
Stands on the blasted heath.   He now prepared
To speak; whereat their doubled ranks they bend
From wing to wing, and half enclose him round
With all his peers: Attention held them mute.
Thrice he assayed, and thrice, in spite of scorn,
Tears, such as Angels weep, burst forth: at last
Words interwove with sighs found out their way:—
   "O myriads of immortal Spirits! O Powers
Matchless, but with the Almighty!—and that strife
Was not inglorious, though the event was dire,
As this place testifies, and this dire change,
Hateful to utter.   But what power of mind,
Foreseeing or presaging, from the depth
Of knowledge past or present, could have feared
How such united force of gods, how such
As stood like these, could ever know repulse?
For who can yet believe, though after loss,
That all these puissant legions, whose exile
Hath emptied Heaven, shall fail to re-ascend,
Self-raised, and re-possess their native seat?
For me, be witness all the host of Heaven,
If counsels different, or danger shunned

M.—C

By me, have lost our hopes.   But He who reigns
Monarch in Heaven till then as one secure
Sat on His throne, upheld by old repute,
Consent or custom, and His regal state
Put forth at full, but still His strength concealed—
Which tempted our attempt, and wrought our fall.
Henceforth His might we know, and know our own,
So as not either to provoke, or dread
New war provoked : our better part remains
To work in close design, by fraud or guile,
What force effected not ; that He no less
At length from us may find, Who overcomes
By force hath overcome but half His foe.
Space may produce new Worlds ; whereof so rife
There went a fame in Heaven that He ere long
Intended to create, and therein plant
A generation whom His choice regard
Should favour equal to the Sons of Heaven.
Thither, if but to pry, shall be perhaps
Our first eruption—thither, or elsewhere ;
For this infernal pit shall never hold
Celestial Spirits in bondage, nor the Abyss
Long under darkness cover.   But these thoughts
Full counsel must mature.   Peace is despaired ;
For who can think submission ?   War, then, war
Open or understood, must be resolved."
     He spake ; and, to confirm his words, out-flew
Millions of flaming swords, drawn from the thighs
Of mighty Cherubim ; the sudden blaze
Far round illumined Hell.   Highly they raged
Against the Highest, and fierce with graspèd arms
Clashed on their sounding shields the din of war,
Hurling defiance toward the vault of Heaven.
     There stood a hill not far, whose grisly top
Belched fire and rolling smoke ; the rest entire
Shone with a glossy scurf—undoubted sign
That in his womb was hid metallic ore,
The work of sulphur.   Thither, winged with speed,
A numerous brigad hastened : as when bands
Of pioneers, with spade and pickaxe armed,
Forerun the royal camp, to trench a field,
Or cast a rampart.   Mammon led them on—
Mammon, the least erected Spirit that fell
From Heaven ; for even in Heaven his looks and thoughts
Were always downward bent, admiring more
The riches of Heaven's pavement, trodden gold,
Than aught divine or holy else enjoyed
In vision beatific.   By him first
Men also, and by his suggestion taught,
Ransacked the Centre, and with impious hands
Rifled the bowels of their mother Earth
For treasures better hid.   Soon had his crew
Opened into the hill a spacious wound,
And digged out ribs of gold.   Let none admire

18

That riches grow in Hell; that soil may best
Deserve the precious bane. And here let those
Who boast in mortal things, and wondering tell
Of Babel, and the works of Memphian kings,
Learn how their greatest monuments of fame,
And strength, and art, are easily outdone
By Spirits reprobate, and in an hour
What in an age they, with incessant toil
And hands innumerable, scarce perform.
Nigh on the plain, in many cells prepared,
That underneath had veins of liquid fire
Sluiced from the lake, a second multitude
With wondrous art founded the massy ore,
Severing each kind, and scummed the bullion-dross.
A third as soon had formed within the ground
A various mould, and from the boiling cells
By strange conveyance filled each hollow nook;
As in an organ, from one blast of wind,
To many a row of pipes the sound-board breathes.
Anon out of the earth a fabric huge
Rose like an exhalation, with the sound
Of dulcet symphonies and voices sweet—
Built like a temple, where pilasters round
Were set, and Doric pillars overlaid
With golden architrave; nor did there want
Cornice or frieze, with bossy sculptures graven:
The roof was fretted gold. Not Babylon
Nor great Alcairo such magnificence
Equalled in all their glories, to enshrine
Belus or Serapis their gods, or seat
Their kings, when Egypt with Assyria strove
In wealth and luxury. The ascending pile
Stood fixed her stately highth; and straight the doors,
Opening their brazen folds, discover, wide
Within, her ample spaces o'er the smooth
And level pavement; from the archèd roof,
Pendent by subtle magic, many a row
Of starry lamps and blazing cressets, fed
With naphtha and asphaltus, yielded light
As from a sky. The hasty multitude
Admiring entered; and the work some praise,
And some the architect. His hand was known
In Heaven by many a towered structure high,
Where sceptred Angels held their residence,
And sat as Princes, whom the supreme King
Exalted to such power, and gave to rule,
Each in his hierarchy, the Orders bright.
Nor was his name unheard or unadored
In ancient Greece; and in Ausonian land
Men called him Mulciber; and how he fell
From Heaven they fabled, thrown by angry Jove
Sheer o'er the crystal battlements; from morn
To noon he fell, from noon to dewy eve,
A summer's day, and with the setting sun

Dropt from the zenith, like a falling star,
On Lemnos, the Ægæan isle. Thus they relate,
Erring; for he with this rebellious rout
Fell long before; nor aught availed him now
To have built in Heaven high towers; nor did he scape
By all his engines, but was headlong sent,
With his industrious crew, to build in Hell.
  Meanwhile the wingèd Haralds, by command
Of sovran power, with awful ceremony
And trumpet's sound, throughout the host proclaim
A solemn council forthwith to be held
At Pandemonium, the high capital
Of Satan and his peers. Their summons called
From every band and squarèd regiment
By place or choice the worthiest; they anon
With hundreds and with thousands trooping came
Attended. All access was thronged; the gates
And porches wide, but chief the spacious hall
(Though like a covered field, where champions bold
Wont ride in armed, and at the Soldan's chair
Defied the best of Panim chivalry
To mortal combat, or career with lance),
Thick swarmed, both on the ground and in the air,
Brushed with the hiss of rustling wings. As bees
In spring-time, when the Sun with Taurus rides,
Pour forth their populous youth about the hive
In clusters; they among fresh dews and flowers
Fly to and fro, or on the smoothèd plank,
The suburb of their straw-built citadel,
New rubbed with balm, expatiate, and confer
Their state-affairs; so thick the aery crowd
Swarmed and were straitened; till, the signal given,
Behold a wonder! They but now who seemed
In bigness to surpass Earth's giant sons,
Now less than smallest dwarfs, in narrow room
Throng numberless—like that pygmean race
Beyond the Indian mount; or faery elves,
Whose midnight revels, by a forest-side
Or fountain, some belated peasant sees,
Or dreams he sees, while overhead the Moon
Sits arbitress, and nearer to the Earth
Wheels her pale course: they, on their mirth and dance
Intent, with jocund music charm his ear;
At once with joy and fear his heart rebounds.
Thus incorporeal Spirits to smallest forms
Reduced their shapes immense, and were at large,
Though without number still, amidst the hall
Of that infernal court. But far within,
And in their own dimensions like themselves,
The great Seraphic Lords and Cherubim
In close recess and secret conclave sat,
A thousand demi-gods on golden seats,
Frequent and full. After short silence then,
And summons read, the great consult began.

THE END OF THE FIRST BOOK.

PARADISE LOST.

BOOK II.

THE ARGUMENT.

The consultation begun, Satan debates whether another battle be to be hazarded for the recovery of Heaven: some advise it, others dissuade. A third proposal is preferred, mentioned before by Satan—to search the truth of that prophecy or tradition in Heaven concerning another world, and another kind of creature, equal, or not much inferior, to themselves, about this time to be created. Their doubt who shall be sent on this difficult search: Satan, their chief, undertakes alone the voyage; is honoured and applauded. The council thus ended, the rest betake them several ways and to several employments, as their inclinations lead them, to entertain the time till Satan return. He passes on his journey to Hell-gates; finds them shut, and who sat there to guard them; by whom at length they are opened, and discover to him the great gulf between Hell and Heaven. With what difficulty he passes through, directed by Chaos, the Power of that place, to the sight of this new World which he sought.

HIGH on a throne of royal state, which far
Outshone the wealth of Ormus and of Ind,
Or where the gorgeous East with richest hand
Showers on her kings barbaric pearl and gold,
Satan exalted sat, by merit raised
To that bad eminence; and, from despair
Thus high uplifted beyond hope, aspires
Beyond thus high, insatiate to pursue
Vain war with Heaven; and, by success untaught,
His proud imaginations thus displayed :—
"Powers and Dominions, Deities of Heaven !—
For, since no deep within her gulf can hold
Immortal vigour, though oppressed and fallen,
I give not Heaven for lost; from this descent
Celestial Virtues rising will appear
More glorious and more dread than from no fall,
And trust themselves to fear no second fate !—
Me though just right, and the fixed laws of Heaven,
Did first create your leader—next, free choice,
With what besides in council or in fight
Hath been achieved of merit—yet this loss,
Thus far at least recovered, hath much more
Established in a safe, unenvied throne,
Yielded with full consent. The happier state

In Heaven, which follows dignity, might draw
Envy from each inferior; but who here
Will envy whom the highest place exposes
Foremost to stand against the Thunderer's aim
Your bulwark, and condemns to greatest share
Of endless pain? Where there is, then, no good
For which to strive, no strife can grow up there
From faction: for none sure will claim in Hell
Precedence; none whose portion is so small
Of present pain that with ambitious mind
Will covet more! With this advantage, then,
To union, and firm faith, and firm accord,
More than can be in Heaven, we now return
To claim our just inheritance of old,
Surer to prosper than prosperity
Could have assured us; and by what best way,
Whether of open war or covert guile,
We now debate. Who can advise may speak."

  He ceased; and next him Moloch, sceptred king,
Stood up—the strongest and the fiercest Spirit
That fought in Heaven, now fiercer by despair.
His trust was with the Eternal to be deemed
Equal in strength, and rather than be less
Cared not to be at all; with that care lost
Went all his fear: of God, or Hell, or worse,
He recked not, and these words thereafter spake:—
  "My sentence is for open war. Of wiles,
More unexpert, I boast not: them let those
Contrive who need, or when they need; not now.
For, while they sit contriving, shall the rest—
Millions that stand in arms, and longing wait
The signal to ascend—sit lingering here,
Heaven's fugitives, and for their dwelling-place
Accept this dark opprobrious den of shame,
The prison of His tyranny who reigns
By our delay? No! let us rather choose,
Armed with Hell-flames and fury, all at once
O'er Heaven's high towers to force resistless way,
Turning our tortures into horrid arms
Against the Torturer; when, to meet the noise
Of His almighty engine, He shall hear
Infernal thunder, and, for lightning, see
Black fire and horror shot with equal rage
Among His Angels, and His throne itself
Mixed with Tartarean sulphur and strange fire,
His own invented torments. But perhaps
The way seems difficult, and steep to scale
With upright wing against a higher foe!
Let such bethink them, if the sleepy drench
Of that forgetful lake benumb not still,
That in our proper motion we ascend
Up to our native seat; descent and fall
To us is adverse. Who but felt of late,
When the fierce foe hung on our broken rear

Insulting, and pursued us through the Deep,
With what compulsion and laborious flight
We sunk thus low? The ascent is easy, then;
The event is feared! Should we again provoke
Our stronger, some worse way His wrath may find
To our destruction, if there be in Hell
Fear to be worse destroyed! What can be worse
Than to dwell here, driven out from bliss, condemned
In this abhorrèd deep to utter woe;
Where pain of unextinguishable fire
Must exercise us without hope of end
The vassals of His anger, when the scourge
Inexorably, and the torturing hour,
Calls us to penance? More destroyed than thus,
We should be quite abolished, and expire.
What fear we then? what doubt we to incense
His utmost ire? which, to the highth enraged,
Will either quite consume us, and reduce
To nothing this essential—happier far
Than miserable to have eternal being!—
Or, if our substance be indeed divine,
And cannot cease to be, we are at worst
On this side nothing; and by proof we feel
Our power sufficient to disturb His Heaven,
And with perpetual inroads to alarm,
Though inaccessible, His fatal throne:
Which, if not victory is yet revenge."
    He ended frowning, and his look denounced
Desperate revenge, and battle dangerous
To less than gods. On the other side up rose
Belial, in act more graceful and humane.
A fairer person lost not Heaven; he seemed
For dignity composed, and high exploit.
But all was false and hollow; though his tongue
Dropt manna, and could make the worse appear
The better reason, to perplex and dash
Maturest counsels: for his thoughts were low—
To vice industrious, but to nobler deeds
Timorous and slothful. Yet he pleased the ear,
And with persuasive accent thus began:—
    " I should be much for open war, O Peers,
As not behind in hate, if what was urged
Main reason to persuade immediate war
Did not dissuade me most, and seem to cast
Ominous conjecture on the whole success;
When he who most excels in fact of arms,
In what he counsels and in what excels
Mistrustful, grounds his courage on despair
And utter dissolution, as the scope
Of all his aim, after some dire revenge.
First, what revenge? The towers of Heaven are filled
With armèd watch, that render all access
Impregnable: oft on the bordering Deep
Encamp their legions, or with obscure wing

23

Scout far and wide into the realm of Night,
Scorning surprise.   Or, could we break our way
By force, and at our heels all Hell should rise
With blackest insurrection to confound
Heaven's purest light, yet our great Enemy,
All incorruptible, would on His throne
Sit unpolluted, and the ethereal mould,
Incapable of stain, would soon expel
Her mischief, and purge off the baser fire,
Victorious.   Thus repulsed, our final hope
Is flat despair; we must exasperate
The Almighty Victor to spend all His rage;
And that must end us; that must be our cure—
To be no more.   Sad cure! for who would lose,
Though full of pain, this intellectual being,
Those thoughts that wander through eternity,
To perish rather, swallowed up and lost
In the wide womb of uncreated Night,
Devoid of sense and motion?   And who knows,
Let this be good, whether our angry Foe
Can give it, or will ever?   How He can
Is doubtful; that He never will is sure.
Will He, so wise, let loose at once His ire,
Belike through impotence or unaware,
To give His enemies their wish, and end
Them in His anger whom His anger saves
To punish endless?   'Wherefore cease we, then?'
Say they who counsel war; 'we are decreed,
Reserved, and destined to eternal woe;
Whatever doing, what can we suffer more,
What can we suffer worse?'   Is this, then, worst—
Thus sitting, thus consulting, thus in arms?
What when we fled amain, pursued and strook
With Heaven's afflicting thunder, and besought
The Deep to shelter us?   This Hell then seemed
A refuge from those wounds.   Or when we lay
Chained on the burning lake?   That sure was worse.
What if the breath that kindled those grim fires,
Awaked, should blow them into sevenfold rage,
And plunge us in the flames; or from above
Should intermitted vengeance arm again
His red right hand to plague us?   What if all
Her stores were opened, and this firmament
Of Hell should spout her cataracts of fire,
Impendent horrors, threatening hideous fall
One day upon our heads; while we perhaps,
Designing or exhorting glorious war,
Caught in a fiery tempest, shall be hurled,
Each on his rock transfixed, the sport and prey
Of racking whirlwinds, or for ever sunk
Under yon boiling ocean, wrapt in chains,
There to converse with everlasting groans,
Unrespited, unpitied, unreprieved,
Ages of hopeless end?   This would be worse.

24

War, therefore, open or concealed, alike
My voice dissuades; for what can force or guile
With Him, or who deceive His mind, whose eye
Views all things at one view?   He from Heaven's highth
All these our motions vain sees and derides,
Not more almighty to resist our might
Than wise to frustrate all our plots and wiles.
Shall we, then, live thus vile—the race of Heaven
Thus trampled, thus expelled, to suffer here
Chains and these torments?   Better these than worse,
By my advice; since fate inevitable
Subdues us, and omnipotent decree,
The Victor's will.   To suffer, as to do,
Our strength is equal; nor the law unjust
That so ordains.   This was at first resolved,
If we were wise, against so great a foe
Contending, and so doubtful what might fall.
I laugh when those who at the spear are bold
And venturous, if that fail them, shrink, and fear
What yet they know must follow—to endure
Exile, or ignominy, or bonds, or pain,
The sentence of their Conqueror.   This is now
Our doom: which if we can sustain and bear,
Our Supreme Foe in time may much remit
His anger, and perhaps, thus far removed,
Not mind us not offending, satisfied
With what is punished; whence these raging fires
Will slacken, if His breath stir not their flames.
Our purer essence then will overcome
Their noxious vapour; or, inured, not feel;
Or, changed at length, and to the place conformed
In temper and in nature, will receive
Familiar the fierce heat; and, void of pain,
This horror will grow mild, this darkness light;
Besides what hope the never-ending flight
Of future days may bring, what chance, what change
Worth waiting—since our present lot appears
For happy though but ill, for ill not worst,
If we procure not to ourselves more woe."
   Thus Belial, with words clothed in reason's garb,
Counselled ignoble ease and peaceful sloth,
Not peace; and after him thus Mammon spake:—
   "Either to disenthrone the King of Heaven
We war, if war be best, or to regain
Our own right lost.   Him to unthrone we then
May hope, when everlasting Fate shall yield
To fickle Chance, and Chaos judge the strife.
The former, vain to hope, argues as vain
The latter; for what place can be for us
Within Heaven's bound, unless Heaven's Lord Supreme
We overpower?   Suppose He should relent,
And publish grace to all, on promise made
Of new subjection; with what eyes could we
Stand in His presence humble, and receive

Strict laws imposed, to celebrate His throne
With warbled hymns, and to His Godhead sing
Forced Halleluiahs, while He lordly sits
Our envied sovran, and His altar breathes
Ambrosial odours and ambrosial flowers,
Our servile offerings?   This must be our task
In Heaven, this our delight.   How wearisome
Eternity so spent in worship paid
To whom we hate!   Let us not then pursue,
By force impossible, by leave obtained
Unacceptable, though in Heaven, our state
Of splendid vassalage; but rather seek
Our own good from ourselves, and from our own
Live to ourselves, though in this vast recess,
Free and to none accountable, preferring
Hard liberty before the easy yoke
Of servile pomp.   Our greatness will appear
Then most conspicuous when great things of small,
Useful of hurtful, prosperous of adverse,
We can create, and in what place soe'er
Thrive under evil, and work ease out of pain
Through labour and endurance.   This deep world
Of darkness do we dread?   How oft amidst
Thick clouds and dark doth Heaven's all-ruling Sire
Choose to reside, His glory unobscured,
And with the majesty of darkness round
Covers His throne, from whence deep thunders roar,
Mustering their rage, and Heaven resembles Hell!
As He our darkness, cannot we His light
Imitate when we please?   This desert soil
Wants not her hidden lustre, gems and gold;
Nor want we skill or art from whence to raise
Magnificence; and what can Heaven show more?
Our torments also may, in length of time,
Become our elements, these piercing fires
As soft as now severe, our temper changed
Into their temper; which must needs remove
The sensible of pain.   All things invite
To peaceful counsels, and the settled state
Of order, how in safety best we may
Compose our present evils, with regard
Of what we are and where, dismissing quite
All thoughts of war.   Ye have what I advise."
   He scarce had finished, when such murmur filled
The assembly as when hollow rocks retain
The sound of blustering winds, which all night long
Had roused the sea, now with hoarse cadence lull
Seafaring men o'erwatched, whose bark by chance,
Or pinnace, anchors in a craggy bay
After the tempest.   Such applause was heard
As Mammon ended, and his sentence pleased,
Advising peace: for such another field
They dreaded worse than Hell; so much the fear
Of thunder and the sword of Michaël

Wrought still within them; and no less desire
To found this nether empire, which might rise,
By policy and long process of time,
In emulation opposite to Heaven.
Which when Beëlzebub perceived—than whom,
Satan except, none higher sat—with grave
Aspect he rose, and in his rising seemed
A pillar of state. Deep on his front engraven
Deliberation sat, and public care;
And princely counsel in his face yet shone,
Majestic, though in ruin. Sage he stood,
With Atlantean shoulders, fit to bear
The weight of mightiest monarchies; his look
Drew audience and attention still as night
Or summer's noontide air, while thus he spake:—
  "Thrones and Imperial Powers, Offspring of Heaven,
Ethereal Virtues! or these titles now
Must we renounce, and, changing style, be called
Princes of Hell? for so the popular vote
Inclines—here to continue, and build up here
A growing empire; doubtless! while we dream,
And know not that the King of Heaven hath doomed
This place our dungeon—not our safe retreat
Beyond His potent arm, to live exempt
From Heaven's high jurisdiction, in new league
Banded against His throne, but to remain
In strictest bondage, though thus far removed,
Under the inevitable curb, reserved
His captive multitude. For He, be sure,
In highth or depth, still first and last will reign
Sole king, and of His kingdom lose no part
By our revolt, but over Hell extend
His empire, and with iron sceptre rule
Us here, as with His golden those in Heaven.
What sit we then projecting peace and war?
War hath determined us and foiled with loss
Irreparable; terms of peace yet none
Vouchsafed or sought; for what peace will be given
To us enslaved, but custody severe,
And stripes and arbitrary punishment
Inflicted? and what peace can we return,
But, to our power, hostility and hate,
Untamed reluctance, and revenge, though slow,
Yet ever plotting how the Conqueror least
May reap His conquest, and may least rejoice
In doing what we most in suffering feel?
Nor will occasion want, nor shall we need
With dangerous expedition to invade
Heaven, whose high walls fear no assault or siege,
Or ambush from the Deep. What if we find
Some easier enterprise? There is a place
(If ancient and prophetic fame in Heaven
Err not)—another World, the happy seat
Of some new race, called Man, about this time

To be created like to us, though less
In power and excellence, but favoured more
Of Him who rules above; so was His will
Pronounced among the gods, and by an oath
That shook Heaven's whole circumference confirmed.
Thither let us bend all our thoughts, to learn
What creatures there inhabit, of what mould
Or substance, how endued, and what their power
And where their weakness: how attempted best,
By force or subtlety.   Though heaven be shut,
And Heaven's high Arbitrator sit secure
In His own strength, this place may lie exposed,
The utmost border of His kingdom, left
To their defence who hold it: here, perhaps,
Some advantageous act may be achieved
By sudden onset—either with Hell-fire
To waste His whole creation, or possess
All as our own, and drive, as we are driven,
The puny habitants; or, if not drive,
Seduce them to our party, that their God
May prove their foe, and with repenting hand
Abolish His own works.   This would surpass
Common revenge, and interrupt His joy
In our confusion, and our joy upraise
In His disturbance; when His darling sons,
Hurled headlong to partake with us, shall curse
Their frail original, and faded bliss—
Faded so soon!   Advise if this be worth
Attempting, or to sit in darkness here
Hatching vain empires."   Thus Beëlzebub
Pleaded his devilish counsel—first devised
By Satan, and in part proposed: for whence,
But from the author of all ill, could spring
So deep a malice, to confound the race
Of mankind in one root, and Earth with Hell
To mingle and involve, done all to spite
The great Creator?   But their spite still serves
His glory to augment.   The bold design
Pleased highly those Infernal States, and joy
Sparkled in all their eyes: with full assent
They vote: whereat his speech he thus renews:—
"Well have ye judged, well ended long debate,
Synod of Gods, and, like to what ye are,
Great things resolved, which from the lowest deep
Will once more lift us up, in spite of fate,
Nearer our ancient seat—perhaps in view
Of those bright confines, whence, with neighbouring arms,
And opportune excursion, we may chance
Re-enter Heaven; or else in some mild zone
Dwell, not unvisited of Heaven's fair light,
Secure, and at the brightening orient beam
Purge off this gloom: the soft delicious air,
To heal the scar of these corrosive fires,
Shall breathe her balm.   But, first, whom shall we send

In search of this new World? whom shall we find
Sufficient? who shall tempt with wandering feet
The dark, unbottomed, infinite Abyss,
And through the palpable obscure find out
His uncouth way, or spread his aery flight,
Upborne with indefatigable wings
Over the vast Abrupt, ere he arrive
The happy Isle? What strength, what art, can then
Suffice, or what evasion bear him safe
Through the strict senteries and stations thick
Of Angels watching round? Here he had need
All circumspection: and we now no less
Choice in our suffrage; for on whom we send
The weight of all, and our last hope, relies."
　　This said, he sat; and expectation held
His look suspense, awaiting who appeared
To second, or oppose, or undertake
The perilous attempt. But all sat mute,
Pondering the danger with deep thoughts; and each
In other's countenance read his own dismay,
Astonished. None among the choice and prime
Of those Heaven-warring champions could be found
So hardy as to proffer or accept,
Alone, the dreadful voyage; till, at last,
Satan, whom now transcendent glory raised
Above his fellows, with monarchal pride
Conscious of highest worth, unmoved thus spake:—
　　"O Progeny of Heaven! Empyreal Thrones!
With reason hath deep silence and demur
Seized us, though undismayed. Long is the way
And hard, that out of Hell leads up to Light.
Our prison strong, this huge convex of fire,
Outrageous to devour, immures us round
Ninefold; and gates of burning adamant,
Barred over us, prohibit all egress.
These passed, if any pass, the void profound
Of unessential Night receives him next,
Wide-gaping, and with utter loss of being
Threatens him, plunged in that abortive gulf.
If thence he scape, into whatever world,
Or unknown region, what remains him less
Than unknown dangers, and as hard escape?
But I should ill become this throne, O Peers,
And this imperial sovranty, adorned
With splendour, armed with power, if aught proposed
And judged of public moment in the shape
Of difficulty or danger, could deter
Me from attempting. Wherefore do I assume
These royalties, and not refuse to reign,
Refusing to accept as great a share
Of hazard as of honour, due alike
To him who reigns, and so much to him due
Of hazard more as he above the rest
High honoured sits? Go, therefore, mighty Powers,

Terror of Heaven, though fallen; intend at home,
While here shall be our home, what best may ease
The present misery, and render Hell
More tolerable; if there be cure or charm
To respite, or deceive, or slack the pain
Of this ill mansion : intermit no watch
Against a wakeful foe, while I abroad
Through all the coasts of dark destruction seek
Deliverance for us all.   This enterprise
None shall partake with me." Thus saying, rose
The Monarch, and prevented all reply;
Prudent lest, from his resolution raised,
Others among the chief might offer now,
Certain to be refused, what erst they feared,
And, so refused, might in opinion stand
His rivals, winning cheap the high repute
Which he through hazard huge must earn.   But they
Dreaded not more the adventure than his voice
Forbidding; and at once with him they rose.
Their rising all at once was as the sound
Of thunder heard remote.   Towards him they bend
With awful reverence prone, and as a God
Extol him equal to the Highest in Heaven.
Nor failed they to express how much they praised
That for the general safety he despised
His own : for neither do the Spirits damned
Lose all their virtue; lest bad men should boast
Their specious deeds on earth, which glory excites,
Or close ambition varnished o'er with zeal.
    Thus they their doubtful consultations dark
Ended, rejoicing in their matchless Chief :
As, when from mountain-tops the dusky clouds
Ascending, while the North-wind sleeps, o'erspread
Heaven's cheerful face, the louring element
Scowls o'er the darkened landskip snow or shower,
If chance the radiant sun, with farewell sweet,
Extend his evening beam, the fields revive,
The birds their notes renew, and bleating herds
Attest their joy, that hill and valley rings.
O shame to men!   Devil with devil damned
Firm concord holds; men only disagree
Of creatures rational, though under hope
Of heavenly grace, and, God proclaiming peace,
Yet live in hatred, enmity, and strife
Among themselves, and levy cruel wars
Wasting the earth, each other to destroy :
As if (which might induce us to accord)
Man had not hellish foes enow besides,
That day and night for his destruction wait!
    The Stygian council thus dissolved; and forth
In order came the grand Infernal Peers :
Midst came their mighty Paramount, and seemed
Alone the antagonist of Heaven, nor less
Than Hell's dread Emperor, with pomp supreme,

And god-like imitated state: him round
A globe of fiery Seraphim enclosed
With bright emblazonry, and horrent arms.
Then of their session ended they bid cry
With trumpet's regal sound the great result:
Toward the four winds four speedy Cherubim
Put to their mouths the sounding alchymy,
By harald's voice explained; the hollow Abyss
Heard far and wide, and all the host of Hell
With defeaning shout returned them loud acclaim.
Thence more at ease their minds, and somewhat raised
By false presumptuous hope, the rangèd Powers
Disband; and, wandering, each his several way
Pursues, as inclination or sad choice
Leads him perplexed, where he may likeliest find
Truce to his restless thoughts, and entertain
The irksome hours, till his great Chief return.
Part on the plain, or in the air sublime,
Upon the wing or in swift race contend,
As at the Olympian games or Pythian fields;
Part curb their fiery steeds, or shun the goal
With rapid wheels, or fronted brigads form:
As when, to warn proud cities, war appears
Waged in the troubled sky, and armies rush
To battle in the clouds; before each van
Prick forth the aery knights, and couch their spears,
Till thickest legions close; with feats of arms
From either end of heaven the welkin burns.
Others, with vast Typhœan rage, more fell,
Rend up both rocks and hills, and ride the air
In whirlwind; Hell scarce holds the wild uproar:—
As when Alcides, from Œchalia crowned
With conquest, felt the envenomed robe, and tore
Through pain up by the roots Thessalian pines,
And Lichas from the top of Œta threw
Into the Euboic sea. Others, more mild,
Retreated in a silent valley, sing
With notes angelical to many a harp
Their own heroic deeds, and hapless fall
By doom of battle, and complain that Fate
Free Virtue should enthrall to Force or Chance.
Their song was partial; but the harmony
(What could it less when Spirits immortal sing?)
Suspended Hell, and took with ravishment
The thronging audience. In discourse more sweet
(For Eloquence the Soul, Song charms the Sense)
Others apart sat on a hill retired,
In thoughts more elevate, and reasoned high
Of Providence, Foreknowledge, Will, and Fate—
Fixed fate, free will, foreknowledge absolute—
And found no end, in wandering mazes lost.
Of good and evil much they argued then,
Of happiness and final misery,
Passion and apathy, and glory and shame:

Vain wisdom all, and false philosophy!—
Yet, with a pleasing sorcery, could charm
Pain for a while or anguish, and excite
Fallacious hope, or arm the obdurèd breast
With stubborn patience as with triple steel.
Another part, in squadrons and gross bands,
On bold adventure to discover wide
That dismal world, if any clime perhaps
Might yield them easier habitation, bend
Four ways their flying march, along the banks
Of four infernal rivers, that disgorge
Into the burning lake their baleful streams—
Abhorrèd Styx, the flood of deadly hate;
Sad Acheron of sorrow, black and deep;
Cocytus, named of lamentation loud
Heard on the rueful stream; fierce Phlegeton,
Whose waves of torrent fire inflame with rage.
Far off from these a slow and silent stream,
Lethe, the river of oblivion, rolls
Her watery labyrinth, whereof who drinks
Forthwith his former state and being forgets—
Forgets both joy and grief, pleasure and pain.
Beyond this flood a frozen continent
Lies dark and wild, beat with perpetual storms
Of whirlwind and dire hail, which on firm land
Thaws not, but gathers heap, and ruin seems
Of ancient pile; all else deep snow and ice,
A gulf profound as that Serbonian bog
Betwixt Damiata and Mount Casius old,
Where armies whole have sunk: the parching air
Burns frore, and cold performs the effect of fire.
Thither, by harpy-footed Furies haled,
At certain revolutions all the damned
Are brought; and feel by turns the bitter change
Of fierce extremes, extremes by change more fierce,
From beds of raging fire to starve in ice
Their soft ethereal warmth, and there to pine
Immovable, infixed, and frozen round
Periods of time,—thence hurried back to fire.
They ferry over this Lethean sound
Both to and fro, their sorrow to augment,
And wish and struggle, as they pass, to reach
The tempting stream, with one small drop to lose
In sweet forgetfulness all pain and woe,
All in one moment, and so near the brink;
But Fate withstands, and, to oppose the attempt,
Medusa with Gorgonian terror guards
The ford, and of itself the water flies
All taste of living wight, as once it fled
The lip of Tantalus. Thus roving on
In confused march forlorn, the adventurous bands,
With shuddering horror pale, and eyes aghast,
Viewed first their lamentable lot, and found
No rest. Through many a dark and dreary vale

They passed, and many a region dolorous,
O'er many a frozen, many a fiery Alp,
Rocks, caves, lakes, fens, bogs, dens, and shades of death—
A universe of death, which God by curse
Created evil, for evil only good;
Where all life dies, death lives, and Nature breeds,
Perverse, all monstrous, all prodigious things,
Abominable, inutterable, and worse
Than fables yet have feigned or fear conceived,
Gorgons, and Hydras, and Chimæras dire.
  Meanwhile the Adversary of God and Man,
Satan, with thoughts inflamed of highest design,
Puts on swift wings, and toward the gates of Hell
Explores his solitary flight: sometimes
He scours the right hand coast, sometimes the left;
Now shaves with level wing the deep, then soars
Up to the fiery concave towering high.
As when far off at sea a fleet descried
Hangs in the clouds, by equinoctial winds
Close sailing from Bengala, or the isles
Of Ternate and Tidore, whence merchants bring
Their spicy drugs; they on the trading flood,
Through the wide Ethiopian to the Cape,
Ply stemming nightly toward the pole: so seemed
Far off the flying Fiend.   At last appear
Hell-bounds, high reaching to the horrid roof,
And thrice threefold the gates; three folds were brass,
Three iron, three of adamantine rock,
Impenetrable, impaled with circling fire,
Yet unconsumed.   Before the gates there sat
On either side a formidable Shape.
The one seemed woman to the waist, and fair,
But ended foul in many a scaly fold,
Voluminous and vast—a serpent armed
With mortal sting.   About her middle round
A cry of Hell-hounds never-ceasing barked
With wide Cerberean mouths full loud, and rung
A hideous peal; yet, when they list, would creep,
If aught disturbed their noise, into her womb,
And kennel there; yet there still barked and howled
Within unseen.   Far less abhorred than these
Vexed Scylla, bathing in the sea that parts
Calabria from the hoarse Trinacrian shore;
Nor uglier follow the night-hag, when, called
In secret, riding through the air she comes,
Lured with the smell of infant blood, to dance
With Lapland witches, while the labouring moon
Eclipses at their charms.   The other Shape—
If shape it might be called that shape had none
Distinguishable in member, joint, or limb;
Or substance might be called that shadow seemed,
For each seemed either—black it stood as Night,
Fierce as ten Furies, terrible as Hell,
And shook a dreadful dart; what seemed his head

M.—D

The likeness of a kingly crown had on.
Satan was now at hand, and from his seat
The monster moving onward came as fast
With horrid strides; Hell trembled as he strode.
The undaunted Fiend what this might be admired—
Admired, not feared (God and His Son except,
Created thing naught valued he nor shunned),
And with disdainful look thus first began:—
"Whence and what art thou, execrable Shape,
That dar'st, though grim and terrible, advance
Thy miscreated front athwart my way
To yonder gates? Through them I mean to pass,
That be assured, without leave asked of thee.
Retire; or taste thy folly, and learn by proof,
Hell-born, not to contend with Spirits of Heaven."
To whom the Goblin, full of wrath, replied:—
"Art thou that Traitor-Angel, art thou he,
Who first broke peace in Heaven and faith, till then
Unbroken, and in proud rebellious arms
Drew after him the third part of Heaven's sons,
Conjured against the Highest—for which both thou
And they, outcast from God, are here condemned
To waste eternal days in woe and pain?
And reckon'st thou thyself with Spirits of Heaven,
Hell-doomed, and breath'st defiance here and scorn,
Where I reign king, and, to enrage thee more,
Thy king and lord? Back to thy punishment,
False fugitive; and to thy speed add wings,
Lest with a whip of scorpions I pursue
Thy lingering, or with one stroke of this dart
Strange horror seize thee, and pangs unfelt before."
So spake the grisly Terror, and in shape,
So speaking, and so threatening, grew tenfold
More dreadful and deform. On the other side,
Incensed with indignation, Satan stood
Unterrified, and like a comet burned,
That fires the length of Ophiuchus huge
In the arctic sky, and from his horrid hair
Shakes pestilence and war. Each at the head
Levelled his deadly aim; their fatal hands
No second stroke intend; and such a frown
Each cast at the other as when two black clouds,
With Heaven's artillery fraught, come rattling on
Over the Caspian,—then stand front to front
Hovering a space, till winds the signal blow
To join their dark encounter in mid-air.
So frowned the mighty combatants that Hell
Grew darker at their frown; so matched they stood;
For never but once more was either like
To meet so great a foe. And now great deeds
Had been achieved, whereof all Hell had rung,
Had not the snaky Sorceress, that sat
Fast by Hell-gate and kept the fatal key,
Risen, and with hideous outcry rushed between.

"O father, what intends thy hand," she cried,
"Against thy only son?   What fury, O son,
Possesses thee to bend that mortal dart
Against thy father's head?   And know'st for whom?
For Him who sits above, and laughs the while
At thee, ordained his drudge to execute
Whate'er his wrath, which He calls justice, bids—
His wrath, which one day will destroy ye both!"
   She spake, and at her words the hellish Pest
Forebore: then these to her Satan returned:—
"So strange thy outcry, and thy words so strange
Thou interposest, that my sudden hand,
Prevented, spares to tell thee yet by deeds
What it intends, till first I know of thee
What thing thou art, thus double-formed, and why,
In this infernal vale first met, thou call'st
Me father, and that phantasm call'st my son.
I know thee not, nor ever saw till now
Sight more detestable than him and thee."
   To whom thus the Portress of Hell-gate replied:—
"Hast thou forgot me, then; and do I seem
Now in thine eye so foul?—once deemed so fair
In Heaven, when at the assembly, and in sight
Of all the Seraphim with thee combined
In bold conspiracy against Heaven's King,
All on a sudden miserable pain
Surprised thee, dim thine eyes, and dizzy swum
In darkness, while thy head flames thick and fast
Threw forth, till on the left side opening wide,
Likest to thee in shape and countenance bright,
Then shining heavenly fair, a goddess armed,
Out of thy head I sprung.   Amazement seized
All the host of Heaven; back they recoiled afraid
At first, and called me *Sin*, and for a sign
Portentous held me; but, familiar grown,
I pleased, and with attractive graces won
The most averse—thee chiefly, who, full oft
Thyself in me thy perfect image viewing,
Becam'st enamoured; and such joy thou took'st
With me in secret that my womb conceived
A growing burden.   Meanwhile war arose,
And fields were fought in Heaven: wherein remained
(For what could else?) to our Almighty Foe
Clear victory; to our part loss and rout
Through all the Empyrean.   Down they fell,
Driven headlong from the pitch of Heaven, down
Into this Deep; and in the general fall
I also: at which time this powerful key
Into my hands was given, with charge to keep
These gates for ever shut, which none can pass
Without my opening.   Pensive here I sat
Alone; but long I sat not, till my womb,
Pregnant by thee, and now excessive grown,
Prodigious motion felt and rueful throes.

At last this odious offspring whom thou seest,
Thine own begotten, breaking violent way,
Tore through my entrails, that, with fear and pain
Distorted, all my nether shape thus grew
Transformed: but he my inbred enemy
Forth issued, brandishing his fatal dart,
Made to destroy.   I fled, and cried out *Death!*
Hell trembled at the hideous name, and sighed
From all her caves, and back resounded *Death!*
I fled; but he pursued (though more, it seems,
Inflamed with lust than rage), and, swifter far,
Me overtook, his mother, all dismayed,
And, in embraces forcible and foul
Engendering with me, of that rape begot
These yelling monsters, that with ceaseless cry
Surround me, as thou saw'st—hourly conceived
And hourly born, with sorrow infinite
To me: for, when they list, into the womb
That bred them they return, and howl, and gnaw
My bowels, their repast; then, bursting forth
Afresh, with conscious terrors vex me round,
That rest or intermission none I find.
Before mine eyes in opposition sits
Grim Death, my son and foe, who sets them on,
And me, his parent, would full soon devour
For want of other prey, but that he knows
His en d with mine involved, and knows that I
Should prove a bitter morsel, and his bane,
Whenever that shall be: so Fate pronounced.
But thou, O father, I forewarn thee, shun
His deadly arrow; neither vainly hope
To be invulnerable in those bright arms,
Though tempered Heavenly; for that mortal dint,
Save He who reigns above, none can resist."
    She finished; and the subtle Fiend his lore
Soon learned, now milder, and thus answered smooth:—
    "Dear daughter—since thou claim'st me for thy sire,
And my fair son here show'st me, the dear pledge
Of dalliance had with thee in Heaven, and joys
Then sweet, now sad to mention, through dire change
Befallen us unforeseen, unthought-of—know,
I come no enemy, but to set free
From out this dark and dismal house of pain
Both him and thee, and all the Heavenly host
Of Spirits that, in our just pretences armed,
Fell with us from on high.   From them I go
This uncouth errand sole, and one for all
Myself expose, with lonely steps to tread
The unfounded Deep, and through the void immense
To search, with wandering quest, a place foretold
Should be—and, by concurring signs, ere now
Created vast and round—a place of bliss
In the purlieus of Heaven; and therein placed
A race of upstart creatures, to supply

Perhaps our vacant room, though more removed,
Lest Heaven, surcharged with potent multitude,
Might hap to move new broils.   Be this, or aught
Than this more secret, now designed, I haste
To know; and, this once known, shall soon return,
And bring ye to the place where thou and Death
Shall dwell at ease, and up and down unseen
Wing silently the buxom air, embalmed
With odours.   There ye shall be fed and filled
Immeasurably; all things shall be your prey."
   He ceased; for both seemed highly pleased, and Death
Grinned horrible a ghastly smile, to hear
His famine should be filled, and blessed his maw
Destined to that good hour.   No less rejoiced
His mother bad, and thus bespake her sire:—
   "The key of this infernal Pit, by due
And by command of Heaven's all-powerful King,
I keep, by Him forbidden to unlock
These adamantine gates; against all force
Death ready stands to interpose his dart,
Fearless to be o'ermatched by living might.
But what owe I to His commands above,
Who hates me, and hath hither thrust me down
Into this gloom of Tartarus profound,
To sit in hateful office here confined,
Inhabitant of Heaven and Heavenly-born—
Here in perpetual agony and pain,
With terrors and with clamours compassed round
Of mine own brood, that on my bowels feed?
Thou art my father, thou my author, thou
My being gav'st me; whom should I obey
But thee? whom follow?   Thou wilt bring me soon
To that new world of light and bliss, among
The gods who live at ease, where I shall reign
At thy right hand voluptuous, as beseems
Thy daughter and thy darling, without end."
   Thus saying, from her side the fatal key,
Sad instrument of all our woe, she took;
And, towards the gate rolling her bestial train,
Forthwith the huge portcullis high up-drew,
Which, but herself, not all the Stygian Powers
Could once have moved; then in the key-hole turns
The intricate wards, and every bolt and bar
Of massy iron or solid rock with ease
Unfastens.   On a sudden open fly,
With impetuous recoil and jarring sound,
The infernal doors, and on their hinges grate
Harsh thunder, that the lowest bottom shook
Of Erebus.   She opened; but to shut
Excelled her power: the gates wide open stood,
That with extended wings a bannered host,
Under spread ensigns marching, might pass through
With horse and chariots ranked in loose array;
So wide they stood, and like a furnace-mouth

Cast forth redounding smoke and ruddy flame.
Before their eyes in sudden view appear
The secrets of the hoary Deep—a dark
Illimitable ocean, without bound,
Without dimension; where length, breadth, and highth,
And time, and place, are lost; where eldest Night
And Chaos, ancestors of Nature, hold
Eternal anarchy, amidst the noise
Of endless wars, and by confusion stand.
For Hot, Cold, Moist, and Dry, four champions fierce,
Strive here for mastery, and to battle bring
Their embryon atoms: they around the flag
Of each his faction, in their several clans,
Light-armed or heavy, sharp, smooth, swift, or slow,
Swarm populous, unnumbered as the sands
Of Barca or Cyrene's torrid soil,
Levied to side with warring winds, and poise
Their lighter wings. To whom these most adhere
He rules a moment: Chaos umpire sits,
And by decision more embroils the fray
By which he reigns: next him, high arbiter,
Chance governs all. Into this wild Abyss,
The womb of Nature, and perhaps her grave,
Of neither Sea, nor Shore, nor Air, nor Fire,
But all these in their pregnant causes mixed
Confusedly, and which thus must ever fight,
Unless the Almighty Maker them ordain
His dark materials to create more worlds—
Into this wild Abyss the wary Fiend
Stood on the brink of Hell and looked a while,
Pondering his voyage; for no narrow frith
He had to cross. Nor was his ear less pealed
With noises loud and ruinous (to compare
Great things with small) than when Bellona storms
With all her battering engines, bent to rase
Some capital city; or less than if this frame
Of Heaven were falling, and these elements
In mutiny had from her axle torn
The steadfast Earth. At last his sail-broad vans
He spreads for flight, and, in the surging smoke
Uplifted, spurns the ground; thence many a league,
As in a cloudy chair, ascending rides
Audacious; but, that seat soon failing, meets
A vast vacuity. All unawares,
Fluttering his pennons vain, plumb-down he drops
Ten thousand fathom deep, and to this hour
Down had been falling, had not, by ill chance,
The strong rebuff of some tumultuous cloud,
Instinct with fire and nitre, hurried him
As many miles aloft. That fury stayed—
Quenched in a boggy Syrtis, neither sea,
Nor good dry land—nigh foundered, on he fares,
Treading the crude consistence, half on foot,
Half flying; behoves him now both oar and sail.

38

As when a gryphon through the wilderness
With wingèd course, o'er hill, or moory dale,
Pursues the Arimaspian, who by stealth
Had from his wakeful custody purloined
The guarded gold; so eagerly the Fiend
O'er bog or steep, through strait, rough, dense, or rare,
With head, hands, wings, or feet, pursues his way,
And swims, or sinks, or wades, or creeps, or flies.
At length a universal hubbub wild
Of stunning sounds, and voices all confused,
Borne through the hollow dark, assaults his ear
With loudest vehemence.   Thither he plies
Undaunted, to meet there whatever Power
Or Spirit of the nethermost Abyss
Might in that noise reside, of whom to ask
Which way the nearest coast of darkness lies
Bordering on light; when straight behold the throne
Of *Chaos*, and his dark pavilion spread
Wide on the wasteful Deep!   With him enthroned
Sat sable-vested *Night*, eldest of things,
The consort of his reign; and by them stood
Orcus and Ades, and the dreaded name
Of Demogorgon; Rumour next, and Chance,
And Tumult, and Confusion, all embroiled,
And Discord with a thousand various mouths.
  To whom Satan, turning boldly, thus:—"Ye Powers
And Spirits of this nethermost Abyss,
Chaos and ancient Night, I come no spy
With purpose to explore or to disturb
The secrets of your realm; but, by constraint
Wandering this darksome desert, as my way
Lies through your spacious empire up to light,
Alone and without guide, half lost, I seek,
What readiest path leads where your gloomy bounds
Confine with Heaven; or, if some other place,
From your dominion won, the Ethereal King
Possesses lately, thither to arrive
I travel this profound.   Direct my course:
Directed, no mean recompense it brings
To your behoof, if I that region lost,
All usurpation thence expelled, reduce
To her original darkness and your sway
(Which is my present journey), and once more
Erect the standard there of ancient Night.
Yours be the advantage all, mine the revenge!"
  Thus Satan; and him thus the Anarch old,
With faltering speech and visage incomposed,
Answered:—"I know thee stranger, who thou art—
That mighty leading Angel, who of late
Made head against Heaven's King, though overthrown.
I saw and heard; for such a numerous host
Fled not in silence through the frighted Deep,
With ruin upon ruin, rout on rout,
Confusion worse confounded; and Heaven-gates

Poured out by millions her victorious bands,
Pursuing. I upon my frontiers here
Keep residence; if all I can will serve
That little which is left so to defend,
Encroached on still, through our intestine broils
Weakening the sceptre of old Night: first, Hell,
Your dungeon, stretching far and wide beneath;
Now lately Heaven and Earth, another world
Hung o'er my realm, linked in a golden chain
To that side Heaven from whence your legions fell!
If that way be your walk, you have not far;
So much the nearer danger. Go, and speed;
Havoc, and spoil, and ruin, are my gain."
    He ceased; and Satan staid not to reply,
But, glad that now his sea should find a shore,
With fresh alacrity and force renewed
Springs upward, like a pyramid of fire,
Into the wild expanse, and through the shock
Of fighting elements, on all sides round
Environed, wins his way; harder beset
And more endangered than when Argo passed
Through Bosporus betwixt the justling rocks,
Or when Ulysses on the larboard shunned
Charybdis, and by the other Whirlpool steered.
So he with difficulty and labour hard
Moved on. With difficulty and labour he;
But, he once passed, soon after, when Man fell,
Strange alteration! Sin and Death amain,
Following his track (such was the will of Heaven),
Paved after him a broad and beaten way
Over the dark Abyss, whose boiling gulf
Tamely endured a bridge of wondrous length,
From Hell continued, reaching the utmost Orb
Of this frail World; by which the Spirits perverse
With easy intercourse pass to and fro
To tempt or punish mortals, except whom
God and good Angels guard by special grace.
    But now at last the sacred influence
Of light appears, and from the walls of Heaven
Shoots far into the bosom of dim Night
A glimmering dawn. Here Nature first begins
Her farthest verge, and Chaos to retire,
As from her outmost works, a broken foe,
With tumult less and with less hostile din;
That Satan with less toil, and now with ease,
Wafts on the calmer wave by dubious light,
And, like a weather-beaten vessel, holds
Gladly the port, though shrouds and tackle torn;
Or in the emptier waste, resembling air,
Weighs his spread wings, at leisure to behold
Far off the empyreal Heaven, extended wide
In circuit, undetermined square or round,
With opal towers and battlements adorned
Of living sapphire, once his native seat

And, fast by, hanging in a golden chain,
This pendent World, in bigness as a star
Of smallest magnitude close by the moon.
Thither, full fraught with mischievous revenge,
Accurst, and in a cursed hour, he hies.

THE END OF THE SECOND BOOK.

PARADISE LOST.

BOOK III.

THE ARGUMENT.

God, sitting on His throne, sees Satan flying towards this World, then newly-created; shows him to the Son, who sat at His right hand; foretells the success of Satan in perverting mankind; clears His own justice and wisdom from all imputation, having created Man free, and able enough to have withstood his Tempter; yet declares His purpose of grace towards him, in regard he fell not of his own malice, as did Satan, but by him seduced. The Son of God renders praises to His Father for the manifestation of His gracious purpose towards Man: but God again declares that grace cannot be extended towards Man without the satisfaction of Divine Justice; Man hath offended the majesty of God by aspiring to Godhead, and therefore, with all his progeny, devoted to death, must die, unless some one can be found sufficient to answer for his offence, and undergo his punishment. The Son of God freely offers Himself a ransom for Man; the Father accepts Him, ordains His incarnation, pronounces His exaltation above all names in Heaven and Earth; commands all the Angels to adore Him. They obey, and, hymning to their harps in full quire, celebrate the Father and the Son. Meanwhile Satan alights upon the bare convex of this World's outermost orb; where wandering he first finds a place since called the Limbo of Vanity: what persons and things fly up thither: thence comes to the gate of Heaven, described ascending by stairs, and the waters above the firmament that flow about it. His passage thence to the orb of the Sun: he finds there Uriel, the regent of that orb, but first changes himself into the shape of a meaner Angel, and, pretending a zealous desire to behold the new Creation, and Man whom God had placed here, inquires of him the place of his habitation, and is directed: Alights first on Mount Niphates.

HAIL, holy Light, offspring of Heaven first-born!
Or of the Eternal co-eternal beam
May I express thee unblamed? since God is light,
And never but in unapproachèd light
Dwelt from eternity—dwelt then in thee,
Bright effluence of bright essence increate!
Or hear'st thou rather pure Ethereal stream,
Whose fountain who shall tell? Before the Sun,
Before the Heavens, thou wert, and at the voice
Of God, as with a mantle, didst invest
The rising World of waters dark and deep,
Won from the void and formless Infinite!
Thee I revisit now with bolder wing,

42

Escaped the Stygian Pool, though long detained
In that obscure sojourn, while in my flight,
Through utter and through middle Darkness borne,
With other notes than to the Orphean lyre
I sung of Chaos and eternal Night,
Taught by the Heavenly Muse to venture down
The dark descent, and up to re-ascend,
Though hard and rare. Thee I revisit safe,
And feel thy sovran vital lamp ; but thou
Revisit'st not these eyes, that roll in vain
To find thy piercing ray, and find no dawn ;
So thick a drop serene hath quenched their orbs,
Or dim suffusion veiled.   Yet not the more
Cease I to wander where the Muses haunt
Clear spring, or shady grove, or sunny hill,
Smit with the love of sacred song ; but chief
Thee, Sion, and the flowery brooks beneath,
That wash thy hallowed feet, and warbling flow,
Nightly I visit : nor sometimes forget
Those other two equalled with me in fate,
So were I equalled with them in renown,
Blind Thamyris and blind Mæonides,
And Tiresias and Phineus, prophets old :
Then feed on thoughts that voluntary move
Harmonious numbers ; as the wakeful bird
Sings darkling, and in shadiest covert hid,
Tunes her nocturnal note.   Thus with the year
Seasons return ; but not to me returns
Day, or the sweet approach of even or morn
Or sight of vernal bloom, or summer's rose,
Or flocks, or herds, or human face divine ;
But cloud instead and ever-during dark
Surrounds me, from the cheerful ways of men
Cut off, and, for the book of knowledge fair,
Presented with a universal blank
Of Nature's works, to me expunged and rased,
And wisdom at one entrance quite shut out.
So much the rather thou, Celestial Light,
Shine inward, and the mind through all her powers
Irradiate ; there plant eyes ; all mist from thence
Purge and disperse, that I may see and tell
Of things invisible to mortal sight.
  Now had the Almighty Father from above,
From the pure Empyrean where He sits
High throned above all highth, bent down His eye,
His own works and their works at once to view :
About Him all the Sanctities of Heaven
Stood thick as stars, and from His sight received
Beatitude past utterance ; on His right
The radiant image of His glory sat,
His only Son.   On Earth He first beheld
Our two first parents, yet the only two
Of mankind, in the Happy Garden placed,
Reaping immortal fruits of joy and love,

Uninterrupted joy, unrivalled love,
In blissful solitude.   He then surveyed
Hell and the gulf between, and Satan there
Coasting the wall of Heaven on this side Night,
In the dun air sublime, and ready now
To stoop, with wearied wings and willing feet,
On the bare outside of this World, that seemed
Firm land imbosomed without firmament,
Uncertain which, in ocean or in air.
Him God beholding from His prospect high,
Wherein past, present, future, He beholds,
Thus to His only Son foreseeing spake :—
  " Only-begotten Son, seest Thou what rage
Transports our Adversary? whom no bounds
Prescribed, no bars of Hell, nor all the chains
Heaped on him there, nor yet the main Abyss
Wide interrupt, can hold ; so bent he seems
On desperate revenge, that shall redound
Upon his own rebellious head.   And now,
Through all restraint broke loose, he wings his way
Not far off Heaven, in the precincts of light,
Directly towards the new-created World,
And Man there placed, with purpose to assay
If him by force he can destroy, or, worse,
By some false guile pervert : And shall pervert ;
For Man will hearken to his glozing lies,
And easily transgress the sole command,
Sole pledge of his obedience : so will fall
He and his faithless progeny.   Whose fault?
Whose but his own? Ingrate, he had of Me
All he could have ; I made him just and right,
Sufficient to have stood, though free to fall.
Such I created all the Ethereal Powers
And Spirits, both them who stood and them who failed ;
Freely they stood who stood, and fell who fell.
Not free, what proof could they have given sincere
Of true allegiance, constant faith, or love,
Where only what they needs must do appeared,
Not what they would? What praise could they receive,
What pleasure I, from such obedience paid,
When Will and Reason (Reason also is Choice),
Useless and vain, of freedom both despoiled,
Made passive both, had served Necessity,
Not Me? They, therefore, as to right belonged
So were created, nor can justly accuse
Their Maker, or their making, or their fate,
As if Predestination overruled
Their will, disposed by absolute decree
Or high foreknowledge.   They themselves decreed
Their own revolt, not I.   If I foreknew,
Foreknowledge had no influence on their fault,
Which had no less proved certain unforeknown.
So without least impulse or shadow of fate,
Or aught by me immutably foreseen,

44

They trespass, authors to themselves in all,
Both what they judge and what they choose ; for so
I formed them free, and free they must remain
Till they enthrall themselves : I else must change
Their nature, and revoke the high decree
Unchangeable, eternal, which ordained
Their freedom ; they themselves ordained their fall.
The first sort by their own suggestion fell,
Self-tempted, self-depraved ; Man falls, deceived
By the other first : Man, therefore, shall find grace ;
The other, none. In mercy and justice both,
Through Heaven and Earth, so shall My glory excel ;
But mercy, first and last, shall brightest shine."
   Thus while God spake ambrosial fragrance filled
All Heaven, and in the blessed Spirits elect
Sense of new joy ineffable diffused.
Beyond compare the Son of God was seen
Most glorious ; in Him all His Father shone
Substantially expressed ; and in His face
Divine compassion visibly appeared,
Love without end, and without measure grace ;
Which uttering, thus He to His Father spake :—
   "O Father, gracious was that word which closed
Thy sovran sentence, that Man should find grace ;
For which both Heaven and Earth shall high extol
Thy praises, with the innumerable sound
Of hymns and sacred songs, wherewith Thy throne
Encompassed shall resound Thee ever blest.
For, should Man finally be lost—should Man,
Thy creature late so loved, Thy youngest son,
Fall circumvented thus by fraud, though joined
With his own folly——! That be from Thee far,
That far be from Thee, Father, who art judge
Of all things made, and judgest only right !
Or shall the Adversary thus obtain
His end, and frustrate Thine ? shall he fulfil
His malice, and Thy goodness bring to naught
Or proud return, though to his heavier doom
Yet with revenge accomplished, and to Hell
Draw after him the whole race of mankind,
By him corrupted ? Or wilt Thou Thyself
Abolish Thy creation, and unmake,
For him, what for Thy glory Thou hast made ?—
So should Thy goodness and Thy greatness both
Be questioned and blasphemed without defence."
   To whom the great Creator thus replied :—
"O Son, in whom My soul hath chief delight,
Son of My bosom, Son who art alone
My word, My wisdom, and effectual might,
All hast Thou spoken as My thoughts are, all
As My eternal purpose hath decreed.
Man shall not quite be lost, but saved who will ;
Yet not of will in him, but grace in Me
Freely vouchsafed. Once more I will renew

His lapsèd powers, though forfeit, and enthralled
By sin to foul exorbitant desires :
Upheld by Me, yet once more he shall stand
On even ground against his mortal foe—
By Me upheld, that he may know how frail
His fallen condition is, and to Me owe
All his deliverance, and to none but Me.
Some I have chosen of peculiar grace,
Elect above the rest ; so is My will :
The rest shall hear Me call, and oft be warned
Their sinful state, and to appease betimes
The incensèd Deity, while offered grace
Invites ; for I will clear their senses dark
What may suffice, and soften stony hearts
To pray, repent, and bring obedience due.
To prayer, repentance, and obedience due,
Though but endeavoured with sincere intent,
Mine ear shall not be slow, Mine eye not shut.
And I will place within them as a guide
My umpire Conscience ; whom if they will hear,
Light after light well used they shall attain,
And to the end persisting safe arrive.
This My long sufferance, and My day of grace,
They who neglect and scorn shall never taste ;
But hard be hardened, blind be blinded more,
That they may stumble on, and deeper fall ;
And none but such from mercy I exclude.——
But yet all is not done. Man disobeying,
Disloyal, breaks his fealty, and sins
Against the high supremacy of Heaven,
Affecting Godhead, and, so losing all,
To expiate his treason hath naught left,
But, to destruction sacred and devote,
He with his whole posterity must die ;—
Die he or Justice must ; unless for him
Some other, able, and as willing, pay
The rigid satisfaction, death for death.
Say, Heavenly Powers, where shall we find such love ?
Which of ye will be mortal, to redeem
Man's mortal crime, and just, the unjust to save ?
Dwells in all Heaven charity so dear ?"
    He asked, but all the Heavenly Quire stood mute,
And silence was in Heaven : on Man's behalf
Patron or intercessor none appeared—
Much less that durst upon his own head draw
The deadly forfeiture, and ransom set.
And now without redemption all mankind
Must have been lost, adjudged to Death and Hell
By doom severe, had not the Son of God,
In whom the fulness dwells of love divine,
His dearest mediation thus renewed :—
    "Father, Thy word is passed, Man shall find grace ;
And shall Grace not find means, that finds her way,
The speediest of Thy wingèd messengers,

To visit all Thy creatures, and to all
Comes unprevented, unimplored, unsought?
Happy for Man, so coming! He her aid
Can never seek, once dead in sins and lost—
Atonement for himself, or offering meet,
Indebted and undone, hath none to bring.
Behold *Me*, then : Me for him, life for life,
I offer ; on Me let Thine anger fall ;
Account Me Man : I for his sake will leave
Thy bosom, and this glory next to Thee
Freely put off, and for him lastly die
Well pleased ; on Me let Death wreak all his rage.
Under his gloomy power I shall not long
Lie vanquished. Thou hast given Me to possess
Life in Myself for ever ; by Thee I live ;
Though now to Death I yield, and am his due,
All that of Me can die, yet, that debt paid,
Thou wilt not leave Me in the loathsome grave
His prey, nor suffer My unspotted soul
For ever with corruption there to dwell ;
But I shall rise victorious, and subdue
My vanquisher, spoiled of his vaunted spoil.
Death his death's wound shall then receive, and stoop
Inglorious, of his mortal sting disarmed ;
I through the ample air in triumph high
Shall lead Hell captive maugre Hell, and show
The powers of Darkness bound. Thou, at the sight
Pleased, out of Heaven shalt look down and smile,
While, by Thee raised, I ruin all My foes—
Death last, and with his carcase glut the grave ;
Then, with the multitude of My redeemed,
Shall enter Heaven, long absent, and return,
Father, to see Thy face, wherein no cloud
Of anger shall remain, but peace assured
And reconcilement : wrath shall be no more
Thenceforth, but in Thy presence joy entire."
  His words here ended ; but his meek aspéct
Silent yet spake, and breathed immortal love
To mortal men, above which only shone
Filial obedience : as a sacrifice
Glad to be offered, He attends the will
Of His great Father. Admiration seized
All Heaven, what this might mean, and whither tend,
Wondering ; but soon the Almighty thus replied :—
  "O Thou in Heaven and Earth the only peace
Found out for mankind under wrath, O Thou
My sole complacence ! well Thou know'st how dear
To Me are all My works ; nor Man the least,
Though last created, that for him I spare
Thee from My bosom and right hand, to save
By losing Thee a while, the whole race lost !
Thou, therefore, whom Thou only canst redeem,
Their nature also to Thy nature join ;
And be Thyself Man among men on Earth,

47

Made flesh, when time shall be, of virgin seed,
By wondrous birth ; be Thou in Adam's room
The head of all mankind, though Adam's son.
As in him perish all men, so in Thee,
As from a second root, shall be restored
As many as are restored ; without Thee, none.
His crime makes guilty all his sons ; Thy merit,
Imputed, shall absolve them who renounce
Their own both righteous and unrighteous deeds,
And live in Thee transplanted, and from Thee
Receive new life. So Man, as is most just,
Shall satisfy for Man, be judged and die,
And dying rise, and, rising, with Him raise
His brethren, ransomed with His own dear life.
So Heavenly love shall undo Hellish hate,
Giving to death, and dying to redeem,
So dearly to redeem what Hellish hate
So easily destroyed, and still destroys
In those who, when they may, accept not grace.
Nor shalt Thou, by descending to assume
Man's nature, lessen or degrade Thine own.
Because Thou hast, though throned in highest bliss
Equal to God, and equally enjoying
God-like fruition, quitted all to save
A world from utter loss, and hast been found
By merit more than birthright Son of God,—
Found worthiest to be so by being good,
Far more than great or high ; because in Thee
Love hath abounded more than glory abounds ;
Therefore Thy humiliation shall exalt
With Thee Thy manhood also to this throne :
Here shalt Thou sit incarnate, here shalt reign
Both God and Man, Son both of God and Man,
Anointed universal King. All power
I give Thee ; reign for ever, and assume
Thy merits ; under Thee, as Head Supreme,
Thrones, Princedoms, Powers, Dominions, I reduce :
All knees to Thee shall bow of them that bide
In Heaven, or Earth, or, under Earth, in Hell.
When Thou, attended gloriously from Heaven,
Shalt in the sky appear, and from Thee send
The summoning Archangels to proclaim
Thy dread tribunal, forthwith from all winds
The living, and forthwith the cited dead
Of all past ages, to the general doom
Shall hasten ; such a peal shall rouse their sleep.
Then, all Thy Saints assembled, Thou shalt judge
Bad men and Angels ; they arraigned shall sink
Beneath Thy sentence ; Hell, her numbers full,
Thenceforth shall be for ever shut. Meanwhile
The World shall burn, and from her ashes spring
New Heaven and Earth, wherein the just shall dwell,
And, after all their tribulations long,
See golden days, fruitful of golden deeds,

With Joy and Love triumphing, and fair Truth.
Then Thou Thy regal sceptre shalt lay by ;
For regal sceptre then no more shall need ;
God shall be all in all.   But all ye Gods,
Adore Him who, to compass all this, dies ;
Adore the Son, and honour Him as Me."
   No sooner had the Almighty ceased but—all
The multitude of Angels, with a shout
Loud as from numbers without number, sweet
As from blest voices, uttering joy—Heaven rung
With jubilee, and loud hosannas filled
The eternal regions.   Lowly reverent
Towards either throne they bow, and to the ground
With solemn adoration down they cast
Their crowns, inwove with amarant and gold,—
Immortal amarant, a flower which once
In Paradise, fast by the Tree of Life,
Began to bloom, but, soon for Man's offence
To Heaven removed where first it grew, there grows
And flowers aloft, shading the Fount of Life,
And where the River of Bliss through midst of Heaven
Rolls o'er Elysian flowers her amber stream !
With these, that never fade, the Spirits elect
Bind their resplendent locks, inwreathed with beams.
Now in loose garlands thick thrown off, the bright
Pavement, that like a sea of jasper shone,
Impurpled with celestial roses smiled.
Then, crowned again, their golden harps they took—
Harps ever tuned, that glittering by their side
Like quivers hung ; and with preamble sweet
Of charming symphony they introduce
Their sacred song, and waken raptures high :
No voice exempt, no voice but well could join
Melodious part ; such concord is in Heaven.
   Thee, Father, first they sung, Omnipotent,
Immutable, Immortal, Infinite,
Eternal King ; Thee, Author of all being,
Fountain of light, Thyself invisible
Amidst the glorious brightness where Thou sitt'st
Throned inaccessible, but when thou shad'st
The full blaze of Thy beams, and through a cloud
Drawn round about Thee like a radiant shrine
Dark with excessive bright thy skirts appear,
Yet dazzle Heaven, that brightest Seraphim
Approach not, but with both wings veil their eyes.
Thee next they sang, of all creation first,
Begotten Son, Divine Similitude,
In whose conspicuous countenance, without cloud
Made visible, the Almighty Father shines,
Whom else no creature can behold : on Thee
Impressed the effulgence of His glory abides ;
Transfused on Thee His ample Spirit rests.
He Heaven of Heavens, and all the Powers therein,
By Thee created ; and by Thee threw down

The aspiring Dominations.   Thou that day
Thy Father's dreadful thunder didst not spare,
Nor stop thy flaming chariot wheels, that shook
Heaven's everlasting frame, while o'er the necks
Thou drov'st of warring Angels disarrayed.
Back from pursuit, Thy Powers with loud acclaim
Thee only extolled, Son of Thy Father's might,
To execute fierce vengeance on His foes.
Not so on Man : Him, through their malice fallen,
Father of mercy and grace, Thou didst not doom
So strictly, but much more to pity incline.
No sooner did Thy dear and only Son
Perceive Thee purposed not to doom frail Man
So strictly, but much more to pity inclined,
He, to appease Thy wrath, and end the strife
Of mercy and justice in Thy face discerned,
Regardless of the bliss wherein He sat
Second to Thee, offered Himself to die
For Man's offence.   O unexampled love !
Love nowhere to be found less than Divine !
Hail, Son of God, Saviour of men !   Thy name
Shall be the copious matter of my song
Henceforth, and never shall my harp Thy praise
Forget, nor from Thy Father's praise disjoin !
     Thus they in Heaven, above the Starry Sphere,
Their happy hours in joy and hymning spent.
Meanwhile, upon the firm opacous globe
Of this round World, whose first convex divides
The luminous inferior Orbs, enclosed
From Chaos and the inroad of Darkness old,
Satan alighted walks.   A globe far off
It seemed ; now seems a boundless continent,
Dark, waste, and wild, under the frown of Night
Starless exposed, and ever-threatening storms
Of Chaos blustering round, inclement sky,
Save on that side which from the wall of Heaven,
Though distant far, some small reflection gains
Of glimmering air less vexed with tempest loud.
Here walked the Fiend at large in spacious field,
As when a vulture, on Imaus bred,
Whose snowy ridge the roving Tartar bounds,
Dislodging from a region scarce of prey,
To gorge the flesh of lambs or yeanling kids
On hills where flocks are fed, flies toward the springs
Of Ganges or Hydaspes, Indian streams,
But in his way lights on the barren plains
Of Sericana, where Chineses drive
With sails and wind their cany waggons light ;
So, on this windy sea of land, the Fiend
Walked up and down alone, bent on his prey :
Alone, for other creature in this place,
Living or lifeless, to be found was none ;—
None yet ; but store hereafter from the Earth
Up hither like aerial vapours flew

Of all things transitory and vain, when sin
With vanity had filled the works of men—
Both all things vain, and all who in vain things
Built their fond hopes of glory or lasting fame,
Or happiness in this or the other life.
All who have their reward on earth, the fruits
Of painful superstition and blind zeal,
Naught seeking but the praise of men, here find
Fit retribution, empty as their deeds ;
All the unaccomplished works of Nature's hand,
Abortive, monstrous, or unkindly mixed,
Dissolved on Earth, fleet hither, and in vain,
Till final dissolution, wander here—
Not in the neighbouring Moon, as some have dreamed :
Those argent fields more likely habitants,
Translated Saints, or middle Spirits hold,
Betwixt the angelical and human kind.
Hither, of ill-joined sons and daughters born,
First from the ancient world those Giants came,
With many a vain exploit, though then renowned ;
The builders next of Babel on the plain
Of Sennaar, and still with vain design
New Babels, had they wherewithal, would build :
Others came single ; he who, to be deemed
A god, leaped fondly into Ætna flames,
Empedocles ; and he who, to enjoy
Plato's Elysium, leaped into the sea,
Cleombrotus ; and many more, too long,
Embryos and idiots, eremites and friars,
White, black, and grey, with all their trumpery.
Here pilgrims roam, that strayed so far to seek
In Golgotha Him dead who lives in Heaven ;
And they who, to be sure of Paradise,
Dying put on the weeds of Dominic,
Or in Franciscan think to pass disguised.
They pass the planets seven, and pass the fixed,
And that crystalline sphere whose balance weighs
The trepidation talked, and that first moved ;
And now Saint Peter at Heaven's wicket seems
To wait them with his keys, and now at foot
Of Heaven's ascent they lift their feet, when, lo !
A violent cross wind from either coast
Blows them transverse, ten thousand leagues awry,
Into the devious air. Then might ye see
Cowls, hoods, and habits, with their wearers, tost
And fluttered into rags ; then reliques, beads,
Indulgences, dispenses, pardons, bulls,
The sport of winds : all these upwhirled aloft,
Fly o'er the backside of the World far off
Into a Limbo large and broad, since called
The Paradise of Fools ; to few unknown
Long after, now unpeopled and untrod.
    All this dark globe the Fiend found as he passed ;
And long he wandered, till at last a gleam

51

Of dawning light turned thitherward in haste
His travelled steps.   Far distant he descries,
Ascending by degrees magnificent
Up to the wall of Heaven, a structure high ;
At top whereof, but far more rich, appeared
The work as of a kingly palace-gate,
With frontispiece of diamond and gold
Embellished ; thick with sparkling orient gems
The portal shone, inimitable on Earth
By model, or by shading pencil drawn.
The stairs were such as whereon Jacob saw
Angels ascending and descending, bands
Of guardians bright, when he from Esau fled
To Padan-Aram, in the field of Luz
Dreaming by night under the open sky,
And waking cried, *This is the gate of Heaven.*
Each stair mysteriously was meant, nor stood
There always, but drawn up to Heaven sometimes
Viewless ; and underneath a bright sea flowed
Of jasper, or of liquid pearl, whereon
Who after came from Earth sailing arrived
Wafted by Angels, or flew o'er the lake
Rapt in a chariot drawn by fiery steeds.
The stairs were then let down, whether to dare
The Fiend by easy ascent, or aggravate
His sad exclusion from the doors of bliss :
Direct against which opened from beneath,
Just o'er the blissful seat of Paradise,
A passage down to the Earth—a passage wide ;
Wider by far than that of after-times
Over Mount Sion, and, though that were large,
Over the Promised Land to God so dear,
By which, to visit oft those happy tribes,
On high behests His Angels to and fro
Passed frequent, and His eye with choice regard
From Paneas, the fount of Jordan's flood,
To Beërsaba, where the Holy Land
Borders on Egypt and the Arabian shore.
So wide the opening seemed, where bounds were set
To darkness, such as bound the ocean wave.
Satan from hence, now on the lower stair,
That scaled by steps of gold to Heaven-gate,
Looks down with wonder at the sudden view
Of all this World at once.   As when a scout,
Through dark and desert ways with peril gone
All night, at last by break of cheerful dawn
Obtains the brow of some high-climbing hill,
Which to his eye discovers unaware
The goodly prospect of some foreign land
First seen, or some renowned metropolis
With glistering spires and pinnacles adorned,
Which now the rising sun gilds with his beams ;
Such wonder seized, though after Heaven seen,
The Spirit malign, but much more envy seized,

At sight of all this World beheld so fair.
Round he surveys (and well might, where he stood
So high above the circling canopy
Of Night's extended shade) from eastern point
Of Libra to the fleecy star that bears
Andromeda far off Atlantic seas
Beyond the horizon ; then from pole to pole
He views in breadth,—and, without longer pause,
Down right into the World's first region throws
His flight precipitant, and winds with ease
Through the pure marble air his oblique way
Amongst innumerable stars, that shone
Stars distant, but nigh-hand seemed other worlds.
Or other worlds they seemed, or happy isles,
Like those Hesperian Gardens famed of old,
Fortunate fields, and groves, and flowery vales ;
Thrice happy isles !   But who dwelt happy there
He staid not to inquire : above them all
The golden Sun, in splendour likest Heaven,
Allured his eye.   Thither his course he bends,
Through the calm firmament (but up or down,
By centre or eccentric, hard to tell,
Or longitude) where the great luminary,
Aloof the vulgar constellations thick,
That from his lordly eye keep distance due,
Dispenses light from far.   They, as they move
Their starry dance in numbers that compute
Days, months, and years, towards his all-cheering lamp
Turn swift their various motions, or are turned
By his magnetic beam, that gently warms
The Universe, and to each inward part
With gentle penetration, though unseen,
Shoots invisible virtue even to the Deep ;
So wondrously was set his station bright.
There lands the Fiend, a spot like which perhaps
Astronomer in the Sun's lucent orb
Through his glazed optic tube yet never saw.
The place he found beyond expression bright,
Compared with aught on Earth, metal or stone—
Not all parts like, but all alike informed
With radiant light, as glowing iron with fire.
If metal, part seemed gold, part silver clear ;
If stone, carbuncle most or chrysolite,
Ruby or topaz, to the twelve that shone
In Aaron's breast-plate, and a stone besides,
Imagined rather oft than elsewhere seen—
That stone, or like to that, which here below
Philosophers in vain so long have sought ;
In vain, though by their powerful art they bind
Volatile Hermes, and call up unbound
In various shapes old Proteus from the sea,
Drained through a limbec to his native form.
What wonder then if fields and regions here
Breathe forth elixir pure, and rivers run

Potable gold, when, with one virtuous touch,
The arch-chemic Sun, so far from us remote,
Produces, with terrestrial humour mixed,
Here in the dark so many precious things
Of colour glorious and effect so rare?
Here matter new to gaze the Devil met
Undazzled.   Far and wide his eye commands;
For sight no obstacle found here, nor shade,
But all sunshine, as when his beams at noon
Culminate from the equator, as they now
Shot upward still direct, whence no way round
Shadow from body opaque can fall; and the air,
Nowhere so clear, sharpened his visual ray
To objects distant far, whereby he soon
Saw within ken a glorious Angel stand,
The same whom John saw also in the Sun.
His back was turned, but not his brightness hid;
Of beaming sunny rays a golden tiar
Circled his head, nor less his locks behind
Illustrious on his shoulders fledge with wings
Lay waving round: on some great charge employed
He seemed, or fixed in cogitation deep.
Glad was the Spirit impure, as now in hope
To find who might direct his wandering flight
To Paradise, the happy seat of Man,
His journey's end, and our beginning woe.
But first he casts to change his proper shape,
Which else might work him danger or delay:
And now a stripling Cherub he appears,
Not of the prime, yet such as in his face
Youth smiled celestial, and to every limb
Suitable grace diffused; so well he feigned.
Under a coronet his flowing hair
In curls on either cheek played; wings he wore
Of many a coloured plume sprinkled with gold,
His habit fit for speed succinct, and held
Before his decent steps a silver wand.
He drew not nigh unheard; the Angel bright,
Ere he drew nigh, his radiant visage turned,
Admonished by his ear, and straight was known
The Archangel Uriel—one of the seven
Who in God's presence, nearest to His throne,
Stand ready at command, and are His eyes
That run through all the Heavens, or down to the Earth
Bear His swift errands over moist and dry,
O'er sea and land.   Him Satan thus accosts:—
"Uriel! for thou of those seven Spirits that stand
In sight of God's high throne, gloriously bright,
The first art wont His great authentic will
Interpreter through highest Heaven to bring,
Where all His Sons thy embassy attend,
And here art likeliest by supreme decree
Like honour to obtain, and as His eye
To visit oft this new Creation round—

Unspeakable desire to see and know
All these His wondrous works, but chiefly Man,
His chief delight and favour, him for whom
All these His works so wondrous He ordained,
Hath brought me from the quires of Cherubim
Alone thus wandering.   Brightest Seraph, tell
In which of all these shining orbs hath Man
His fixèd seat—or fixèd seat hath none,
But all these shining orbs his choice to dwell—
That I may find him, and with secret gaze
Or open admiration him behold
On whom the great Creator hath bestowed
Worlds, and on whom hath all these graces poured;
That both in him and all things, as is meet,
The Universal Maker we may praise;
Who justly hath driven out His rebel foes
To deepest Hell, and, to repair that loss,
Created this new happy race of Men
To serve Him better: Wise are all His ways!"
   So spake the false dissembler unperceived;
For neither man nor angel can discern
Hypocrisy—the only evil that walks
Invisible, except to God alone,
By His permissive will, through Heaven and Earth;
And oft, though Wisdom wake, Suspicion sleeps
At Wisdom's gate, and to Simplicity
Resigns her charge, while goodness thinks no ill
Where no ill seems: which now for once beguiled
Uriel, though Regent of the Sun, and held
The sharpest-sighted Spirit of all in Heaven;
Who to the fraudulent impostor foul,
In his uprightness, answer thus returned :—
   "Fair Angel, thy desire, which tends to know
The works of God, thereby to glorify
The great Work-master, leads to no excess
That reaches blame, but rather merits praise
The more it seems excess, that led thee hither
From thy empyreal mansion thus alone,
To witness with thine eyes what some perhaps,
Contented with report, hear only in Heaven;
For wonderful indeed are all His works,
Pleasant to know, and worthiest to be all
Had in remembrance always with delight!
But what created mind can comprehend
Their number, or the wisdom infinite
That brought them forth, but hid their causes deep?
I saw when, at His word, the formless mass,
This World's material mould, came to a heap:
Confusion heard His voice, and wild Uproar
Stood ruled, stood vast Infinitude confined;
Till, at His second bidding, Darkness fled,
Light shone, and order from disorder sprung.
Swift to their several quarters hasted then
The cumbrous elements—Earth, Flood, Air, Fire;

55

And this ethereal quintessence of Heaven
Flew upward, spirited with various forms,
That rolled orbicular, and turned to stars
Numberless, as thou seest, and how they move:
Each had his place appointed, each his course;
The rest in circuit walls this Universe.
Look downward on that globe, whose hither side
With light from hence, though but reflected, shines:
That place is Earth, the seat of Man; that light
His day, which else, as the other hemisphere,
Night would invade; but there the neighbouring Moon
(So call that opposite fair star) her aid
Timely interposes, and, her monthly round
Still ending, still renewing, through mid-heaven,
With borrowed light her countenance triform
Hence fills and empties, to enlighten the Earth,
And in her pale dominion checks the night.
That spot to which I point is Paradise,
Adam's abode; those lofty shades his bower.
Thy way thou canst not miss; me mine requires."
   Thus said, he turned; and Satan, bowing low,
As to superior Spirits is wont in Heaven,
Where honour due and reverence none neglects,
Took leave, and toward the coast of Earth beneath,
Down from the ecliptic, sped with hoped success,
Throws his steep flight in many an aery wheel,
Nor staid till on Niphates' top he lights.

THE END OF THE THIRD BOOK.

PARADISE LOST.

BOOK IV.

THE ARGUMENT.

Satan, now in prospect of Eden, and nigh the place where he must now attempt the bold enterprise which he undertook alone against God and Man, falls into many doubts with himself, and many passions—fear, envy, and despair; but at length confirms himself in evil; journeys on to Paradise, whose outward prospect and situation is described; overleaps the bounds; sits, in the shape of a cormorant, on the Tree of Life, as highest in the Garden, to look about him. The Garden described; Satan's first sight of Adam and Eve; his wonder at their excellent form and happy state, but with resolution to work their fall; overhears their discourse; thence gathers that the Tree of Knowledge was forbidden them to eat of under penalty of death, and thereon intends to found his temptation by seducing them to transgress; then leaves them a while to know further of their state by some other means. Meanwhile Uriel, descending on a sunbeam, warns Gabriel, who had in charge the gate of Paradise, that some evil Spirit had escaped the Deep, and passed at noon by his Sphere, in the shape of a good Angel, down to Paradise, discovered after by his furious gestures in the mount. Gabriel promises to find him ere morning. Night coming on, Adam and Eve discourse of going to their rest: their bower described; their evening worship. Gabriel, drawing forth his bands of night-watch to walk the rounds of Paradise, appoints two strong Angels to Adam's bower, lest the evil Spirit should be there doing some harm to Adam or Eve sleeping; there they find him at the ear of Eve, tempting her in a dream, and bring him, though unwilling, to Gabriel; by whom questioned, he scornfully answers; prepares resistance; but, hindered by a sign from Heaven, flies out of Paradise.

O FOR that warning voice, which he who saw
The Apocalypse heard cry in Heaven aloud,
Then when the Dragon, put to second rout,
Came furious down to be revenged on men,
Woe to the inhabitants on Earth! that now,
While time was, our first parents had been warned
The coming of their secret foe, and scaped,
Haply so scaped, his mortal snare! For now
Satan, now first inflamed with rage, came down,
The tempter, ere the accuser, of mankind,
To wreak on innocent frail Man his loss
Of that first battle, and his flight to Hell.
Yet not rejoicing in his speed, though bold
Far off and fearless, nor with cause to boast,

Begins his dire attempt ; which, nigh the birth
Now rolling, boils in his tumultuous breast,
And like a devilish engine back recoils
Upon himself.   Horror and doubt distract
His troubled thoughts, and from the bottom stir
The hell within him ; for within him Hell
He brings, and round about him, nor from Hell
One step, no more than from himself, can fly
By change of place.   Now conscience wakes despair
That slumbered ; wakes the bitter memory
Of what he was, what is, and what must be
Worse ; of worse deeds worse sufferings must ensue !
Sometimes towards Eden, which now in his view
Lay pleasant, his grieved look he fixes sad ;
Sometimes towards Heaven and the full-blazing Sun,
Which now sat high in his meridian tower :
Then, much revolving, thus in sighs began :—
   "O thou that, with surpassing glory crowned,
Look'st from thy sole dominion like the god
Of this new World—at whose sight all the stars
Hide their diminished heads—to thee I call,
But with no friendly voice, and add thy name,
O Sun, to tell thee how I hate thy beams,
That bring to my remembrance from what state
I fell, how glorious once above thy sphere,
Till pride and worse ambition threw me down,
Warring in Heaven against Heaven's matchless King !
Ah, wherefore ?   He deserved no such return
From me, whom He created what I was
In that bright eminence, and with His good
Upbraided none ; nor was His service hard.
What could be less than to afford Him praise,
The easiest recompense, and pay Him thanks,
How due ?   Yet all His good proved ill in me,
And wrought but malice.   Lifted up so high,
I sdained subjection, and thought one step higher
Would set me highest, and in a moment quit
The debt immense of endless gratitude,
So burdensome, still paying, still to owe ;
Forgetful what from Him I still received ;
And understood not that a grateful mind
By owing owes not, but still pays, at once
Indebted and discharged—what burden then ?
Oh, had His powerful destiny ordained
Me some inferior Angel, I had stood
Then happy ; no unbounded hope had raised
Ambition.   Yet why not ?   Some other Power
As great might have aspired, and me, though mean,
Drawn to his part.   But other Powers as great
Fell not, but stand unshaken, from within
Or from without to all temptations armed !
Hadst thou the same free will and power to stand ?
Thou hadst.   Whom hast thou then, or what, to accuse,
But Heaven's free love dealt equally to all ?

Be then His love accursed, since, love or hate,
To me alike it deals eternal woe.
Nay, cursed be thou ; since against His thy will
Chose freely what it now so justly rues.
Me miserable ! which way shall I fly
Infinite wrath and infinite despair ?
Which way I fly is Hell ; myself am Hell ;
And, in the lowest deep, a lower deep
Still threatening to devour me opens wide,
To which the Hell I suffer seems a Heaven.
O, then, at last relent ! Is there no place
Left for repentance, none for pardon left ?
None left but by submission ; and that word
Disdain forbids me, and my dread of shame
Among the Spirits beneath, whom I seduced
With other promises and other vaunts
Than to submit, boasting I could subdue
The Omnipotent. Ay me ! they little know
How dearly I abide that boast so vain,
Under what torments inwardly I groan.
While they adore me on the throne of Hell,
With diadem and sceptre high advanced,
The lower still I fall, only supreme
In misery : such joy ambition finds !
But say I could repent, and could obtain,
By act of grace, my former state ; how soon
Would highth recall high thoughts, how soon unsay
What feigned submission swore ! Ease would recant
Vows made in pain, as violent and void
(For never can true reconcilement grow
Where wounds of deadly hate have pierced so deep) ;
Which would but lead me to a worse relapse
And heavier fall : so should I purchase dear
Short intermission, bought with double smart.
This knows my Punisher ; therefore as far
From granting He, as I from begging, peace.
All hope excluded thus, behold, instead
Of us, outcast, exiled, His new delight,
Mankind, created, and for him this World !
So farewell hope, and, with hope, farewell fear,
Farewell remorse ! All good to me is lost ;
Evil, be thou my Good : by thee at least
Divided empire with Heaven's King I hold,
By thee, and more than half perhaps will reign ;
As Man ere long, and this new World, shall know."
    Thus while he spake, each passion dimmed his face,
Thrice changed with pale—ire, envy, and despair ;
Which marred his borrowed visage, and betrayed
Him counterfeit, if any eye beheld :
For Heavenly minds from such distempers foul
Are ever clear. Whereof he soon aware
Each perturbation smoothed with outward calm,
Artificer of fraud ; and was the first
That practised falsehood under saintly show,

Deep malice to conceal, couched with revenge :
Yet not enough had practised to deceive
Uriel, once warned ; whose eye pursued him down
The way he went, and on the Assyrian mount
Saw him disfigured, more than could befall
Spirit of happy sort : his gestures fierce
He marked and mad demeanour, then alone,
As he supposed, all unobserved, unseen.
    So on he fares, and to the border comes
Of Eden, where delicious Paradise,
Now nearer, crowns with her enclosure green,
As with a rural mound, the champain head
Of a steep wilderness, whose hairy sides
With thicket overgrown, grotesque and wild,
Access denied : and overhead up-grew
Insuperable highth of loftiest shade,
Cedar, and pine, and fir, and branching palm,
A sylvan scene, and, as the ranks ascend
Shade above shade, a woody theatre
Of stateliest view.   Yet higher than their tops
The verdurous wall of Paradise up-sprung ;
Which to our general sire gave prospect large
Into his nether empire neighbouring round.
And higher than that wall a circling row
Of goodliest trees, loaden with fairest fruit,
Blossoms and fruits at once of golden hue,
Appeared, with gay enamelled colours mixed ;
On which the sun more glad impressed his beams
Than in fair evening cloud, or humid bow,
When God hath showered the earth : so lovely seemed
That landskip.   And of pure now purer air
Meets his approach, and to the heart inspires
Vernal delight and joy, able to drive
All sadness but despair.   Now gentle gales,
Fanning their odoriferous wings, dispense
Native perfumes, and whisper whence they stole
Those balmy spoils.   As, when to them who sail
Beyond the Cape of Hope, and now are past
Mozambic, off at sea north-east winds blow
Sabean odours from the spicy shore
Of Araby the Blest, with such delay
Well pleased they slack their course, and many a league
Cheered with the grateful smell old Ocean smiles ;
So entertained those odorous sweets the Fiend
Who came their bane, though with them better pleased
Than Asmodëus with the fishy fume
That drove him, though enamoured, from the spouse
Of Tobit's son, and with a vengeance sent
From Media post to Egypt, there fast bound.
    Now to the ascent of that steep savage hill
Satan had journeyed on, pensive and slow ;
But further way found none ; so thick entwined,
As one continued brake, the undergrowth
Of shrubs and tangling bushes had perplexed

All path of man or beast that passed that way.
One gate there only was, and that looked east
On the other side.   Which when the Arch-Felon saw,
Due entrance he disdained, and, in contempt,
At one slight bound high overleaped all bound
Of hill or highest wall, and sheer within
Lights on his feet.   As when a prowling wolf,
Whom hunger drives to seek new haunt for prey,
Watching where shepherds pen their flocks at eve,
In hurdled cotes amid the field secure,
Leaps o'er the fence with ease into the fold ;
Or as a thief, bent to unhoard the cash
Of some rich burgher, whose substantial doors,
Cross-barred and bolted fast, fear no assault,
In at the window climbs, or o'er the tiles ;
So clomb this first grand Thief into God's fold :
So since into His Church lewd hirelings climb.
Thence up he flew, and on the Tree of Life,
The middle tree and highest there that grew,
Sat like a cormorant ; yet not true life
Thereby regained, but sat devising death
To them who lived : nor on the virtue thought
Of that life-giving plant, but only used
For prospect what, well used, had been the pledge
Of immortality.   So little knows
Any, but God alone, to value right
The good before him, but perverts best things
To worst abuse, or to their meanest use.
Beneath him, with new wonder, now he views,
To all delight of human sense exposed,
In narrow room Nature's whole wealth : yea, more !—
A Heaven on Earth : for blissful Paradise
Of God the garden was, by Him in the east
Of Eden planted.   Eden stretched her line
From Auran eastward to the royal towers
Of great Seleucia, built by Grecian kings,
Or where the sons of Eden long before
Dwelt in Telassar.   In this pleasant soil
His far more pleasant garden God ordained.
Out of the fertile ground He caused to grow
All trees of noblest kind for sight, smell, taste ;
And all amid them stood the Tree of Life,
High eminent, blooming ambrosial fruit
Of vegetable gold ; and next to life,
Our death, the Tree of Knowledge, grew fast by—
Knowledge of good, bought dear by knowing ill.
Southward through Eden went a river large,
Nor changed his course, but through the shaggy hill
Passed underneath ingulfed : for God had thrown
That mountain, as His garden-mould, high raised
Upon the rapid current, which, through veins
Of porous earth with kindly thirst up-drawn,
Rose a fresh fountain, and with many a rill
Watered the garden : thence united fell

Down the steep glade, and met the nether flood,
Which from his darksome passage now appears,
And now, divided into four main streams,
Runs diverse, wandering many a famous realm
And country whereof here needs no account ;
But rather to tell how, if Art could tell
How, from that sapphire fount the crispèd brooks,
Rolling on orient pearl and sands of gold,
With mazy error under pendent shades
Ran nectar, visiting each plant, and fed
Flowers worthy of Paradise, which not nice Art
In beds and curious knots, but Nature boon
Poured forth profuse on hill, and dale, and plain,
Both where the morning sun first warmly smote
The open field, and where the unpierced shade
Imbrowned the noontide bowers.   Thus was this place,
A happy rural seat of various view :
Groves whose rich trees wept odorous gums and balm ;
Others whose fruit, burnished with golden rind,
Hung amiable—Hesperian fables true,
If true, here only—and of delicious taste.
Betwixt them lawns, or level downs, and flocks
Grazing the tender herb, were interposed,
Or palmy hillock ; or the flowery lap
Of some irriguous valley spread her store,
Flowers of all hue, and without thorn the rose.
Another side, umbrageous grots and caves
Of cool recess, o'er which the mantling vine
Lays forth her purple grape, and gently creeps
Luxuriant ; meanwhile murmuring waters fall
Down the slope hills dispersed, or in a lake,
That to the fringèd bank with myrtle crowned
Her crystal mirror holds, unite their streams.
The birds their quire apply ; airs, vernal airs,
Breathing the smell of field and grove, attune
The trembling leaves, while universal Pan,
Knit with the Graces and the Hours in dance,
Led on the eternal Spring.   Not that fair field
Of Enna, where Proserpin gathering flowers,
Herself a fairer flower, by gloomy Dis
Was gathered—which cost Ceres all that pain
To seek her through the world—nor that sweet grove
Of Daphne, by Orontes and the inspired
Castalian spring, might with this Paradise
Of Eden strive ; nor that Nyseian isle,
Girt with the river Triton, where old Cham,
Whom Gentiles Ammon call and Libyan Jove,
Hid Amalthea, and her florid son,
Young Bacchus, from his stepdame Rhea's eye ;
Nor, where Abassin kings their issue guard,
Mount Amara (though this by some supposed
True Paradise) under the Ethiop line
By Nilus' head, enclosed with shining rock,
A whole day's journey high, but wide remote

62

From this Assyrian garden, where the Fiend
Saw undelighted all delight, all kind
Of living creatures, new to sight and strange.
Two of far nobler shape, erect, and tall,
God-like erect, with native honour clad
In naked majesty, seemed lords of all,
And worthy seemed ; for in their looks divine
The image of their glorious Maker shone,
Truth, wisdom, sanctitude severe and pure—
Severe, but in true filial freedom placed,
Whence true authority in men : though both
Not equal, as their sex not equal seemed ;
For contemplation he and valour formed,
For softness she and sweet attractive grace ;
He for God only, she for God in him.
His fair large front and eye sublime declared
Absolute rule ; and hyacinthine locks
Round from his parted forelock manly hung
Clustering, but not beneath his shoulders broad :
She, as a veil down to the slender waist,
Her unadornèd golden tresses wore
Dishevelled, but in wanton ringlets waved
As the vine curls her tendrils—which implied
Subjection, but required with gentle sway,
And by her yielded, by him best received
Yielded, with coy submission, modest pride,
And sweet, reluctant, amorous delay.
Nor those mysterious parts were then concealed ;
Then was not guilty shame. Dishonest shame
Of Nature's works, honour dishonourable,
Sin-bred, how have ye troubled all mankind
With shows instead, mere shows of seeming pure,
And banished from man's life his happiest life,
Simplicity and spotless innocence !
So passed they naked on, nor shunned the sight
Of God or Angel ; for they thought no ill :
So hand in hand they passed, the loveliest pair
That ever since in love's embraces met—
Adam the goodliest man of men since born
His sons ; the fairest of her daughters Eve.
Under a tuft of shade that on a green
Stood whispering soft, by a fresh fountain-side,
They sat them down ; and, after no more toil
Of their sweet gardening labour than sufficed
To recommend cool Zephyr, and make ease
More easy, wholesome thirst and appetite
More grateful, to their supper-fruits they fell—
Nectarine fruits, which the compliant boughs
Yielded them, sidelong as they sat recline
On the soft downy bank damasked with flowers.
The savoury pulp they chew, and in the rind,
Still as they thirsted, scoop the brimming stream ;
Nor gentle purpose, nor endearing smiles
Wanted, nor youthful dalliance, as beseems

Fair couple linked in happy nuptial league,
Alone as they. About them frisking played
All beasts of the earth, since wild, and of all chase
In wood or wilderness, forest or den.
Sporting the lion ramped, and in his paw
Dandled the kid ; bears, tigers, ounces, pards,
Gambolled before them; the unwieldy elephant,
To make them mirth, used all his might, and wreathed
His lithe proboscis ; close the serpent sly,
Insinuating, wove with Gordian twine
His braided train, and of his fatal guile
Gave proof unheeded. Others on the grass
Couched, and, now filled with pasture, gazing sat,
Or bedward ruminating ; for the sun,
Declined, was hastening now with prone career
To the Ocean Isles, and in the ascending scale
Of Heaven the stars that usher evening rose:
When Satan, still in gaze as first he stood,
Scarce thus at length failed speech recovered sad :—
   " O Hell ! what do mine eyes with grief behold?
Into our room of bliss thus high advanced
Creatures of other mould—Earth-born perhaps,
Not Spirits, yet to Heavenly Spirits bright
Little inferior—whom my thoughts pursue
With wonder, and could love ; so lively shines
In them divine resemblance, and such grace
The hand that formed them on their shape hath poured.
Ah ! gentle pair, ye little think how nigh
Your change approaches, when all these delights
Will vanish, and deliver ye to woe—
More woe, the more your taste is now of joy:
Happy, but for so happy ill secured
Long to continue, and this high seat, your Heaven,
Ill fenced for Heaven to keep out such a foe
As now is entered ; yet no purposed foe
To you, whom I could pity thus forlorn,
Though I unpitied. League with you I seek,
And mutual amity, so strait, so close,
That I with you must dwell, or you with me,
Henceforth. My dwelling, haply, may not please,
Like this fair Paradise, your sense ; yet such
Accept your Maker's work ; He gave it me,
Which I as freely give. Hell shall unfold,
To entertain you two, her widest gates,
And send forth all her kings ; there will be room,
Not like these narrow limits, to receive
Your numerous offspring ; if no better place,
Thank Him who puts me, loath, to this revenge
On you, who wrong me not, for him who wronged.
And, should I at your harmless innocence
Melt, as I do, yet public reason just—
Honour and empire with revenge enlarged
By conquering this new World—compels me now
To do what else, though damned, I should abhor."

So spake the Fiend, and with necessity,
The tyrant's plea, excused his devilish deeds.
Then from his lofty stand on that high tree
Down he alights among the sportful herd
Of those four-footed kinds, himself now one,
Now other, as their shape served best his end
Nearer to view his prey, and, unespied,
To mark what of their state he more might learn
By word or action marked.   About them round
A lion now he stalks with fiery glare;
Then as a tiger, who by chance hath spied
In some purlieu two gentle fawns at play,
Straight crouches close ; then, rising, changes oft
His couchant watch, as one who chose his ground,
Whence rushing he might surest seize them both
Griped in each paw: when Adam, first of men,
To first of women, Eve, thus moving speech,
Turned him all ear to hear new utterance flow:—
   "Sole partner and sole part of all these joys,
Dearer thyself than all, needs must the Power
That made us, and for us this ample World,
Be infinitely good, and of His good
As liberal and free as infinite ;
That raised us from the dust, and placed us here
In all this happiness, who at His hand
Have nothing merited, nor can perform
Aught whereof He hath need ; He who requires
From us no other service than to keep
This one, this easy charge—of all the trees
In Paradise that bear delicious fruit
So various, not to taste that only Tree
Of Knowledge, planted by the Tree of Life ;
So near grows Death to Life, whate'er Death is—
Some dreadful thing no doubt; for well thou know'st
God hath pronounced it Death to taste that Tree:
The only sign of our obedience left
Among so many signs of power and rule
Conferred upon us, and dominion given
Over all other creatures that possess
Earth, Air, and Sea.   Then let us not think hard
One easy prohibition, who enjoy
Free leave so large to all things else, and choice
Unlimited of manifold delights ;
But let us ever praise Him, and extol
His bounty, following our delightful task,
To prune these growing plants, and tend these flowers ;
Which, were it toilsome, yet with thee were sweet."
   To whom thus Eve replied :—" O thou for whom
And from whom I was formed flesh of thy flesh,
And without whom am to no end, my guide
And head ! what thou hast said is just and right.
For we to Him, indeed, all praises owe,
And daily thanks— I chiefly, who enjoy
So far the happier lot, enjoying thee

M.—F

Pre-eminent by so much odds, while thou
Like consort to thyself canst nowhere find.
That day I oft remember, when from sleep
I first awaked, and found myself reposed,
Under a shade, on flowers, much wondering where
And what I was, whence thither brought, and how.
Not distant far from thence a murmuring sound
Of waters issued from a cave, and spread
Into a liquid plain ; then stood unmoved,
Pure as the expanse of Heaven. I thither went
With unexperienced thought, and laid me down
On the green bank, to look into the clear
Smooth lake, that to me seemed another sky.
As I bent down to look, just opposite
A shape within the watery gleam appeared,
Bending to look on me. I started back,
It started back ; but pleased I soon returned,
Pleased it returned as soon with answering looks
Of sympathy and love. There I had fixed
Mine eyes till now, and pined with vain desire,
Had not a voice thus warned me : 'What thou seest,
What there thou seest, fair creature, is thyself ;
With thee it came and goes : but follow me,
And I will bring thee where no shadow stays
Thy coming, and thy soft embraces—he
Whose image thou art ; him thou shalt enjoy
Inseparably thine ; to him shalt bear
Multitudes like thyself, and thence be called
Mother of human race.' What could I do,
But follow straight, invisibly thus led ?
Till I espied thee, fair, indeed, and tall,
Under a platane ; yet methought less fair,
Less winning soft, less amiably mild,
Than that smooth watery image. Back I turned ;
Thou, following, criedst aloud, 'Return, fair Eve ;
Whom fliest thou ? Whom thou fliest, of him thou art,
His flesh, his bone ; to give thee being I lent
Out of my side to thee, nearest my heart,
Substantial life, to have thee by my side
Henceforth an individual solace dear :
Part of my soul I seek thee, and thee claim
My other half.' With that thy gentle hand
Seized mine : I yielded, and from that time see
How beauty is excelled by manly grace
And wisdom, which alone is truly fair."
  So spake our general mother, and, with eyes
Of conjugal attraction unreproved,
And meek surrender, half-embracing leaned
On our first father; half her swelling breast
Naked met his, under the flowing gold
Of her loose tresses hid. He, in delight
Both of her beauty and submissive charms,
Smiled with superior love, as Jupiter
On Juno smiles when he impregns the clouds

That shed May flowers, and pressed her matron lip
With kisses pure.   Aside the Devil turned
For envy ; yet with jealous leer malign
Eyed them askance, and to himself thus plained :—
    "Sight hateful, sight tormenting !   Thus these two,
Imparadised in one another's arms,
The happier Eden, shall enjoy their fill
Of bliss on bliss ; while I to Hell am thrust,
Where neither joy nor love, but fierce desire,
Among our other torments not the least,
Still unfulfilled, with pain of longing pines !
Yet let me not forget what I have gained
From their own mouths.   All is not theirs, it seems ;
One fatal tree there stands, of Knowledge called,
Forbidden them to taste.   Knowledge forbidden ?
Suspicious, reasonless !   Why should their Lord
Envy them that ?   Can it be sin to know ?
Can it be death ?   And do they only stand
By ignorance ?   Is that their happy state,
The proof of their obedience and their faith ?
O fair foundation laid whereon to build
Their ruin !   Hence I will excite their minds
With more desire to know, and to reject
Envious commands, invented with design
To keep them low, whom knowledge might exalt
Equal with gods.   Aspiring to be such,
They taste and die : what likelier can ensue ?
But first with narrow search I must walk round
This garden, and no corner leave unspied ;
A chance but chance may lead where I may meet
Some wandering Spirit of Heaven, by fountain-side,
Or in thick shade retired, from him to draw
What further would be learned.   Live while ye may,
Yet happy pair ; enjoy, till I return,
Short pleasures ; for long woes are to succeed ! "
    So saying, his proud step he scornful turned,
But with sly circumspection, and began
Through wood, through waste, o'er hill, o'er dale, his roam.
Meanwhile in utmost longitude, where Heaven
With Earth and Ocean meets, the setting Sun
Slowly descended, and with right aspect
Against the eastern gate of Paradise
Levelled his evening rays.   It was a rock
Of alabaster, piled up to the clouds,
Conspicuous far, winding with one ascent
Accessible from Earth, one entrance high ;
The rest was craggy cliff, that overhung
Still as it rose, impossible to climb.
Betwixt these rocky pillars Gabriel sat,
Chief of the angelic guards, awaiting night ;
About him exercised heroic games
The unarmed youth of Heaven ; but nigh at hand
Celestial armoury, shields, helms, and spears,
Hung high, with diamond flaming and with gold.

Thither came Uriel, gliding through the even
On a sunbeam, swift as a shooting star
In autumn thwarts the night, when vapours fired
Impress the air, and shows the mariner
From what point of his compass to beware
Impetuous winds.   He thus began in haste :—
" Gabriel, to thee thy course by lot hath given
Charge and strict watch that to this happy place
No evil thing approach or enter in.
This day at highth of noon came to my sphere
A Spirit, zealous, as he seemed, to know
More of the Almighty's works, and chiefly Man,
God's latest image.   I descried his way
Bent all on speed, and marked his aery gait,
But in the mount that lies from Eden north,
Where he first lighted, soon discerned his looks
Alien from Heaven, with passions foul obscured.
Mine eye pursued him still, but under shade
Lost sight of him.   One of the banished crew,
I fear, hath ventured from the Deep, to raise
New troubles ; him thy care must be to find."
   To whom the winged Warrior thus returned :—
" Uriel, no wonder if thy perfect sight,
Amid the Sun's bright circle where thou sitt'st,
See far and wide.   In at this gate none pass
The vigilance here placed, but such as come
Well known from Heaven ; and since meridian hour
No creature thence.   If Spirit of other sort,
So minded, have o'erleaped these earthy bounds
On purpose, hard thou know'st it to exclude
Spiritual substance with corporeal bar.
But, if within the circuit of these walks,
In whatsoever shape, he lurk of whom
Thou tell'st, by morrow dawning I shall know."
   So promised he ; and Uriel to his charge
Returned on that bright beam, whose point now raised
Bore him slope downward to the Sun, now fallen
Beneath the Azores ; whether the Prime Orb,
Incredible how swift, had thither rolled
Diurnal, or this less volúbil Earth,
By shorter flight to the east, had left him there
Arraying with reflected purple and gold
The clouds that on his western throne attend.
   Now came still Evening on, and Twilight gray
Had in her sober livery all things clad ;
Silence accompanied ; for beast and bird,
They to their grassy couch, these to their nests
Were slunk, all but the wakeful nightingale.
She all night long her amorous descant sung :
Silence was pleased.   Now glowed the firmament
With living sapphires ; Hesperus, that led
The starry host, rode brightest, till the Moon,
Rising in clouded majesty, at length
Apparent queen, unveiled her peerless light,

And o'er the dark her silver mantle threw ;
When Adam thus to Eve :—" Fair consort, the hour
Of night, and all things now retired to rest,
Mind us of like repose ; since God hath set
Labour and rest, as day and night, to men
Successive, and the timely dew of sleep,
Now falling with soft slumberous weight, inclines
Our eye-lids.   Other creatures all day long
Rove idle, unemployed, and less need rest ;
Man hath his daily work of body or mind
Appointed, which declares his dignity,
And the regard of Heaven on all his ways ;
While other animals unactive range,
And of their doings God takes no account.
To-morrow, ere fresh morning streak the east
With first approach of light, we must be risen,
And at our pleasant labour, to reform
Yon flowery arbours, yonder alleys green,
Our walk at noon, with branches overgrown,
That mock our scant manuring, and require
More hands than ours to lop their wanton growth.
Those blossoms also, and those dropping gums,
That lie bestrewn, unsightly and unsmooth,
Ask riddance, if we mean to tread with ease.
Meanwhile, as Nature wills, Night bids us rest."
    To whom thus Eve, with perfect beauty adorned :—
" My author and disposer, what thou bidd'st
Unargued I obey.   So God ordains :
God is thy law, thou mine : to know no more
Is woman's happiest knowledge, and her praise.
With thee conversing, I forget all time,
All seasons, and their change ; all please alike.
Sweet is the breath of Morn, her rising sweet,
With charm of earliest birds ; pleasant the Sun,
When first on this delightful land he spreads
His orient beams, on herb, tree, fruit, and flower,
Glistening with dew : fragrant the fertile Earth
After soft showers ; and sweet the coming-on
Of grateful Evening mild ; then silent Night,
With this her solemn bird, and this fair Moon,
And these the gems of Heaven, her starry train :
But neither breath of Morn, when she ascends
With charm of earliest birds ; nor rising Sun
On this delightful land ; nor herb, fruit, flower,
Glistering with dew ; nor fragrance after showers ;
Nor grateful Evening mild ; nor silent Night,
With this her solemn bird ; nor walk by moon,
Or glittering star-light, without thee is sweet.
But wherefore all night long shine these ? for whom
This glorious sight, when sleep hath shut all eyes ?"
    To whom our general ancestor replied :—
" Daughter of God and Man, accomplished Eve,
Those have their course to finish round the Earth
By morrow evening, and from land to land

In order, though to nations yet unborn,
Ministering light prepared, they set and rise ;
Lest total Darkness should by night regain
Her old possession, and extinguish life
In nature and all things ; which these soft fires
Not only enlighten, but with kindly heat
Of various influence foment and warm,
Temper or nourish, or in part shed down
Their stellar virtue on all kinds that grow
On Earth, made hereby apter to receive
Perfection from the Sun's more potent ray.
These, then, though unbeheld in deep of night,
Shine not in vain. Nor think, though men were none,
That Heaven would want spectators, God want praise.
Millions of spiritual creatures walk the Earth
Unseen, both when we wake, and when we sleep :
All these with ceaseless praise His works behold
Both day and night. How often, from the steep
Of echoing hill or thicket, have we heard
Celestial voices to the midnight air,
Sole, or responsive each to other's note,
Singing their great Creator ! Oft in bands
While they keep watch, or nightly rounding walk,
With heavenly touch of instrumental sounds
In full harmonic number joined, their songs
Divide the night, and lift our thoughts to Heaven."
   Thus talking, hand in hand alone they passed
On to their blissful bower. It was a place
Chosen by the sovran Planter, when He framed
All things to Man's delightful use. The roof
Of thickest covert was inwoven shade,
Laurel and myrtle, and what higher grew
Of firm and fragrant leaf ; on either side
Acanthus, and each odorous bushy shrub
Fenced up the verdant wall ; each beauteous flower,
Iris all hues, roses, and jessamine,
Reared high their flourished heads between, and wrought
Mosaic ; under foot the violet,
Crocus, and hyacinth, with rich inlay
Broidered the ground, more coloured than with stone
Of costliest emblem. Other creature here,
Beast, bird, insect, or worm, durst enter none ;
Such was their awe of Man. In shadier bower
More sacred and sequestered, though but feigned,
Pan or Sylvanus never slept, nor Nymph
Nor Faunus haunted. Here, in close recess,
With flowers, garlands, and sweet-smelling herbs,
Espousèd Eve decked first her nuptial bed,
And heavenly choirs the hymenæan sung,
What day the genial Angel to our sire
Brought her, in naked beauty more adorned,
More lovely, than Pandora, whom the gods
Endowed with all their gifts ; and, O ! too like
In sad event, when, to the unwiser son

Of Japhet brought by Hermes, she ensnared
Mankind with her fair looks, to be avenged
On him who had stole Jove's authentic fire.
   Thus at their shady lodge arrived, both stood,
Both turned, and under open sky adored
The God that made both Sky, Air, Earth, and Heaven,
Which they beheld, the Moon's resplendent globe,
And starry Pole :—"Thou also madest the Night,
Maker Omnipotent ; and Thou the Day,
Which we, in our appointed work employed,
Have finished, happy in our mutual help
And mutual love, the crown of all our bliss
Ordained by Thee ; and this delicious place,
For us too large, where Thy abundance wants
Partakers, and uncropt falls to the ground.
But Thou hast promised from us two a race
To fill the Earth, who shall with us extol
Thy goodness infinite, both when we wake,
And when we seek, as now, Thy gift of sleep."
   This said unanimous, and other rites
Observing none, but adoration pure,
Which God likes best, into their inmost bower
Handed they went ; and, eased the putting-off
These troublesome disguises which we wear,
Straight side by side were laid ; nor turned, I ween,
Adam from his fair spouse, nor Eve the rites
Mysterious of connubial love refused :
Whatever hypocrites austerely talk
Of purity, and place, and innocence,
Defaming as impure what God declares
Pure, and commands to some, leaves free to all.
Our Maker bids increase ; who bids abstain
But our destroyer, foe to God and Man ?
Hail, wedded Love, mysterious law, true source
Of human offspring, sole propriety
In Paradise of all things common else !
By thee adulterous lust was driven from men
Among the bestial herds to range : by thee,
Founded in reason, loyal, just, and pure,
Relations dear, and all the charities
Of father, son, and brother, first were known.
Far be it that I should write thee sin or blame,
Or think thee unbefitting holiest place,
Perpetual fountain of domestic sweets,
Whose bed is undefiled and chaste pronounced,
Present, or past, as saints and patriarchs used.
Here Love his golden shafts employs, here lights
His constant lamp, and waves his purple wings,
Reigns here and revels ; not in the bought smile
Of harlots—loveless, joyless, unendeared,
Casual fruition ; nor in court amours,
Mixed dance, or wanton mask, or midnight ball,
Or serenate, which the starved lover sings
To his proud fair, best quitted with disdain.

These, lulled by nightingales, embracing slept,
And on their naked limbs the flowery roof
Showered roses, which the morn repaired.   Sleep on,
Blest pair ! and, O ! yet happiest, if ye seek
No happier state, and know to know no more !
　Now had Night measured with her shadowy cone
Half-way up-hill this vast sublunar vault,
And from their ivory port the Cherubim
Forth issuing at the accustomed hour, stood armed
To their night-watches in warlike parade ;
When Gabriel to his next in power thus spake :—
　"Uzziel, half these draw off, and coast the south
With strictest watch ; these other wheel the north :
Our circuit meets full west."   As flame they part,
Half wheeling to the shield, half to the spear.
From these, two strong and subtle Spirits he called
That near him stood, and gave them thus in charge :—
　"Ithuriel and Zephon, with winged speed
Search through this Garden ; leave unsearched no nook ;
But chiefly where those two fair creatures lodge,
Now laid perhaps asleep, secure of harm.
This evening from the Sun's decline arrived
Who tells of some infernal Spirit seen
Hitherward bent (who could have thought ?), escaped
The bars of Hell, on errand bad, no doubt :
Such, where ye find, seize fast, and hither bring."
　So saying, on he led his radiant files,
Dazzling the moon ; these to the bower direct
In search of whom they sought.   Him there they found
Squat like a toad, close at the ear of Eve,
Assaying by his devilish art to reach
The organs of her fancy, and with them forge
Illusions as he list, phantasms and dreams ;
Or if, inspiring venom, he might taint
The animal spirits, that from pure blood arise
Like gentle breaths from rivers pure, thence raise,
At least distempered, discontented thoughts,
Vain hopes, vain aims, inordinate desires,
Blown up with high conceits engendering pride.
Him thus intent Ithuriel with his spear
Touched lightly ; for no falsehood can endure
Touch of celestial temper, but returns
Of force to its own likeness.   Up he starts,
Discovered and surprised.   As, when a spark
Lights on a heap of nitrous powder, laid
Fit for the tun, some magazine to store
Against a rumoured war, the smutty grain,
With sudden blaze diffused, inflames the air :
So started up, in his own shape, the Fiend.
Back stept those two fair Angels, half amazed
So sudden to behold the grisly King ;
Yet thus, unmoved with fear, accost him soon :—
　"Which of those rebel Spirits adjudged to Hell
Com'st thou, escaped thy prison ? and, transformed,

72

Why satt'st thou like an enemy in wait,
Here watching at the head of these that sleep ?"
  "Know ye not, then," said Satan, filled with scorn,
"Know ye not me ? Ye knew me once no mate
For you, there sitting where ye durst not soar !
Not to know me argues yourselves unknown,
The lowest of your throng ; or, if ye know,
Why ask ye, and superfluous begin
Your message, like to end as much in vain ?"
  To whom thus Zephon, answering scorn with scorn :—
"Think not, revolted Spirit, thy shape the same,
Or undiminished brightness, to be known
As when thou stood'st in Heaven upright and pure.
That glory then, when thou no more wast good,
Departed from thee ; and thou resemblest now
Thy sin and place of doom obscure and foul.
But come ; for thou, be sure, shalt give account
To Him who sent us, whose charge is to keep
This place inviolable, and these from harm."
  So spake the Cherub ; and his grave rebuke,
Severe in youthful beauty, added grace
Invincible. Abashed the Devil stood,
And felt how awful goodness is, and saw
Virtue in her shape how lovely—saw, and pined
His loss ; but chiefly to find here observed
His lustre visibly impaired ; yet seemed
Undaunted. "If I must contend," said he,
"Best with the best—the sender, not the sent ;
Or all at once : more glory will be won,
Or less be lost." "Thy fear," said Zephon bold,
"Will save us trial what the least can do
Single against thee wicked, and thence weak."
  The Fiend replied not, overcome with rage ;
But, like a proud steed reined, went haughty on,
Champing his iron curb. To strive or fly
He held it vain ; awe from above had quelled
His heart, not else dismayed. Now drew they nigh
The western point, where those half-rounding guards
Just met, and, closing, stood in squadron joined,
Awaiting next command. To whom their chief,
Gabriel, from the front thus called aloud :—
  "O friends, I hear the tread of nimble feet
Hasting this way, and now by glimpse discern
Ithuriel and Zephon through the shade ;
And with them comes a third, of regal port,
But faded splendour wan, who by his gait
And fierce demeanour seems the Prince of Hell—
Not likely to part hence without contest.
Stand firm, for in his look defiance lours."
  He scarce had ended, when those two approached,
And brief related whom they brought, where found,
How busied, in what form and posture couched.
To whom, with stern regard, thus Gabriel spake :—
"Why hast thou, Satan, broke the bounds prescribed

73

To thy transgressions, and disturbed the charge
Of others, who approve not to transgress
By thy example, but have power and right
To question thy bold entrance on this place ;
Employed, it seems, to violate sleep, and those
Whose dwelling God hath planted here in bliss ?"
    To whom thus Satan, with contemptuous brow :—
"Gabriel, thou hadst in Heaven the esteem of wise ;
And such I held thee ; but this question asked
Puts me in doubt. Lives there who loves his pain ?
Who would not, finding way, break loose from Hell,
Though thither doomed ? Thou wouldst thyself, no doubt,
And boldly venture to whatever place
Farthest from pain, where thou mightst hope to change
Torment with ease, and soonest recompense
Dole with delight ; which in this place I sought :
To thee no reason, who know'st only good,
But evil hast not tried. And wilt object
His will who bound us ? Let Him surer bar
His iron gates, if He intends our stay
In that dark durance. Thus much what was asked :
The rest is true ; they found me where they say ;
But that implies not violence or harm."
    Thus he in scorn. The warlike Angel moved,
Disdainfully half smiling, thus replied :—
"O loss of one in Heaven to judge of wise,
Since Satan fell, whom folly overthrew,
And now returns him from his prison scaped,
Gravely in doubt whether to hold them wise
Or not who ask what boldness brought him hither
Unlicensed from his bounds in Hell prescribed !
So wise he judges it to fly from pain
However, and to scape his punishment !
So judge thou still, presumptuous, till the wrath,
Which thou incurr'st by flying, meet thy flight
Sevenfold, and scourge that wisdom back to Hell,
Which taught thee yet no better that no pain
Can equal anger infinite provoked.
But wherefore thou alone ? Wherefore with thee
Came not all Hell broke loose ? Is pain to them
Less pain, less to be fled ? or thou than they
Less hardy to endure ? Courageous chief,
The first in flight from pain, hadst thou alleged
To thy deserted host this cause of flight,
Thou surely hadst not come sole fugitive."
    To which the Fiend thus answered, frowning stern :—
"Not that I less endure, or shrink from pain,
Insulting Angel ! well thou know'st I stood
Thy fiercest, when in battle to thy aid
The blasting volleyed thunder made all speed
And seconded thy else not dreaded spear.
But still thy words at random, as before,
Argue thy inexperience what behoves,
From hard assays and ill successes past,

74

A faithful leader—not to hazard all
Through ways of danger by himself untried
I, therefore, I alone, first undertook
To wing the desolate Abyss, and spy
This new-created World, whereof in Hell
Fame is not silent, here in hope to find
Better abode, and my afflicted Powers
To settle here on Earth, or in mid Air ;
Though for possession put to try once more
What thou and thy gay legions dare against ;
Whose easier business were to serve their Lord
High up in Heaven, with songs to hymn His throne,
And practised distances to cringe, not fight."—
   To whom the Warrior-Angel soon replied :—
" To say and straight unsay, pretending first
Wise to fly pain, professing next the spy,
Argues no leader, but a liar traced,
Satan ; and couldst thou 'faithful' add ?   O name,
O sacred name of faithfulness profaned !
Faithful to whom ? to thy rebellious crew ?
Army of fiends, fit body to fit head !
Was this your discipline and faith engaged,
Your military obedience, to dissolve
Allegiance to the acknowledged Power Supreme ?
And thou, sly hypocrite, who now wouldst seem
Patron of liberty, who more than thou
Once fawned, and cringed, and servilely adored
Heaven's awful Monarch ? wherefore, but in hope
To dispossess Him, and thyself to reign ?
But mark what I areed thee now : Avaunt !
Fly thither whence thou fledd'st.   If from this hour
Within these hallowed limits thou appear,
Back to the Infernal Pit I drag thee chained,
And seal thee so as henceforth not to scorn
The facile gates of Hell too slightly barred."
   So threatened he ; but Satan to no threats
Gave heed, but waxing more in rage, replied :—
" Then, when I am thy captive, talk of chains,
Proud limitary Cherub ! but ere then
Far heavier load thyself expect to feel
From my prevailing arm, though Heaven's King
Ride on thy wings, and thou with thy compeers,
Used to the yoke, draw'st His triumphant wheels
In progress through the road of Heaven star-paved."
   While thus he spake, the angelic squadron bright
Turned fiery red, sharpening in moonèd horns
Their phalanx, and began to hem him round
With ported spears, as thick as when a field
Of Ceres ripe for harvest waving bends
Her bearded grove of ears which way the wind
Sways them ; the careful ploughman doubting stands
Lest on the threshing-floor his hopeful sheaves
Prove chaff.   On the other side, Satan, alarmed,
Collecting all his might, dilated stood,

Like Teneriff or Atlas, unremoved :
His stature reached the sky, and on his crest
Sat Horror plumed ; nor wanted in his grasp
What seemed both spear and shield.   Now dreadful deeds
Might have ensued ; nor only Paradise,
In this commotion, but the starry cope
Of Heaven perhaps, or all the Elements
At least, had gone to wrack, disturbed and torn
With violence of this conflict, had not soon
The Eternal, to prevent such horrid fray,
Hung forth in Heaven His golden scales, yet seen
Betwixt Astræa and the Scorpion sign,
Wherein all things created first He weighed,
The pendulous round Earth with balanced air
In counterpoise, now ponders all events,
Battles and realms.   In these He put two weights,
The sequel each of parting and of fight :
The latter quick up flew, and kicked the beam ;
Which Gabriel spying thus bespake the Fiend :—
   "Satan, I know thy strength, and thou know'st mine,
Neither our own, but given ; what folly then
To boast what arms can do ! since thine no more
Than Heaven permits, nor mine, though doubled now
To trample thee as mire.   For proof look up,
And read thy lot in yon celestial sign,
Where thou art weighed, and shown how light, how weak
If thou resist."   The Fiend looked up, and knew
His mounted scale aloft : nor more ; but fled
Murmuring ; and with him fled the shades of Night.

THE END OF THE FOURTH BOOK.

PARADISE LOST.

BOOK V.

THE ARGUMENT.

Morning approached, Eve relates to Adam her troublesome dream; he likes it not, yet comforts her: they come forth to their day labours: their morning hymn at the door of their bower. God, to render Man inexcusable, sends Raphael to admonish him of his obedience, of his free estate, of his enemy near at hand, who he is, and why his enemy, and whatever else may avail Adam to know. Raphael comes down to Paradise; his appearance described; his coming discerned by Adam afar off, sitting at the door of his bower; he goes out to meet him, brings him to his lodge, entertains him with the choicest fruits of Paradise, got together by Eve; their discourse at table. Raphael performs his message, minds Adam of his state and of his enemy; relates, at Adam's request, who that enemy is, and how he came to be so, beginning from his first revolt in Heaven, and the occasion thereof; how he drew his legions after him to the parts of the North, and there incited them to rebel with him, persuading all but only Abdiel, a seraph, who in argument dissuades and opposes him, then forsakes him.

Now Morn, her rosy steps in the eastern clime
Advancing, sowed the earth with orient pearl,
When Adam waked, so customed; for his sleep
Was aery light, from pure digestion bred,
And temperate vapours bland, which the only sound
Of leaves and fuming rills, Aurora's fan,
Lightly dispersed, and the shrill matin song
Of birds on every bough. So much the more
His wonder was to find unwakened Eve,
With tresses discomposed, and glowing cheek,
As through unquiet rest. He, on his side
Leaning half raised, with looks of cordial love
Hung over her enamoured, and beheld
Beauty which, whether waking or asleep,
Shot forth peculiar graces; then, with voice
Mild as when Zephyrus on Flora breathes,
Her hand soft touching, whispered thus :—"Awake,
My fairest, my espoused, my latest found,
Heaven's last, best gift, my ever-new delight!
Awake! the morning shines, and the fresh field
Calls us; we lose the prime to mark how spring
Our tended plants, how blows the citron grove,
What drops the myrrh, and what the balmy reed,

How Nature paints her colours, how the bee
Sits on the bloom extracting liquid sweet."
   Such whispering waked her, but with startled eye
On Adam ; whom embracing, thus she spake :—
  "O sole in whom my thoughts find all repose,
My glory, my perfection ! glad I see
Thy face, and morn returned ; for I this night
(Such night till this I never passed) have dreamed,
If dreamed, not, as I oft am wont, of thee,
Works of day passed, or morrow's next design ;
But of offence and trouble, which my mind
Knew never till this irksome night. Methought
Close at mine ear one called me forth to walk
With gentle voice ; I thought it thine. It said,
'Why sleep'st thou, Eve ? now is the pleasant time,
The cool, the silent, save where silence yields
To the night-warbling bird, that now awake
Tunes sweetest his love-laboured song ; now reigns
Full-orbed the moon, and, with more pleasing light,
Shadowy, sets off the face of things—in vain,
If none regard. Heaven wakes with all his eyes ;
Whom to behold but thee, Nature's desire,
In whose sight all things joy, with ravishment
Attracted by thy beauty still to gaze ?'
I rose as at thy call, but found thee not :
To find thee I directed then my walk ;
And on, methought, alone I passed through ways
That brought me on a sudden to the tree
Of interdicted knowledge. Fair it seemed,
Much fairer to my fancy than by day ;
And, as I wondering looked, beside it stood
One shaped and winged like one of those from Heaven
By us oft seen : his dewy locks distilled
Ambrosia. On that tree he also gazed ;
And, 'O fair plant,' said he, 'with fruit surcharged,
Deigns none to ease thy load, and taste thy sweet,
Nor God nor Man ? Is knowledge so despised ?
Or envy, or what reserve forbids to taste ?
Forbid who will, none shall from me withhold
Longer thy offered good, why else set here ?'
This said, he paused not, but with venturous arm
He plucked, he tasted. Me damp horror chilled
At such bold words vouched with a deed so bold ;
But he thus, overjoyed : ' O fruit divine,
Sweet of thyself, but much more sweet thus cropt,
Forbidden here, it seems, as only fit
For gods, yet able to make gods of men !
And why not gods of men, since good, the more
Communicated, more abundant grows,
The author not impaired, but honoured more ?
Here, happy creature, fair angelic Eve !
Partake thou also : happy though thou art,
Happier thou may'st be, worthier canst not be.
Taste this, and be henceforth among the gods

78

Thyself a goddess ; not to Earth confined,
But sometimes in the Air, as we ; sometimes
Ascend to Heaven, by merit thine, and see
What life the gods live there, and such live thou.'
So saying, he drew nigh, and to me held,
Even to my mouth of that same fruit held part
Which he had plucked : the pleasant savoury smell
So quickened appetite that I, methought,
Could not but taste.   Forthwith up to the clouds
With him I flew, and underneath beheld
The Earth outstretched immense, a prospect wide
And various.   Wondering at my flight and change
To this high exaltation, suddenly
My guide was gone, and I, methought, sunk down,
And fell asleep ; but, O, how glad I waked
To find this but a dream !"   Thus Eve her night
Related, and thus Adam answered sad :—
   "Best image of myself, and dearer half,
The trouble of thy thoughts this night in sleep
Affects me equally ; nor can I like
This uncouth dream—of evil sprung, I fear ;
Yet evil whence ?   In thee can harbour none,
Created pure.   But know that in the soul
Are many lesser faculties, that serve
Reason as chief.   Among these Fancy next
Her office holds ; of all external things,
Which the five watchful senses represent,
She forms imaginations, aery shapes,
Which reason, joining or disjoining, frames
All what we affirm or what deny, and call
Our knowledge or opinion ; then retires
Into her private cell when Nature rests.
Oft, in her absence, mimic Fancy wakes
To imitate her ; but, misjoining shapes,
Wild work produces oft, and most in dreams,
Ill matching words and deeds long past or late.
Some such resemblances, methinks, I find
Of our last evening's talk in this thy dream,
But with addition strange.   Yet be not sad :
Evil into the mind of God or Man
May come and go, so unapproved, and leave
No spot or blame behind ; which gives me hope
That what in sleep thou didst abhor to dream
Waking thou never wilt consent to do.
Be not disheartened, then, nor cloud those looks,
That wont to be more cheerful and serene
Than when fair Morning first smiles on the world ;
And let us to our fresh employments rise
Among the groves, the fountains, and the flowers,
That open now their choicest bosomed smells,
Reserved from night, and kept for thee in store."
   So cheered he his fair spouse ; and she was cheered,
But silently a gentle tear let fall
From either eye, and wiped them with her hair :

Two other precious drops that ready stood,
Each in their crystal sluice, he, ere they fell,
Kissed as the gracious signs of sweet remorse
And pious awe, that feared to have offended.
  So all was cleared, and to the field they haste.
But first from under shady arborous roof
Soon as they forth were come to open sight
Of day-spring, and the Sun—who, scarce uprisen,
With wheels yet hovering o'er the ocean-brim,
Shot parallel to the Earth his dewy ray,
Discovering in wide landskip all the east
Of Paradise and Eden's happy plains—
Lowly they bowed, adoring, and began
Their orisons, each morning duly paid
In various style ; for neither various style
Nor holy rapture wanted they to praise
Their Maker, in fit strains pronounced, or sung
Unmeditated ; such prompt eloquence
Flowed from their lips, in prose or numerous verse,
More tuneable than needed lute or harp
To add more sweetness: And they thus began:—
  " These are Thy glorious works, Parent of good,
Almighty ! Thine this universal frame,
Thus wondrous fair: Thyself how wondrous then!
Unspeakable ! who sitt'st above these heavens
To us invisible, or dimly seen
In these Thy lowest works ; yet these declare
Thy goodness beyond thought, and power divine.
Speak, ye who best can tell, ye Sons of Light,
Angels—for ye behold Him, and with songs
And choral symphonies, day without night,
Circle His throne rejoicing—ye in Heaven ;
On Earth join, all ye creatures, to extol
Him first, Him last, Him midst, and without end.
Fairest of Stars, last in the train of Night,
If better thou belong not to the Dawn,
Sure pledge of day, that crown'st the smiling morn
With thy bright circlet, praise Him in thy sphere
While day arises, that sweet hour of prime.
Thou Sun, of this great World both eye and soul,
Acknowledge Him thy greater ; sound His praise
In thy eternal course, both when thou climb'st
And when high noon hast gained, and when thou fall'st.
Moon, that now meet'st the orient Sun, now fliest,
With the fixed Stars, fixed in their orb that flies ;
And ye five other wandering Fires, that move
In mystic dance, not without song, resound
His praise who out of Darkness called up Light.
Air, and ye Elements, the eldest birth
Of Nature's womb, that in quaternion run
Perpetual circle, multiform, and mix
And nourish all things, let your ceaseless change
Vary to our great Maker still new praise.
Ye Mists and Exhalations, that now rise

From hill or steaming lake, dusky or gray,
Till the sun paint your fleecy skirts with gold,
In honour to the World's great Author rise;
Whether to deck with clouds the uncoloured sky,
Or wet the thirsty earth with falling showers,
Rising or falling, still advance His praise.
His praise, ye Winds, that from four quarters blow,
Breathe soft or loud ; and wave your tops, ye Pines,
With every Plant, in sign of worship wave.
Fountains, and ye, that warble, as ye flow,
Melodious murmurs, warbling tune His praise.
Join voices, all ye living Souls.   Ye Birds,
That, singing, up to Heaven-gate ascend,
Bear on your wings and in your notes His praise.
Ye that in waters glide, and ye that walk
The earth, and stately tread, or lowly creep,
Witness if *I* be silent, morn or even,
To hill or valley, fountain, or fresh shade,
Made vocal by my song, and taught His praise.
Hail, universal Lord!   Be bounteous still
To give us only good; and, if the night
Have gathered aught of evil, or concealed,
Disperse it, as now light dispels the dark."
   So prayed they innocent, and to their thoughts
Firm peace recovered soon, and wonted calm.
On to their morning's rural work they haste,
Among sweet dews and flowers, where any row
Of fruit-trees, over-woody, reached too far
Their pampered boughs, and needed hands to check
Fruitless embraces: or they led the vine
To wed her elm; she, spoused, about him twines
Her marriageable arms, and with her brings
Her dower, the adopted clusters, to adorn
His barren leaves.   Them thus employed beheld
With pity Heaven's high King, and to Him called
Raphael, the sociable Spirit, that deigned
To travel with Tobias, and secured
His marriage with the seven-times-wedded maid.
   "Raphael," said He, " thou hear'st what stir on Earth
Satan, from Hell scaped through the darksome Gulf,
Hath raised in Paradise, and how disturbed
This night the human pair ; how he designs
In them at once to ruin all mankind.
Go, therefore; half this day, as friend with friend,
Converse with Adam, in what bower or shade
Thou find'st him from the heat of noon retired
To respite his day-labour with repast
Or with repose ; and such discourse bring on
As may advise him of his happy state—
Happiness in his power left free to will,
Left to his own free will, his will though free
Yet mutable.   Whence warn him to beware
He swerve not, too secure: tell him withal
His danger, and from whom: what enemy,

M.—G

Late fallen himself from Heaven, is plotting now
The fall of others from like state of bliss.
By violence? no, for that shall be withstood;
But by deceit and lies. This let him know,
Lest, wilfully transgressing, he pretend
Surprisal, unadmonished, unforewarned."
 So spake the Eternal Father, and fulfilled
All justice. Nor delayed the wingèd Saint
After his charge received; but from among
Thousand celestial Ardours, where he stood
Veiled with his gorgeous wings, upspringing light,
Flew through the midst of Heaven. The angelic quires,
On each hand parting, to his speed gave way
Through all the empyreal road, till, at the gate
Of Heaven arrived, the gate self-opened wide,
On golden hinges turning, as by work
Divine the sovran Architect had framed.
From hence—no cloud or, to obstruct his sight,
Star interposed, however small—he sees,
Not unconform to other shining globes,
Earth, and the Garden of God, with cedars crowned
Above all hills; as when by night the glass
Of Galileo, less assured, observes
Imagined lands and regions in the Moon;
Or pilot from amidst the Cyclades
Delos or Samos first appearing kens,
A cloudy spot. Down thither prone in flight
He speeds, and through the vast ethereal sky
Sails between worlds and worlds, with steady wing
Now on the polar winds; then with quick fan
Winnows the buxom air, till, within soar
Of towering eagles, to all the fowls he seems
A phœnix, gazed by all, as that sole bird,
When, to enshrine his relics in the Sun's
Bright temple, to Egyptian Thebes he flies.
At once on the eastern cliff of Paradise
He lights, and to his proper shape returns,
A Seraph winged. Six wings he wore, to shade
His lineaments divine: the pair that clad
Each shoulder broad came mantling o'er his breast
With regal ornament; the middle pair
Girt like a starry zone his waist, and round
Skirted his loins and thighs with downy gold
And colours dipt in heaven; the third his feet
Shadowed from either heel with feathered mail,
Sky-tinctured grain. Like Maia's son he stood,
And shook his plumes, that heavenly fragrance filled
The circuit wide. Straight knew him all the bands
Of Angels under watch, and to his state
And to his message high in honour rise;
For on some message high they guessed him bound.
Their glittering tents he passed, and now is come
Into the blissful field, through groves of myrrh,
And flowering odours, cassia, nard, and balm,

A wilderness of sweets; for Nature here
Wantoned as in her prime, and played at will
Her virgin fancies, pouring forth more sweet,
Wild above rule or art, enormous bliss.
Him, through the spicy forest onward come,
Adam discerned, as in the door he sat
Of his cool bower, while now the mounted Sun
Shot down direct his fervid rays, to warm
Earth's inmost womb, more warmth than Adam needs;
And Eve, within, due at her hour, prepared
For dinner savoury fruits, of taste to please
True appetite, and not disrelish thirst
Of nectarous draughts between, from milky stream,
Berry or grape : to whom thus Adam called :—
    "Haste hither, Eve, and, worth thy sight, behold
Eastward among those trees what glorious Shape
Comes this way moving ; seems another morn
Risen on mid-noon.   Some great behest from Heaven
To us perhaps he brings, and will vouchsafe
This day to be our guest.   But go with speed,
And what thy stores contain bring forth, and pour
Abundance fit to honour and receive
Our heavenly stranger ; well we may afford
Our givers their own gifts, and large bestow
From large bestowed, where Nature multiplies
Her fertile growth, and by disburdening grows
More fruitful ; which instructs us not to spare."
    To whom thus Eve :—"Adam, Earth's hallowed mould,
Of God inspired, small store will serve where store,
All seasons, ripe for use hangs on the stalk ;
Save what, by frugal storing, firmness gains
To nourish, and superfluous moist consumes.
But I will haste, and from each bough and brake,
Each plant and juciest gourd, will pluck such choice
To entertain our Angel-guest as he,
Beholding, shall confess that here on Earth
God hath dispensed His bounties as in Heaven."
    So saying, with dispatchful looks in haste
She turns, on hospitable thoughts intent
What choice to choose for delicacy best,
What order so contrived as not to mix
Tastes, not well joined, inelegant, but bring
Taste after taste upheld with kindliest change :
Bestirs her then, and from each tender stalk
Whatever Earth, all-bearing mother, yields
In India East or West, or middle shore
In Pontus or the Punic coast, or where
Alcinöus reigned, fruit of all kinds, in coat
Rough or smooth rined, or bearded husk, or shell,
She gathers, tribute large, and on the board
Heaps with unsparing hand.   For drink the grape
She crushes, inoffensive must, and meaths
From many a berry, and from sweet kernels pressed
She tempers dulcet creams—nor these to hold

Wants her fit vessels pure ; then strews the ground
With rose and odours from the shrub unfumed.
  Meanwhile our primitive great Sire, to meet
His godlike guest, walks forth, without more train
Accompanied than with his own complete
Perfections ; in himself was all his state,
More solemn than the tedious pomp that waits
On princes, when their rich retinue long
Of horses led and grooms besmeared with gold
Dazzles the crowd and sets them all agape.
Nearer his presence, Adam, though not awed,
Yet with submiss approach and reverence meek,
As to a superior nature, bowing low,
Thus said :—"Native of Heaven (for other place
None can than Heaven such glorious Shape contain),
Since, by descending from the Thrones above,
Those happy places thou hast deigned a while
To want, and honour these, vouchsafe with us,
Two only, who yet by sovran gift possess
This spacious ground, in yonder shady bower
To rest, and what the Garden choicest bears
To sit and taste, till this meridian heat
Be over, and the sun more cool decline."
  Whom thus the angelic Virtue answered mild :—
"Adam, I therefore came ; nor art thou such
Created, or such place hast here to dwell,
As may not oft invite, though Spirits of Heaven,
To visit thee.   Lead on, then, where thy bower
O'ershades ; for these mid-hours, till evening rise,
I have at will."   So to the sylvan lodge
They came, that like Pomona's arbour smiled,
With flowerets decked and fragrant smells.   But Eve,
Undecked, save with herself, more lovely fair
Than wood-nymph, or the fairest goddess feigned
Of three that in Mount Ida naked strove,
Stood to entertain her guest from Heaven ; no veil
She needed, virtue-proof ; no thought infirm
Altered her cheek.   On whom the Angel "Hail !"
Bestowed—the holy salutation used
Long after to blest Mary, second Eve :—
  "Hail ! Mother of mankind, whose fruitful womb
Shall fill the world more numerous with thy sons
Than with these various fruits the trees of God
Have heaped this table !"   Raised of grassy turf
Their table was, and mossy seats had round,
And on her ample square, from side to side,
All Autumn piled, though Spring and Autumn here
Danced hand-in-hand.   A while discourse they hold—
No fear lest dinner cool—when thus began
Our Author :—"Heavenly Stranger, please to taste
These bounties, which our Nourisher, from whom
All perfect good, unmeasured-out, descends,
To us for food and for delight hath caused
The Earth to yield : unsavoury food, perhaps,

To Spiritual Natures ; only this I know,
That one Celestial Father gives to all."
    To whom the Angel :—"Therefore, what He gives
(Whose praise be ever sung) to Man, in part
Spiritual, may of purest Spirits be found
No ingrateful food : and food alike those pure
Intelligential substances require
As doth your Rational ; and both contain
Within them every lower faculty
Of sense, whereby they hear, see, smell, touch, taste,
Tasting concoct, digest, assimilate,
And corporeal to incorporeal turn.
For know, whatever was created needs
To be sustained and fed. Of Elements
The grosser feeds the purer : Earth the Sea ;
Earth and the Sea feed Air ; the Air those Fires
Ethereal, and, as lowest, first the Moon ;
Whence in her visage round those spots, unpurged
Vapours not yet into her substance turned.
Nor doth the Moon no nourishment exhale
From her moist continent to higher Orbs.
The Sun, that light imparts to all, receives
From all his alimental recompense
In humid exhalations, and at even
Sups with the Ocean. Though in Heaven the trees
Of life ambrosial fruitage bear, and vines
Yield nectar—though from off the boughs each morn
We brush mellifluous dews and find the ground
Covered with pearly grain—yet God hath here
Varied His bounty so with new delights
As may compare with Heaven ; and to taste
Think not I shall be nice." So down they sat,
And to their viands fell ; nor seemingly
The Angel, nor in mist—the common gloss
Of theologians—but with keen dispatch
Of real hunger, and concoctive heat
To transubstantiate : what redounds transpires
Through Spirits with ease ; nor wonder, if by fire
Of sooty coal the empiric alchemist
Can turn, or holds it possible to turn,
Metals of drossiest ore to perfect gold,
As from the mine. Meanwhile at table Eve
Ministered naked, and their flowing cups
With pleasant liquors crowned. O innocence
Deserving Paradise ! If ever, then,
Then had the Sons of God excuse to have been
Enamoured at that sight. But in those hearts
Love unlibidinous reigned, nor jealousy
Was understood, the injured lover's hell.
    Thus when with meats and drinks they had sufficed,
Nor burdened nature, sudden mind arose
In Adam not to let the occasion pass,
Given him by this great conference, to know
Of things above his world, and of their being

Who dwell in Heaven, whose exellence he saw
Transcend his own so far, whose radiant forms,
Divine effulgence, whose high power so far
Exceeded human ; and his wary speech
Thus to the empyreal minister he framed :—
  "Inhabitant with God, now know I well
Thy favour, in this honour done to Man ;
Under whose lowly roof thou hast vouchsafed
To enter, and these earthly fruits to taste,
Food not of Angels, yet accepted so
As that more willingly thou couldst not seem
At Heaven's high feasts to have fed ; yet what compare !"
  To whom the wingèd Hierarch replied :—
"O Adam, one Almighty is, from whom
All things proceed, and up to Him return,
If not depraved from good, created all
Such to perfection ; one first matter all,
Endued with various forms, various degrees
Of substance, and, in things that live, of life ;
But more refined, more spiritous and pure,
As nearer to Him placed, or nearer tending
Each in their several active spheres assigned,
Till body up to spirit work, in bounds
Proportioned to each kind. So from the root
Springs lighter the green stalk, from thence the leaves
More aery, last the bright consummate flower
Spirits odorous breathes : flowers and their fruit,
Man's nourishment, by gradual scale sublimed,
To vital spirits aspire, to animal,
To intellectual ; give both life and sense,
Fancy and understanding ; whence the Soul
Reason receives, and Reason is her being,
Discursive, or Intuitive : Discourse
Is oftest yours, the latter most is ours,
Differing but in degree, of kind the same.
Wonder not, then, what God for you saw good
If I refuse not, but convert, as you,
To proper substance. Time may come when Men
With Angels may participate, and find
No inconvenient diet, nor too light fare ;
And from these corporal nutriments, perhaps,
Your bodies may at last turn all to spirit,
Improved by tract of time, and wing'd ascend
Ethereal, as we, or may at choice
Here or in heavenly paradises dwell,
If ye be found obedient, and retain
Unalterably firm His love entire
Whose progeny you are. Meanwhile enjoy,
Your fill, what happiness this happy state
Can comprehend, incapable of more."
  To whom the Patriarch of Mankind replied :—
"O favourable Spirit, propitious guest,
Well hast thou taught the way that might direct
Our knowledge, and the scale of Nature set
86

BOOK V

From centre to circumference, whereon,
In contemplation of created things,
By steps we may ascend to God. But say,
What meant that caution joined, *If ye be found
Obedient?* Can we want obedience, then,
To Him, or possibly His love desert,
Who formed us from the dust, and placed us here
Full to the utmost measure of what bliss
Human desires can seek or apprehend?"
   To whom the Angel:—"Son of Heaven and Earth,
Attend! That thou art happy, owe to God;
That thou continuest such, owe to thyself,
That is, to thy obedience; therein stand.
This was that caution given thee; be advised.
God made thee perfect, not immutable;
And good He made thee; but to persevere
He left it in thy power—ordained thy will
By nature free, not over-ruled by fate
Inextricable, or strict necessity.
Our voluntary service He requires,
Not our necessitated. Such with Him
Finds no acceptance, nor can find; for how
Can hearts not free be tried whether they serve
Willing or no, who will but what they must
By destiny, and can no other choose?
Myself, and all the Angelic Host, that stand
In sight of God enthroned, our happy state
Hold, as you yours, while our obedience holds.
On other surety none: freely we serve,
Because we freely love, as in our will
To love or not; in this we stand or fall.
And some are fallen, to disobedience fallen,
And so from Heaven to deepest Hell. O fall
From what high state of bliss into what woe!"
   To whom our great Progenitor:—"Thy words
Attentive, and with more delighted ear,
Divine instructor, I have heard, than when
Cherubic songs by night from neighbouring hills
Aërial music send. Nor knew I not
To be, both will and deed, created free.
Yet that we never shall forget to love
Our Maker, and obey Him Whose command
Single is yet so just, my constant thoughts
Assured me, and still assure; though what thou tell'st
Hath passed in Heaven some doubt within me move,
But more desire to hear, if thou consent,
The full relation, which must needs be strange,
Worthy of sacred silence to be heard.
And we have yet large day, for scarce the Sun
Hath finished half his journey, and scarce begins
His other half in the great zone of Heaven."
   Thus Adam made request; and Raphael,
After short pause assenting, thus began:—
   "High matter thou enjoin'st me, O prime of Men—

87

Sad task and hard; for how shall I relate
To human sense the invisible exploits
Of warring Spirits? how, without remorse,
The ruin of so many, glorious once
And perfect while they stood? how, last, unfold
The secrets of another world, perhaps
Not lawful to reveal? Yet for thy good
This is dispensed; and what surmounts the reach
Of human sense I shall delineate so,
By likening spiritual to corporal forms,
As may express them best—though what if Earth
Be but the shadow of Heaven, and things therein
Each to other like more than on Earth is thought!
   "As yet this World was not, and Chaos wild
Reigned where these heavens now roll, where Earth now rests
Upon her centre poised, when on a day
(For Time, though in Eternity, applied
To motion, measures all things durable
By present, past, and future), on such day
As Heaven's great year brings forth, the empyreal host
Of Angels, by imperial summons called,
Innumerable before the Almighty's throne
Forthwith from all the ends of Heaven appeared
Under their hierarchs in orders bright.
Ten thousand thousand ensigns high advanced,
Standards and gonfalons, 'twixt van and rear
Stream in the air, and for distinction serve
Of hierarchies, of orders, and degrees;
Or in their glittering tissues bear emblazed
Holy memorials, acts of zeal and love
Recorded eminent. Thus when in orbs
Of circuit inexpressible they stood,
Orb within orb, the Father Infinite,
By Whom in bliss embosomed sat the Son,
Amidst, as from a flaming mount, whose top
Brightness had made invisible, thus spake:—
   "'Hear, all ye Angels, Progeny of Light,
Thrones, Dominations, Princedoms, Virtues, Powers,
Hear My decree, which unrevoked shall stand:
This day I have begot Whom I declare
My only Son, and on this holy hill
Him have anointed, Whom ye now behold
At My right hand. Your head I Him appoint,
And by Myself have sworn to Him shall bow
All knees in Heaven, and shall confess Him Lord.
Under His great vicegerent reign abide,
United as one individual soul,
For ever happy. Him who disobeys
Me disobeys, breaks union, and, that day,
Cast out from God and blessed vision, falls
Into utter darkness, deep engulfed, his place
Ordained without redemption, without end.'
   "So spake the Omnipotent, and with His words
All seemed well pleased; all seemed, but were not all.

That day, as other solemn days, they spent
In song and dance about the sacred hill—
Mystical dance, which yonder starry sphere
Of planets and of fixed in all her wheels
Resembles nearest ; mazes intricate,
Eccentric, intervolved, yet regular
Then most when most irregular they seem ;
And in their motions harmony divine
So smooths her charming tones that God's own ear
Listens delighted.   Evening now approached
(For we have also our evening and our morn—
We ours for change delectable, not need),
Forthwith from dance to sweet repast they turn
Desirous : all in circles as they stood,
Tables are set, and on a sudden piled
With Angels' food ; and rubied nectar flows
In pearl, in diamond, and massy gold,
Fruit of delicious vines, the growth of Heaven.
On flowers reposed, and with fresh flowerets crowned,
They eat, they drink, and in communion sweet
Quaff immortality and joy, secure
Of surfeit where full measure only bounds
Excess, before the all-bounteous King, Who showered
With copious hand, rejoicing in their joy.
Now when ambrosial Night, with clouds exhaled
From that high mount of God whence light and shade
Spring both, the face of brightest Heaven had changed
To grateful twilight (for Night comes not there
In darker veil), and roseate dews disposed
All but the unsleeping eyes of God to rest,
Wide over all the plain, and wider far
Than all this globous Earth in plain outspread
(Such are the courts of God), the angelic throng,
Dispersed in bands and files, their camp extend
By living streams among the trees of life—
Pavilions numberless and sudden reared,
Celestial tabernacles, where they slept,
Fanned with cool winds ; save those who, in their course,
Melodious hymns about the sovran throne
Alternate all night long.   But not so waked
Satan—so call him now ; his former name
Is heard no more in Heaven.   He, of the first,
If not the first Archangel, great in power,
In favour, and pre-eminence, yet fraught
With envy against the Son of God, that day
Honoured by His great Father, and proclaimed
Messiah, King Anointed, could not bear,
Through pride, that sight, and thought himself impaired.
Deep malice thence conceiving and disdain,
Soon as midnight brought on the dusky hour
Friendliest to sleep and silence, he resolved
With all his legions to dislodge, and leave
Unworshipped, unobeyed, the Throne supreme,
Contemptuous, and, his next subordinate

Awakening, thus to him in secret spake :—
" ' Sleep'st thou, companion dear ? what sleep can close
Thy eyelids ? and rememberest what decree,
Of yesterday, so late hath passed the lips
Of Heaven's Almighty?   Thou to me thy thoughts
Wast wont, I mine to thee was wont, to impart ;
Both waking we were one ; how, then, can now
Thy sleep dissent ?   New laws thou seest imposed ;
New laws from Him who reigns new minds may raise
In us who serve—new counsels, to debate
What doubtful may ensue.   More in this place
To utter is not safe.   Assemble thou
Of all those myriads which we lead the chief ;
Tell them that, by command, ere yet dim Night
Her shadowy cloud withdraws, I am to haste,
And all who under me their banners wave,
Homeward with flying march where we possess
The quarters of the North, there to prepare
Fit entertainment to receive our King,
The great Messiah, and His new commands,
Who speedily, through all the Hierarchies
Intends to pass triumphant, and give laws.'
    " So spake the false Archangel, and infused
Bad influence into the unwary breast
Of his associate.   He together calls,
Or several one by one, the regent Powers,
Under him regent ; tells, as he was taught,
That, the Most High commanding, now ere Night,
Now ere dim Night had disencumbered Heaven,
The great hierarchal standard was to move ;
Tells the suggested cause, and casts between
Ambiguous words and jealousies, to sound
Or taint integrity.   But all obeyed
The wonted signal, and superior voice
Of their great Potentate ; for great indeed
His name, and high was his degree in Heaven :
His countenance, as the morning-star that guides
The starry flock, allured them, and with lies
Drew after him the third part of Heaven's host.
Meanwhile, the Eternal Eye, Whose sight discerns
Abstrusest thoughts, from forth His holy mount,
And from within the golden lamps that burn
Nightly before Him, saw without their light
Rebellion rising—saw in whom, how spread
Among the Sons of Morn, what multitudes
Were banded to oppose His high decree ;
And, smiling, to His only Son thus said :—
    " ' Son, Thou in Whom My glory I behold
In full resplendence, Heir of all My might,
Nearly it now concerns Us to be sure
Of Our omnipotence, and with what arms
We mean to hold what anciently We claim
Of deity or empire : such a foe
Is rising, who intends to erect his throne

90

Equal to Ours, throughout the spacious North ;
Nor so content, hath in his thought to try
In battle what Our power is or Our right.
Let Us advise, and to this hazard draw
With speed what force is left, and all employ
In Our defence, lest unawares We lose
This Our high place, Our Sanctuary, Our hill.'
  " To whom the Son, with calm aspéct and clear
Lightening divine, ineffable, serene,
Made answer :—'Mighty Father, Thou Thy foes
Justly hast in derision, and secure
Laugh'st at their vain designs and tumults vain—
Matter to Me of glory, whom their hate
Illustrates, when they see all regal power
Given Me to quell their pride, and in event
Know whether I be dextrous to subdue
Thy rebels, or be found the worst in Heaven.'
  "So spake the Son ; but Satan with His Powers
Far was advanced on winged speed, an host
Innumerable as the stars of night,
Or stars of morning, dew-drops which the sun
Impearls on every leaf and every flower.
Regions they passed, the mighty regencies
Of Seraphim and Potentates and Thrones
In their triple degrees—regions to which
All thy dominion, Adam, is no more
Than what this garden is to all the earth
And all the sea, from one entire globose
Stretched into longitude ; which having passed,
At length into the limits of the North
They came, and Satan to his royal seat
High on a hill, far-blazing, as a mount
Raised on a mount, with pyramids and towers
From diamond quarries hewn and rocks of gold—
The palace of great Lucifer (so call
That structure, in the dialect of men
Interpreted) which, not long after, he,
Affecting all equality with God,
In imitation of that mount whereon
Messiah was declared in sight of Heaven,
The Mountain of the Congregation called ;
For thither he assembled all his train,
Pretending so commanded to consult
About the great reception of their King
Thither to come, and with calumnious art
Of counterfeited truth thus held their ears :—
  "'Thrones, Dominations, Princedoms, Virtues, Powers—
If these magnific titles yet remain
Not merely titular, since by decree
Another now hath to Himself engrossed
All power, and us eclipsed under the name
Of King Anointed ; for Whom all this haste
Of midnight march, and hurried meeting here,
This only to consult, how we may best,

With what may be devised of honours new,
Receive Him coming to receive from us
Knee-tribute yet unpaid, prostration vile !
Too much to one ! but double how endured—
To One and to His image now proclaimed ?
But what if better counsels might erect
Our minds, and teach us to cast off this yoke !
Will ye submit your necks, and choose to bend
The supple knee ? Ye will not, if I trust
To know ye right, or if ye know yourselves
Natives and Sons of Heaven possessed before
By none, and, if not equal all, yet free,
Equally free ; for orders and degrees
Jar not with liberty, but well consist.
Who can in reason, then, or right, assume
Monarchy over such as live by right
His equals—if in power and splendour less,
In freedom equal ? or can introduce
Law and edict on us, who without law
Err not ? much less for this to be our Lord,
And look for adoration, to the abuse
Of those imperial titles which assert
Our being ordained to govern, not to serve !'
  " Thus far his bold discourse without control
Had audience, when, among the Seraphim,
Abdiel, than whom none with more zeal adored
The Deity, and divine commands obeyed,
Stood up, and in a flame of zeal severe
The current of his fury thus opposed :—
  "'O argument blasphemous, false, and proud—
Words which no ear ever to hear in Heaven
Expected ; least of all from thee, ingrate,
In place thyself so high above thy peers !
Canst thou with impious obloquy condemn
The just decree of God, pronounced and sworn,
That to His only Son, by right endued
With regal sceptre, every soul in Heaven
Shall bend the knee, and in that honour due
Confess Him rightful King ? Unjust, thou say'st,
Flatly unjust, to bind with laws the free
And equal over equals to let reign,
One over all with unsucceeded power !
Shalt thou give law to God ? shalt thou dispute
With Him the points of liberty, who made
Thee what thou art, and formed the Powers of Heaven
Such as He pleased, and circumscribed their being ?
Yet, by experience taught, we know how good,
And of our good and of our dignity
How provident He is—how far from thought
To make us less ; bent rather to exalt
Our happy state, under one head more near
United. But—to grant it thee unjust
That equal over equals monarch reign—
Thyself, though great and glorious, dost thou count,

Or all angelic nature joined in one,
Equal to Him, begotten Son, by Whom,
As by His Word, the mighty Father made
All things, even thee, and all the Spirits of Heaven
By Him created in their bright degrees,
Crowned them with glory, and to their glory named
Thrones, Dominations, Princedoms, Virtues, Powers?—
Essential Powers; nor by His reign obscured,
But more illustrious made; since He, the head,
One of our number thus reduced becomes;
His laws our laws; all honour to Him done
Returns our own. Cease, then, this impious rage,
And tempt not these; but hasten to appease
The incensèd Father and the incensèd Son
While pardon may be found, in time besought.'
   "So spake the fervent Angel; but his zeal
None seconded, as out of season judged,
Or singular and rash. Whereat rejoiced
The Apostate, and, more haughty, thus replied:—
   "'That we were formed, then, say'st thou? and the work
Of secondary hands, by task transferred
From Father to His Son? Strange point and new!
Doctrine which we would know whence learned! Who saw
When this creation was? Remember'st thou
Thy making, while the Maker gave thee being?
We know no time when we were not as now;
Know none before us, self-begot, self-raised
By our own quickening power when fatal course
Had circled his full orb, the birth mature
Of this our native Heaven, Ethereal Sons.
Our puissance is our own; our own right hand
Shall teach us highest deeds, by proof to try
Who is our equal. Then thou shalt behold
Whether by supplication we intend
Address, and to begirt the Almighty Throne
Beseeching or besieging. This report,
These tidings, carry to the Anointed King;
And fly, ere evil intercept thy flight.'
   "He said; and, as the sound of waters deep,
Hoarse murmur echoed to his words applause
Through the infinite host. Nor less for that
The flaming Seraph, fearless, though alone,
Encompassed round with foes, thus answered bold:—
   "'O alienate from God, O Spirit accursed,
Forsaken of all good! I see thy fall
Determined, and thy hapless crew involved
In this perfidious fraud, contagion spread
Both of thy crime and punishment. Henceforth
No more be troubled how to quit the yoke
Of God's Messiah. Those indulgent laws
Will not be now vouchsafed; other decrees
Against thee are gone forth without recall;
That golden sceptre which thou didst reject
Is now an iron rod to bruise and break

Thy disobedience.   Well thou didst advise;
Yet not for thy advice or threats I fly
These wicked tents devoted, lest the wrath
Impendent, raging into sudden flame,
Distinguish not: for soon expect to feel
His thunder on thy head, devouring fire.
Then who created thee lamenting learn
When who can uncreate thee thou shalt know.'
   "So spake the Seraph Abdiel, faithful found;
Among the faithless faithful only he;
Among innumerable false unmoved,
Unshaken, unseduced, unterrified,
His loyalty he kept, his love, his zeal;
Nor number nor example with him wrought
To swerve from truth, or change his constant mind,
Though single.   From amidst them forth he passed,
Long way through hostile scorn, which he sustained
Superior, nor of violence feared aught;
And with retorted scorn his back he turned
On those proud towers, to swift destruction doomed."

THE END OF THE FIFTH BOOK.

PARADISE LOST.

BOOK VI.

THE ARGUMENT.

Raphael continues to relate how Michael and Gabriel were sent forth to battle against Satan and his Angels. The first fight described: Satan and his Powers retire under night. He calls a council; invents devilish engines, which, in the second day's fight, put Michael and his Angels to some disorder; but they at length, pulling up mountains, overwhelmed both the force and machines of Satan. Yet, the tumult not so ending, God, on the third day, sends Messiah His Son, for whom He had reserved the glory of that victory. He, in the power of His Father, coming to the place, and causing all His legions to stand still on either side, with His chariot and thunder driving into the midst of His enemies, pursues them, unable to resist, towards the wall of Heaven; which opening, they leap down with horror and confusion into the place of punishment prepared for them in the Deep. Messiah returns with triumph to His Father.

"All night the dreadless Angel, unpursued,
Through Heaven's wide champaign held his way, till Morn,
Waked by the circling Hours, with rosy hand
Unbarred the gates of Light. There is a cave
Within the Mount of God, fast by His throne,
Where Light and Darkness in perpetual round
Lodge and dislodge by turns—which makes through Heaven
Grateful vicissitude, like day and night;
Light issues forth, and at the other door
Obsequious Darkness enters, till her hour
To veil the heaven, though darkness there might well
Seem twilight here. And now went forth the Morn
Such as in highest heaven, arrayed in gold
Empyreal; from before her vanished Night,
Shot through with orient beams; when all the plain
Covered with thick embattled squadrons bright,
Chariots, and flaming arms, and fiery steeds,
Reflecting blaze on blaze, first met his view.
War he perceived, war in procinct, and found
Already known what he for news had thought
To have reported. Gladly then he mixed
Among those friendly Powers, who him received
With joy and acclamations loud, that one,
That of so many myriads fallen yet one,
Returned not lost. On to the sacred hill

They led him, high applauded, and present
Before the seat supreme; from whence a voice,
From midst a golden cloud, thus mild was heard :—
" 'Servant of God, well done ! Well hast thou fought
The better fight, who single hast maintained
Against revolted multitudes the cause
Of truth, in word mightier than they in arms,
And for the testimony of truth hast borne
Universal reproach, far worse to bear
Than violence ; for this was all thy care—
To stand approved in sight of God, though worlds
Judged thee perverse. The easier conquest now
Remains thee—aided by this host of friends,
Back on thy foes more glorious to return
Than scorned thou didst depart ; and to subdue
By force who reason for their law refuse—
Right reason for their law, and for their King
Messiah, who by right of merit reigns.
Go, Michael, of celestial armies prince,
And thou in military prowess next,
Gabriel ; lead forth to battle these My sons
Invincible ; lead forth My armed Saints,
By thousands and by millions ranged for fight,
Equal in number to that godless crew
Rebellious. Them with fire and hostile arms
Fearless assault ; and, to the brow of Heaven
Pursuing, drive them out from God and bliss
Into their place of punishment, the gulf
Of Tartarus, which ready opens wide
His fiery chaos to receive their fall.'
    " So spake the Sovran Voice ; and clouds began
To darken all the hill, and smoke to roll
In dusky wreaths reluctant flames, the sign
Of wrath awaked ; nor with less dread the loud
Ethereal trumpet from on high gan blow.
At which command the Powers Militant
That stood for Heaven, in mighty quadrate joined
Of union irresistible, moved on
In silence their bright legions to the sound
Of instrumental harmony, that breathed
Heroic ardour to adventurous deeds
Under their godlike leaders, in the cause
Of God and His Messiah. On they move,
Indissolubly firm ; nor obvious hill,
Nor straitening vale, nor wood, nor stream, divides
Their perfect ranks ; for high above the ground
Their march was, and the passive air upbore
Their nimble tread. As when the total kind
Of birds, in orderly array on wing,
Came summoned over Eden to receive
Their names of thee ; so over many a tract
Of Heaven they marched, and many a province wide,
Tenfold the length of this terrene. At last,
Far in the horizon, to the north, appeared

From skirt to skirt a fiery region, stretched
In battailous aspect; and, nearer view,
Bristled with upright beams innumerable
Of rigid spears, and helmets thronged, and shields
Various, with boastful argument portrayed,
The banded Powers of Satan hasting on
With furious expedition: for they weened
That self-same day, by fight or by surprise,
To win the Mount of God, and on His throne
To set the envier of His state, the proud
Aspirer. But their thoughts proved fond and vain
In the mid-way; though strange to us it seemed
At first that Angel should with Angel war,
And in fierce hosting meet, who wont to meet
So oft in festivals of joy and love
Unanimous, as sons of one great Sire,
Hymning the Eternal Father. But the shout
Of battle now began, and rushing sound
Of onset ended soon each milder thought.
High in the midst, exalted as a God,
The Apostate in his sun-bright chariot sat,
Idol of majesty divine, enclosed
With flaming Cherubim and golden shields ;
Then lighted from his gorgeous throne—for now
'Twixt host and host but narrow space was left,
A dreadful interval, and front to front
Presented stood in terrible array
Of hideous length. Before the cloudy van,
On the rough edge of battle ere it joined,
Satan, with vast and haughty strides advanced,
Came towering, armed in adamant and gold.
Abdiel that sight endured not, where he stood
Among the mightiest, bent on highest deeds,
And thus his own undaunted heart explores :—
    "'O Heaven ! that such resemblance of the Highest
Should yet remain, where faith and realty
Remain not ! Wherefore should not strength and might
There fail where virtue fails, or weakest prove
Where boldest, though to sight unconquerable?
His puissance, trusting in the Almighty's aid,
I mean to try, whose reason I have tried
Unsound and false ; nor is it aught but just
That he who in debate of truth hath won
Should win in arms, in both disputes alike
Victor. Though brutish that contést and foul,
When reason hath to deal with force, yet so
Most reason is that reason overcome.'
    "So pondering, and from his armed peers
Forth-stepping opposite, half-way he met
His daring foe, at this prevention more
Incensed, and thus securely him defied :—
    "'Proud, art thou met ? Thy hope was to have reached
The highth of thy aspiring unopposed—
The throne of God unguarded, and His side

M.—H   97

Abandoned at the terror of thy power
Or potent tongue.   Fool ! not to think how vain
Against the Omnipotent to rise in arms ;
Who, out of smallest things, could without end
Have raised incessant armies to defeat
Thy folly ; or with solitary hand,
Reaching beyond all limit, at one blow,
Unaided could have finished thee, and whelmed
Thy legions under darkness !   But thou seest
All are not of thy train ; there be who faith
Prefer, and piety to God, though then
To thee not visible when I alone
Seemed in thy world erroneous to dissent
From all : my Sect thou seest ; now learn too late
How few sometimes may know when thousands err.'
  "Whom the grand Foe, with scornful eye askance,
Thus answered :—' Ill for thee, but in wished hour
Of my revenge, first sought for, thou return'st
From flight, seditious Angel, to receive
Thy merited reward, the first assay
Of this right hand provoked, since first that tongue,
Inspired with contradiction, durst oppose
A third part of the Gods, in synod met
Their deities to assert : who, while they feel
Vigour divine within them, can allow
Omnipotence to none.   But well thou com'st
Before thy fellows, ambitious to win
From me some plume, that thy success may show
Destruction to the rest.   This pause between
(Unanswered lest thou boast) to let thee know.—
At first I thought that Liberty and Heaven
To heavenly souls had been all one ; but now
I see that most through sloth had rather serve,
Ministering Spirits, trained up in feast and song :
Such hast thou armed, the minstrelsy of Heaven—
Servility with freedom to contend,
As both their deeds compared this day shall prove.'
  "To whom, in brief, thus Abdiel stern replied :—
' Apostate ! still thou err'st, nor end wilt find
Of erring, from the path of truth remote.
Unjustly thou deprav'st it with the name
Of servitude, to serve whom God ordains,
Or Nature : God and Nature bid the same,
When He who rules is worthiest, and excels
Them whom He governs.   This is servitude—
To serve the unwise, or him who hath rebelled
Against his worthier, as thine now serve thee,
Thyself not free, but to thyself enthralled ;
Yet lewdly dar'st our ministering upbraid.
Reign thou in Hell, thy kingdom ; let me serve
In Heaven God ever blest, and His divine
Behests obey, worthiest to be obeyed.
Yet chains in Hell, not realms, expect : meanwhile,
From me returned, as erst thou saidst, from flight,

This greeting on thy impious crest receive.'
  "So saying, a noble stroke he lifted high,
Which hung not, but so swift with tempest fell
On the proud crest of Satan that no sight,
Nor motion of swift thought, less could his shield,
Such ruin intercept. Ten paces huge
He back recoiled ; the tenth on bended knee
His massy spear upstayed : as if, on earth,
Winds under ground, or waters forcing way,
Sidelong had pushed a mountain from his seat,
Half-sunk with all his pines. Amazement seized
The rebel Thrones, but greater rage, to see
Thus foiled their mightiest ; ours joy filled, and shout,
Presage of victory, and fierce desire
Of battle : whereat Michael bid sound
The Archangel trumpet. Through the vast of Heaven
It sounded, and the faithful armies rung
Hosannah to the Highest ; nor stood at gaze
The adverse legions, nor less hideous joined
The horrid shock. Now storming fury rose,
And clamour such as heard in Heaven till now
Was never ; arms on armour clashing brayed
Horrible discord, and the madding wheels
Of brazen chariots raged ; dire was the noise
Of conflict ; overhead the dismal hiss
Of fiery darts in flaming volleys flew,
And, flying, vaulted either host with fire.
So under fiery cope together rushed
Both battles main with ruinous assault
And inextinguishable rage. All Heaven
Resounded ; and, had Earth been then, all Earth
Had to her centre shook. What wonder, when
Millions of fierce encountering Angels fought
On either side, the least of whom could wield
These elements, and arm him with the force
Of all their regions ? How much more of power
Army against army numberless to raise
Dreadful combustion warring, and disturb,
Though not destroy, their happy native seat ;
Had not the Eternal King Omnipotent
From His stronghold of Heaven high overruled
And limited their might, though numbered such
As each divided legion might have seemed
A numerous host, in strength each armed hand
A legion ! Led in fight, yet leader seemed
Each warrior single as in chief ; expert
When to advance, or stand, or turn the sway
Of battle, open when, and when to close
The ridges of grim war. No thought of flight,
None of retreat, no unbecoming deed
That argued fear ; each on himself relied
As only in his arm the moment lay
Of victory. Deeds of eternal fame
Were done, but infinite ; for wide was spread

That war, and various : sometimes on firm ground
A standing fight ; then, soaring on main wing,
Tormented all the air ; all air seemed then
Conflicting fire. Long time in even scale
The battle hung ; till Satan, who that day
Prodigious power had shown, and met in arms
No equal, ranging through the dire attack
Of fighting Seraphim confused, at length
Saw where the sword of Michael smote, and felled
Squadrons at once : with huge two-handed sway
Brandished aloft, the horrid edge came down
Wide-wasting. Such destruction to withstand
He hasted, and opposed the rocky orb
Of tenfold adamant, his ample shield,
A vast circumference. At his approach
The great Archangel from his warlike toil
Surceased, and, glad, as hoping here to end
Intestine war in Heaven, the Arch-foe subdued,
Or captive dragged in chains, with hostile frown
And visage all inflamed, first thus began :—
  "'Author of Evil, unknown till thy revolt,
Unnamed in Heaven, now plenteous as thou seest
These acts of hateful strife—hateful to all,
Though heaviest, by just measure, on thyself
And thy adherents—how hast thou disturbed
Heaven's blessed peace, and into Nature brought
Misery, uncreated till the crime
Of thy rebellion ! how hast thou instilled
Thy malice into thousands, once upright
And faithful, now proved false ! But think not here
To trouble holy rest ; Heaven casts thee out
From all her confines ; Heaven, the seat of bliss,
Brooks not the works of violence and war.
Hence, then, and Evil go with thee along,
Thy offspring, to the place of Evil, Hell—
Thou and thy wicked crew ! there mingle broils !
Ere this avenging sword begin thy doom,
Or some more sudden vengeance, winged from God,
Precipitate thee with augmented pain.'
  "So spake the Prince of Angels ; to whom thus
The Adversary :—'Nor think thou with wind
Of airy threats to awe whom yet with deeds
Thou canst not. Hast thou turned the least of these
To flight—or, if to fall, but that they rise
Unvanquished—easier to transact with me
That thou shouldst hope, imperious, and with threats
To chase me hence ? Err not that so shall end
The strife which thou call'st evil, but we style
The strife of glory ; which we mean to win,
Or turn this Heaven itself into the Hell
Thou fablest ; here, however, to dwell free,
If not to reign. Meanwhile, thy utmost force—
And join Him named Almighty to thy aid—
I fly not, but have sought thee far and nigh.'

"They ended parle, and both addressed for fight
Unspeakable ; for who, though with the tongue
Of Angels, can relate, or to what things
Liken on Earth conspicious, that may lift
Human imagination to such highth
Of godlike power ? for likest gods they seemed,
Stood they or moved, in stature, motion, arms,
Fit to decide the empire of great Heaven.
Now waved their fiery swords, and in the air
Made horrid circles ; two broad suns their shields
Blazed opposite, while Expectation stood
In horror ; from each hand with speed retired,
Where erst was thickest fight, the Angelic throng,
And left large field, unsafe within the wind
Of such commotion : such as (to set forth
Great things by small) if, Nature's concord broke,
Among the constellations war were sprung,
Two planets, rushing from aspéct malign
Of fiercest opposition, in mid sky
Should combat, and their jarring spheres confound.
Together both, with next to almighty arm
Uplifted imminent, one stroke they aimed
That might determine, and not need repeat
As not of power, at once ; nor odds appeared
In might or swift prevention.   But the sword
Of Michael from the armoury of God
Was given him tempered so that neither keen
Nor solid might resist that edge : it met
The sword of Satan, with steep force to smite
Descending, and in half cut sheer ; nor stayed,
But, with swift wheel reverse, deep entering, shared
All his right side.   Then Satan first knew pain,
And writhed him to and fro convolved ; so sore
The griding sword with discontinuous wound
Passed through him.   But the ethereal substance closed,
Not long divisible : and from the gash
A stream of nectarous humour issuing flowed
Sanguine, such as celestial Spirits may bleed,
And all his armour stained, erewhile so bright.
Forthwith, on all sides, to his aid was run
By Angels many and strong, who interposed
Defence, while others bore him on their shields
Back to his chariot where it stood retired
From off the files of war : there they him laid
Gnashing for anguish, and despite, and shame
To find himself not matchless, and his pride
Humbled by such rebuke, so far beneath
His confidence to equal God in power.
Yet soon he healed ; for Spirits, that live throughout
Vital in every part—not, as frail Man,
In entrails, heart or head, liver or reins—
Cannot but by annihilating die ;
Nor in their liquid texture mortal wound
Receive, no more than can the fluid air :

All heart they live, all head, all eye, all ear,
All intellect, all sense ; and as they please
They limb themselves, and colour, shape, or size
Assume, as likes them best, condense or rare.
" Meanwhile, in other parts, like deeds deserved
Memorial, where the might of Gabriel fought,
And with fierce ensigns pierced the deep array
Of Moloch, furious king, who him defied,
And at his chariot-wheels to drag him bound
Threatened, nor from the Holy One of Heaven
Refrained his tongue blasphémous, but anon,
Down cloven to the waist, with shattered arms
And uncouth pain fled bellowing.   On each wing
Uriel and Raphaël his vaunting foe,
Though huge and in a rock of diamond armed,
Vanquished—Adramelech and Asmadai,
Two potent Thrones, that to be less than Gods
Disdained, but meaner thoughts learned in their flight,
Mangled with ghastly wounds through plate and mail.
Nor stood unmindful Abdiel to annoy
The atheist crew, but with redoubled blow
Ariel, and Arioch, and the violence
Of Ramiel, scorched and blasted, overthrew.
I might relate of thousands, and their names
Eternize here on Earth ; but those elect
Angels, contented with their fame in Heaven,
Seek not the praise of men : the other sort,
In might though wondrous and in acts of war,
Nor of renown less eager, yet by doom
Cancelled from Heaven and sacred memory,
Nameless in dark oblivion let them dwell.
For strength from truth divided, and from just,
Illaudable, nought merits but dispraise
And ignominy, yet to glory aspires,
Vain-glorious, and through infamy seeks fame :
Therefore eternal silence be their doom !
" And now, their mightiest quelled, the battle swerved,
With many an inroad gored ; deformed rout
Entered, and foul disorder ; all the ground
With shivered armour strown, and on a heap
Chariot and charioteer lay overturned,
And fiery foaming steeds ; what stood recoiled,
O'er-wearied, through the faint Satanic host,
Defensive scarce, or with pale fear surprised—
Then first with fear surprised and sense of pain—
Fled ignominious, to such evil brought
By sin of disobedience, till that hour
Not liable to fear, or flight, or pain.
Far otherwise the inviolable Saints
In cubic phalanx firm advanced entire,
Invulnerable, impenetrably armed ;
Such high advantages their innocence
Gave them above their foes—not to have sinned,
Not to have disobeyed ; in fight they stood

Unwearied, unobnoxious to be pained
By wound, though from their place by violence moved.
  "Now Night her course began, and, over Heaven
Inducing darkness, grateful truce imposed,
And silence on the odious din of war.
Under her cloudy covert both retired,
Victor and vanquished. On the foughten field
Michael and his Angels prevalent
Encamping, placed in guard their watches round,
Cherubic waving fires : on the other part,
Satan with his rebellious disappeared,
Far in the dark dislodged, and, void of rest,
His potentates to council called by night,
And in the midst thus undismayed began :—
  "'O now in danger tried, now known in arms
Not to be overpowered, companions dear,
Found worthy not of liberty alone—
Too mean pretence—but, what we more affect,
Honour, dominion, glory, and renown ;
Who have sustained one day in doubtful fight
(And, if one day, why not eternal days ?)
What Heaven's Lord had powerfullest to send
Against us from about His throne, and judged
Sufficient to subdue us to His will,
But proves not so : then fallible, it seems,
Of future we may deem Him, though till now
Omniscient thought ! True is, less firmly armed,
Some disadvantage we endured, and pain—
Till now not known, but, known, as soon contemned ;
Since now we find this our empyreal form
Incapable of mortal injury,
Imperishable, and, though pierced with wound,
Soon closing, and by native vigour healed.
Of evil, then, so small as easy think
The remedy : perhaps more valid arms,
Weapons more violent, when next we meet,
May serve to better us and worse our foes,
Or equal what between us made the odds
In nature none. If other hidden cause
Left them superior, while we can preserve
Unhurt our minds, and understanding sound,
Due search and consultation will disclose.'
  "He sat ; and in the assembly next upstood
Nisroch, of Principalities the prime.
As one he stood escaped from cruel fight
Sore toiled, his riven arms to havoc hewn,
And, cloudy in aspéct, thus answering spake :—
  "'Deliverer from new Lords, leader to free
Enjoyment of our right as Gods ! yet hard
For Gods, and too unequal work, we find
Against unequal arms to fight in pain,
Against unpained, impassive ; from which evil
Ruin must needs ensue. For what avails
Valour or strength, though matchless, quelled with pain,

Which all subdues, and makes remiss the hands
Of mightiest? Sense of pleasure we may well
Spare out of life perhaps, and not repine,
But live content—which is the calmest life;
But pain is perfect misery, the worst
Of evils, and, excessive, overturns
All patience. He who, therefore, can invent
With what more forcible we may offend
Our yet unwounded enemies, or arm
Ourselves with like defence, to me deserves
No less than for deliverance what we owe.'
  "Whereto, with look composed, Satan replied:—
'Not uninvented that, which thou aright
Believ'st so main to our success, I bring.
Which of us who beholds the bright surfáce
Of this ethereous mould whereon we stand—
This continent of spacious Heaven, adorned
With plant, fruit, flower ambrosial, gems and gold—
Whose eye so superficially surveys
These things as not to mind from whence they grow
Deep under ground: materials dark and crude,
Of spiritous and fiery spume, till, touched
With Heaven's ray, and tempered, they shoot forth
So beauteous, opening to the ambient light?
These in their dark nativity the Deep
Shall yield us, pregnant with infernal flame;
Which, into hollow engines long and round
Thick-rammed, at the other bore with touch of fire
Dilated and infuriate, shall send forth
From far, with thundering noise, among our foes
Such implements of mischief as shall dash
To pieces and o'erwhelm whatever stands
Adverse, that they shall fear we have disarmed
The Thunderer of his only dreaded bolt.
Nor long shall be our labour; yet ere dawn
Effect shall end our wish. Meanwhile revive;
Abandon fear; to strength and counsel joined
Think nothing hard, much less to be despaired.'
  "He ended; and his words their drooping cheer
Enlightened, and their languished hope revived.
The invention all admired, and each how he
To be the inventor missed; so easy it seemed
Once found, which yet unfound most would have thought
Impossible! Yet, haply, of thy race,
In future days, if malice should abound,
Some one, intent on mischief, or inspired
With devilish machination, might devise
Like instrument to plague the sons of men
For sin, on war and mutual slaughter bent.
Forthwith from council to the work they flew;
None arguing stood; innumerable hands
Were ready; in a moment up they turned
Wide the celestial soil, and saw beneath
The originals of Nature in their crude

Conception ; sulphurous and nitrous foam
They found, they mingled, and, with subtle art
Concocted and adusted, they reduced
To blackest grain, and into store conveyed.
Part hidden veins digged up (nor hath this Earth
Entrails unlike) of mineral and stone,
Whereof to found their engines and their balls
Of missive ruin ; part incentive reed
Provide, pernicious with one touch to fire.
So all ere day-spring, under conscious Night,
Secret they finished, and in order set,
With silent circumspection, unespied.
  "Now, when fair Morn orient in Heaven appeared,
Up rose the victor Angels, and to arms
The matin trumpet sung. In arms they stood
Of golden panoply, refulgent host,
Soon banded ; others from the dawning hills
Looked round, and scouts each coast light-armèd scour,
Each quarter, to descry the distant foe,
Where lodged, or whither fled, or if for fight,
In motion or in halt. Him soon they met
Under spread ensigns moving nigh, in slow
But firm battalion : back with speediest sail
Zophiel, of Cherubim the swiftest wing,
Came flying, and in mid air aloud thus cried :—
  "'Arm, Warriors, arm for fight ! The foe at hand,
Whom fled we thought, will save us long pursuit
This day ; fear not his flight ; so thick a cloud
He comes, and settled in his face I see
Sad resolution and secure. Let each
His adamantine coat gird well, and each
Fit well his helm, gripe fast his orbed shield,
Borne even or high ; for this day will pour down,
If I conjecture aught, no drizzling shower,
But rattling storm of arrows barbed with fire.'
  "So warned he them, aware themselves, and soon
In order, quit of all impediment.
Instant, without disturb, they took alarm,
And onward move embattled : when, behold,
Not distant far, with heavy pace the foe
Approaching gross and huge, in hollow cube
Training his devilish enginry, impaled
On every side with shadowing squadrons deep,
To hide the fraud. At interview both stood
A while ; but suddenly at head appeared
Satan, and thus was heard commanding loud :—
  "'Vanguard, to right and left the front unfold,
That all may see who hate us how we seek
Peace and composure, and with open breast
Stand ready to receive them, if they like
Our overture, and turn not back perverse :
But that I doubt. However, witness Heaven !
Heaven, witness thou anon ! while we discharge
Freely our part. Ye, who appointed stand,

Do as you have in charge, and briefly touch
What we propound, and loud that all may hear.'
  "So scoffing in ambiguous words, he scarce
Had ended, when to right and left the front
Divided, and to either flank retired ;
Which to our eyes discovered, new and strange,
A triple mounted row of pillars laid
On wheels (for like to pillars most they seemed,
Or hollowed bodies make of oak or fir,
With branches lopt, in wood or mountain felled).
Brass, iron, stony mould, had not their mouths
With hideous orifice gaped on us wide,
Portending hollow truce. At each, behind,
A Seraph stood, and in his hand a reed
Stood waving tipt with fire ; while we, suspense,
Collected stood within our thoughts amused.
Not long ! for sudden all at once their reeds
Put forth, and to a narrow vent applied
With nicest touch.   Immediate in a flame,
But soon obscured with smoke, all Heaven appeared,
From those deep-throated engines belched, whose roar
Embowelled with outrageous noise the air,
And all her entrails tore, disgorging foul
Their devilish glut, chained thunderbolts and hail
Of iron globes ; which on the victor host
Levelled, with such impetuous fury smote,
That whom they hit none on their feet might stand,
Though standing else as rocks, but down they fell
By thousands, Angel on Archangel rolled,
The sooner for their arms.   Unarmed, they might
Have easily, as Spirits, evaded swift
By quick contraction or remove ; but now
Foul dissipation followed, and forced rout ;
Nor served it to relax their serried files.
What should they do ? If on they rushed, repulse
Repeated, and indecent overthrow
Doubled, would render them yet more despised,
And to their foes a laughter—for in view
Stood ranked of Seraphim another row,
In posture to displode their second tire
Of thunder ; back defeated to return
They worse abhorred. Satan beheld their plight,
And to his mates thus in derision called :—
  "'O friends, why come not on these victors proud ?
Erewhile they fierce were coming ; and, when we,
To entertain them fair with open front
And breast (what could we more ?), propounded terms
Of composition, straight they changed their minds,
Flew off, and into strange vagaries fell,
As they would dance. Yet for a dance they seemed
Somewhat extravagant and wild ; perhaps
For joy of offered peace. But I suppose,
If our proposals once again were heard,
We should compel them to a quick result.'

"To whom thus Belial, in like gamesome mood :—
'Leader, the terms we sent were terms of weight,
Of hard contents, and full of force urged home,
Such as we might perceive amused them all,
And stumbled many. Who receives them right
Had need from head to foot well understand ;
Not understood, this gift they have besides—
They show us when our foes walk not upright.'
  "So they among themselves in pleasant vein
Stood scoffing, highthened in their thoughts beyond
All doubt of victory ; Eternal Might
To match with their inventions they presumed
So easy, and of His thunder made a scorn,
And all His host derided, while they stood
A while in trouble. But they stood not long ;
Rage prompted them at length, and found them arms
Against such hellish mischief fit to oppose.
Forthwith (behold the excellence, the power,
Which God hath in His mighty Angels placed !)
Their arms away they threw, and to the hills
(For Earth hath this variety from Heaven
Of pleasure situate in hill and dale)
Light as the lightning-glimpse they ran, they flew ;
From their foundations, loosening to and fro,
They plucked the seated hills, with all their load,
Rocks, waters, woods, and, by the shaggy tops
Uplifting, bore them in their hands. Amaze,
Be sure, and terror, seized the rebel host,
When coming towards them so dread they saw
The bottom of the mountains upward turned,
Till on those cursed engines' triple row
They saw them whelmed, and all their confidence
Under the weight of mountains buried deep ;
Themselves invaded next, and on their heads
Main promontories flung, which in the air
Came shadowing, and oppressed whole legions armed.
Their armour helped their harm, crushed in and bruised,
Into their substance pent—which wrought them pain
Implacable, and many a dolorous groan,
Long struggling underneath, ere they could wind
Out of such prison, though Spirits of purest light,
Purest at first, now gross by sinning grown.
The rest, in imitation, to like arms
Betook them, and the neighbouring hills uptore ;
So hills amid the air encountered hills,
Hurled to and fro with jaculation dire,
That underground they fought in dismal shade :
Infernal noise ! war seemed a civil game
To this uproar ; horrid confusion heaped
Upon confusion rose. And now all Heaven
Had gone to wrack, with ruin overspread,
Had not the Almighty Father, where He sits
Shrined in His sanctuary of Heaven secure,
Consulting on the sum of things, foreseen

This tumult, and permitted all, advised,
That His great purpose He might so fulfil,
To honour His Anointed Son, avenged
Upon His enemies, and to declare
All power on Him transferred.   Whence to His Son,
The assessor of His throne, He thus began :—
  "'Effulgence of My glory, Son beloved,
Son in Whose face invisible is beheld
Visibly, what by Deity I am,
And in Whose hand what by decree I do,
Second Omnipotence! two days are passed,
Two days, as we compute the days of Heaven,
Since Michael and his Powers went forth to tame
These disobedient.   Sore hath been their fight,
As likeliest was when two such foes met armed :
For to themselves I left them; and Thou know'st
Equal in their creation they were formed,
Save what sin hath impaired—which yet hath wrought
Insensibly, for I suspend their doom:
Whence in perpetual fight they needs must last
Endless, and no solution will be found.
War wearied hath performed what war can do,
And to disordered rage let loose the reins,
With mountains, as with weapons, armed; which makes
Wild work in Heaven, and dangerous to the main.
Two days are, therefore, passed; the third is Thine:
For Thee I have ordained it, and thus far
Have suffered, that the glory may be Thine
Of ending this great war, since none but Thou
Can end it.   Into Thee such virtue and grace
Immense I have transfused, that all may know
In Heaven and Hell Thy power above compare,
And this perverse commotion governed thus,
To manifest Thee worthiest to be Heir
Of all things—to be Heir, and to be King
By sacred unction, Thy deserved right.
Go, then, Thou Mightiest, in Thy Father's might;
Ascend My chariot; guide the rapid wheels
That shake Heaven's basis; bring forth all My war;
My bow and thunder, My almighty arms,
Gird on, and sword upon Thy puissant thigh;
Pursue these Sons of Darkness, drive them out
From all Heaven's bounds into the utter Deep;
There let them learn, as likes them, to despise
God, and Messiah His anointed King.'
  "He said, and on His Son with rays direct
Shone full.   He all His Father full expressed
Ineffably into His face received;
And thus the Filial Godhead answering spake:—
  "'O Father, O Supreme of Heavenly Thrones,
First, Highest, Holiest, Best, Thou always seek'st
To glorify Thy Son; I always Thee,
As is most just.   This I My glory account,
My exaltation, and My whole delight,

That Thou in Me, well pleased, declar'st Thy will
Fulfilled, which to fulfil is all My bliss.
Sceptre and power, Thy giving, I assume,
And gladlier shall resign when in the end
Thou shalt be all in all, and I in Thee
For ever, and in Me all whom Thou lov'st.
But whom Thou hat'st I hate, and can put on
Thy terrors, as I put Thy mildness on,
Image of Thee in all things: and shall soon,
Armed with Thy might, rid Heaven of these rebelled,
To their prepared ill mansion driven down,
To chains of darkness and the undying worm,
That from Thy just obedience could revolt,
Whom to obey is happiness entire.
Then shall Thy Saints, unmixed, and from the impure
Far separate, circling Thy holy Mount,
Unfeigned halleluiahs to Thee sing,
Hymns of high praise, and I among them chief.'
    "So said, He, o'er His sceptre bowing, rose
From the right hand of Glory where He sat;
And the third sacred morn began to shine,
Dawning through Heaven.   Forth rushed with whirlwind sound
The chariot of Paternal Deity,
Flashing thick flames, wheel within wheel; undrawn,
Itself instinct with spirit, but convoyed
By four cherubic Shapes.   Four faces each
Had wondrous; as with stars, their bodies all
And wings were set with eyes; with eyes the wheels
Of beryl, and careering fires between;
Over their heads a crystal firmament,
Whereon a sapphire throne, inlaid with pure
Amber and colours of the showery arch.
He, in celestial panoply all armed
Of radiant Urim, work divinely wrought,
Ascended; at His right hand Victory
Sat eagle-winged; beside Him hung His bow,
And quiver, with three-bolted thunder stored;
And from about Him fierce effusion rolled
Of smoke and bickering flame and sparkles dire.
Attended with ten thousand thousand Saints,
He onward came; far off His coming shone;
And twenty thousand (I their number heard)
Chariots of God, half on each hand, were seen.
He on the wings of Cherub rode sublime
On the crystalline sky, in sapphire throned—
Illustrious far and wide, but by His own
First seen.   Them unexpected joy surprised
When the great ensign of Messiah blazed
Aloft, by Angels borne, His sign in Heaven;
Under whose conduct Michael soon reduced
His army, circumfused on either wing,
Under their Head embodied all in one.
Before Him Power Divine His way prepared;
At His command the uprooted hills retired

Each to his place; they heard His voice, and went
Obsequious; Heaven His wonted face renewed,
And with fresh flowerets hill and valley smiled.
  " This saw His hapless foes, but stood obdured,
And to rebellious fight rallied their Powers,
Insensate, hope conceiving from despair.
In Heavenly Spirits could such perverseness dwell?
But to convince the proud what signs avail,
Or wonders move the obdurate to relent?
They, hardened more by what might most reclaim,
Grieving to see His glory, at the sight
Took envy, and, aspiring to His highth,
Stood re-embattled fierce, by force or fraud
Weening to prosper, and at length prevail
Against God and Messiah, or to fall
In universal ruin last; and now
To final battle drew, disdaining flight,
Or faint retreat : when the great Son of God
To all His host on either hand thus spake :—
  " ' Stand still in bright array, ye Saints ; here stand,
Ye Angels armed! this day from battle rest.
Faithful hath been your warfare, and of God
Accepted, fearless in His righteous cause ;
And, as ye have received, so have ye done,
Invincibly.   But of this cursed crew
The punishment to other hand belongs ;
Vengeance is His, or whose He sole appoints.
Number to this day's work is not ordained,
Nor multitude ; stand only and behold
God's indignation on these godless poured
By Me.   Not you, but Me, they have despised,
Yet envied ; against Me is all their rage,
Because the Father, to Whom in Heaven supreme
Kingdom and power and glory appertains,
Hath honoured Me, according to His will.
Therefore to Me their doom He hath assigned,
That they may have their wish, to try with Me
In battle which the stronger proves—they all,
Or I alone against them ; since by strength
They measure all, of other excellence
Not emulous, nor care who them excels ;
Nor other strife with them do I vouchsafe.'
  " So spake the Son, and into terror changed
His countenance, too severe to be beheld,
And full of wrath bent on His enemies.
At once the Four spread out their starry wings
With dreadful shade contiguous, and the orbs
Of His fierce chariot rolled, as with the sound
Of torrent floods, or of a numerous host.
He on His impious foes right onward drove,
Gloomy as Night.   Under His burning wheels
The steadfast Empyrean shook throughout,
All but the throne itself of God.   Full soon
Among them He arrived, in His right hand

Grasping ten thousand thunders, which He sent
Before Him, such as in their souls infixed
Plagues.   They, astonished, all resistance lost,
All courage; down their idle weapons dropt;
O'er shields, and helms, and helmed heads He rode
Of Thrones and mighty Seraphim prostráte,
That wished the mountains now might be again
Thrown on them, as a shelter from His ire.
Nor less on either side tempestuous fell
His arrows, from the four-fold visaged Four,
Distinct with eyes, and from the living wheels,
Distinct alike with multitude of eyes;
One spirit in them ruled, and every eye
Glared lightning, and shot forth pernicious fire
Among the accursed, that withered all their strength,
And of their wonted vigour left them drained,
Exhausted, spiritless, afflicted, fallen.
Yet half His strength He put not forth, but checked
His thunder in mid-volley; for He meant
Not to destroy, but root them out of Heaven.
The overthrown He raised, and, as a herd
Of goats or timorous flock together thronged,
Drove them before Him thunderstruck, pursued
With terrors and with furies to the bounds
And crystal wall of Heaven; which, opening wide,
Rolled inward, and a spacious gap disclosed
Into the wasteful Deep.   The monstrous sight
Strook them with horror backward; but far worse
Urged them behind: headlong themselves they threw
Down from the verge of Heaven: eternal wrath
Burnt after them to the bottomless pit.
    "Hell heard the unsufferable noise; Hell saw
Heaven ruining from Heaven, and would have fled
Affrighted; but strict Fate had cast too deep
Her dark foundations, and too fast had bound.
Nine days they fell; confounded Chaos roared,
And felt tenfold confusion in their fall
Through his wild Anarchy; so huge a rout
Encumbered him with ruin.   Hell at last,
Yawning, received them whole, and on them closed—
Hell, their fit habitation, fraught with fire
Unquenchable, the house of woe and pain.
Disburdened Heaven rejoiced, and soon repaired
Her mural breach, returning whence it rolled.
Sole Victor, from the expulsion of His foes
Messiah His triumphal chariot turned.
To meet Him all His saints, who silent stood
Eye-witnesses of His almighty acts,
With jubilee advanced; and, as they went,
Shaded with branching palm, each order bright
Sung triumph, and Him sung victorious King,
Son, Heir, and Lord, to Him dominion given,
Worthiest to reign.   He celebrated rode,
Triumphant through mid Heaven, into the courts

And temple of His mighty Father throned
On high; Who into glory Him received,
Where now He sits at the right hand of bliss.
"Thus, measuring things in Heaven by things on Earth,
At thy request, and that thou may'st beware
By what is past, to thee I have revealed
What might have else to human race been hid—
The discord which befell, and war in Heaven
Among the Angelic Powers, and the deep fall
Of those too high aspiring who rebelled
With Satan: he who envies now thy state,
Who now is plotting how he may seduce
Thee also from obedience, that, with him
Bereaved of happiness, thou may'st partake
His punishment, eternal misery;
Which would be all his solace and revenge,
As a despite done against the Most High,
Thee once to gain companion of his woe.
But listen not to his temptations; warn
Thy weaker; let it profit thee to have heard,
By terrible example, the reward
Of disobedience. Firm they might have stood,
Yet fell. Remember, and fear to transgress."

THE END OF THE SIXTH BOOK

PARADISE LOST.

BOOK VII.

THE ARGUMENT.

Raphael, at the request of Adam, relates how and wherefore this World
was first created :—that God, after the expelling of Satan and his Angels out
of Heaven, declared His pleasure to create another World, and other creatures
to dwell therein ; sends His Son with glory, and attendance of Angels, to
perform the work of creation in six days : the Angels celebrate with hymns
the performance thereof, and His re-ascension into Heaven.

DESCEND from Heaven, Urania, by that name
If rightly thou art called, whose voice divine
Following, above the Olympian hill I soar,
Above the flight of Pegasean wing !
The meaning, not the name, I call ; for thou
Nor of the Muses nine, nor on the top
Of old Olympus dwell'st ; but, heavenly-born,
Before the hills appeared or fountain flowed,
Thou with Eternal Wisdom didst converse,
Wisdom thy sister, and with her didst play
In presence of the Almighty Father, pleased
With thy celestial song.   Up led by thee,
Into the Heaven of Heavens I have presumed,
An earthly guest, and drawn empyreal air,
Thy tempering.   With like safety guided down,
Return me to my native element ;
Lest, from this flying steed unreined (as once
Bellerophon, though from a lower clime)
Dismounted, on the Aleian field I fall,
Erroneous there to wander and forlorn.
Half yet remains unsung, but narrower bound
Within the visible Diurnal Sphere.
Standing on Earth, not rapt above the pole,
More safe I sing with mortal voice unchanged
To hoarse or mute, though fallen on evil days,
On evil days though fallen, and evil tongues,
In darkness, and with dangers compassed round,
And solitude ; yet not alone, while thou
Visit'st my slumbers nightly, or when Morn
Purples the East.   Still govern thou my song,
Urania, and fit audience find, though few.

M.—I

But drive far off the barbarous dissonance
Of Bacchus and his revellers, the race
Of that wild rout that tore the Thracian bard
In Rhodope, where woods and rocks had ears
To rapture, till the savage clamour drowned
Both harp and voice ; nor could the Muse defend
Her son. So fail not thou who thee implores ;
For thou art heavenly, she an empty dream.
   Say, Goddess, what ensued when Raphael,
The affable Archangel, had forewarned
Adam, by dire example, to beware
Apostasy, by what befell in Heaven
To those apostates, lest the like befall
In Paradise to Adam or his race,
Charged not to touch the interdicted Tree,
If they transgress, and slight that sole command,
So easily obeyed amid the choice
Of all tastes else to please their appetite,
Though wandering. He, with his consorted Eve,
The story heard attentive, and was filled
With admiration and deep muse, to hear
Of things so high and strange—things to their thought
So unimaginable as hate in Heaven,
And war so near the peace of God in bliss,
With such confusion ; but the evil, soon
Driven back, redounded as a flood on those
From whom it sprung, impossible to mix
With blessedness. Whence Adam soon repealed
The doubts that in his heart arose ; and, now
Led on, yet sinless, with desire to know,
What nearer might concern him—how this World
Of heaven and earth conspicuous first began ;
When, and whereof, created ; for what cause ;
What within Eden, or without, was done
Before his memory—as one whose drouth,
Yet scarce allayed, still eyes the current stream,
Whose liquid murmur heard new thirst excites,
Proceeded thus to ask his Heavenly Guest :—
   "Great things, and full of wonder in our ears,
Far differing from this World, thou hast revealed,
Divine Interpreter ! by favour sent
Down from the Empyrean to forewarn
Us timely of what might else have been our loss,
Unknown, which human knowledge could not reach ;
For which to the infinitely Good we owe
Immortal thanks, and His admonishment
Receive with solemn purpose to observe
Immutably His sovran will, the end
Of what we are. But, since thou hast vouchsafed
Gently, for our instruction, to impart
Things above Earthly thought, which yet concerned
Our knowing, as to highest Wisdom seemed,
Deign to descend now lower, and relate
What may no less perhaps avail us known—

How first began this Heaven which we behold
Distant so high, with moving fires adorned
Innumerable ; and this which yields or fills
All space, the ambient Air, wide interfused,
Embracing round this florid Earth ; what cause
Moved the Creator, in His holy rest
Through all eternity, so late to build
In Chaos ; and, the work begun, how soon
Absolved : if unforbid thou may'st unfold
What we not to explore the secrets ask
Of his eternal empire, but the more
To magnify His works the more we know.
And the great Light of Day yet wants to run
Much of his race, though steep.   Suspense in heaven
Held by thy voice, thy potent voice he hears,
And longer will delay, to hear thee tell
His generation, and the rising birth
Of Nature from the unapparent Deep :
Or, if the Star of Evening and the Moon
Haste to thy audience, Night with her will bring
Silence, and Sleep listening to thee will watch ;
Or we can bid his absence till thy song
End, and dismiss thee ere the morning shine."
   Thus Adam his illustrious guest besought ;
And thus the godlike Angel answered mild :—
   "This also thy request, with caution asked,
Obtain ; though to recount almighty works
What words or tongue of Seraph can suffice,
Or heart of man suffice to comprehend ?
Yet what thou canst attain, which best may serve
To glorify the Maker, and infer
Thee also happier, shall not be withheld
Thy hearing.   Such commission from above
I have received, to answer thy desire
Of knowledge within bounds ; beyond abstain
To ask, nor let thine own inventions hope
Things not revealed, which the invisible King,
Only omniscient, hath suppressed in night,
To none communicable in Earth or Heaven.
Enough is left besides to search and know ;
But Knowledge is as food, and needs no less
Her temperance over appetite, to know
In measure what the mind may well contain ;
Oppresses else with surfeit, and soon turns
Wisdom to folly, as nourishment to wind.
   "Know then that, after Lucifer from Heaven
(So call him, brighter once amidst the host
Of Angels than that star the stars among)
Fell with his flaming legions through the Deep
Into his place, and the great Son returned
Victorious with His Saints, the Omnipotent
Eternal Father from His throne beheld
Their multitude, and to His Son thus spake :—
   "'At least Our envious foe hath failed, who thought

All like himself rebellious ; by whose aid
This inaccessible high strength, the seat
Of Deity supreme, Us dispossessed,
He trusted to have seized, and into fraud
Drew many whom their place knows here no more.
Yet far the greater part have kept, I see,
Their station ; Heaven, yet populous, retains
Number sufficient to possess her realms,
Though wide, and this high temple to frequent
With ministeries due and solemn rites.
But, lest his heart exalt him in the harm
Already done, to have dispeopled Heaven—
My damage fondly deemed—I can repair
That detriment, if such it be to lose
Self-lost, and in a moment will create
Another world ; out of one man a race
Of men innumerable, there to dwell,
Not here, till, by degrees of merit raised,
They open to themselves at length the way
Up hither, under long obedience tried,
And Earth be changed to Heaven, and Heaven to Earth,
One kingdom, joy and union without end.
Meanwhile inhabit lax, ye Powers of Heaven ;
And Thou, My Word, begotten Son, by Thee
This I perform ; speak Thou, and be it done !
My overshadowing Spirit and might with Thee
I send along ; ride forth, and bid the Deep
Within appointed bounds be Heaven and Earth.
Boundless the Deep, because I am who fill
Infinitude ; nor vacuous the space,
Though I, uncircumscribed, Myself retire,
And put not forth My goodness, which is free
To act or not.   Necessity and Chance
Approach not Me, and what I will is Fate.'
   "So spake the Almighty ; and to what He spake
His Word, the Filial Godhead, gave effect.
Immediate are the acts of God, more swift
Than time or motion, but to human ears
Cannot without process of speech be told,
So told as earthly notion can receive.
Great triumph and rejoicing was in Heaven
When such was heard declared the Almighty's will.
Glory they sung to the Most High, good-will
To future men, and in their dwellings peace—
Glory to Him whose just avenging ire
Had driven out the ungodly from His sight
And the habitations of the just ; to Him
Glory and praise whose wisdom had ordained
Good out of evil to create—instead
Of Spirits malign, a better race to bring
Into their vacant room, and thence diffuse
His good to worlds and ages infinite.
   "So sang the Hierarchies.   Meanwhile the Son
On His great expedition now appeared,

Girt with omnipotence, with radiance crowned
Of majesty divine, sapience and love
Immense ; and all His Father in Him shone.
About His chariot numberless were poured
Cherub and Seraph, Potentates and Thrones,
And Virtues, winged Spirits, and chariots winged
From the armoury of God, where stand of old
Myriads, between two brazen mountains lodged
Against a solemn day, harnessed at hand,
Celestial equipage ; and now came forth
Spontaneous, for within them Spirit lived,
Attendant on their Lord.   Heaven opened wide
Her ever-during gates, harmonious sound
On golden hinges moving, to let forth
The King of Glory, in His powerful Word
And Spirit coming to create new worlds.
On Heavenly ground they stood, and from the shore
They viewed the vast immeasurable Abyss,
Outrageous as a sea, dark, wasteful, wild,
Up from the bottom turned by furious winds
And surging waves, as mountains to assault
Heaven's height, and with the centre mix the pole.
   " ' Silence, ye troubled waves, and, thou Deep, peace ! '
Said then the omnific Word : ' Your discord end ! '
Nor stayed ; but, on the wings of Cherubim
Uplifted, in paternal glory rode
Far into Chaos and the World unborn ;
For Chaos heard His voice.   Him all His train
Followed in bright procession, to behold
Creation, and the wonders of His might.
Then stayed the fervid wheels, and in His hand
He took the golden compasses, prepared
In God's eternal store, to circumscribe
This Universe, and all created things.
One foot He centred, and the other turned
Round through the vast profundity obscure,
And said, ' Thus far extend, thus far thy bounds ;
This be thy just circumference, O World ! '
Thus God the Heaven created, thus the Earth,
Matter unformed and void.   Darkness profound
Covered the Abyss ; but on the watery calm
His brooding wings the Spirit of God outspread,
And vital virtue infused, and vital warmth,
Throughout the fluid mass, but downward purged
The black, tartareous cold, infernal dregs,
Adverse to life ; then founded, then conglobed,
Like things to like, the rest to several place
Disparted, and between spun out the Air,
And Earth, self-balanced, on her centre hung.
   " ' Let there be Light ! ' said God ; and forthwith Light
Ethereal, first of things, quintessence pure,
Sprung from the Deep, and from her native East
To journey through the aery gloom began,
Sphered in a radiant cloud—for yet the Sun

117

Was not; she in a cloudy tabernacle
Sojourned the while.   God saw the Light was good;
And light from darkness by the hemisphere
Divided : Light the Day, and Darkness Night,
He named.   Thus was the first Day even and morn;
Nor passed uncelebrated, nor unsung
By the celestial quires, when orient light
Exhaling first from darkness they beheld,
Birth-day of Heaven and Earth.   With joy and shout
The hollow universal orb they filled,
And touched their golden harps, and hymning praised
God and His works ; Creator Him they sung,
Both when first evening was, and when first morn.
  "Again God said, 'Let there be firmament
Amid the waters, and let it divide
The waters from the waters !'   And God made
The firmament, expanse of liquid, pure,
Transparent, elemental air, diffused
In circuit to the uttermost convex
Of this great round—partition firm and sure,
The waters underneath from those above
Dividing ; for as Earth, so He the World
Built on circumfluous waters calm, in wide
Crystalline ocean, and the loud misrule
Of Chaos far removed, lest fierce extremes
Contiguous might distemper the whole frame :
And Heaven He named the Firmament.   So even
And morning chorus sung the second Day.
  "The Earth was formed, but, in the womb as yet
Of waters, embryon immature, involved,
Appeared not ; over all the face of Earth
Main ocean flowed, not idle, but, with warm
Prolific humour softening all her globe,
Fermented the great mother to conceive,
Satiate with genial moisture ; when God said,
'Be gathered now, ye waters under heaven,
Into one place, and let dry land appear !'
Immediately the mountains huge appear
Emergent, and their broad bare backs upheave
Into the clouds ; their tops ascend the sky.
So high as heaved the tumid hills, so low
Down sunk a hollow bottom broad and deep,
Capacious bed of waters.   Thither they
Hasted with glad precipitance, uprolled,
As drops on dust conglobing, from the dry :
Part rise in crystal wall, or ridge direct,
For haste ; such flight the great command impressed
On the swift floods.   As armies at the call
Of trumpet (for of armies thou hast heard)
Troop to the standard, so the watery throng,
Wave rolling after wave, where way they found—
If steep, with torrent rapture, if through plain,
Soft-ebbing ; nor withstood them rock or hill ;
But they, or underground, or circuit wide

With serpent error wandering, found their way,
And on the washy ooze deep channels wore :
Easy, ere God had bid the ground be dry,
All but within those banks where rivers now
Stream, and perpetual draw their humid train.
The dry land Earth, and the great receptacle
Of congregated waters He called Seas ;
And saw that it was good, and said, 'Let the Earth
Put forth the verdant grass, herb yielding seed,
And fruit-tree yielding fruit after her kind,
Whose seed is in herself upon the Earth !'
He scarce had said when the bare Earth, till then
Desert and bare, unsightly, unadorned,
Brought forth the tender grass, whose verdure clad
Her universal face with pleasant green ;
Then herbs of every leaf, that sudden flowered,
Opening their various colours, and made gay
Her bosom, smelling sweet ; and, these scarce blown,
Forth flourished thick the clustering vine, forth crept
The smelling gourd, up stood the corny reed
Embattled in her field : add the humble shrub,
And bush with frizzled hair implicit : last
Rose, as in dance, the stately trees, and spread
Their branches hung with copious fruit, or gemmed
Their blossoms.   With high woods the hills were crowned,
With tufts the valleys and each fountain-side,
With borders long the rivers, that Earth now
Seemed like to Heaven, a seat where gods might dwell,
Or wander with delight, and love to haunt
Her sacred shades ; though God had yet not rained
Upon the Earth, and man to till the ground
None was, but from the Earth a dewy mist
Went up and watered all the ground, and each
Plant of the field, which ere it was in the Earth
God made, and every herb before it grew
On the green stem.   God saw that it was good ;
So even and morn recorded the third Day.
   "Again the Almighty spake, 'Let there be Lights
High in the expanse of Heaven, to divide
The Day from Night ; and let them be for signs,
For seasons, and for days, and circling years ;
And let them be for lights, as I ordain
Their office in the firmament of heaven,
To give light on the Earth !' and it was so.
And God made two great lights, great for their use
To Man, the greater to have rule by day,
The less by night, altern ; and made the Stars,
And set them in the firmament of heaven
To illuminate the Earth, and rule the day
In their vicissitude, and rule the night,
And light from darkness to divide.   God saw,
Surveying His great work, that it was good :
For, of celestial bodies, first the Sun
A mighty sphere he framed, unlightsome first,

Though of ethereal mould ; then formed the Moon
Globose, and every magnitude of Stars,
And sowed with stars the heaven thick as a field.
Of light by far the greater part He took,
Transplanted from her cloudy shrine, and placed
In the Sun's orb, made porous to receive
And drink the liquid light, firm to retain
Her gathered beams, great palace now of Light.
Hither, as to their fountain, other stars
Repairing in their golden urns draw light,
And hence the morning planet gilds her horns ;
By tincture or reflection they augment
Their small peculiar, though from human sight
So far remote, with diminution seen.
First in his east the glorious lamp was seen,
Regent of day, and all the horizon round
Invested with bright rays, jocund to run
His longitude through heaven's high road ; the grey
Dawn, and the Pleiades, before him danced,
Shedding sweet influence.   Less bright the Moon,
But opposite in levelled west, was set
His mirror, with full face borrowing her light
From him ; for other light she needed none
In that aspect, and still that distance keeps
Till night ; then in the east her turn she shines,
Revolved on heaven's great axle, and her reign
With thousand lesser lights dividual holds,
With thousand thousand stars, that then appeared
Spangling the hemisphere.   Then first adorned
With her bright luminaries, that set and rose,
Glad evening and glad morn crowned the fourth Day.
    "And God said, ' Let the waters generate
Reptile with spawn abundant, living soul ;
And let Fowl fly above the earth, with wings
Displayed on the open firmament of heaven !'
And God created the great whales, and each
Soul living, each that crept, which plenteously
The waters generated by their kinds,
And every bird of wing after his kind,
And saw that it was good, and blessed them, saying,
' Be fruitful, multiply, and, in the seas,
And lakes, and running streams, the waters fill ;
And let the fowl be multiplied on the earth !'
Forthwith the sounds and seas, each creek and bay,
With fry innumerable swarm, and shoals
Of fish that, with their fins and shining scales,
Glide under the green wave in sculls that oft
Bank the mid-sea.   Part, single or with mate,
Graze the sea-weed, their pasture, and through groves
Of coral stray, or, sporting with quick glance,
Show to the sun their waved coats dropt with gold,
Or, in their pearly shells at ease, attend
Moist nutriment, or under rocks their food
In jointed armour watch ; on smooth the seal

120

And bended dolphins play : part, huge of bulk,
Wallowing unwieldy, enormous in their gait,
Tempest the ocean.   There leviathan,
Hugest of living creatures, on the deep
Stretched like a promontory, sleeps or swims,
And seems a moving land, and at his gills
Draws in, and at his trunk spouts out, a sea.
Meanwhile the tepid caves, and fens, and shores,
Their brood as numerous hatch from the egg, that soon,
Bursting with kindly rupture, forth disclosed
Their callow young ; but feathered soon and fledge
They summed their pens, and, soaring the air sublime,
With clang despised the ground, under a cloud
In prospect.   There the eagle and the stork
On cliffs and cedar-tops their eyries build.
Part loosely wing the region ; part, more wise,
In common, ranged in figure, wedge their way,
Intelligent of seasons, and set forth
Their aery caravan, high over seas
Flying, and over lands, with mutual wing
Easing their flight : so steers the prudent crane
Her annual voyage, borne on winds : the air
Floats as they pass, fanned with unnumbered plumes.
From branch to branch the smaller birds with song
Solaced the woods, and spread their painted wings,
Till even ; nor then the solemn nightingale
Ceased warbling, but all night tuned her soft lays.
Others, on silver lakes and rivers, bathed
Their downy breast ; the swan, with arched neck
Between her white wings mantling proudly, rows
Her state with oary feet ; yet oft they quit
The dank, and, rising on stiff pennons, tower
The mid aerial sky.   Others on ground
Walked firm—the crested cock, whose clarion sounds
The silent hours, and the other, whose gay train
Adorns him, coloured with the florid hue
Of rainbows and starry eyes.   The waters thus
With Fish replenished, and the air with Fowl,
Evening and morn solemnized the fifth Day.
   "The sixth, and of Creation last, arose
With evening harps and matin ; when God said,
'Let the Earth bring forth soul living in her kind,
Cattle, and creeping things, and beasts of the earth,
Each in their kind !'   The Earth obeyed, and, straight
Opening her fertile womb, teemed at a birth
Innumerous living creatures, perfect forms,
Limbed and full-grown.   Out of the ground up rose,
As from his lair, the wild beast, where he wons
In forest wild, in thicket, brake, or den—
Among the trees in pairs they rose, they walked ;
The cattle in the fields and meadows green :
Those rare and solitary, these in flocks
Pasturing at once and in broad herds, up-sprung.
The grassy clods now calved ; now half appeared

The tawny lion, pawing to get free
His hinder parts—then springs, as broke from bonds,
And rampant shakes his brinded mane ; the ounce,
The libbard, and the tiger, as the mole
Rising, the crumbled earth above them threw
In hillocks ; the swift stag from underground
Bore up his branching head ; scarce from his mould
Behemoth, biggest born of earth, upheaved
His vastness ; fleeced the flocks and bleating rose,
As plants ; ambiguous between sea and land,
The river-horse and scaly crocodile.
At once came forth whatever creeps the ground,
Insect or worm.   Those waved their limber fans
For wings, and smallest lineaments exact
In all the liveries decked of summer's pride,
With spots of gold and purple, azure and green ;
These as a line their long dimension drew,
Streaking the ground with sinuous trace ; not all
Minims of nature ; some of serpent kind,
Wondrous in length and corpulence, involved
Their snaky folds, and added wings.   First crept
The parsimonious emmet, provident
Of future, in small room large heart enclosed—
Pattern of just equality perhaps
Hereafter—joined in her popular tribes
Of commonalty.   Swarming next appeared
The female bee, that feeds her husband drone
Deliciously, and builds her waxen cells
With honey stored.   The rest are numberless,
And thou their natures know'st, and gav'st them names,
Needless to thee repeated ; nor unknown
The serpent, subtlest beast of all the field,
Of huge extent sometimes, with brazen eyes
And hairy mane terrific, though to thee
Not noxious, but obedient at thy call.
   " Now Heaven in all her glory shone, and rolled
Her motions, as the great First Mover's hand
First wheeled their course ; Earth, in her rich attire
Consummate, lovely smiled ; Air, Water, Earth,
By fowl, fish, beast, was flown, was swum, was walked,
Frequent ; and of the sixth Day yet remained.
There wanted yet the master-work, the end
Of all yet done—a creature who, not prone
And brute as other creatures, but endued
With sanctity of reason, might erect
His stature, and, upright with front serene
Govern the rest, self-knowing, and from thence
Magnanimous to correspond with Heaven,
But grateful to acknowledge whence his good
Descends ; thither with heart, and voice, and eyes
Directed in devotion, to adore
And worship God Supreme, who made him chief
Of all His works.   Therefore the Omnipotent
Eternal Father (for where is not He

Present?) thus to his Son audibly spake:—
'Let us make now Man in our image, Man
In our similitude, and let them rule
Over the fish and fowl of sea and air,
Beast of the field, and over all the earth,
And every creeping thing that creeps the ground!'
This said, He formed thee, Adam, thee, O Man,
Dust of the ground, and in thy nostrils breathed
The breath of life; in His own image He
Created thee, in the image of God
Express, and thou becam'st a living soul.
Male He created thee, but thy consort
Female, for race; then blessed mankind, and said,
'Be fruitful, multiply, and fill the Earth;
Subdue it, and throughout dominion hold
Over fish of the sea, and fowl of the air,
And every living thing that moves on the Earth!'
Wherever thus created—for no place
Is yet distinct by name—thence, as thou know'st,
He brought thee into this delicious grove,
This Garden, planted with the trees of God,
Delectable both to behold and taste,
And freely all their pleasant fruit for food
Gave thee. All sorts are here that all the earth yields,
Variety without end; but of the tree
Which tasted works knowledge of good and evil
Thou may'st not; in the day thou eat'st, thou diest.
Death is the penalty imposed; beware,
And govern well thy appetite, lest Sin
Surprise thee, and her black attendant, Death.
"Here finished He, and all that He had made
Viewed, and, behold! all was entirely good.
So even and morn accomplished the sixth Day;
Yet not till the Creator, from His work
Desisting, though unwearied, up returned,
Up to the Heaven of Heavens, His high abode,
Thence to behold this new-created World,
The addition of His empire, how it showed
In prospect from His throne, how good, how fair,
Answering His great idea. Up He rode
Followed with acclamation, and the sound
Symphonious of ten thousand harps, that tuned
Angelic harmonies. The Earth, the Air
Resounded (thou remember'st, for thou heard'st),
The heavens and all the constellations rung,
The planets in their stations listening stood,
While the bright pomp ascended jubilant.
'Open, ye everlasting gates!' they sung;
'Open, ye Heavens, your living doors! let in
The great Creator, from His work returned
Magnificent, His six days' work, a World!
Open, and henceforth oft; for God will deign
To visit oft the dwellings of just men
Delighted, and with frequent intercourse

Thither will send His winged messengers
On errands of supernal grace.' So sung
The glorious train ascending. He through Heaven,
That opened wide her blazing portals, led
To God's eternal house direct the way—
A broad and ample road, whose dust is gold,
And pavement stars, as stars to thee appear
Seen in the Galaxy, that milky way
Which nightly as a circling zone thou seest
Powdered with stars. And now on Earth the seventh
Evening arose in Eden—for the sun
Was set, and twilight from the east came on,
Forerunning night—when at the holy mount
Of Heaven's high-seated top, the imperial throne
Of Godhead, fixed for ever firm and sure,
The Filial Power arrived, and sat Him down
With His great Father; for He also went
Invisible, yet stayed (such privilege
Hath Omnipresence) and the work ordained,
Author and end of all things, and, from work
Now resting, blessed and hallowed the seventh Day,
As resting on that day from all His work;
But not in silence holy kept: the harp
Had work, and rested not; the solemn pipe
And dulcimer, all organs of sweet stop,
All sounds on fret by string or golden wire,
Tempered soft tunings, intermixed with voice
Choral or unison; of incense clouds,
Fuming from golden censers, hid the Mount.
Creation and the Six Days' acts they sung:—
'Great are Thy works, Jehovah! infinite
Thy power! what thought can measure Thee, or tongue
Relate Thee—greater now in Thy return
Than from the Giant-angels? Thee that day
Thy thunders magnified; but to create
Is greater than created to destroy.
Who can impair Thee, mighty King, or bound
Thy empire? Easily the proud attempt
Of Spirits apostate, and their counsels vain,
Thou hast repelled, while impiously they thought
Thee to diminish, and from Thee withdraw
The number of Thy worshippers. Who seeks
To lessen Thee, against his purpose, serves
To manifest the more Thy might; his evil
Thou usest, and from thence creat'st more good.
Witness this new-made World, another Heaven
From Heaven-gate not far, founded in view
On the clear hyaline, the glassy sea;
Of amplitude almost immense, with stars
Numerous, and every star perhaps a world
Of destined habitation—but Thou know'st
Their seasons; among these the seat of men,
Earth, with her nether ocean circumfused,
Their pleasant dwelling-place. Thrice happy men

And sons of men, whom God hath thus advanced,
Created in His image, there to dwell
And worship Him, and in reward to rule
Over His works, on earth, in sea, or air,
And multiply a race of worshippers
Holy and just! thrice happy, if they know
Their happiness, and persevere upright!'
  "So sung they, and the Empyrean rung
With halleluiahs. Thus was Sabbath kept.
And thy request think now fulfilled, that asked
How first this World and face of things began,
And what before thy memory was done
From the beginning, that posterity,
Informed by thee, might know. If else thou seek'st
Aught, not surpassing human measure, say."

THE END OF THE SEVENTH BOOK.

PARADISE LOST.

BOOK VIII.

THE ARGUMENT.

Adam inquires concerning celestial motions; is doubtfully answered, and exhorted to search rather things more worthy of knowledge. Adam assents, and, still desirous to detain Raphael, relates to him what he remembered since his own creation—his placing in Paradise; his talk with God concerning solitude and fit society; his first meeting and nuptials with Eve. His discourse with the Angel thereupon; who, after admonitions repeated, departs.

THE Angel ended, and in Adam's ear
So charming left his voice that he a while
Thought him still speaking, still stood fixed to hear;
Then, as new-waked, thus gratefully replied:—
"What thanks sufficient, or what recompense
Equal, have I to render thee, divine
Historian, who thus largely hast allayed
The thirst I had of knowledge, and vouchsafed
This friendly condescension to relate
Things else by me unsearchable—now heard
With wonder, but delight, and, as is due,
With glory attributed to the high
Creator? Something yet of doubt remains,
Which only thy solution can resolve.
When I behold this goodly frame, this World,
Of Heaven and Earth consisting, and compute
Their magnitudes—this Earth, a spot, a grain,
An atom, with the Firmament compared
And all her numbered stars, that seem to roll
Spaces incomprehensible (for such
Their distance argues, and their swift return
Diurnal) merely to officiate light
Round this opacous Earth, this punctual spot,
One day and night, in all their vast survey
Useless besides—reasoning, I oft admire
How Nature, wise and frugal, could commit
Such disproportions, with superfluous hand
So many nobler bodies to create,
Greater so manifold, to this one use,
For aught appears, and on their Orbs impose
Such restless revolution day by day

Repeated, while the sedentary Earth,
That better might with far less compass move,
Served by more noble than herself, attains
Her end without least motion, and receives,
As tribute, such a sumless journey brought
Of incorporeal speed, her warmth and light:
Speed, to describe whose swiftness number fails."
   So spake our Sire, and by his countenance seemed
Entering on studious thoughts abstruse; which Eve
Perceiving, where she sat retired in sight,
With lowliness majestic from her seat,
And grace that won who saw to wish her stay,
Rose, and went forth among her fruits and flowers,
To visit how they prospered, bud and bloom,
Her nursery; they at her coming sprung,
And, touched by her fair tendance, gladlier grew.
Yet went she not as not with such discourse
Delighted, or not capable her ear
Of what was high. Such pleasure she reserved,
Adam relating, she sole auditress;
Her husband the relater she preferred
Before the Angel, and of him to ask
Chose rather; he, she knew, would intermix
Grateful digressions, and solve high dispute
With conjugal caresses: from his lip
Not words alone pleased her. Oh, when meet now
Such pairs, in love and mutual honour joined?
With goddess-like demeanour forth she went,
Not unattended; for on her as Queen
A pomp of winning Graces waited still.
And from about her shot darts of desire
Into all eyes, to wish her still in sight.
And Raphael now to Adam's doubt proposed
Benevolent and facile thus replied :—
   "To ask or search I blame thee not; for Heaven
Is as the Book of God before thee set,
Wherein to read His wondrous works, and learn
His seasons, hours, or days, or months, or years.
This to attain, whether Heaven move or Earth
Imports not, if thou reckon right; the rest
From Man or Angel the great Architect
Did wisely to conceal, and not divulge
His secrets, to be scanned by them who ought
Rather admire. Or, if they list to try
Conjecture, He His fabric of the Heavens
Hath left to their disputes—perhaps to move
His laughter at their quaint opinions wide
Hereafter, when they come to model Heaven,
And calculate the stars; how they will wield
The mighty frame; how build, unbuild, contrive
To save appearances; how gird the Sphere
With Centric and Eccentric scribbled o'er,
Cycle and Epicycle, Orb in Orb.
Already by thy reasoning this I guess,

Who art to lead thy offspring, and supposest
That bodies bright and greater should not serve
The less not bright, nor Heaven such journeys run,
Earth sitting still, when she alone receives
The benefit. Consider, first, that great
Or bright infers not excellence. The Earth,
Though, in comparison of Heaven, so small,
Nor glistering, may of solid good contain
More plenty than the Sun that barren shines,
Whose virtue on itself works no effect,
But in the fruitful earth; there first received
His beams, unactive else, their vigour find.
Yet not to Earth are those bright luminaries
Officious, but to thee, Earth's habitant.
And, for the Heaven's wide circuit, let it speak
The Maker's high magnificence, who built
So spacious, and His line stretched out so far,
That Man may know he dwells not in his own—
An edifice too large for him to fill,
Lodged in a small partition, and the rest
Ordained for uses to his Lord best known.
The swiftness of those Circles attribute,
Though numberless, to His omnipotence,
That to corporeal substances could add
Speed almost spiritual. Me thou think'st not slow,
Who since the morning-hour set out from Heaven
Where God resides, and ere mid-day arrived
In Eden—distance inexpressible
By numbers that have name. But this I urge,
Admitting motion in the Heavens, to show
Invalid that which thee to doubt it moved;
Not that I so affirm, though so it seem
To thee who hast thy dwelling here on Earth.
God, to remove His ways from human sense,
Placed Heaven from Earth so far, that earthly sight,
If it presume, might err in things too high,
And no advantage gain. What if the Sun
Be centre to the World, and other Stars,
By his attractive virtue and their own
Incited, dance about him various rounds?
Their wandering course, now high, now low, then hid,
Progressive, retrograde, or standing still,
In six thou seest; and what if, seventh to these,
The planet Earth, so steadfast though she seem,
Insensibly three different motions move?
Which else to several spheres thou must ascribe,
Moved contrary with thwart obliquities,
Or save the Sun his labour, and that swift
Nocturnal and diurnal rhomb supposed,
Invisible else above all stars, the wheel
Of Day and Night; which needs not thy belief,
If Earth, industrious of herself, fetch Day,
Travelling east, and with her part averse
From the Sun's beam meet Night, her other part

Still luminous by his ray.   What if that light,
Sent from her through the wide transpicuous air,
To the terrestrial Moon be as a star,
Enlightening her by day, as she by night
This Earth—reciprocal, if land be there,
Fields and inhabitants?   Her spots thou seest
As clouds, and clouds may rain, and rain produce
Fruits in her softened soil, for some to eat
Allotted there; and other Suns, perhaps,
With their attendant Moons, thou wilt descry,
Communicating male and female light—
Which two great sexes animate the World,
Stored in each Orb perhaps with some that live.
For such vast room in Nature unpossessed
By living soul, desert and desolate,
Only to shine, yet scarce to contribute
Each Orb a glimpse of light, conveyed so far
Down to this habitable, which returns
Light back to them, is obvious to dispute.
But whether thus these things, or whether not—
Whether the Sun, predominant in heaven,
Rise on the Earth, or Earth rise on the Sun;
He from the east his flaming road begin,
Or she from west her silent course advance
With inoffensive pace that spinning sleeps
On her soft axle, while she paces even,
And bears thee soft with the smooth air along—
Solicit not thy thoughts with matters hid:
Leave them to God above; Him serve and fear.
Of other creatures as Him pleases best,
Wherever placed, let Him dispose; joy thou
In what He gives to thee, this Paradise
And thy fair Eve; Heaven is for thee too high
To know what passes there.   Be lowly wise;
Think only what concerns thee and thy being;
Dream not of other worlds, what creatures there
Live, in what state, condition, or degree—
Contented that thus far hath been revealed
Not of Earth only, but of highest Heaven."
   To whom thus Adam, cleared of doubt, replied:—
"How fully hast thou satisfied me, pure
Intelligence of Heaven, Angel serene,
And, freed from intricacies, taught to live
The easiest way, nor with perplexing thoughts
To interrupt the sweet of life, from which
God hath bid dwell far off all anxious cares,
And not molest us, unless we ourselves
Seek them with wandering thoughts, and notions vain!
But apt the mind or fancy is to rove
Unchecked; and of her roving is no end,
Till, warned, or by experience taught, she learn
That not to know at large of things remote
From use, obscure and subtle, but to know
That which before us lies in daily life,

M.—K

Is the prime wisdom : what is more is fume,
Or emptiness, or fond impertinence,
And renders us in things that most concern
Unpractised, unprepared, and still to seek.
Therefore from this high pitch let us descend
A lower flight, and speak of things at hand
Useful ; whence, haply, mention may arise
Of something not unseasonable to ask,
By sufferance, and thy wonted favour, deigned.
Thee I have heard relating what was done
Ere my remembrance ; now hear me relate
My story, which, perhaps, thou hast not heard.
And day is yet not spent ; till then thou seest
How subtly to detain thee I devise,
Inviting thee to hear while I relate—
Fond, were it not in hope of thy reply.
For, while I sit with thee, I seem in Heaven ;
And sweeter thy discourse is to my ear
Than fruits of palm-tree, pleasantest to thirst
And hunger both, from labour, at the hour
Of sweet repast.   They satiate, and soon fill,
Though pleasant ; but thy words, with grace divine
Imbued, bring to their sweetness no satiety."
     To whom thus Raphael answered, heavenly meek :—
"Nor are thy lips ungraceful, Sire of Men,
Nor tongue ineloquent ; for God on thee
Abundantly His gifts hath also poured,
Inward and outward both, His image fair :
Speaking, or mute, all comeliness and grace
Attends thee, and each word, each motion, forms.
Nor less think we in Heaven of thee on Earth
Than of our fellow-servant, and inquire
Gladly into the ways of God with Man ;
For God, we see, hath honoured thee, and set
On Man His equal love.   Say, therefore, on ;
For I that day was absent, as befell,
Bound on a voyage uncouth and obscure,
Far on excursion toward the gates of Hell,
Squared in full legion (such command we had),
To see that none thence issued forth a spy
Or enemy, while God was in His work,
Lest He, incensed at such eruption bold,
Destruction with Creation might have mixed.
Not that they durst without His leave attempt ;
But us He sends upon His high behests
For state, as sovran King, and to inure
Our prompt obedience.   Fast we found, fast shut,
The dismal gates, and barricadoed strong,
But, long ere our approaching, heard within
Noise, other than the sound of dance or song—
Torment, and loud lament, and furious rage.
Glad we returned up to the coasts of Light
Ere Sabbath-evening ; so we had in charge.
But thy relation now ; for I attend,

Pleased with thy words no less than thou with mine."
 So spake the godlike Power, and thus our Sire :—
"For Man to tell how human life began
Is hard ; for who himself beginning knew ?
Desire with thee still longer to converse
Induced me. As new-waked from soundest sleep,
Soft on the flowery herb I found me laid,
In balmy sweat, which with his beams the Sun
Soon dried, and on the reeking moisture fed.
Straight toward Heaven my wondering eyes I turned,
And gazed a while the ample sky, till, raised
By quick instinctive motion, up I sprung,
As thitherward endeavouring, and upright
Stood on my feet. About me round I saw
Hill, dale, and shady woods, and sunny plains,
And liquid lapse of murmuring streams ; by these,
Creatures that lived and moved, and walked or flew,
Birds on the branches warbling : all things smiled ;
With fragrance and with joy my heart o'erflowed.
Myself I then perused, and limb by limb
Surveyed, and sometimes went, and sometimes ran
With supple joints, as lively vigour led ;
But who I was, or where, or from what cause,
Knew not. To speak I tried, and forthwith spake ;
My tongue obeyed, and readily could name
Whate'er I saw. 'Thou Sun,' said I, 'fair light,
And thou enlightened Earth, so fresh and gay,
Ye hills and dales, ye rivers, woods, and plains,
And ye that live and move, fair creatures, tell,
Tell, if ye saw, how came I thus, how here !
Not of myself ; by some great Maker then,
In goodness and in power pre-eminent.
Tell me, how may I know Him, how adore,
From whom I have that thus I move and live,
And feel that I am happier than I know !'
While thus I called, and strayed I knew not whither,
From where I first drew air, and first beheld
This happy light, when answer none returned,
On a green shady bank, profuse of flowers,
Pensive I sat me down. There gentle sleep
First found me, and with soft oppression seized
My drowsed sense, untroubled, though I thought
I then was passing to my former state
Insensible, and forthwith to dissolve :
When suddenly stood at my head a dream,
Whose inward apparition gently moved
My fancy to believe I yet had being,
And lived. One came, methought, of shape divine,
And said, 'Thy mansion wants thee, Adam ; rise,
First Man, of men innumerable ordained
First father ! called by thee, I come thy guide
To the Garden of bliss, thy seat prepared.'
So saying, by the hand he took me, raised,
And over fields and waters, as in air

Smooth sliding without step, last led me up
A woody mountain, whose high top was plain,
A circuit wide, enclosed, with goodliest trees
Planted, with walks and bowers, that what I saw
Of Earth before scarce pleasant seemed.   Each tree
Loaden with fairest fruit, that hung to the eye
Tempting, stirred in me sudden appetite
To pluck and eat ; whereat I waked, and found
Before mine eyes all real, as the dream
Had lively shadowed.   Here had new begun
My wandering, had not He who was my guide
Up hither from among the trees appeared,
Presence Divine.   Rejoicing, but with awe,
In adoration at His feet I fell
Submiss.   He reared me, and, 'Whom thou sought'st I am,'
Said mildly, 'Author of all this thou seest
Above, or round about thee, or beneath.
This Paradise I give thee ; count it thine
To till and keep, and of the fruit to eat.
Of every tree that in the Garden grows
Eat freely with glad heart ; fear here no dearth.
But of the tree whose operation brings
Knowledge of good and ill, which I have set,
The pledge of thy obedience and thy faith,
Amid the garden by the Tree of Life—
Remember what I warn thee—shun to taste,
And shun the bitter consequence : for know,
The day thou eat'st thereof, My sole command
Transgressed, inevitably thou shalt die,
From that day mortal, and this happy state
Shalt lose, expelled from hence into a world
Of woe and sorrow.'   Sternly He pronounced
The rigid interdiction, which resounds
Yet dreadful in mine ear, though in my choice
Not to incur ; but soon his clear aspéct
Returned, and gracious purpose thus renewed :—
'Not only these fair bounds, but all the Earth
To thee and to thy race I give ; as lords
Possess it, and all things that therein live,
Or live in sea or air, beast, fish, and fowl.
In sign whereof, each bird and beast behold
After their kinds ; I bring them to receive
From thee their names, and pay thee fealty
With low subjection.   Understand the same
Of fish within their watery residence,
Not hither summoned, since they cannot change
Their element to draw the thinner air.'
As thus He spake, each bird and beast behold
Approaching two and two—these cowering low
With blandishment ; each bird stooped on his wing.
I named them as they passed, and understood
Their nature ; with such knowledge God endued
My sudden apprehension.   But in these
I found not what methought I wanted still,

And to the Heavenly Vision thus presumed :—
   "'O, by what name—for Thou above all these,
Above mankind, or aught than mankind higher,
Surpassest far my naming—how may I
Adore Thee, Author of this Universe,
And all this good to Man, for whose well-being
So amply, and with hands so liberal,
Thou hast provided all things ? But with me
I see not who partakes. In solitude
What happiness ? who can enjoy alone,
Or, all enjoying, what contentment find ?'
Thus I, presumptuous ; and the Vision bright,
As with a smile more brightened, thus replied :—
   "'What call'st thou solitude ? Is not the Earth
With various living creatures, and the Air,
Replenished, and all these at thy command
To come and play before thee ? Know'st thou not
Their language and their ways ? They also know,
And reason not contemptibly ; with these
Find pastime, and bear rule ; thy realm is large.'
So spake the Universal Lord, and seemed
So ordering. I, with leave of speech implored,
And humble deprecation, thus replied :—
   "'Let not my words offend Thee, Heavenly Power ;
My Maker, be propitious while I speak.
Hast Thou not made me here Thy substitute,
And these inferior far beneath me set ?
Among unequals what society
Can sort, what harmony or true delight ?
Which must be mutual, in proportion due
Given and received ; but, in disparity,
The one intense, the other still remiss,
Cannot well suit with either, but soon prove
Tedious alike. Of fellowship I speak
Such as I seek, fit to participate
All rational delight, wherein the brute
Cannot be human consort. They rejoice
Each with their kind, lion with lioness ;
So fitly them in pairs Thou hast combined :
Much less can bird with beast, or fish with fowl,
So well converse, nor with the ox the ape ;
Worse, then, can man with beast, and least of all.'
   "Whereto the Almighty answered, not displeased :—
'A nice and subtle happiness, I see,
Thou to thyself proposest, in the choice
Of thy associates, Adam, and wilt taste
No pleasure, though in pleasure, solitary.
What think'st thou, then, of Me, and this My state ?
Seem I to thee sufficiently possessed
Of happiness, or not, Who am alone
From all eternity ? for none I know
Second to Me or like, equal much less.
How have I, then, with whom to hold converse,
Save with the creatures which I made, and those

To Me inferior infinite descents
Beneath what other creatures are to thee?'
"He ceased.   I lowly answered :—'To attain
The highth and depth of Thy eternal ways
All human thoughts come short, Supreme of Things!
Thou in Thyself art perfect, and in Thee
Is no deficience found.   Not so is Man,
But in degree—the cause of his desire
By conversation with his like to help
Or solace his defects.   No need that Thou
Shouldst propagate, already infinite,
And through all numbers absolute, though One ;
But Man by number is to manifest
His single imperfection, and beget
Like of his like, his image multiplied,
In unity defective ; which requires
Collateral love, and dearest amity.
Thou, in Thy secrecy although alone,
Best with Thyself accompanied, seek'st not
Social communication—yet, so pleased,
Canst raise Thy creature to what highth Thou wilt
Of union or communion, deified ;
I, by conversing, cannot these erect
From prone, nor in their ways complacence find.'
Thus I emboldened spake, and freedom used
Permissive, and acceptance found ; which gained
This answer from the gracious Voice Divine :—
"'Thus far to try thee, Adam, I was pleased,
And find thee knowing not of beasts alone,
Which thou hast rightly named, but of thyself—
Expressing well the spirit within thee free,
My image, not imparted to the brute ;
Whose fellowship, therefore, unmeet for thee,
Good reason was thou freely shouldst dislike.
And be so minded still.   I, ere thou spak'st,
Knew it not good for Man to be alone,
And no such company as then thou saw'st
Intended thee—for trial only brought,
To see how thou couldst judge of fit and meet.
What next I bring shall please thee, be assured,
Thy likeness, thy fit help, thy other self,
Thy wish exactly to thy heart's desire.'
"He ended, or I heard no more ; for now
My earthly, by His heavenly overpowered,
Which it had long stood under, strained to the highth
In that celestial colloquy sublime,
As with an object that excels the sense,
Dazzled and spent, sunk down, and sought repair
Of sleep, which instantly fell on me, called
By Nature as in aid, and closed mine eyes.
Mine eyes he closed, but open left the cell
Of fancy, my internal sight ; by which,
Abstract as in a trance, methought I saw,
Though sleeping, where I lay, and saw the Shape

134

Still glorious before whom awake I stood ;
Who, stooping, opened my left side, and took
From thence a rib, with cordial spirits warm,
And life-blood streaming fresh ; wide was the wound,
But suddenly with flesh filled up and healed.
The rib He formed and fashioned with His hands ;
Under His forming hands a creature grew,
Man-like, but different sex, so lovely fair
That what seemed fair in all the world seemed now
Mean, or in her summed up, in her contained
And in her looks, which from that time infused
Sweetness into my heart unfelt before,
And into all things from her air inspired
The spirit of love and amorous delight.
She disappeared, and left me dark ; I waked
To find her, or for ever to deplore
Her loss, and other pleasures all abjure :
When, out of hope, behold her not far off,
Such as I saw her in my dream, adorned
With what all Earth or Heaven could bestow
To make her amiable.   On she came,
Led by her Heavenly Maker, though unseen
And guided by His voice, nor uninformed
Of nuptial sanctity and marriage rites.
Grace was in all her steps, heaven in her eye,
In every gesture dignity and love.
I, overjoyed, could not forbear aloud :—
  " 'This turn hath made amends ; Thou hast fulfilled
Thy words, Creator bounteous and benign,
Giver of all things fair—but fairest this
Of all Thy gifts !—nor enviest.   I now see
Bone of my bone, flesh of my flesh, my Self
Before me.   Woman is her name, of Man
Extracted ; for this cause he shall forego
Father and mother, and to his wife adhere,
And they shall be one flesh, one heart, one soul.'
  " She heard me thus ; and, though divinely brought,
Yet innocence and virgin modesty,
Her virtue, and the conscience of her worth,
That would be wooed, and not unsought be won,
Not obvious, not obtrusive, but retired,
The more desirable—or, to say all,
Nature herself, though pure of sinful thought—
Wrought in her so, that, seeing me, she turned.
I followed her ; she what was honour knew,
And with obsequious majesty approved
My pleaded reason.   To the nuptial bower
I led her blushing like the Morn ; all Heaven,
And happy constellations, on that hour
Shed their selectest influence ; the Earth
Gave sign of gratulation, and each hill ;
Joyous the birds ; fresh gales and gentle airs
Whispered it to the woods, and from their wings
Flung rose, flung odours from the spicy shrub,

Disporting, till the amorous bird of night
Sung spousal, and bid haste the Evening-star
On his hill-top to light the bridal lamp.
   "Thus have I told thee all my state, and brought
My story to the sum of earthly bliss
Which I enjoy, and must confess to find
In all things else delight indeed, but such
As, used or not, works in the mind no change,
Nor vehement desire—these delicacies
I mean of taste, sight, smell, herbs, fruits, and flowers,
Walks, and the melody of birds : but here,
Far otherwise, transported I behold,
Transported touch; here passion first I felt,
Commotion strange, in all enjoyments else
Superior and unmoved, here only weak
Against the charm of beauty's powerful glance.
Or Nature failed in me, and left some part
Not proof enough such object to sustain,
Or, from my side subducting, took perhaps
More than enough—at least on her bestowed
Too much of ornament, in outward show
Elaborate, of inward less exact.
For well I understand in the prime end
Of Nature her the inferior, in the mind
And inward faculties, which most excel ;
In outward also her resembling less
His image who made both, and less expressing
The character of that dominion given
O'er other creatures.　Yet when I approach
Her loveliness, so absolute she seems
And in herself complete, so well to know
Her own, that what she wills to do or say
Seems wisest, virtuousest, discreetest, best.
All higher Knowledge in her presence falls
Degraded ; Wisdom in discourse with her
Loses, discountenanced, and like Folly shows;
Authority and Reason on her wait,
As one intended first, not after made
Occasionally; and, to consummate all,
Greatness of mind and nobleness their seat
Build in her loveliest, and create an awe
About her, as a guard angelic placed."
   To whom the Angel, with contracted brow:—
"Accuse not Nature ! she hath done her part;
Do thou but thine ! and be not diffident
Of Wisdom; she deserts thee not, if thou
Dismiss not her, when most thou need'st her nigh,
By attributing overmuch to things
Less excellent, as thou thyself perceiv'st.
For, what admir'st thou, what transports thee so?
An outside—fair, no doubt, and worthy well
Thy cherishing, thy honouring, and thy love;
Not thy subjection.　Weigh with her thyself ;
Then value.　Oft-times nothing profits more

Than self-esteem, grounded on just and right
Well managed.   Of that skill the more thou know'st,
The more she will acknowledge thee her head,
And to realities yield all her shows—
Made so adorn for thy delight the more,
So awful, that with honour thou may'st love
Thy mate, who sees when thou art seen least wise.
But, if the sense of touch, whereby mankind
Is propagated, seem such dear delight
Beyond all other, think the same vouchsafed
To cattle and each beast; which would not be
To them made common and divulged, if aught
Therein enjoyed were worthy to subdue
The Soul of Man, or passion in him move.
What higher in her society thou find'st
Attractive, human, rational, love still:
In loving thou dost well; in passion not,
Wherein true Love consists not.   Love refines
The thoughts, and heart enlarges—hath his seat
In Reason, and is judicious, is the scale
By which to Heavenly Love thou may'st ascend,
Not sunk in carnal pleasure; for which cause
Among the beasts no mate for thee was found."
   To whom thus, half abashed, Adam replied:—
"Neither her outside formed so fair, nor aught
In procreation, common to all kinds
(Though higher of the genial bed by far,
And with mysterious reverence, I deem),
So much delights me as those graceful acts,
Those thousand decencies, that daily flow
From all her words and actions, mixed with love
And sweet compliance, which declare unfeigned
Union of mind, or in us both one soul—
Harmony to behold in wedded pair
More grateful than harmonious sound to the ear.
Yet these subject not; I to thee disclose
What inward thence I feel, not therefore foiled,
Who meet with various objects, from the sense
Variously representing, yet, still free,
Approve the best, and follow what I approve.
To love thou blam'st me not—for Love, thou say'st,
Leads up to Heaven, is both the way and guide;
Bear with me, then, if lawful what I ask.
Love not the Heavenly Spirits, and how their love
Express they—by looks only, or do they mix
Irradiance, virtual or immediate touch?"
   To whom the Angel, with a smile that glowed
Celestial rosy-red, Love's proper hue,
Answered:—"Let it suffice thee that thou know'st
Us happy, and without Love no happiness.
Whatever pure thou in the body enjoy'st
(And pure thou wert created) we enjoy
In eminence, and obstacle find none
Of membrane, joint, or limb, exclusive bars.

Easier than air with air, if Spirits embrace,
Total they mix, union of pure with pure
Desiring, nor restrained conveyance need
As flesh to mix with flesh, or soul with soul.
But I can now no more; the parting Sun
Beyond the Earth's green Cape and verdant Isles
Hesperean sets, my signal to depart.
Be strong, live happy, and love! but first of all
Him whom to love is to obey, and keep
His great command; take heed lest passion sway
Thy judgment to do aught which else free-will
Would not admit; thine and of all thy sons
The weal or woe in thee is placed; beware!
I in thy persevering shall rejoice,
And all the Blest. Stand fast; to stand or fall
Free in thine own arbitrement it lies.
Perfect within, no outward aid require;
And all temptation to transgress repel."
  So saying, he arose; whom Adam thus
Followed with benediction:—"Since to part,
Go, Heavenly Guest, Ethereal Messenger,
Sent from whose sovran goodness I adore!
Gentle to me and affable hath been
Thy condescension, and shall be honoured ever
With grateful memory. Thou to Mankind
Be good and friendly still, and oft return!"
  So parted they, the Angel up to Heaven
From the thick shade, and Adam to his bower.

THE END OF THE EIGHTH BOOK.

PARADISE LOST.

BOOK IX.

THE ARGUMENT.

Satan, having compassed the Earth, with meditated guile returns as a mist by night into Paradise; enters into the Serpent sleeping. Adam and Eve in the morning go forth to their labours, which Eve proposes to divide in several places, each labouring apart: Adam consents not, alleging the danger lest that enemy of whom they were forewarned should attempt her found alone. Eve, loth to be thought not circumspect or firm enough, urges her going apart, the rather desirous to make trial of her strength; Adam at last yields. The Serpent finds her alone: his subtle approach, first gazing, then speaking, with much flattery extolling Eve above all other creatures. Eve, wondering to hear the Serpent speak, asks how he attained to human speech and such understanding not till now; the Serpent answers that by tasting of a certain tree in the Garden he attained both to speech and reason, till then void of both. Eve requires him to bring her to that tree, and finds it to be the Tree of Knowledge forbidden: the Serpent, now grown bolder, with many wiles and arguments induces her at length to eat. She, pleased with the taste, deliberates a while whether to impart thereof to Adam or not, at last brings him of the fruit; relates what persuaded her to eat thereof. Adam, at first amazed, but perceiving her lost, resolves, through vehemence of love, to perish with her, and, extenuating the trespass, eats also of the fruit. The effects thereof in them both; they seek to cover their nakedness; then fall to variance and accusation of one another.

No more of talk where God or Angel Guest
With Man, as with his friend, familiar used
To sit indulgent, and with him partake
Rural repast, permitting him the while
Venial discourse unblamed.   I now must change
Those notes to tragic—foul distrust, and breach
Disloyal, on the part of man, revolt
And disobedience; on the part of Heaven,
Now alienated, distance and distaste,
Anger and just rebuke, and judgment given,
That brought into this World a world of woe,
Sin and her shadow Death, and Misery,
Death's harbinger.   Sad task! yet argument
Not less but more heroic than the wrath
Of stern Achilles on his foe pursued
Thrice fugitive about Troy wall; or rage
Of Turnus for Lavinia disespoused;
Or Neptune's ire, or Juno's, that so long

Perplexed the Greek, and Cytherea's son:
If answerable style I can obtain
Of my celestial Patroness, who deigns
Her nightly visitation unimplored,
And dictates to me slumbering, or inspires
Easy my unpremeditated verse,
Since first this subject for heroic song
Pleased me, long choosing and beginning late,
Not sedulous by nature to indite
Wars, hitherto the only argument
Heroic deemed, chief mastery to dissect
With long and tedious havoc fabled knights
In battles feigned (the better fortitude
Of patience and heroic martyrdom
Unsung), or to describe races and games,
Or tilting furniture, emblazoned shields,
Impresses quaint, caparisons and steeds,
Bases and tinsel trappings, gorgeous knights
At joust and tournament; then marshalled feast
Served up in hall with sewers and seneshals:
The skill of artifice or office mean;
Not that which justly gives heroic name
To person or to poem! Me, of these
Nor skilled nor studious, higher argument
Remains, sufficient of itself to raise
That name, unless an age too late, or cold
Climate, or years, damp my intended wing
Depressed; and much they may if all be mine,
Not hers who brings it nightly to my ear.
  The Sun was sunk, and after him the Star
Of Hesperus, whose office is to bring
Twilight upon the Earth, short arbiter
'Twixt day and night, and now from end to end
Night's hemisphere had veiled the horizon round,
When Satan, who late fled before the threats
Of Gabriel out of Eden, now improved
In meditated fraud and malice, bent
On Man's destruction, maugre what might hap
Of heavier on himself, fearless returned.
By night he fled, and at midnight returned
From compassing the Earth—cautious of day
Since Uriel, Regent of the Sun, descried
His entrance, and forewarned the Cherubim
That kept their watch. Thence, full of anguish, driven,
The space of seven continued nights he rode
With darkness—thrice the equinoctial line
He circled, four times crossed the car of Night
From pole to pole, traversing each colure—
On the eighth returned, and on the coast averse
From entrance or cherubic watch by stealth
Found unsuspected way. There was a place
(Now not, though Sin, not Time, first wrought the change)
Where Tigris, at the foot of Paradise,
Into a gulf shot under ground, till part

BOOK IX

Rose up a fountain by the Tree of Life.
In with the river sunk, and with it rose,
Satan, involved in rising mist; then sought
Where to lie hid. Sea he had searched and land
From Eden over Pontus, and the Pool
Mæotis, up beyond the river Ob;
Downward as far antarctic; and, in length,
West from Orontes to the ocean barred
At Darien, thence to the land where flows
Ganges and Indus. Thus the orb he roamed
With narrow search, and with inspection deep
Considered every creature, which of all
Most opportune might serve his wiles, and found
The Serpent subtlest beast of all the field.
Him, after long debate, irresolute
Of thoughts revolved, his final sentence chose
Fit vessel, fittest imp of fraud, in whom
To enter, and his dark suggestions hide
From sharpest sight; for in the wily snake
Whatever sleights none would suspicious mark,
As from his wit and native subtlety
Proceeding, which, in other beasts observed,
Doubt might beget of diabolic power
Active within beyond the sense of brute.
Thus he resolved, but first from inward grief
His bursting passion into plaints thus poured :—
   "O Earth, how like to Heaven, if not preferred
More justly, seat worthier of Gods, as built
With second thoughts, reforming what was old!
For what God, after better, worse would build ?
Terrestrial Heaven, danced round by other Heavens,
That shine, yet bear their bright officious lamps,
Light above light, for thee alone, as seems,
In thee concentring all their precious beams
Of sacred influence! As God in Heaven
Is centre, yet extends to all, so thou
Centring receiv'st from all those orbs; in thee,
Not in themselves, all their known virtue appears,
Productive in herb, plant, and nobler birth
Of creatures animate with gradual life
Of growth, sense, reason, all summed up in Man.
With what delight could I have walked thee round,
If I could joy in aught—sweet interchange
Of hill and valley, rivers, woods, and plains,
Now land, now sea, and shores with forest crowned,
Rocks, dens, and caves! But I in none of these
Find place or refuge; and the more I see
Pleasures about me, so much more I feel
Torment within me, as from the hateful siege
Of contraries; all good to me becomes
Bane, and in Heaven much worse would be my state.
But neither here seek I, no, nor in Heaven,
To dwell, unless by mastering Heaven's Supreme;
Nor hope to be myself less miserable

By what I seek, but others to make such
As I, though thereby worse to me redound.
For only in destroying I find ease
To my relentless thoughts ; and him destroyed,
Or won to what may work his utter loss,
For whom all this was made, all this will soon
Follow, as to him linked in weal or woe :
In woe, then, that destruction wide may range !
To me shall be the glory sole among
The Infernal Powers, in one day to have marred
What He, Almighty styled, six nights and days
Continued making, and who knows how long
Before had been contriving ? though perhaps
Not longer than since I in one night freed
From servitude inglorious well nigh half
The Angelic Name, and thinner left the throng
Of His adorers. He, to be avenged,
And to repair His numbers thus impaired—
Whether such virtue, spent of old, now failed
More Angels to create (if they at least
Are His created), or to spite us more—
Determined to advance into our room
A creature formed of earth, and him endow,
Exalted from so base original,
With heavenly spoils, our spoils. What He decreed
He effected ; Man He made, and for him built
Magnificent this World, and Earth his seat,
Him Lord pronounced, and, O indignity !
Subjected to his service Angel-wings
And flaming ministers, to watch and tend
Their earthly charge. Of these the vigilance
I dread, and to elude, thus wrapt in mist
Of midnight vapour, glide obscure, and pry
In every bush and brake, where hap may find
The Serpent sleeping, in whose mazy folds
To hide me, and the dark intent I bring.
O foul descent ! that I, who erst contended
With Gods to sit the highest, am now constrained
Into a beast, and, mixed with bestial slime,
This essence to incarnate and imbrute,
That to the highth of deity aspired !
But what will not ambition and revenge
Descend to ? Who aspires must down as low
As high he soared, obnoxious, first or last,
To basest things. Revenge, at first though sweet,
Bitter ere long back on itself recoils.
Let it ; I reck not, so it light well aimed,
Since higher I fall short, on him who next
Provokes my envy, this new favourite
Of Heaven, this Man of Clay, son of despite,
Whom, us the more to spite, his Maker raised
From dust : spite then with spite is best repaid."
  So saying, through each thicket, dank or dry,
Like a black mist low-creeping, he held on

142

His midnight search, where soonest he might find
The Serpent. Him fast sleeping soon he found,
In labyrinth of many a round self-rolled,
His head the midst, well stored with subtle wiles :
Not yet in horrid shade or dismal den,
Nor nocent yet, but on the grassy herb,
Fearless, unfeared, he slept. In at his mouth
The Devil entered, and his brutal sense,
In heart or head, possessing soon inspired
With act intelligential; but his sleep
Disturbed not, waiting close the approach of morn.
  Now, whenas sacred light began to dawn
In Eden on the humid flowers, that breathed
Their morning incense, when all things that breathe
From the Earth's great altar send up silent praise
To the Creator, and His nostrils fill
With grateful smell, forth came the human pair,
And joined their vocal worship to the quire
Of creatures wanting voice; that done, partake
The season, prime for sweetest scents and airs;
Then commune how that day they best may ply
Their growing work—for much their work outgrew
The hands' dispatch of two gardening so wide :
And Eve first to her husband thus began :—
  "Adam, well may we labour still to dress
This Garden, still to tend plant, herb, and flower,
Our pleasant task enjoined; but, till more hands
Aid us, the work under our labour grows,
Luxurious by restraint: what we by day
Lop overgrown, or prune, or prop, or bind,
One night or two with wanton growth derides,
Tending to wild. Thou, therefore, now advise,
Or hear what to my mind first thoughts present.
Let us divide our labours—thou where choice
Leads thee, or where most needs, whether to wind
The woodbine round this arbour, or direct
The clasping ivy where to climb; while I
In yonder spring of roses intermixed
With myrtle find what to redress till noon.
For, while so near each other thus all day
Our task we choose, what wonder if so near
Looks intervene and smiles, or objects new
Casual discourse draw on, which intermits
Our day's work, brought to little, though begun
Early, and the hour of supper comes unearned!"
  To whom mild answer Adam thus returned :—
"Sole Eve, associate sole, to me beyond
Compare above all living creatures dear!
Well hast thou motioned, well thy thoughts employed
How we might best fulfil the work which here
God hath assigned us, nor of me shalt pass
Unpraised; for nothing lovelier can be found
In woman than to study household good,
And good works in her husband to promote.

143

Yet not so strictly hath our Lord imposed
Labour as to debar us when we need
Refreshment, whether food, or talk between,
Food of the mind, or this sweet intercourse
Of looks and smiles; for smiles from reason flow
To brute denied, and are of love the food—
Love, not the lowest end of human life.
For not to irksome toil, but to delight,
He made us, and delight to reason joined.
These paths and bowers doubt not but our joint hands
Will keep from wilderness with ease, as wide
As we need walk, till younger hands ere long
Assist us. But, if much converse perhaps
Thee satiate, to short absence I could yield;
For solitude sometimes is best society,
And short retirement urges sweet return.
But other doubt possesses me, lest harm
Befall thee, severed from me; for thou know'st
What hath been warned us—what malicious foe,
Envying our happiness, and of his own
Despairing, seeks to work us woe and shame
By sly assault, and somewhere nigh at hand
Watches, no doubt, with greedy hope to find
His wish and best advantage, us asunder,
Hopeless to circumvent us joined, where each
To other speedy aid might lend at need.
Whether his first design be to withdraw
Our fealty from God, or to disturb
Conjugal love—than which perhaps no bliss
Enjoyed by us excites his envy more—
Or this, or worse, leave not the faithful side
That gave thee being, still shades thee and protects.
The wife, where danger or dishonour lurks,
Safest and seemliest by her husband stays,
Who guards her, or with her the worst endures."
    To whom the virgin majesty of Eve,
As one who loves, and some unkindness meets,
With sweet austere composure thus replied:—
  "Offspring of Heaven and Earth, and all Earth's lord!
That such an enemy we have, who seeks
Our ruin, both by thee informed I learn,
And from the parting Angel overheard,
As in a shady nook I stood behind,
Just then returned at shut of evening flowers.
But that thou shouldst my firmness therefore doubt
To God or thee, because we have a foe
May tempt it, I expected not to hear.
His violence thou fear'st not, being such
As we, not capable of death or pain,
Can either not receive, or can repel.
His fraud is, then, thy fear; which plain infers
Thy equal fear that my firm faith and love
Can by his fraud be shaken or seduced:
Thoughts, which how found they harbour in thy breast,

Adam ! misthought of her to thee so dear ?"
　　To whom, with healing words, Adam replied :—
"Daughter of God and Man, immortal Eve !—
For such thou art, from sin and blame entire—
Not diffident of thee do I dissuade
Thy absence from my sight, but to avoid
The attempt itself, intended by our foe.
For he who tempts, though in vain, at least asperses
The tempted with dishonour foul, supposed
Not incorruptible of faith, not proof
Against temptation.　Thou thyself with scorn
And anger wouldst resent the offered wrong,
Though ineffectual found ; misdeem not, then,
If such affront I labour to avert
From thee alone, which on us both at once
The enemy, though bold, will hardly dare ;
Or, daring, first on me the assault shall light.
Nor thou his malice and false guile contemn—
Subtle he needs must be who could seduce
Angels—nor think superfluous others' aid.
I from the influence of thy looks receive
Access in every virtue—in thy sight
More wise, more watchful, stronger, if need were
Of outward strength ; while shame, thou looking on,
Shame to be overcome or overreached,
Would utmost vigour raise, and raised unite.
Why shouldst not thou like sense within thee feel
When I am present, and thy trial choose
With me, best witness of thy virtue tried ?"
　　So spake domestic Adam in his care
And matrimonial love ; but Eve, who thought
Less attributed to her faith sincere,
Thus her reply with accent sweet renewed :—
"If this be our condition, thus to dwell
In narrow circuit straitened by a foe,
Subtle or violent, we not endued
Single with like defence wherever met,
How are we happy, still in fear of harm ?
But harm precedes not sin : only our foe
Tempting affronts us with his foul esteem
Of our integrity ; his foul esteem
Sticks no dishonour on our front, but turns
Foul on himself ; then wherefore shunned or feared
By us, who rather double honour gain
From his surmise proved false, find peace within,
Favour from Heaven, our witness, from the event ?
And what is faith, love, virtue, unassayed
Alone, without exterior help sustained ?
Let us not then suspect our happy state
Left so imperfect by the Maker wise
As not secure to single or combined.
Frail is our happiness, if this be so ;
And Eden were no Eden, thus exposed."
　　To whom thus Adam fervently replied :—

M.—L　　　　　　　　　　　　　　　　145

"O Woman, best are all things as the will
Of God ordained them; his creating hand
Nothing imperfect or deficient left
Of all that he created—much less Man,
Or aught that might his happy state secure,
Secure from outward force. Within himself
The danger lies, yet lies within his power;
Against his will he can receive no harm.
But God left free the Will; for what obeys
Reason is free; and Reason he made right,
But bid her well beware, and still erect,
Lest, by some fair appearing good surprised,
She dictate false, and misinform the Will
To do what God expressly hath forbid.
Not then mistrust, but tender love, enjoins
That I should mind thee oft; and mind thou me.
Firm we subsist, yet possible to swerve,
Since Reason not impossibly may meet
Some specious object by the foe suborned,
And fall into deception unaware,
Not keeping strictest watch, as she was warned.
Seek not temptation, then, which to avoid
Were better, and most likely if from me
Thou sever not : trial will come unsought.
Wouldst thou approve thy constancy, approve
First thy obedience; the other who can know,
Not seeing thee attempted, who attest?
But, if thou think trial unsought may find
Us both securer than thus warned thou seem'st,
Go; for thy stay, not free, absents thee more.
Go in thy native innocence; rely
On what thou hast of virtue; summon all :
For God towards thee hath done his part : do thine."
    So spake the Patriarch of Mankind; but Eve
Persisted; yet submiss, though last, replied :—
    "With thy permission, then, and thus forewarned,
Chiefly by what thy own last reasoning words
Touched only, that our trial, when least sought,
May find us both perhaps far less prepared,
The willinger I go, nor much expect
A foe so proud will first the weaker seek :
So bent, the more shall shame him his repulse."
    Thus saying, from her husband's hand her hand
Soft she withdrew, and, like a wood-nymph light,
Oread or Dryad, or of Delia's train,
Betook her to the groves, but Delia's self
In gait surpassed and goddess-like deport,
Though not as she with bow and quiver armed,
But with such gardening tools as Art, yet rude,
Guiltless of fire had formed, or Angels brought.
To Pales, or Pomona, thus adorned,
Likest she seemed—Pomona when she fled
Vertumnus—or to Ceres in her prime,
Yet virgin of Proserpina from Jove.

Her long with ardent look his eye pursued
Delighted, but desiring more her stay.
Oft he to her his charge of quick return
Repeated ; she to him as oft engaged
To be returned by noon amid the bower,
And all things in best order to invite
Noontide repast, or afternoon's repose.
O much deceived, much failing, hapless Eve,
Of thy presumed return ! event perverse !
Thou never from that hour in Paradise
Found'st either sweet repast or sound repose ;
Such ambush, hid among sweet flowers and shades,
Waited, with hellish rancour imminent,
To intercept thy way, or send thee back
Despoiled of innocence, of faith, of bliss.
For now, and since first break of dawn, the Fiend,
Mere serpent in appearance, forth was come,
And on his quest where likeliest he might find
The only two of mankind, but in them
The whole included race, his purposed prey.
In bower and field he sought, where any tuft
Of grove or garden-plot more pleasant lay,
Their tendance or plantation for delight ;
By fountain or by shady rivulet
He sought them both, but wished his hap might find
Eve separate ; he wished, but not with hope
Of what so seldom chanced, when to his wish,
Beyond his hope, Eve separate he spies,
Veiled in a cloud of fragrance, where she stood,
Half-spied, so thick the roses bushing round
About her glowed, oft stooping to support
Each flower of tender stalk, whose head, though gay
Carnation, purple, azure, or specked with gold,
Hung drooping unsustained.   Them she upstays
Gently with myrtle band, mindless the while
Herself, though fairest unsupported flower,
From her best prop so far, and storm so nigh.
Nearer he drew, and many a walk traversed
Of stateliest covert, cedar, pine, or palm ;
Then voluble and bold, now hid, now seen
Among thick-woven arborets, and flowers
Imbordered on each bank, the hand of Eve :
Spot more delicious than those gardens feigned
Or of revived Adonis, or renowned
Alcinous, host of old Laertes' son,
Or that, not mystic, where the sapient king
Held dalliance with his fair Egyptian spouse.
Much he the place admired, the person more.
As one who, long in populous city pent,
Where houses thick and sewers annoy the air,
Forth issuing on a summer's morn, to breathe
Among the pleasant villages and farms
Adjoined, from each thing met conceives delight—
The smell of grain, or tedded grass, or kine,

Or dairy, each rural sight, each rural sound—
If chance with nymph-like step fair virgin pass,
What pleasing seemed for her now pleases more,
She most, and in her look sums all delight:
Such pleasure took the Serpent to behold
This flowery plat, the sweet recess of Eve
Thus early, thus alone.   Her heavenly form
Angelic, but more soft and feminine,
Her graceful innocence, her every air
Of gesture or least action, overawed
His malice, and with rapine sweet bereaved
His fierceness of the fierce intent it brought.
That space the Evil One abstracted stood
From his own evil, and for the time remained
Stupidly good, of enmity disarmed,
Of guile, of hate, of envy, of revenge.
But the hot hell that always in him burns,
Though in mid Heaven, soon ended his delight,
And tortures him now more, the more he sees
Of pleasure not for him ordained.   Then soon
Fierce hate he recollects, and all his thoughts
Of mischief, gratulating, thus excites :—
   "Thoughts, whither have ye led me? with what sweet
Compulsion thus transported to forget
What hither brought us? hate, not love, nor hope
Of Paradise for Hell, hope here to taste
Of pleasure, but all pleasure to destroy,
Save what is in destroying ; other joy
To me is lost.   Then let me not let pass
Occasion which now smiles.   Behold alone
The Woman, opportune to all attempts—
Her husband, for I view far round, not nigh,
Whose higher intellectual more I shun,
And strength, of courage haughty, and of limb
Heroic built, though of terrestrial mould ;
Foe not informidable, exempt from wound—
I not ; so much hath Hell debased, and pain
Enfeebled me, to what I was in Heaven.
She fair, divinely fair, fit love for Gods,
Not terrible, though terror be in love,
And beauty, not approached by stronger hate,
Hate stronger under show of love well feigned—
The way which to her ruin now I tend."
   So spake the Enemy of Mankind, enclosed
In serpent, inmate bad, and toward Eve
Addressed his way—not with indented wave,
Prone on the ground, as since, but on his rear,
Circular base of rising folds, that towered
Fold above fold, a surging maze ; his head
Crested aloft, and carbuncle his eyes ;
With burnished neck of verdant gold, erect
Amidst his circling spires, that on the grass
Floated redundant.   Pleasing was his shape
And lovely ; never since of serpent kind

Lovelier—not those that in Illyria changed
Hermione and Cadmus, or the god
In Epidaurus ; nor to which transformed
Ammonian Jove, or Capitoline, was seen,
He with Olympias, this with her who bore
Scipio, the highth of Rome.   With tract oblique
At first, as one who sought access but feared
To interrupt, sidelong he works his way.
As when a ship, by skilful steersman wrought
Nigh river's mouth or foreland, where the wind
Veers oft, as oft so steers, and shifts her sail,
So varied he, and of his tortuous train
Curled many a wanton wreath in sight of Eve,
To lure her eye.   She, busied, heard the sound
Of rustling leaves, but minded not, as used
To such disport before her through the field
From every beast, more duteous at her call
Than at Circean call the herd disguised.
He, bolder now, uncalled before her stood,
But as in gaze admiring.   Oft he bowed
His turret crest and sleek enamelled neck,
Fawning, and licked the ground whereon she trod.
His gentle dumb expression turned at length
The eye of Eve to mark his play ; he, glad
Of her attention gained, with serpent-tongue
Organic, or impulse of vocal air,
His fraudulent temptation thus began :—
  " Wonder not, sovran mistress (if perhaps
Thou canst who art sole wonder), much less arm
Thy looks, the heaven of mildness, with disdain,
Displeased that I approach thee thus, and gaze
Insatiate, I thus single, nor have feared
Thy awful brow, more awful thus retired.
Fairest resemblance of thy Maker fair,
Thee all things living gaze on, all things thine
By gift, and thy celestial beauty adore,
With ravishment beheld—there best beheld
Where universally admired.   But here,
In this enclosure wild, these beasts among,
Beholders rude, and shallow to discern
Half what in thee is fair, one man except,
Who sees thee (and what is one ?) who shouldst be seen
A Goddess among Gods, adored and served
By Angels numberless, thy daily train ? "
  So glozed the Tempter, and his proem tuned.
Into the heart of Eve his words made way,
Though at the voice much marvelling ; at length,
Not unamazed, she thus in answer spake :—
  " What may this mean ?   Language of Man pronounced
By tongue of brute, and human sense expressed !
The first at least of these I thought denied
To beasts, whom God on their creation-day
Created mute to all articulate sound ;
The latter I demur, for in their looks

Much reason, and in their actions, oft appears.
Thee, Serpent, subtlest beast of all the field
I knew, but not with human voice endued ;
Redouble, then, this miracle, and say,
How cam'st thou speakable of mute, and how
To me so friendly grown above the rest
Of brutal kind that daily are in sight :
Say, for such wonder claims attention due."
　　To whom the guileful Tempter thus replied :—
"Empress of this fair World, resplendent Eve !
Easy to me it is to tell thee all
What thou command'st, and right thou shouldst be obeyed.
I was at first as other beasts that graze
The trodden herb, of abject thoughts and low,
As was my food, nor aught but food discerned
Or sex, and apprehended nothing high :
Till on a day, roving the field, I chanced
A goodly tree far distant to behold,
Loaden with fruit of fairest colours mixed,
Ruddy and gold.　I nearer drew to gaze ;
When from the boughs a savoury odour blown,
Grateful to appetite, more pleased my sense
Than smell of sweetest fennel or the teats
Of ewe or goat dropping with milk at even,
Unsucked of lamb or kid, that tend their play.
To satisfy the sharp desire I had
Of tasting those fair apples, I resolved
Not to defer ; hunger and thirst at once,
Powerful persuaders, quickened at the scent
Of that alluring fruit, urged me so keen.
About the mossy trunk I wound me soon ;
For high from ground, the branches would require
Thy utmost reach, or Adam's : round the tree
All other beasts that saw, with like desire
Longing and envying stood, but could not reach.
Amid the tree now got, where plenty hung
Tempting so nigh, to pluck and eat my fill
I spared not ; for such pleasure till that hour
At feed or fountain never had I found.
Sated at length, ere long I might perceive
Strange alteration in me, to degree
Of Reason in my inward powers, and Speech
Wanted not long, though to this shape retained.
Thenceforth to speculations high or deep
I turned my thoughts, and with capacious mind
Considered all things visible in Heaven,
Or Earth, or Middle, all things fair and good.
But all that fair and good in thy divine
Semblance, and in thy beauty's heavenly ray,
United I beheld—no fair to thine
Equivalent or second ; which compelled
Me thus, though importune perhaps, to come
And gaze, and worship thee of right declared
Sovran of creatures, universal Dame ! "

150

So talked the spirited sly Snake; and Eve,
Yet more amazed, unwary thus replied:—
"Serpent, thy overpraising leaves in doubt
The virtue of that fruit, in thee first proved.
But say, where grows the tree? from hence how far?
For many are the trees of God that grow
In Paradise, and various, yet unknown
To us; in such abundance lies our choice
As leaves a greater store of fruit untouched,
Still hanging incorruptible, till men
Grow up to their provision, and more hands
Help to disburden Nature of her bearth."
    To whom the wily Adder, blithe and glad:—
"Empress, the way is ready, and not long—
Beyond a row of myrtles, on a flat,
Fast by a fountain, one small thicket past
Of blowing myrrh and balm.   If thou accept
My conduct, I can bring thee thither soon."
    "Lead, then," said Eve.   He, leading, swiftly rolled
In tangles, and made intricate seem straight,
To mischief swift.   Hope elevates, and joy
Brightens his crest.   As when a wandering fire,
Compact of unctuous vapour, which the night
Condenses, and the cold environs round,
Kindled through agitation to a flame
(Which oft, they say, some evil spirit attends),
Hovering and blazing with delusive light,
Misleads the amazed night-wanderer from his way
To bogs and mires, and oft through pond or pool,
There swallowed up and lost, from succour far:
So glistered the dire Snake, and into fraud
Led Eve, our credulous mother, to the Tree
Of Prohibition, root of all our woe;
Which, when she saw, thus to her guide she spake:—
    "Serpent, we might have spared our coming hither,
Fruitless to me, though fruit be here to excess,
The credit of whose virtue rests with thee—
Wondrous, indeed, if cause of such effects!
But of this tree we may not taste nor touch;
God so commanded, and left that command
Sole daughter of His voice: the rest, we live
Law to ourselves; our Reason is our Law."
    To whom the Tempter guilefully replied:—
"Indeed!   Hath God then said that of the fruit
Of all these garden-trees ye shall not eat,
Yet lords declared of all in Earth or Air?"
    To whom thus Eve, yet sinless:—"Of the fruit
Of each tree in the garden we may eat;
But of the fruit of this fair tree, amidst
The Garden, God hath said, 'Ye shall not eat
Thereof, nor shall ye touch it, lest ye die.'"
    She scarce had said, though brief, when now more bold
The Tempter, but with show of zeal and love
To Man, and indignation at his wrong,

151

New part puts on, and, as to passion moved,
Fluctuates disturbed, yet comely, and in act
Raised, as of some great matter to begin.
As when of old some orator renowned
In Athens or free Rome, where eloquence
Flourished, since mute, to some great cause addressed,
Stood in himself collected, while each part,
Motion, each act, won audience ere the tongue
Sometimes in highth began, as no delay
Of preface brooking through his zeal of right:
So standing, moving, or to highth upgrown,
The Tempter, all impassioned, thus began:—
    "O sacred, wise, and wisdom-giving Plant,
Mother of science! now I feel thy power
Within me clear, not only to discern
Things in their causes, but to trace the ways
Of highest agents, deemed however wise.
Queen of this Universe! do not believe
Those rigid threats of death.   Ye shall not die.
How should ye? By the fruit? it gives you life
To knowledge. By the Threatener? look on me,
Me who have touched and tasted, yet both live,
And life more perfect have attained than Fate
Meant me, by venturing higher than my lot.
Shall that be shut to Man which to the Beast
Is open? or will God incense His ire
For such a petty trespass, and not praise
Rather your dauntless virtue, whom the pain
Of death denounced, whatever thing Death be,
Deterred not from achieving what might lead
To happier life, knowledge of Good and Evil?
Of good, how just! of evil—if what is evil
Be real, why not known, since easier shunned?
God, therefore, cannot hurt ye, and be just;
Not just, not God; not feared then, nor obeyed:
Your fear itself of death removes the fear.
Why, then, was this forbid? Why but to awe,
Why but to keep ye low and ignorant,
His worshippers? He knows that in the day
Ye eat thereof your eyes, that seem so clear,
Yet are but dim, shall perfectly be then
Opened and cleared, and ye shall be as Gods,
Knowing both good and evil, as they know.
That ye should be as Gods, since I as Man,
Internal Man, is but proportion meet—
I, of brute, human; ye, of human, Gods.
So ye shall die perhaps, by putting off
Human, to put on Gods—death to be wished,
Though threatened, which no worse than this can bring!
And what are Gods, that Man may not become
As they, participating godlike food?
The Gods are first, and that advantage use
On our belief, that all from them proceeds.
I question it; for this fair Earth I see,

152

Warmed by the Sun, producing every kind;
Them nothing. If they all things, who enclosed
Knowledge of good and evil in this tree,
That whoso eats thereof forthwith attains
Wisdom without their leave? and wherein lies
The offence, that Man should thus attain to know?
What can your knowledge hurt Him, or this tree
Impart against His will, if all be His?
Or is it envy? and can envy dwell
In Heavenly breasts? These, these and many more
Causes import your need of this fair fruit.
Goddess humane, reach, then, and freely taste!"

　　He ended; and his words, replete with guile,
Into her heart too easy entrance won.
Fixed on the fruit she gazed, which to behold
Might tempt alone; and in her ears the sound
Yet rung of his persuasive words, impregned
With reason, to her seeming, and with truth.
Meanwhile the hour of noon drew on, and waked
An eager appetite, raised by the smell
So savoury of that fruit, which with desire,
Inclinable now grown to touch or taste,
Solicited her longing eye; yet first,
Pausing a while, thus to herself she mused :—
　　"Great are thy virtues, doubtless, best of fruits,
Though kept from Man, and worthy to be admired,
Whose taste, too long forborne, at first assay
Gave elocution to the mute, and taught
The tongue not made for speech to speak thy praise.
Thy praise He also who forbids thy use
Conceals not from us, naming thee the Tree
Of Knowledge, knowledge both of good and evil;
Forbids us then to taste. But His forbidding
Commends thee more, while it infers the good
By thee communicated, and our want;
For good unknown sure is not had, or, had
And yet unknown, is as not had at all.
In plain, then, what forbids He but to know?
Forbids us good, forbids us to be wise!
Such prohibitions bind not. But, if Death
Bind us with after-bands, what profits then
Our inward freedom? In the day we eat
Of this fair fruit, our doom is we shall die!
How dies the Serpent? He hath eaten, and lives,
And knows, and speaks, and reasons, and discerns,
Irrational till then. For us alone
Was death invented? or to us denied
This intellectual food, for beasts reserved?
For beasts it seems; yet that one beast which first
Hath tasted envies not, but brings with joy
The good befallen him, author unsuspect,
Friendly to Man, far from deceit or guile.
What fear I, then? rather, what know to fear
Under this ignorance of good and evil,

Of God or Death, of law or penalty?
Here grows the cure of all, this fruit divine,
Fair to the eye, inviting to the taste,
Of virtue to make wise. What hinders, then,
To reach, and feed at once both body and mind?"
  So saying, her rash hand in evil hour
Forth-reaching to the fruit, she plucked, she eat.
Earth felt the wound, and Nature from her seat,
Sighing through all her works, gave signs of woe
That all was lost. Back to the thicket slunk
The guilty Serpent, and well might, for Eve,
Intent now only on her taste, naught else
Regarded; such delight till then, as seemed,
In fruit she never tasted, whether true,
Or fancied so through expectation high
Of knowledge; nor was Godhead from her thought.
Greedily she ingorged without restraint,
And knew not eating death. Satiate at length,
And hightened as with wine, jocund and boon,
Thus to herself she pleasingly began :—
  "O sovran, virtuous, precious of all trees
In Paradise! of operation blest
To sapience, hitherto obscured, infamed,
And thy fair fruit let hang, as to no end
Created! but henceforth my early care,
Not without song, each morning, and due praise,
Shall tend thee, and the fertile burden ease
Of thy full branches, offered free to all;
Till, dieted by thee, I grow mature
In knowledge, as the Gods who all things know.
Though others envy what they cannot give—
For, had the gift been theirs, it had not here
Thus grown! Experience, next to thee I owe,
Best guide : not following thee, I had remained
In ignorance; thou open'st Wisdom's way,
And giv'st access, though secret she retire.
And I perhaps am secret : Heaven is high—
High, and remote to see from thence distinct
Each thing on Earth; and other care perhaps
May have diverted from continual watch
Our great Forbidder, safe with all His spies
About Him. But to Adam in what sort
Shall I appear? Shall I to him make known
As yet my change, and give him to partake
Full happiness with me, or rather not,
But keep the odds of knowledge in my power
Without co-partner? so to add what wants
In female sex, the more to draw his love,
And render me more equal, and perhaps—
A thing not undesirable—sometime
Superior; for, inferior, who is free?
This may be well; but what if God have seen,
And death ensue? Then I shall be no more;
And Adam, wedded to another Eve,

Shall live with her enjoying, I extinct !
A death to think ! Confirmed, then, I resolve
Adam shall share with me in bliss or woe.
So dear I love him that with him all deaths
I could endure, without him live no life."
  So saying, from the tree her step she turned,
But first low reverence done, as to the Power
That dwelt within, whose presence had infused
Into the plant sciential sap, derived
From nectar, drink of Gods. Adam the while,
Waiting desirous her return, had wove
Of choicest flowers a garland, to adorn
Her tresses, and her rural labours crown,
As reapers oft are wont their harvest-queen.
Great joy he promised to his thoughts, and new
Solace in her return, so long delayed ;
Yet oft his heart, divine of something ill,
Misgave him. He the faltering measure felt,
And forth to meet her went, the way she took
That morn when first they parted. By the Tree
Of Knowledge he must pass ; there he her met,
Scarce from the tree returning, in her hand
A bough of fairest fruit, that downy smiled,
New gathered, and ambrosial smell diffused.
To him she hasted ; in her face excuse
Came prologue, and apology to prompt,
Which, with bland words at will, she thus addressed :—
  "Hast thou not wondered, Adam, at my stay ?
Thee I have missed, and thought it long, deprived
Thy presence—agony of love till now
Not felt, nor shall be twice ; for never more
Mean I to try, what rash untried I sought,
The pain of absence from thy sight. But strange
Hath been the cause, and wonderful to hear.
This tree is not, as we are told, a tree
Of danger tasted, nor to evil unknown
Opening the way, but of divine effect
To open eyes, and make them Gods who taste ;
And hath been tasted such. The Serpent, wise,
Or not restrained as we, or not obeying,
Hath eaten of the fruit, and is become
Not dead, as we are threatened, but thenceforth
Endued with human voice and human sense,
Reasoning to admiration, and with me
Persuasively hath so prevailed that I
Have also tasted, and have also found
The effects to correspond—opener mine eyes,
Dim erst, dilated spirits, ampler heart,
And growing up to Godhead ; which for thee
Chiefly I sought, without thee can despise.
For bliss, as thou hast part, to me is bliss ;
Tedious, unshared with thee, and odious soon.
Thou, therefore, also taste, that equal lot
May join us, equal joy, as equal love ;

Lest, thou not tasting, different degree
Disjoin us, and I then too late renounce
Deity for thee, when fate will not permit."
   Thus Eve with countenance blithe her story told ;
But in her cheek distemper flushing glowed.
On the other side, Adam, soon as he heard
The fatal trespass done by Eve, amazed,
Astonied stood and blank, while horror chill
Ran through his veins, and all his joints relaxed.
From his slack hand the garland wreathed for Eve
Down dropt, and all the faded roses shed.
Speechless he stood and pale, till thus at length
First to himself he inward silence broke :—
   " O fairest of Creation, last and best
Of all God's works, creature in whom excelled
Whatever can to sight or thought be formed,
Holy, divine, good, amiable, or sweet !
How art thou lost ! how on a sudden lost,
Defaced, deflowered, and now to death devote !
Rather, how hast thou yielded to transgress
The strict forbiddance, how to violate
The sacred fruit forbidden ? Some cursed fraud
Of enemy hath beguiled thee, yet unknown,
And me with thee hath ruined ; for with thee
Certain my resolution is to die.
How can I live without thee ? how forego
Thy sweet converse, and love so dearly joined,
To live again in these wild woods forlorn ?
Should God create another Eve, and I
Another rib afford, yet loss of thee
Would never from my heart. No, no ! I feel
The link of Nature draw me : flesh of flesh,
Bone of my bone thou art, and from thy state
Mine never shall be parted, bliss or woe."
   So having said, as one from sad dismay
Recomforted, and, after thoughts disturbed,
Submitting to what seemed remediless,
Thus in calm mood his words to Eve he turned :—
   " Bold deed thou hast presumed, adventurous Eve,
And peril great provoked, who thus hast dared
Had it been only coveting to eye
That sacred food, sacred to abstinence ;
Much more to taste it, under ban to touch.
But past who can recall, or done undo ?
Not God Omnipotent, nor Fate ! Yet so
Perhaps thou shalt not die ; perhaps the fact
Is not so heinous now—foretasted fruit,
Profaned first by the Serpent, by him first
Made common and unhallowed ere our taste,
Nor yet on him found deadly. He yet lives—
Lives, as thou saidst, and gains to live, as Man,
Higher degree of life : inducement strong
To us, as likely, tasting, to attain
Proportional ascent ; which cannot be

But to be Gods, or Angels, demi-gods.
Nor can I think that God, Creator wise,
Though threatening, will in earnest so destroy
Us, his prime creatures, dignified so high,
Set over all His works ; which, in our fall,
For us created, needs with us must fail,
Dependent made.   So God shall uncreate,
Be frustrate, do, undo, and labour lose—
Not well conceived of God ; who, though His power
Creation could repeat, yet would be loth
Us to abolish, lest the Adversary
Triumph and say : 'Fickle their state whom God
Most favours ; who can please Him long ?   Me first
He ruined, now Mankind ; whom will He next ?'—
Matter of scorn not to be given the Foe.
However, I with thee have fixed my lot,
Certain to undergo like doom.   If death
Consort with thee, death is to me as life ;
So forcible within my heart I feel
The bond of Nature draw me to my own—
My own in thee ; for what thou art is mine.
Our state cannot be severed ; we are one,
One flesh ; to lose thee were to lose myself."
    So Adam ; and thus Eve to him replied :—
" O glorious trial of exceeding love,
Illustrious evidence, example high !
Engaging me to emulate ; but, short
Of thy perfection, how shall I attain,
Adam ? from whose dear side I boast me sprung,
And gladly of our union hear thee speak,
One heart, one soul in both ; whereof good proof
This day affords, declaring thee resolved,
Rather than death, or aught than death more dread,
Shall separate us, linked in love so dear,
To undergo with me one guilt, one crime,
If any be, of tasting this fair fruit ;
Whose virtue (for of good still good proceeds,
Direct, or by occasion) hath presented
This happy trial of thy love, which else
So eminently never had been known.
Were it I thought death menaced would ensue
This my attempt, I would sustain alone
The worst, and not persuade thee—rather die
Deserted than oblige thee with a fact
Pernicious to thy peace, chiefly assured
Remarkably so late of thy so true,
So faithful, love unequalled.   But I feel
Far otherwise the event—not death, but life
Augmented, opened eyes, new hopes, new joys,
Taste so divine that what of sweet before
Hath touched my sense flat seems to this and harsh.
On my experience, Adam, freely taste,
And fear of death deliver to the winds."
    So saying, she embraced him, and for joy

157

Tenderly wept, much won that he his love
Had so ennobled as of choice to incur
Divine displeasure for her sake, or death.
In recompense (for such compliance bad
Such recompense best merits), from the bough
She gave him of that fair enticing fruit
With liberal hand.   He scrupled not to eat,
Against his better knowledge, not deceived,
But fondly overcome with female charm.
Earth trembled from her entrails, as again
In pangs, and Nature gave a second groan ;
Sky loured, and, muttering thunder, some sad drops
Wept at completing of the mortal Sin
Original ; while Adam took no thought,
Eating his fill, nor Eve to iterate
Her former trespass feared, the more to soothe
Him with her loved society ; that now,
As with new wine intoxicated both,
They swim in mirth, and fancy that they feel
Divinity within them breeding wings
Wherewith to scorn the Earth.   But that false fruit
Far other operation first displayed,
Carnal desire inflaming.   He on Eve
Began to cast lascivious eyes ; she him
As wantonly repaid ; in lust they burn,
Till Adam thus 'gan Eve to dalliance move :—
   " Eve, now I see thou art exact of taste
And elegant—of sapience no small part ;
Since to each meaning savour we apply,
And palate call judicious.   I the praise
Yield thee ; so well this day thou hast purveyed.
Much pleasure we have lost, while we abstained
From this delightful fruit, nor known till now
True relish, tasting.   If such pleasure be
In things to us forbidden, it might be wished
For this one tree had been forbidden ten.
But come ; so well refreshed, now let us play,
As meet is, after such delicious fare ;
For never did thy beauty, since the day
I saw thee first and wedded thee, adorned
With all perfections, so inflame my sense
With ardour to enjoy thee, fairer now
Than ever—bounty of this virtuous tree ! "
   So said he, and forbore not glance or toy
Of amorous intent, well understood
Of Eve, whose eye darted contagious fire.
Her hand he seized, and to a shady bank,
Thick overhead with verdant roof embowered,
He led her, nothing loth ; flowers were the couch,
Pansies, and violets, and asphodel,
And hyacinth—Earth's freshest, softest lap.
There they their fill of love and love's disport
Took largely, of their mutual guilt the seal,
The solace of their sin, till dewy sleep

158

Oppressed them, wearied with their amorous play.
　Soon as the force of that fallacious fruit,
That with exhilarating vapour bland
About their spirits had played, and inmost powers
Made err, was now exhaled, and grosser sleep,
Bred of unkindly fumes, with conscious dreams
Encumbered, now had left them, up they rose
As from unrest, and, each the other viewing,
Soon found their eyes how opened, and their minds
How darkened.　Innocence, that as a veil
Had shadowed them from knowing ill, was gone;
Just confidence, and native righteousness,
And honour, from about them, naked left
To guilty Shame : he covered, but his robe
Uncovered more.　So rose the Danite strong,
Herculean Samson, from the harlot-lap
Of Philistean Dalilah, and waked
Shorn of his strength ; they destitute and bare
Of all their virtue.　Silent, and in face
Confounded, long they sat, as strucken mute ;
Till Adam, though not less than Eve abashed,
At length gave utterance to these words constrained :—
　"O Eve, in evil hour thou didst give ear
To that false Worm, of whomsoever taught
To counterfeit Man's voice—true in our fall,
False in our promised rising ; since our eyes
Opened we find indeed, and find we know
Both good and evil, good lost and evil got :
Bad fruit of knowledge, if this be to know,
Which leaves us naked thus, of honour void,
Of innocence, of faith, of purity,
Our wonted ornaments now soiled and stained,
And in our faces evident the signs
Of foul concupiscence ; whence evil store,
Even shame, the last of evils ; of the first
Be sure, then.　How shall I behold the face
Henceforth of God or Angel, erst with joy
And rapture so oft beheld ?　Those Heavenly Shapes
Will dazzle now this earthly with their blaze
Insufferably bright.　Oh, might I here
In solitude live savage, in some glade
Obscured, where highest woods, impenetrable
To star or sunlight, spread their umbrage broad,
And brown as evening !　Cover me, ye pines !
Ye cedars, with innumerable boughs
Hide me, where I may never see them more !
But let us now, as in bad plight, devise
What best may, for the present, serve to hide
The parts of each from other that seem most
To shame obnoxious, and unseemliest seen—
Some tree, whose broad smooth leaves, together sewed,
And girded on our loins, may cover round
Those middle parts, that this new comer, Shame,
There sit not, and reproach us as unclean."

159

So counselled he, and both together went
Into the thickest wood.   There soon they chose
The fig-tree—not that kind for fruit renowned,
But such as, at this day, to Indians known,
In Malabar or Decan spreads her arms
Branching so broad and long that in the ground
The bended twigs take root, and daughters grow
About the mother tree, a pillared shade
High overarched, and echoing walks between :
There oft the Indian herdsman, shunning heat,
Shelters in cool, and tends his pasturing herds
At loop-holes cut through thickest shade.   Those leaves
They gathered, broad as Amazonian targe,
And with what skill they had together sewed,
To gird their waist—vain covering, if to hide
Their guilt and dreaded shame !   O, how unlike
To that first naked glory !   Such of late
Columbus found the American, so girt
With feathered cincture, naked else and wild,
Among the trees on isles and woody shores.
Thus fenced, and, as they thought, their shame in part
Covered, but not at rest or ease of mind,
They sat them down to weep.   Nor only tears
Rained at their eyes, but high winds worse within
Began to rise, high passions—anger, hate,
Mistrust, suspicion, discord—and shook sore
Their inward state of mind, calm region once
And full of peace, now tost and turbulent :
For Understanding ruled not, and the Will
Heard not her lore, both in subjection now
To sensual Appetite, who, from beneath
Usurping over sovran Reason, claimed
Superior sway.   From thus distempered breast
Adam, estranged in look and altered style,
Speech intermitted thus to Eve renewed :—
" Would thou hadst hearkened to my words, and stayed
With me, as I besought thee, when that strange
Desire of wandering, this unhappy morn,
I know not whence possessed thee !   We had then
Remained still happy—not, as now, despoiled
Of all our good, shamed, naked, miserable !
Let none henceforth seek needless cause to approve
The faith they owe ; when earnestly they seek
Such proof, conclude they then begin to fail."
    To whom, soon moved with touch of blame, thus Eve :—
" What words have passed thy lips, Adam severe ?
Imput'st thou that to my default, or will
Of wandering, as thou call'st it, which who knows
But might as ill have happened thou being by,
Or to thyself perhaps ?   Hadst thou been there,
Or here the attempt, thou couldst not have discerned
Fraud in the Serpent, speaking as he spake ;
No ground of enmity between us known
Why he should mean me ill or seek to harm.

Was I to have never parted from thy side?
As good have grown there still, a lifeless rib.
Being as I am, why didst not thou, the head,
Command me absolutely not to go,
Going into such danger, as thou saidst?
Too facile then, thou didst not much gainsay,
Nay, didst permit, approve, and fair dismiss.
Hadst thou been firm and fixed in thy dissent,
Neither had I transgressed, nor thou with me."
    To whom, then first incensed, Adam replied:—
"Is this the love, is this the recompense
Of mine to thee, ingrateful Eve, expressed
Immutable when thou wert lost, not I—
Who might have lived, and joyed immortal bliss,
Yet willingly chose rather death with thee?
And am I now upbraided as the cause
Of thy transgressing? not enough severe,
It seems, in thy restraint! What could I more?
I warned thee, I admonished thee, foretold
The danger, and the lurking enemy
That lay in wait; beyond this had been force,
And force upon free will hath here no place.
But confidence then bore thee on, secure
Either to meet no danger, or to find
Matter of glorious trial; and perhaps
I also erred in overmuch admiring
What seemed in thee so perfect that I thought
No evil durst attempt thee. But I rue
That error now, which is become my crime,
And thou the accuser. Thus it shall befall
Him who, to worth in women overtrusting,
Lets her will rule; restraint she will not brook;
And, left to herself, if evil thence ensue,
She first his weak indulgence will accuse."
    Thus they in mutual accusation spent
The fruitless hours, but neither self-condemning;
And of their vain contest appeared no end.

THE END OF THE NINTH BOOK.

PARADISE LOST.

BOOK X.

THE ARGUMENT.

Man's transgression known, the guardian Angels forsake Paradise, and
return up to Heaven to approve their vigilance, and are approved; God
declaring that the entrance of Satan could not be by them prevented. He
sends His Son to judge the transgressors; who descends, and gives sentence
accordingly; then, in pity, clothes them both, and re-ascends. Sin and
Death, sitting till then at the Gates of Hell, by wondrous sympathy feeling
the success of Satan in this new World, and the sin by Man there committed, resolve to sit no longer confined in Hell, but to follow Satan, their
sire, up to the place of Man: to make the way easier from Hell to this
World to and fro, they pave a broad highway or bridge over Chaos, according to the track that Satan first made; then, preparing for Earth, they meet
him, proud of his success, returning to Hell; their mutual gratulation.
Satan arrives at Pandemonium; in full assembly relates, with boasting, his
success against Man: instead of applause is entertained with a general hiss
by all his audience, transformed, with himself also, suddenly into Serpents,
according to his doom given in Paradise; then, deluded with a show of the
Forbidden Tree springing up before them, they, greedily reaching to take of
the fruit, chew dust and bitter ashes. The proceedings of Sin and Death:
God foretells the final victory of His Son over them, and the renewing of
all things; but, for the present, commands His Angels to make several
alterations in the Heavens and Elements. Adam, more and more perceiving
his fallen condition, heavily bewails, rejects the condolement of Eve; she
persists, and at length appeases him: then, to evade the curse likely to fall
on their offspring, proposes to Adam violent ways; which he approves not,
but, conceiving better hope, puts her in mind of the late promise made
them, that her seed should be revenged on the Serpent, and exhorts her,
with him, to seek peace of the offended Deity by repentance and supplication.

MEANWHILE the heinous and despiteful act
Of Satan done in Paradise, and how
He, in the Serpent, had perverted Eve,
Her husband she, to taste the fatal fruit,
Was known in Heaven; for what can 'scape the eye
Of God all-seeing, or deceive His heart
Omniscient? who, in all things wise and just,
Hindered not Satan to attempt the mind
Of Man, with strength entire and free will armed
Complete to have discovered and repulsed
Whatever wiles of foe or seeming friend.
For still they knew, and ought to have still remembered,
The high injunction not to taste that fruit,

Whoever tempted; which they not obeying
Incurred (what could they less?) the penalty,
And, manifold in sin, deserved to fall.
Up into Heaven from Paradise in haste
The Angelic guards ascended, mute and sad
For Man; for of his state by this they knew,
Much wondering how the subtle Fiend had stolen
Entrance unseen. Soon as the unwelcome news
From Earth arrived at Heaven-gate, displeased
All were who heard; dim sadness did not spare
That time celestial visages, yet, mixed
With pity, violated not their bliss.
About the new-arrived, in multitudes,
The Ethereal people ran, to hear and know
How all befell. They towards the throne supreme,
Accountable, made haste, to make appear,
With righteous plea, their utmost vigilance,
And easily approved; when the Most High,
Eternal Father, from His secret cloud
Amidst, in thunder uttered thus His voice:—

"Assembled Angels, and ye Powers returned
From unsuccessful charge, be not dismayed
Nor troubled at these tidings from the Earth,
Which your sincerest care could not prevent,
Foretold so lately what would come to pass,
When first this Tempter crossed the gulf from Hell.
I told ye then he should prevail, and speed
On his bad errand—Man should be seduced,
And flattered out of all, believing lies
Against his Maker; no decree of mine,
Concurring to necessitate his fall,
Or touch with lightest moment of impulse
His free will, to her own inclining left
In even scale. But fallen he is; and now
What rests, but that the mortal sentence pass
On his transgression, Death denounced that day?
Which he presumes already vain and void,
Because not yet inflicted, as he feared,
By some immediate stroke, but soon shall find
Forbearance no acquittance ere day end.
Justice shall not return, as bounty, scorned.
But whom send I to judge them? whom but Thee,
Vicegerent Son? To Thee I have transferred
All judgment, whether in Heaven, or Earth, or Hell.
Easy it may be seen that I intend
Mercy colleague with justice, sending Thee,
Man's friend, his Mediator, his designed
Both ransom and Redeemer voluntary,
And destined Man himself to judge Man fallen."
So spake the Father; and, unfolding bright
Toward the right hand His glory, on the Son
Blazed forth unclouded deity. He full
Resplendent all His Father manifest
Expressed, and thus divinely answered mild:—

"Father Eternal, Thine is to decree;
Mine both in Heaven and Earth to do Thy will
Supreme, that Thou in Me, Thy Son beloved,
May'st ever rest well pleased. I go to judge
On Earth these Thy transgressors; but Thou know'st,
Whoever judged, the worst on Me must light,
When time shall be; for so I undertook
Before Thee, and, not repenting, this obtain
Of right, that I may mitigate their doom
On Me derived. Yet I shall temper so
Justice with mercy as may illustrate most
Them fully satisfied, and Thee appease.
Attendance none shall need, nor train, where none
Are to behold the judgment but the judged,
Those two; the third best absent is condemned,
Convict by flight, and rebel to all law;
Conviction to the Serpent none belongs."
    Thus saying, from His radiant seat He rose
Of high collateral glory. Him Thrones and Powers,
Princedoms, and Domination ministrant,
Accompanied to Heaven-gate, from whence
Eden, and all the coast in prospect lay.
Down He descended straight; the speed of Gods
Time counts not, though with swiftest minutes winged.
    Now was the Sun in western cadence low
From noon, and gentle airs due at their hour
To fan the Earth now waked, and usher in
The evening cool, when He, from wrath more cool,
Came, the mild Judge and Intercessor both
To sentence Man. The voice of God they heard
Now walking in the Garden, by soft winds
Brought to their ears, while day declined; they heard,
And from His presence hid themselves among
The thickest trees, both man and wife, till God,
Approaching, thus to Adam called aloud:—
    "Where art thou, Adam, wont with joy to meet
My coming, seen far off? I miss thee here,
Not pleased, thus entertained with solitude,
Where obvious duty erewhile appeared unsought.
Or come I less conspicuous, or what change
Absents thee, or what chance detains? Come forth!"
    He came, and with him Eve, more loth, though first
To offend, discountenanced both, and discomposed.
Love was not in their looks, either to God
Or to each other, but apparent guilt,
And shame, and perturbation, and despair,
Anger, and obstinacy, and hate, and guile.
Whence Adam, faltering long, thus answered brief:—
    "I heard thee in the Garden, and, of thy voice
Afraid, being naked, hid myself." To whom
The gracious Judge, without revile, replied:—
    "My voice thou oft hast heard, and hast not feared,
But still rejoiced; how is it now become
So dreadful to thee? That thou art naked who

Hath told thee? Hast thou eaten of the tree
Whereof I gave thee charge thou shouldst not eat?"
To whom thus Adam, sore beset, replied :—
    "O Heaven! in evil strait this day I stand
Before my Judge—either to undergo
Myself the total crime, or to accuse
My other self, the partner of my life,
Whose failing, while her faith to me remains,
I should conceal, and not expose to blame
By my complaint. But strict necessity
Subdues me, and calamitous constraint,
Lest on my head both sin and punishment,
However insupportable, be all
Devolved ; though, should I hold my peace, yet Thou
Wouldst easily detect what I conceal.
This Woman, whom Thou mad'st to be my help,
And gav'st me as Thy perfect gift, so good,
So fit, so acceptable, so divine,
That from her hand I could suspect no ill,
And what she did, whatever in itself,
Her doing seemed to justify the deed—
She gave me of the tree, and I did eat."
To whom the Sovran Presence thus replied :—
    "Was she thy God, that her thou didst obey
Before His voice? or was she made thy guide,
Superior, or but equal, that to her
Thou didst resign thy manhood, and the place
Wherein God set thee above her, made of thee
And for thee, whose perfection far excelled
Hers in all real dignity? Adorned
She was indeed, and lovely, to attract
Thy love, not thy subjection ; and her gifts
Were such as under government well seemed—
Unseemly to bear rule ; which was thy part
And person, hadst thou known thyself aright."
    So having said, He thus to Eve in few :—
"Say, Woman, what is this which thou hast done?"
    To whom sad Eve, with shame nigh overwhelmed,
Confessing soon, yet not before her Judge
Bold or loquacious, thus abashed replied :—
"The Serpent me beguiled, and I did eat."
    Which when the Lord God heard, without delay
To judgment he proceedèd on the accused
Serpent, though brute, unable to transfer
The guilt on him who made him instrument
Of mischief, and polluted from the end
Of his creation—justly then accursed,
As vitiated in nature. More to know
Concerned not Man (since he no further knew),
Nor altered his offence ; yet God at last
To Satan, first in sin, his doom applied,
Though in mysterious terms, judged as then best ;
And on the Serpent thus His curse let fall :—
    "Because thou hast done this, thou art accursed

Above all cattle, each beast of the field;
Upon thy belly grovelling thou shalt go,
And dust shalt eat all the days of thy life.
Between thee and the Woman I will put
Enmity, and between thine and her seed;
Her seed shall bruise thy head, thou bruise his heel."
So spake this oracle—then verified
When Jesus, Son of Mary, second Eve,
Saw Satan fall like lightning down from Heaven,
Prince of the Air; then, rising from His grave,
Spoiled Principalities and Powers, triumphed
In open show, and, with ascension bright,
Captivity led captive through the Air,
The realm itself of Satan, long usurped,
Whom He shall tread at last under our feet,
Even He who now foretold his fatal bruise,
And to the Woman thus His sentence turned:—
 "Thy sorrow I will greatly multiply
By thy conception; children thou shalt bring
In sorrow forth, and to thy husband's will
Thine shall submit; he over thee shall rule."
 On Adam last thus judgment He pronounced:—
"Because thou hast hearkened to the voice of thy wife,
And eaten of the tree concerning which
I charged thee, saying, *Thou shalt not eat thereof,*
Curs'd is the ground for thy sake; thou in sorrow
Shalt eat thereof all the days of thy life;
Thorns also and thistles it shall bring thee forth
Unbid; and thou shalt eat the herb of the field;
In the sweat of thy face thou shalt eat bread,
Till thou return unto the ground; for thou
Out of the ground wast taken: know thy birth,
For dust thou art, and shalt to dust return."
 So judged He Man, both Judge and Saviour sent,
And the instant stroke of death, denounced that day,
Removed far off; then, pitying how they stood
Before Him naked to the air, that now
Must suffer change, disdained not to begin
Thenceforth the form of servant to assume.
As when He washed His servants' feet, so now,
As father of His family, He clad
Their nakedness with skins of beasts, or slain,
Or, as the snake, with youthful coat repaid;
And thought not much to clothe His enemies.
Nor He their outward only with the skins
Of beasts, but inward nakedness, much more
Opprobrious, with His robe of righteousness
Arraying, covered from His Father's sight.
To Him with swift ascent He up returned,
Into His blissful bosom reassumed
In glory as of old; to Him, appeased,
All, though all-knowing, what had passed with Man
Recounted, mixing intercession sweet.
 Meanwhile, ere thus was sinned and judged on Earth,

Within the gates of Hell sat Sin and Death,
In counterview within the gates, that now
Stood open wide, belching outrageous flame
Far into Chaos, since the Fiend passed through,
Sin opening; who thus now to Death began:—
    " O Son, why sit we here, each other viewing
Idly, while Satan, our great author, thrives
In other worlds, and happier seat provides
For us, his offspring dear? It cannot be
But that success attends him; if mishap,
Ere this he had returned, with fury driven
By his avengers, since no place like this
Can fit his punishment, or their revenge.
Methinks I feel new strength within me rise,
Wings growing, and dominion given me large
Beyond this Deep—whatever draws me on,
Or sympathy, or some connatural force,
Powerful at greatest distance to unite
With secret amity things of like kind
By secretest conveyance. Thou, my shade
Inseparable, must with me along;
For Death from Sin no power can separate.
But, lest the difficulty of passing back
Stay his return perhaps over this gulf
Impassable, impervious, let us try
(Adventurous work, yet to thy power and mine
Not unagreeable!) to found a path
Over this main from Hell to that new World
Where Satan now prevails—a monument
Of merit high to all the infernal host,
Easing their passage hence, for intercourse
Or transmigration, as their lot shall lead.
Nor can I miss the way, so strongly drawn
By this new-felt attraction and instinct."
    Whom thus the meagre Shadow answered soon :—
" Go whither fate and inclination strong
Leads thee; I shall not lag behind, nor err
The way, thou leading: such a scent I draw
Of carnage, prey innumerable, and taste
The savour of death from all things there that live.
Nor shall I to the work thou enterprisest
Be wanting, but afford thee equal aid."
    So saying, with delight he snuffed the smell
Of mortal change on Earth. As when a flock
Of ravenous fowl, though many a league remote,
Against the day of battle, to a field
Where armies lie encamped come flying, lured
With scent of living carcases designed
For death the following day in bloody fight;
So scented the grim Feature, and upturned
His nostril wide into the murky air,
Sagacious of his quarry from so far.
Then both, from out Hell-gates, into the waste
Wide anarchy of Chaos, damp and dark,

Flew diverse, and, with power (their power was great)
Hovering upon the waters, what they met
Solid or slimy, as in raging sea
Tossed up and down, together crowded drove,
From each side shoaling, towards the mouth of Hell;
As when two polar winds, blowing adverse
Upon the Cronian sea, together drive
Mountains of ice, that stop the imagined way
Beyond Petsora eastward to the rich
Cathaian coast.   The aggregated soil
Death with his mace petrific, cold and dry,
As with a trident smote, and fixed as firm
As Delos, floating once; the rest his look
Bound with Gorgonian rigour not to move,
And with asphaltic slime; broad as the gate,
Deep to the roots of Hell the gathered beach
They fastened, and the mole immense wrought on
Over the foaming Deep high-arched, a bridge
Of length prodigious, joining to the wall
Immovable of this now fenceless World,
Forfeit to Death—from hence a passage broad,
Smooth, easy, inoffensive, down to Hell.
So, if great things to small may be compared,
Xerxes, the liberty of Greece to yoke,
From Susa, his Memnonian palace high,
Came to the sea, and, over Hellespont
Bridging his way, Europe with Asia joined,
And scourged with many a stroke the indignant waves.
Now had they brought the work by wondrous art
Pontifical—a ridge of pendent rock
Over the vexed Abyss, following the track
Of Satan, to the self-same place where he
First lighted from his wing and landed safe
From out of Chaos—to the outside bare
Of this round World.   With pins of adamant
And chains they made all fast, too fast they made
And durable; and now in little space
The confines met of empyrean Heaven
And of this World, and on the left hand Hell,
With long reach interposed; three several ways
In sight to each of these three places led.
And now their way to Earth they had descried,
To Paradise first tending, when, behold;
Satan, in likeness of an Angel bright,
Betwixt the Centaur and the Scorpion steering
His zenith, while the Sun in Aries rose!
Disguised he came; but those his children dear
Their parent soon discerned, though in disguise.
He, after Eve seduced, unminded slunk
Into the wood fast by, and, changing shape
To observe the sequel, saw his guileful act
By Eve, though all unweeting, seconded
Upon her husband—saw their shame that sought
Vain covertures; but, when he saw descend

The Son of God to judge them, terrified
He fled, not hoping to escape, but shun
The present—fearing, guilty, what His wrath
Might suddenly inflict; that past, returned
By night, and, listening where the hapless pair
Sat in their sad discourse and various plaint,
Thence gathered his own doom; which understood
Not instant, but of future time, with joy
And tidings fraught, to Hell he now returned,
And at the brink of Chaos, near the foot
Of this new wondrous pontifice, unhoped
Met who to meet him came, his offspring dear.
Great joy was at their meeting, and at sight
Of that stupendous bridge his joy increased.
Long he admiring stood, till Sin, his fair
Enchanting daughter, thus the silence broke :—
    "O Parent, these are thy magnific deeds,
Thy trophies! which thou view'st as not thine own;
Thou art their author and prime architect.
For I no sooner in my heart divined
(My heart, which by a secret harmony
Still moves with thine, joined in connexion sweet)
That thou on Earth hadst prospered, which thy looks
Now also evidence, but straight I felt—
Though distant from thee worlds between, yet felt—
That I must after thee with this thy son;
Such fatal consequence unites us three.
Hell could no longer hold us in her bounds,
Nor this unvoyageable gulf obscure
Detain from following thy illustrious track.
Thou hast achieved our liberty, confined
Within Hell-gates till now; thou us empowered
To fortify thus far, and overlay
With this portentous bridge the dark Abyss.
Thine now is all this World; thy virtue hath won
What thy hands builded not; thy wisdom gained,
With odds, what war hath lost, and fully avenged
Our foil in Heaven. Here thou shalt monarch reign,
There didst not; there let Him still victor sway,
As battle hath adjudged, from this new World
Retiring, by his own doom alienated,
And henceforth monarchy with thee divide
Of all things, parted by the empyreal bounds,
His quadrature, from thy orbicular World,
Or try thee now more dangerous to His throne."
    Whom thus the Prince of Darkness answered glad :—
"Fair daughter, and thou, son and grandchild both,
High proof ye now have given to be the race
Of Satan (for I glory in the name,
Antagonist of Heaven's Almighty King),
Amply have merited of me, of all
The Infernal Empire, that so near Heaven's door
Triumphal with triumphal act have met,
Mine with this glorious work, and made one realm

Hell and this World—one realm, one continent
Of easy thoroughfare.   Therefore, while I
Descend through Darkness, on your road with ease,
To my associate Powers, them to acquaint
With these successes, and with them rejoice,
You two this way, among these numerous orbs,
All yours, right down to Paradise descend;
There dwell, and reign in bliss; thence on the Earth
Dominion exercise and in the air,
Chiefly on Man, sole lord of all declared;
Him first make sure your thrall, and lastly kill.
My substitutes I send ye, and create
Plenipotent on Earth, of matchless might
Issuing from me.   On your joint vigour now
My hold of this new kingdom all depends,
Through Sin to Death exposed by my exploit.
If your joint power prevail, the affairs of Hell
No detriment need fear; go, and be strong."
    So saying, he dismissed them; they with speed
Their course through thickest constellations held,
Spreading their bane; the blasted stars looked wan,
And planets, planet-strook, real eclipse
Then suffered.   The other way Satan went down
The causey to Hell-gate; on either side
Disparted Chaos overbuilt exclaimed,
And with rebounding surge the bars assailed,
That scorned his indignation.   Through the gate,
Wide open and unguarded, Satan passed,
And all about found desolate; for those
Appointed to sit there had left their charge,
Flown to the upper World; the rest were all
Far to the inland retired, about the walls
Of Pandemonium, city and proud seat
Of Lucifer, so by allusion called
Of that bright star to Satan paragoned.
There kept their watch the legions, while the Grand
In council sat, solicitous what chance
Might intercept their Emperor sent; so he
Departing gave command, and they observed.
As when the Tartar from his Russian foe,
By Astracan, over the snowy plains,
Retires, or Bactrian Sophi, from the horns
Of Turkish crescent, leaves all waste beyond
The realm of Aladule, in his retreat
To Tauris or Casbeen; so these, the late
Heaven-banished host, left desert utmost Hell
Many a dark league, reduced in careful watch
Round their metropolis, and now expecting
Each hour their great Adventurer from the search
Of foreign worlds.   He through the midst unmarked,
In show plebeian Angel militant
Of lowest order, passed, and, from the door
Of that Plutonian hall, invisible
Ascended his high throne, which, under state

Of richest texture spread, at the upper end
Was placed in regal lustre. Down a while
He sat, and round about him saw, unseen.
At last, as from a cloud, his fulgent head
And shape star-bright appeared, or brighter clad
With what permissive glory since his fall
Was left him, or false glitter.   All amazed
At that so sudden blaze, the Stygian throng
Bent their aspect, and whom they wished beheld,
Their mighty Chief returned : loud was the acclaim.
Forth rushed in haste the great consulting Peers,
Raised from their dark Divan, and with like joy
Congratulant approached him, who with hand
Silence, and with these words attention, won :—
      "Thrones, Dominations, Princedoms, Virtues, Powers !—
For in possession such, not only of right,
I call ye, and declare ye now, returned,
Successful beyond hope, to lead ye forth
Triumphant out of this infernal pit
Abominable, accursed, the house of woe,
And dungeon of our tyrant !   Now possess,
As lords, a spacious World, to our native Heaven
Little inferior, by my adventure hard
With peril great achieved.   Long were to tell
What I have done, what suffered, with what pain
Voyaged the unreal, vast, unbounded Deep
Of horrible confusion—over which
By Sin and Death a broad way now is paved,
To expedite your glorious march ; but I
Toiled out my uncouth passage, forced to ride
The untractable Abyss, plunged in the womb
Of unoriginal Night and Chaos wild,
That, jealous of their secrets, fiercely opposed
My journey strange, with clamorous uproar
Protesting Fate supreme ; thence how I found
The new-created World, which fame in Heaven
Long had foretold, a fabric wonderful,
Of absolute perfection ; therein Man
Placed in a paradise, by our exile
Made happy.   Him by fraud I have seduced
From his Creator, and, the more to increase
Your wonder, with an apple !   He, thereat
Offended—worth your laughter !—hath given up
Both His beloved Man and all His World
To Sin and Death a prey, and so to us,
Without our hazard, labour, or alarm,
To range in, and to dwell, and over Man
To rule, as over all he should have ruled.
True is, me also He hath judged ; or rather
Me not, but the brute Serpent, in whose shape
Man I deceived.   That which to me belongs
Is enmity, which He will put between
Me and Mankind : I am to bruise his heel ;
His seed—when is not set—shall bruise my head !

A world who would not purchase with a bruise,
Or much more grievous pain ? Ye have the account
Of my performance; what remains, ye Gods,
But up and enter now into full bliss ?"
  So having said, a while he stood, expecting
Their universal shout and high applause
To fill his ear; when, contrary, he hears,
On all sides, from innumerable tongues
A dismal universal hiss, the sound
Of public scorn.   He wondered, but not long
Had leisure, wondering at himself now more.
His visage drawn he felt to sharp and spare,
His arms clung to his ribs, his legs entwining
Each other, till, supplanted, down he fell,
A monstrous serpent on his belly prone,
Reluctant, but in vain; a greater power
Now ruled him, punished in the shape he sinned,
According to his doom.   He would have spoke,
But hiss for hiss returned with forked tongue
To forked tongue; for now were all transformed
Alike, to serpents all, as accessories
To his bold riot.   Dreadful was the din
Of hissing through the hall, thick-swarming now
With complicated monsters, head and tail—
Scorpion, and Asp, and Amphisbæna dire,
Cerastes horned, Hydrus, and Ellops drear,
And Dipsas (not so thick swarmed once the soil
Bedropt with blood of Gorgon, or the isle
Ophiusa) ; but still greatest he the midst,
Now Dragon grown, larger than whom the Sun
Engendered in the Pythian vale on slime,
Huge Python; and his power no less he seemed
Above the rest still to retain.   They all
Him followed, issuing forth to the open field,
Where all yet left of that revolted rout,
Heaven-fallen, in station stood or just array,
Sublime with expectation when to see
In triumph issuing forth their glorious Chief.
They saw, but other sight instead—a crowd
Of ugly serpents ! Horror on them fell,
And horrid sympathy ; for what they saw
They felt themselves now changing.   Down their arms,
Down fell both spear and shield ; down they as fast,
And the dire hiss renewed, and the dire form
Catched by contagion, like in punishment
As in their crime.   Thus was the applause they meant
Turned to exploding hiss, triumph to shame
Cast on themselves from their own mouths.   There stood
A grove hard by, sprung up with this their change,
His will who reigns above, to aggravate
Their penance, laden with fair fruit, like that
Which grew in Paradise, the bait of Eve
Used by the Tempter.   On that prospect strange
Their earnest eyes they fixed, imagining

For one forbidden tree a multitude
Now risen, to work them further woe or shame ;
Yet, parched with scalding thirst and hunger fierce,
Though to delude them sent, could not abstain,
But on they rolled in heaps, and, up the trees
Climbing, sat thicker than the snaky locks
That curled Megæra. Greedily they plucked
The fruitage fair to sight, like that which grew
Near that bituminous lake where Sodom flamed ;
This, more delusive, not the touch, but taste
Deceived ; they, fondly thinking to allay
Their appetite with gust, instead of fruit
Chewed bitter ashes, which the offended taste
With spattering noise rejected. Oft they assayed,
Hunger and thirst constraining ; drugged as oft,
With hatefulest disrelish writhed their jaws
With soot and cinders filled ; so oft they fell
Into the same illusion, not as Man
Whom they triumphed once lapsed. Thus were they
     plagued,
And, worn with famine, long and ceaseless hiss,
Till their lost shape, permitted, they resumed—
Yearly enjoined, some say, to undergo
This annual humbling certain numbered days,
To dash their pride, and joy for Man seduced.
However, some tradition they dispersed
Among the Heathen of their purchase got,
And fabled how the Serpent, whom they called
Ophion, with Eurynome (the wide-
Encroaching Eve perhaps), had first the rule
Of high Olympus, thence by Saturn driven
And Ops, ere yet Dictæan Jove was born.
    Meanwhile in Paradise the Hellish pair
Too soon arrived—Sin, there in power before
Once actual, now in body, and to dwell
Habitual habitant ; behind her Death,
Close following pace for pace, not mounted yet
On his pale horse ; to whom Sin thus began :—
    "Second of Satan sprung, all-conquering Death !
What think'st thou of our empire now ? though earned
With travail difficult, not better far
Than still at Hell's dark threshold to have sat watch,
Unnamed, undreaded, and thyself half-starved ?"
    Whom thus the Sin-born Monster answered soon :—
"To me, who with eternal famine pine,
Alike is Hell, or Paradise, or Heaven—
There best where most with ravin I may meet :
Which here, though plenteous, all too little seems
To stuff this maw, this vast unhide-bound corpse."
    To whom the incestuous Mother thus replied :—
"Thou, therefore, on these herbs, and fruits, and flowers,
Feed first ; on each beast next, and fish, and fowl—
No homely morsels ; and whatever thing
The scythe of Time mows down devour unspared ;

173

Till I, in Man residing through the race,
His thoughts, his looks, words, actions, all infect,
And season him thy last and sweetest prey."
   This said, they both betook them several ways,
Both to destroy, or unimmortal make
All kinds, and for destruction to mature
Sooner or later; which the Almighty seeing,
From His transcendent seat the Saints among,
To those bright Orders uttered thus His voice :—
   "See with what heat these dogs of Hell advance
To waste and havoc yonder World, which I
So fair and good created, and had still
Kept in that state, had not the folly of Man
Let in these wasteful furies, who impute
Folly to me (so doth the Prince of Hell
And his adherents), that with so much ease
I suffer them to enter and possess
A place so heavenly, and, conniving, seem
To gratify my scornful enemies,
That laugh, as if, transported with some fit
Of passion, I to them had quitted all,
At random yielded up to their misrule;
And know not that I called and drew them thither,
My Hell-hounds, to lick up the draff and filth
Which Man's polluting sin with taint hath shed
On what was pure; till, crammed and gorged, nigh burst
With sucked and glutted offal, at one sling
Of thy victorious arm, well-pleasing Son,
Both Sin and Death, and yawning Grave, at last
Through Chaos hurled, obstruct the mouth of Hell
For ever, and seal up his ravenous jaws.
Then Heaven and Earth, renewed, shall be made pure
To sanctity that shall receive no stain :
Till then the curse pronounced on both precedes."
   He ended, and the Heavenly audience loud
Sung Halleluiah, as the sound of seas,
Through multitude that sung:—"Just are Thy ways.
Righteous are Thy decrees on all Thy works;
Who can extenuate Thee? Next, to the Son,
Destined restorer of Mankind, by whom
New Heaven and Earth shall to the ages rise,
Or down from Heaven descend." Such was their song,
While the Creator, calling forth by name
His mighty Angels, gave them several charge,
As sorted best with present things. The Sun
Had first his precept so to move, so shine,
As might affect the Earth with cold and heat
Scarce tolerable, and from the north to call
Decrepit winter, from the south to bring
Solstitial summer's heat. To the blanc Moon
Her office they prescribed; to the other five
Their planetary motions and aspécts,
In sextile, square, and trine, and opposite,
Of noxious efficacy, and when to join

In synod unbenign; and taught the fixed
Their influence malignant when to shower—
Which of them, rising with the Sun or falling,
Should prove tempestuous. To the winds they set
Their corners, when with bluster to confound
Sea, air, and shore; the thunder when to roll
With terror through the dark aerial hall.
Some say He bid His Angels turn askance
The poles of Earth twice ten degrees and more
From the Sun's axle; they with labour pushed
Oblique the centric Globe; some say the Sun
Was bid turn reins from the equinoctial road
Like distant breadth—to Taurus with the seven
Atlantic Sisters, and the Spartan Twins,
Up to the Tropic Crab; thence down amain
By Leo, and the Virgin, and the Scales,
As deep as Capricorn; to bring in change
Of seasons to each clime. Else had the spring
Perpetual smiled on Earth with vernant flowers,
Equal in days and nights, except to those
Beyond the polar circles; to them day
Had unbenighted shone, while the low Sun,
To recompense his distance, in their sight
Had rounded still the horizon, and not known
Or east or west—which had forbid the snow
From cold Estotiland, and south as far
Beneath Magellan. At that tasted fruit,
The Sun, as from Thyestean banquet, turned
His course intended; else how had the world
Inhabited, though sinless, more than now
Avoided pinching cold and scorching heat?
These changes in the heavens, though slow, produced
Like change on sea and land—sideral blast,
Vapour, and mist, and exhalation hot,
Corrupt and pestilent. Now from the north
Of Norumbega, and the Samoed shore,
Bursting their brazen dungeon, armed with ice,
And snow, and hail, and stormy gust and flaw,
Boreas and Cæcias and Argestes loud
And Thrascias rend the woods, and seas upturn;
With adverse blasts upturns them from the south
Notus and Afer, black with thundrous clouds
From Serraliona; thwart of these, as fierce
Forth rush the Levant and the Ponent winds,
Eurus and Zephyr, with their lateral noise,
Sirocco and Libecchio. Thus began
Outrage from lifeless things; but Discord first,
Daughter of Sin, among the irrational
Death introduced through fierce antipathy.
Beast now with beast 'gan war, and fowl with fowl,
And fish with fish. To graze the herb all leaving
Devoured each other! nor stood much in awe
Of Man, but fled him, or with countenance grim
Glared on him passing. These were from without

The growing miseries ; which Adam saw
Already in part, though hid in gloomiest shade,
To sorrow abandoned, but worse felt within,
And, in a troubled sea of passion tost,
Thus to disburden sought with sad complaint :—
  "O miserable of happy ! Is this the end
Of this new glorious World, and me so late
The glory of that glory ? who now, become
Accursed of blessed, hide me from the face
Of God, whom to behold was then my highth
Of happiness ! Yet well, if here would end
The misery ! I deserved it, and would bear
My own deservings. But this will not serve :
All that I eat or drink, or shall beget,
Is propagated curse. O voice, once heard
Delightfully, '*Increase and multiply*';
Now death to hear ! for what can I increase
Or multiply but curses on my head ?
Who, of all ages to succeed, but, feeling
The evil on him brought by me, will curse
My head ? 'Ill fare our Ancestor impure !
For this we may thank Adam !' but his thanks
Shall be the execration. So, besides
Mine own that bide upon me, all from me
Shall with a fierce reflux on me redound—
On me, as on their natural centre, light ;
Heavy, though in their place. O fleeting joys
Of Paradise, dear bought with lasting woes !
Did I request Thee, Maker, from my clay
To mould me Man ? Did I solicit Thee
From darkness to promote me, or here place
In this delicious Garden ? As my will
Concurred not to my being, it were but right
And equal to reduce me to my dust,
Desirous to resign and render back
All I received, unable to perform
Thy terms too hard, by which I was to hold
The good I sought not. To the loss of that,
Sufficient penalty, why hast Thou added
The sense of endless woes ? Inexplicable
Thy justice seems. Yet, to say truth, too late
I thus contest ; then should have been refused
Those terms, whatever, when they were proposed.
Thou didst accept them : wilt thou enjoy the good,
Then cavil the conditions ? And, though God
Made thee without thy leave, what if thy son
Prove disobedient, and, reproved, retort,
'Wherefore didst thou beget me ? I sought it not !'
Wouldst thou admit for his contempt of thee
That proud excuse ? yet him not thy election,
But natural necessity, begot.
God made thee of choice His own, and of His own
To serve Him ; thy reward was of His grace ;
Thy punishment, then, justly is at His will.

Be it so, for I submit ; His doom is fair,
That dust I am, and shall to dust return.
O welcome hour whenever ! Why delays
His hand to execute what His decree
Fixed on this day ? Why do I overlive ?
Why am I mocked with death, and lengthened out
To deathless pain ? How gladly would I meet
Mortality, my sentence, and be earth
Insensible ! how glad would lay me down
As in my mother's lap ! There I should rest,
And sleep secure ; His dreadful voice no more
Would thunder in my ears ; no fear of worse
To me and to my offspring would torment me
With cruel expectation. Yet one doubt
Pursues me still—lest all I cannot die ;
Lest that pure breath of life, the Spirit of Man
Which God inspired, cannot together perish
With this corporeal clod. Then, in the grave,
Or in some other dismal place, who knows
But I shall die a living death ? O thought
Horrid, if true ! Yet why ? It was but breath
Of life that sinned : what dies but what had life
And sin ? The body properly hath neither.
All of me, then, shall die : let this appease
The doubt, since human reach no further knows.
For, though the Lord of all be infinite,
Is His wrath also ? Be it, Man is not so,
But mortal doomed. How can He exercise
Wrath without end on Man, whom death must end ?
Can He make deathless death ? That were to make
Strange contradiction ; which to God Himself
Impossible is held, as argument
Of weakness, not of power. Will He draw out,
For anger's sake, finite to infinite
In punished Man, to satisfy His rigour
Satisfied never ? That were to extend
His sentence beyond dust and Nature's law ;
By which all causes else according still
To the reception of their matter act,
Not to the extent of their own sphere. But say
That death be not one stroke, as I supposed,
Bereaving sense, but endless misery
From this day onward, which I feel begun
Both in me and without me, and so last
To perpetuity——Ay me ! that fear
Comes thundering back with dreadful revolution
On my defenceless head ! Both Death and I
Am found eternal, and incorporate both :
Nor I on my part single ; in me all
Posterity stands cursed. Fair patrimony
That I must leave ye, sons ! Oh, were I able
To waste it all myself, and leave ye none !
So disinherited, how would ye bless
Me, now your curse ! Ah, why should all Mankind,

M.—N

For one man's fault, thus guiltless be condemned?
If guiltless! But from me what can proceed
But all corrupt—both mind and will depraved
Not to do only, but to will the same
With me? How can they, then, acquitted stand
In sight of God? Him, after all disputes,
Forced I absolve. All my evasions vain
And reasonings, though through mazes, lead me still
But to my own conviction; first and last
On me, me only, as the source and spring
Of all corruption, all the blame lights due.
So might the wrath! Fond wish! couldst thou support
That burden, heavier than the Earth to bear—
Than all the world much heavier, though divided
With that bad Woman? Thus, what thou desir'st,
And what thou fear'st, alike destroys all hope
Of refuge, and concludes thee miserable
Beyond all past example and future—
To Satan only like, both crime and doom.
O Conscience! into what abyss of fears
And horrors hast thou driven me; out of which
I find no way, from deep to deeper plunged!"
    Thus Adam to himself lamented loud
Through the still night—not now, as ere Man fell,
Wholesome and cool and mild, but with black air
Accompanied, with damps and dreadful gloom;
Which to his evil conscience represented
All things with double terror. On the ground
Outstretched he lay, on the cold ground, and oft
Cursed his creation; Death as oft accused
Of tardy execution, since denounced
The day of his offence. "Why comes not Death,"
Said he, "with one thrice-acceptable stroke
To end me? Shall Truth fail to keep her word,
Justice divine not hasten to be just?
But Death comes not at call; Justice divine
Mends not her slowest pace for prayers or cries.
O woods, O fountains, hillocks, dales, and bowers!
With other echo late I taught your shades
To answer, and resound far other song."
Whom thus afflicted when sad Eve beheld,
Desolate where she sat, approaching nigh,
Soft words to his fierce passion she assayed;
But her, with stern regard, he thus repelled:—
    "Out of my sight, thou serpent! That name best
Befits thee, with him leagued, thyself as false
And hateful; nothing wants, but that thy shape
Like his, and colour serpentine, may show
Thy inward fraud, to warn all creatures from thee
Henceforth, lest that too heavenly form, pretended
To hellish falsehood, snare them. But for thee
I had persisted happy, had not thy pride
And wandering vanity, when least was safe,
Rejected my forewarning, and disdained

178

Not to be trusted—longing to be seen,
Though by the Devil himself; him overweening
To overreach; but, with the Serpent meeting,
Fooled and beguiled; by him thou, I by thee,
To trust thee from my side, imagined wise,
Constant, mature, proof against all assaults,
And understood not all was but a show,
Rather than solid virtue, all but a rib
Crooked by nature—bent, as now appears,
More to the part sinister—from me drawn;
Well if thrown out, as supernumerary
To my just number found! Oh, why did God,
Creator wise, that peopled highest Heaven
With Spirits masculine, create at last
This novelty on Earth, this fair defect
Of Nature, and not fill the World at once
With men as Angels, without feminine;
Or find some other way to generate
Mankind? This mischief had not then befallen,
And more that shall befall—innumerable
Disturbances on Earth through female snares,
And strait conjunction with this sex. For either
He never shall find out fit mate, but such
As some misfortune brings him, or mistake;
Or whom he wishes most shall seldom gain,
Through her perverseness, but shall see her gained
By a far worse, or, if she love, withheld
By parents; or his happiest choice too late
Shall meet, already linked and wedlock-bound
To a fell adversary, his hate or shame:
Which infinite calamity shall cause
To human life, and household peace confound."

He added not, and from her turned; but Eve,
Not so repulsed, with tears that ceased not flowing,
And tresses all disordered, at his feet
Fell humble, and, embracing them, besought
His peace, and thus proceeded in her plaint:—

"Forsake me not thus, Adam! witness Heaven
What love sincere and reverence in my heart
I bear thee, and unweeting have offended,
Unhappily deceived! Thy suppliant
I beg, and clasp thy knees; bereave me not
Whereon I live, thy gentle looks, thy aid,
Thy counsel in this uttermost distress,
My only strength and stay. Forlorn of thee,
Whither shall I betake me, where subsist?
While yet we live, scarce one short hour perhaps,
Between us two let there be peace; both joining,
As joined in injuries, one enmity
Against a foe by doom express assigned us,
That cruel Serpent. On me exercise not
Thy hatred for this misery befallen—
On me already lost, me than thyself
More miserable. Both have sinned; but thou

179

Against God only; I against God and thee,
And to the place of judgment will return,
There with my cries importune Heaven, that all
The sentence, from thy head removed, may light
On me, sole cause to thee of all this woe,
Me, me only, just object of His ire."
  She ended, weeping; and her lowly plight,
Immovable till peace obtained from fault
Acknowledged and deplored, in Adam wrought
Commiseration. Soon his heart relented
Towards her, his life so late, and sole delight,
Now at his feet submissive in distress—
Creature so fair his reconcilement seeking,
His counsel whom she had displeased, his aid.
As one disarmed, his anger all he lost,
And thus with peaceful words upraised her soon:—
  "Unwary, and too desirous, as before
So now, of what thou know'st not, who desir'st
The punishment all on thyself! Alas!
Bear thine own first, ill able to sustain
His full wrath whose thou feel'st as yet least part,
And my displeasure bear'st so ill. If prayers
Could alter high decrees, I to that place
Would speed before thee, and be louder heard,
That on my head all might be visited,
Thy frailty and infirmer sex forgiven,
To me committed, and by me exposed.
But rise; let us no more contend, nor blame
Each other, blamed enough elsewhere, but strive
In offices of love how we may lighten
Each other's burden in our share of woe;
Since this day's death denounced, if aught I see,
Will prove no sudden, but a slow-paced evil,
A long day's dying, to augment our pain,
And to our seed (O hapless seed!) derived."
  To whom thus Eve, recovering heart, replied:—
"Adam, by sad experiment I know
How little weight my words with thee can find,
Found so erroneous, thence by just event
Found so unfortunate. Nevertheless,
Restored by thee, vile as I am, to place
Of new acceptance, hopeful to regain
Thy love, the sole contentment of my heart,
Living or dying from thee I will not hide
What thoughts in my unquiet breast are risen,
Tending to some relief of our extremes,
Or end, though sharp and sad, yet tolerable,
As in our evils, and of easier choice.
If care of our descent perplex us most,
Which must be born to certain woe, devoured
By Death at last (and miserable it is
To be to others cause of misery,
Our own begotten, and of our loins to bring
Into this cursed world a woeful race,

That, after wretched life, must be at last
Food for so foul a monster), in thy power
It lies, yet ere conception, to prevent
The race unblest, to being yet unbegot.
Childless thou art; childless remain. So Death
Shall be deceived his glut, and with us two
Be forced to satisfy his ravenous maw.
But, if thou judge it hard and difficult,
Conversing, looking, loving, to abstain
From love's due rites, nuptial embraces sweet,
And with desire to languish without hope
Before the present object languishing
With like desire—which would be misery
And torment less than none of what we dread—
Then, both our selves and seed at once to free
From what we fear for both, let us make short;
Let us seek Death, or, he not found, supply
With our own hands his office on ourselves.
Why stand we longer shivering under fears
That show no end but death, and have the power,
Of many ways to die the shortest choosing,
Destruction with destruction to destroy?"
   She ended here, or vehement despair
Broke off the rest; so much of death her thoughts
Had entertained as dyed her cheeks with pale.
But Adam, with such counsel nothing swayed,
To better hopes his more attentive mind
Labouring had raised, and thus to Eve replied:—
   "Eve, thy contempt of life and pleasure seems
To argue in thee something more sublime
And excellent than what thy mind contemns:
But self-destruction therefore sought refutes
That excellence thought in thee, and implies
Not thy contempt, but anguish and regret
For loss of life and pleasure overloved.
Or, if thou covet death, as utmost end
Of misery, so thinking to evade
The penalty pronounced, doubt not but God
Hath wiselier armed His vengeful ire than so
To be forestalled. Much more I fear lest death
So snatched will not exempt us from the pain
We are by doom to pay; rather such acts
Of contumacy will provoke the Highest
To make death in us live. Then let us seek
Some safer resolution—which methinks
I have in view, calling to mind with heed
Part of our sentence, that thy seed shall bruise
The Serpent's head. Piteous amends! unless
Be meant whom I conjecture, our grand foe,
Satan, who in the Serpent hath contrived
Against us this deceit. To crush his head
Would be revenge indeed—which will be lost
By death brought on ourselves, or childless days
Resolved as thou proposest; so our foe

Shall 'scape his punishment ordained, and we
Instead shall double ours upon our heads.
No more be mentioned, then, of violence
Against ourselves, and wilful barrenness
That cuts us off from hope, and savours only
Rancour and pride, impatience and despite,
Reluctance against God and His just yoke
Laid on our necks.   Remember with what mild
And gracious temper He both heard and judged,
Without wrath or reviling.   We expected
Immediate dissolution, which we thought
Was meant by death that day ; when, lo ! to thee
Pains only in child-bearing were foretold,
And bringing forth, soon recompensed with joy,
Fruit of thy womb.   On me the curse aslope
Glanced on the ground.   With labour I must earn
My bread ; what harm ?   Idleness had been worse ;
My labour will sustain me ; and, lest cold
Or heat should injure us, His timely care
Hath, unbesought, provided, and His hands
Clothed us unworthy, pitying while He judged.
How much more, if we pray Him, will His ear
Be open, and His heart to pity incline,
And teach us further by what means to shun
The inclement seasons, rain, ice, hail, and snow !
Which now the sky, with various face, begins
To show us in this mountain, while the winds
Blow moist and keen, shattering the graceful locks
Of these fair spreading trees ; which bids us seek
Some better shroud, some better warmth to cherish
Our limbs benumbed—ere this diurnal star
Leave cold the night, how we his gathered beams
Reflected may with matter sere foment,
Or by collision of two bodies grind
The air attrite to fire ; as late the clouds,
Justling, or pushed with winds, rude in their shock,
Tine the slant lightning, whose thwart flame, driven down,
Kindles the gummy bark of fir or pine,
And sends a comfortable heat from far,
Which might supply the Sun.   Such fire to use,
And what may else be remedy or cure
To evils which our own misdeeds have wrought,
He will instruct us praying, and of grace
Beseeching Him ; so as we need not fear
To pass commodiously this life, sustained
By Him with many comforts, till we end
In dust, our final rest and native home.
What better can we do than, to the place
Repairing where He judged us, prostrate fall
Before Him reverent, and there confess
Humbly our faults, and pardon beg, with tears
Watering the ground, and with our sighs the air
Frequenting, sent from hearts contrite, in sign
Of sorrow unfeigned and humiliation meek ?

Undoubtedly He will relent, and turn
From His displeasure, in whose look serene,
When angry most He seemed and most severe,
What else but favour, grace, and mercy shone ?"
  So spake our Father penitent ; nor Eve
Felt less remorse. They, forthwith to the place
Repairing where He judged them, prostrate fell
Before Him reverent, and both confessed
Humbly their faults, and pardon begged, with tears
Watering the ground, and with their sighs the air
Frequenting, sent from hearts contrite, in sign
Of sorrow unfeigned and humiliation meek.

THE END OF THE TENTH BOOK.

PARADISE LOST.

BOOK XI.

THE ARGUMENT.

The Son of God presents to His Father the prayers of our first parents now repenting, and intercedes for them. God accepts them, but declares that they must no longer abide in Paradise; sends Michael with a band of Cherubim to dispossess them, but first to reveal to Adam future things: Michael's coming down. Adam shows to Eve certain ominous signs: he discerns Michael's approach; goes out to meet him: the Angel denounces their departure. Eve's lamentation. Adam pleads, but submits: the Angel leads him up to a high hill; sets before him in vision what shall happen till the Flood.

THUS they, in lowliest plight, repentant stood
Praying; for from the mercy-seat above
Prevenient grace descending had removed
The stony from their hearts, and made new flesh
Regenerate grow instead, that sighs now breathed
Unutterable, which the Spirit of prayer
Inspired, and winged for Heaven with speedier flight
Than loudest oratory. Yet their port
Not of mean suitors; nor important less
Seemed their petition than when the ancient pair
In fables old, less ancient yet than these,
Deucalion and chaste Pyrrha, to restore
The race of mankind drowned, before the shrine
Of Themis stood devout. To Heaven their prayers
Flew up, nor missed the way, by envious winds
Blown vagabond or frustrate: in they passed
Dimensionless through heavenly doors; then, clad
With incense, where the golden altar fumed,
By their great Intercessor, came in sight
Before the Father's throne. Them the glad Son
Presenting thus to intercede began :—
  "See, Father, what first-fruits on Earth are sprung
From Thy implanted grace in Man—these sighs
And prayers, which in this golden censer mixed
With incense, I, Thy Priest, before Thee bring;
Fruits of more pleasing savour, from Thy seed
Sown with contrition in his heart, than those
Which, his own hand manuring, all the trees
Of Paradise could have produced, ere fallen
From innocence. Now, therefore, bend thine ear

184

To supplication ; hear his sighs, though mute ;
Unskilful with what words to pray, let Me
Interpret for him, Me his advocate
And propitiation ; all his works on Me,
Good or not good, ingraft ; my merit those
Shall perfect, and for these My death shall pay.
Accept Me, and in Me from these receive
The smell of peace toward Mankind ; let him live,
Before Thee reconciled, at least his days
Numbered, though sad, till death, his doom (which I
To mitigate thus plead, not to reverse),
To better life shall yield him, where with Me
All My redeemed may dwell in joy and bliss,
Made one with Me, as I with Thee am one."
    To whom the Father, without cloud, serene :—
" All Thy request for Man, accepted Son,
Obtain ; all Thy request was My decree.
But longer in that Paradise to dwell
The law I gave to Nature him forbids ;
Those pure immortal elements, that know
No gross, no unharmonious mixture foul,
Eject him, tainted now, and purge him off,
As a distemper, gross, to air as gross,
And mortal food, as may dispose him best
For dissolution wrought by sin, that first
Distempered all things, and of incorrupt
Corrupted. I, at first, with two fair gifts
Created him endowed—with Happiness
And Immortality ; that fondly lost,
This other served but to eternize woe,
Till I provided Death : so Death becomes
His final remedy, and, after life
Tried in sharp tribulation, and refined
By faith and faithful works, to second life,
Waked in the renovation of the just,
Resigns him up with Heaven and Earth renewed.
But let Us call to synod all the Blest
Through Heaven's wide bounds ; from them I will not hide
My judgments—how with Mankind I proceed,
As how with peccant Angels late they saw,
And in their state, though firm, stood more confirmed."
    He ended, and the Son gave signal high
To the bright Minister that watched. He blew
His trumpet, heard in Oreb since perhaps
When God descended, and perhaps once more
To sound at general doom. The angelic blast
Filled all the regions : from their blissful bowers
Of amarantine shade, fountain or spring,
By the waters of life, where'er they sat
In fellowships of joy, the Sons of Light
Hasted, resorting to the summons high,
And took their seats, till from His throne supreme
The Almighty thus pronounced His sovran will :—
    " O Sons, like one of us Man is become

To know both good and evil, since his taste
Of that defended fruit ; but let him boast
His knowledge of good lost and evil got,
Happier had it sufficed him to have known
Good by itself and evil not at all.
He sorrows now, repents, and prays contrite—
My motions in him ; longer than they move,
His heart I know how variable and vain,
Self-left.   Lest, therefore, his now bolder hand
Reach also of the Tree of Life, and eat,
And live for ever, dream at least to live
For ever, to remove him I decree,
And send him from the Garden forth, to till
The ground whence he was taken, fitter soil.
Michael, this My behest have thou in charge :
Take to thee from among the Cherubim
Thy choice of flaming warriors, lest the Fiend,
Or in behalf of Man, or to invade
Vacant possession, some new trouble raise ;
Haste thee, and from the Paradise of God
Without remorse drive out the sinful pair,
From hallowed ground the unholy, and denounce
To them, and to their progeny, from thence
Perpetual banishment.   Yet, lest they faint
At the sad sentence rigorously urged
(For I behold them softened, and with tears
Bewailing their excess), all terror hide.
If patiently thy bidding they obey,
Dismiss them not disconsolate ; reveal
To Adam what shall come in future days,
As I shall thee enlighten ; intermix
My covenant in the Woman's seed renewed.
So send them forth, though sorrowing, yet in peace ;
And on the east side of the Garden place,
Where entrance up from Eden easiest climbs,
Cherubic watch, and of a sword the flame
Wide-waving, all approach far off to fright,
And guard all passage to the Tree of Life ;
Lest Paradise a receptacle prove
To Spirits foul, and all my trees their prey,
With whose stolen fruit Man once more to delude."
  He ceased, and the Archangelic Power prepared
For swift descent ; with him the cohort bright
Of Watchful Cherubim.   Four faces each
Had, like a double Janus ; all their shape
Spangled with eyes more numerous than those
Of Argus, and more wakeful than to drowse,
Charmed with Arcadian pipe, the pastoral reed
Of Hermes, or his opiate rod.   Meanwhile,
To resalute the World with sacred light,
Leucothea waked, and with fresh dews embalmed
The earth, when Adam and first matron Eve
Had ended now their orisons, and found
Strength added from above, new hope to spring

Out of despair, joy, but with fear yet linked ;
Which thus to Eve his welcome words renewed :—
  "Eve, easily may faith admit that all
The good which we enjoy from Heaven descends ;
But that from us aught should ascend to Heaven
So prevalent as to concern the mind
Of God high-blest, or to incline His will,
Hard to belief may seem.   Yet this will prayer,
Or one short sigh of human breath, upborne
Even to the seat of God.   For, since I sought
By prayer the offended Deity to appease,
Kneeled and before Him humbled all my heart,
Methought I saw Him placable and mild,
Bending His ear ; persuasion in me grew
That I was heard with favour ; peace returned
Home to my breast, and to my memory
His promise that thy seed shall bruise our Foe ;
Which, then not minded in dismay, yet now
Assures me that the bitterness of death
Is past, and we shall live.   Whence hail to thee !
Eve rightly called, Mother of all Mankind,
Mother of all things living, since by thee
Man is to live, and all things live for Man."
  To whom thus Eve with sad demeanour meek :—
"Ill-worthy I such title should belong
To me, transgressor, who, for thee ordained
A help, became thy snare ; to me reproach
Rather belongs, distrust and all dispraise.
But infinite in pardon was my Judge,
That I, who first brought death on all, am graced
The source of life ; next favourable thou,
Who highly thus to entitle me vouchsaf'st,
Far other name deserving.   But the field
To labour calls us, now with sweat imposed,
Though after sleepless night ; for see ! the Morn,
All unconcerned with our unrest, begins
Her rosy progress smiling.   Let us forth,
I never from thy side henceforth to stray,
Where'er our day's work lies, though now enjoined
Laborious, till day droop.   While here we dwell,
What can be toilsome in these pleasant walks?
Here let us live, though in fallen state, content."
  So spake, so wished, much-humbled Eve ; but Fate
Subscribed not.   Nature first gave signs, impressed
On bird, beast, air—air suddenly eclipsed,
After short blush of morn.   Nigh in her sight
The bird of Jove, stooped from his aery tour,
Two birds of gayest plume before him drove ;
Down from a hill the beast that reigns in woods,
First hunter then, pursued a gentle brace,
Goodliest of all the forest, hart and hind ;
Direct to the eastern gate was bent their flight.
Adam observed, and, with his eye the chase
Pursuing, not unmoved to Eve thus spake :—

" O Eve, some further change awaits us nigh,
Which Heaven by these mute signs in Nature shows,
Forerunners of His purpose, or to warn
Us, haply too secure of our discharge
From penalty because from death released
Some days: how long, and what till then our life,
Who knows, or more than this, that we are dust,
And thither must return, and be no more ?
Why else this double object in our sight,
Of flight pursued in the air and o'er the ground
One way the self-same hour ?   Why in the east
Darkness ere day's mid-course, and morning-light
More orient in yon western cloud, that draws
O'er the blue firmament a radiant white,
And slow descends, with something Heavenly fraught ? "
      He erred not ; for, by this, the Heavenly bands
Down from a sky of jasper lighted now
In Paradise, and on a hill made halt—
A glorious apparition, had not doubt
And carnal fear that day dimmed Adam's eye.
Not that more glorious, when the Angels met
Jacob in Mahanaim, where he saw
The field pavilioned with his guardians bright ;
Nor that which on the flaming mount appeared
In Dothan, covered with a camp of fire,
Against the Syrian king, who, to surprise
One man, assassin-like, had levied war,
War unproclaimed.   The princely Hierarch
In their bright stand there left his Powers to seize
Possession of the Garden ; he alone,
To find where Adam sheltered, took his way,
Not unperceived of Adam ; who to Eve,
While the great visitant approached, thus spake :—
      " Eve, now expect great tidings, which, perhaps,
Of us will soon determine, or impose
New laws to be observed ; for I descry,
From yonder blazing cloud that veils the hill,
One of the Heavenly host, and, by his gait,
None of the meanest—some great Potentate
Or of the Thrones above, such majesty
Invests him coming ; yet not terrible,
That I should fear, nor sociably mild,
As Raphael, that I should much confide,
But solemn and sublime ; whom, not to offend,
With reverence I must meet, and thou retire."
      He ended ; and the Archangel soon drew nigh,
Not in his shape celestial, but as man
Clad to meet man.   Over his lucid arms
A military vest of purple flowed,
Livelier than Melibœan, or the grain
Of Sarra, worn by kings and heroes old
In time of truce ; Iris had dipt the woof.
His starry helm unbuckled showed him prime
In manhood where youth ended ; by his side,

As in a glistering zodiac, hung the sword,
Satan's dire dread, and in his hand the spear.
Adam bowed low ; he, kingly, from his state
Inclined not, but his coming thus declared :—
   " Adam, Heaven's high behest no preface needs.
Sufficient that thy prayers are heard, and Death,
Then due by sentence when thou didst transgress,
Defeated of his seizure many days,
Given thee of grace, wherein thou may'st repent,
And one bad act with many deeds well done
May'st cover. Well may then thy Lord, appeased,
Redeem thee quite from Death's rapacious claim ;
But longer in this Paradise to dwell
Permits not. To remove thee I am come,
And send thee from the Garden forth, to till
The ground whence thou wast taken, fitter soil."
He added not ; for Adam at the news
Heart-strook, with chilling gripe of sorrow stood,
That all his senses bound ; Eve, who unseen
Yet all had heard, with audible lament
Discovered soon the place of her retire :—
   " O unexpected stroke, worse than of Death !
Must I thus leave thee, Paradise ? thus leave
Thee, native soil ? these happy walks and shades,
Fit haunt of Gods, where I had hope to spend,
Quiet, though sad, the respite of that day
That must be mortal to us both ? O flowers,
That never will in other climate grow,
My early visitation, and my last
At even, which I bred up with tender hand
From the first opening bud, and gave ye names,
Who now shall rear ye to the Sun, or rank
Your tribes, and water from the ambrosial fount ?
Thee, lastly, nuptial bower, by me adorned
With what to sight or smell was sweet, from thee
How shall I part, and whither wander down
Into a lower world, to this obscure
And wild ? How shall we breathe in other air
Less pure, accustomed to immortal fruits ?"
   Whom thus the Angel interrupted mild :—
" Lament not, Eve, but patiently resign
What justly thou hast lost ; nor set thy heart,
Thus over-fond, on that which is not thine.
Thy going is not lonely ; with thee goes
Thy husband ; him to follow thou art bound ;
Where he abides, think there thy native soil."
   Adam, by this from the cold sudden damp
Recovering, and his scattered spirits returned,
To Michael thus his humble words addressed :—
   " Celestial, whether among the Thrones, or named
Of them the highest—for such of shape may seem
Prince above princes—gently hast thou told
Thy message, which might else in telling wound,
And in performing end us. What besides

Of sorrow, and dejection, and despair,
Our frailty can sustain, thy tidings bring—
Departure from this happy place, our sweet
Recess, and only consolation left
Familiar to our eyes ; all places else
Inhospitable appear, and desolate,
Nor knowing us, nor known.   And, if by prayer
Incessant I could hope to change the will
Of Him who all things can, I would not cease
To weary Him with my assiduous cries ;
But prayer against His absolute decree
No more avails than breath against the wind,
Blown stifling back on him that breathes it forth :
Therefore to His great bidding I submit.
This most afflicts me—that, departing hence,
As from His face I shall be hid, deprived
His blessed countenance.   Here I could frequent,
With worship, place by place where He vouchsafed
Presence Divine, and to my sons relate,
'On this mount He appeared ; under this tree
Stood visible ; among these pines His voice
I heard ; here with Him at this fountain talked.'
So many grateful altars I would rear
Of grassy turf, and pile up every stone
Of lustre from the brook, in memory
Or monument to ages, and thereon
Offer sweet-smelling gums, and fruits, and flowers.
In yonder nether world where shall I seek
His bright appearances, or footstep trace ?
For, though I fled Him angry, yet, recalled
To life prolonged and promised race, I now
Gladly behold though but His utmost skirts
Of glory, and far off His steps adore."
      To whom thus Michael, with regard benign :—
" Adam, thou know'st Heaven His, and all the Earth,
Not this rock only ; His omnipresence fills
Land, sea, and air, and every kind that lives,
Fomented by His virtual power and warmed.
All the Earth He gave thee to possess and rule,
No despicable gift ; surmise not, then,
His presence to these narrow bounds confined
Of Paradise or Eden.   This had been
Perhaps thy capital seat, from whence had spread
All generations, and had hither come,
From all the ends of the Earth, to celebrate
And reverence thee their great progenitor.
But this pre-eminence thou hast lost, brought down
To dwell on even ground now with thy sons :
Yet doubt not but in valley and in plain
God, is, as here, and will be found alike
Present, and of His presence many a sign
Still following thee, still compassing thee round
With goodness and paternal love, His face
Express, and of His steps the track divine.

Which that thou may'st believe, and to be confirmed
Ere thou from hence depart, know I am sent
To show thee what shall come in future days
To thee and to thy offspring.   Good with bad
Expect to hear, supernal grace contending
With sinfulness of men—thereby to learn
True patience, and to temper joy with fear
And pious sorrow, equally inured
By moderation either state to bear,
Prosperous or adverse : so shalt thou lead
Safest thy life, and best prepared endure
Thy mortal passage when it comes.   Ascend
This hill ; let Eve (for I have drenched her eyes)
Here sleep below while thou to foresight wak'st,
As once thou slept'st while she to life was formed."
     To whom thus Adam gratefully replied :—
"Ascend ; I follow thee, safe guide, the path
Thou lead'st me, and to the hand of Heaven submit,
However chastening—to the evil turn
My obvious breast, arming to overcome
By suffering, and earn rest from labour won,
If so I may attain."   So both ascend
In the visions of God.   It was a hill,
Of Paradise the highest, from whose top
The hemisphere of Earth in clearest ken
Stretched out to the amplest reach of prospect lay.
Not higher that hill, nor wider looking round,
Whereon for different cause the Tempter set
Our second Adam, in the wilderness,
To show Him all Earth's kingdoms and their glory.
His eye might there command wherever stood
City of old or modern fame, the seat
Of mightiest empire, from the destined walls
Of Cambalu, seat of Cathaian Can,
And Samarchand by Oxus, Temir's throne,
To Paquin, of Sinæan kings, and thence
To Agra and Lahor of Great Mogul,
Down to the golden Chersonese, or where
The Persian in Ecbatan sat, or since
In Hispahan, or where the Russian Ksar
In Mosco, or the Sultan in Bizance,
Turchestan-born ; nor could his eye not ken
The empire of Negus to his utmost port
Ercoco, and the less maritime kings,
Mombaza, and Quiloa, and Melind,
And Sofala (thought Ophir), to the realm
Of Congo, and Angola farthest south,
Or thence from Niger flood to Atlas mount,
The kingdoms of Almansor, Fez and Sus,
Marocco, and Algiers, and Tremisen ;
On Europe thence, and where Rome was to sway
The world : in spirit perhaps he also saw
Rich Mexico, the seat of Montezume,
And Cusco in Peru, the richer seat

Of Atabalipa, and yet unspoiled
Guiana, whose great city Geryon's sons
Call El Dorado.   But to nobler sights
Michael from Adam's eyes the film removed
Which that false fruit that promised clearer sight
Had bred ; then purged with euphrasy and rue
The visual nerve, for he had much to see,
And from the well of life three drops instilled.
So deep the power of these ingredients pierced,
Even to the inmost seat of mental sight,
That Adam, now enforced to close his eyes,
Sunk down, and all his spirits became entranced.
But him the gentle Angel by the hand
Soon raised, and his attention thus recalled :—
   "Adam, now ope thine eyes, and first behold
The effects which thy original crime hath wrought
In some to spring from thee, who never touched
The excepted tree, nor with the Snake conspired,
Nor sinned thy sin, yet from that sin derive
Corruption to bring forth more violent deeds."
   His eyes he opened, and beheld a field,
Part arable and tilth, whereon were sheaves
New-reaped, the other part sheep-walks and folds ;
I' the midst an altar as the landmark stood,
Rustic, of grassy sord.   Thither anon
A sweaty reaper from his tillage brought
First-fruits, the green ear and the yellow sheaf,
Unculled, as came to hand.   A shepherd next,
More meek, came with the firstlings of his flock,
Choicest and best ; then, sacrificing, laid
The inwards and their fat, with incense strewed,
On the cleft wood, and all due rites performed.
His offering soon propitious fire from heaven
Consumed, with nimble glance and grateful steam ;
The other's not, for his was not sincere :
Whereat he inly raged, and, as they talked,
Smote him into the midriff with a stone
That beat out life ; he fell, and, deadly pale,
Groaned out his soul, with gushing blood effused.
Much at that sight was Adam in his heart
Dismayed, and thus in haste to the Angel cried :—
   "O Teacher, some great mischief hath befallen
To that meek man, who well had sacrificed :
Is piety thus and pure devotion paid ?"
   To whom Michael thus, he also moved, replied :—
"These two are brethren, Adam, and to come
Out of thy loins.   The unjust the just hath slain,
For envy that his brother's offering found
From Heaven acceptance ; but the bloody fact
Will be avenged, and the other's faith approved
Lose no reward, though here thou see him die,
Rolling in dust and gore."   To which our Sire :—
   "Alas, both for the deed and for the cause !
But have I now seen Death ?   Is this the way

I must return to native dust ?   O sight
Of terror, foul and ugly to behold !
Horrid to think, how horrible to feel !"
    To whom thus Michael :—" Death thou hast seen
In his first shape on Man ; but many shapes
Of Death, and many are the ways that lead
To his grim cave—all dismal, yet to sense
More terrible at the entrance than within.
Some, as thou saw'st, by violent stroke shall die,
By fire, flood, famine ; by intemperance more
In meats and drinks, which on the Earth shall bring
Diseases dire, of which a monstrous crew
Before thee shall appear, that thou may'st know
What misery the inabstinence of Eve
Shall bring on men."   Immediately a place
Before his eyes appeared, sad, noisome, dark ;
A lazar-house it seemed, wherein were laid
Numbers of all diseased—all maladies
Of ghastly spasm, or racking torture, qualms
Of heart-sick agony, all feverous kinds,
Convulsions, epilepsies, fierce catarrhs,
Intestine stone and ulcer, colic pangs,
Demoniac phrenzy, moping melancholy,
And moonstruck madness, pining atrophy,
Marasmus, and wide wasting pestilence,
Dropsies and asthmas, and joint-racking rheums.
Dire was the tossing, deep the groans ; Despair
Tended the sick, busiest from couch to couch ;
And over them triumphant Death his dart
Shook, but delayed to strike, though oft invoked
With vows, as their chief good and final hope.
Sight so deform what heart of rock could long
Dry-eyed behold ?   Adam could not, but wept,
Though not of woman born : compassion quelled
His best of man, and gave him up to tears
A space, till firmer thoughts restrained excess,
And, scarce recovering words, his plaint renewed :—
    " O miserable Mankind, to what fall
Degraded, to what wretched state reserved !
Better end here unborn.   Why is life given
To be thus wrested from us ? rather why
Obtruded on us thus ? who, if we knew
What we receive, would either not accept
Life offered, or soon beg to lay it down,
Glad to be so dismissed in peace.   Can thus
The image of God in Man, created once
So goodly and erect, though faulty since,
To such unsightly sufferings be debased
Under inhuman pains ?   Why should not Man,
Retaining still divine similitude
In part, from such deformities be free,
And for his Maker's image' sake exempt ?"
    " Their Maker's image," answered Michael, " then
Forsook them, when themselves they vilified

M.—O   193

To serve ungoverned Appetite, and took
His image whom they served—a brutish vice,
Inductive mainly to the sin of Eve.
Therefore so abject is their punishment,
Disfiguring not God's likeness, but their own ;
Or, if His likeness, by themselves defaced
While they pervert pure Nature's healthful rules
To loathsome sickness—worthily, since they
God's image did not reverence in themselves."
  " I yield it just," said Adam, "and submit.
But is there yet no other way, besides
These painful passages, how we may come
To death, and mix with our connatural dust ?"
  "There is," said Michael, "if thou well observe
The rule of *Not too much*, by temperance taught
In what thou eat'st and drink'st, seeking from thence
Due nourishment, not gluttonous delight,
Till many years over thy head return.
So may'st thou live, till, like ripe fruit, thou drop
Into thy mother's lap, or be with ease
Gathered, not harshly plucked, for death mature.
This is old age ; but then thou must outlive
Thy youth, thy strength, thy beauty, which will change
To withered, weak, and grey ; thy senses then,
Obtuse, all taste of pleasure must forego
To what thou hast ; and, for the air of youth,
Hopeful and cheerful, in thy blood will reign
A melancholy damp of cold and dry,
To weigh thy spirits down, and last consume
The balm of life."   To whom our Ancestor :—
  "Henceforth I fly not death, nor would prolong
Life much—bent rather how I may be quit,
Fairest and easiest, of this cumbrous charge,
Which I must keep till my appointed day
Of rendering up, and patiently attend
My dissolution." Michaël replied :—
  "Nor love thy life, nor hate ; but what thou liv'st
Live well ; how long or short permit to Heaven.
And now prepare thee for another sight."
  He looked, and saw a spacious plain, whereon
Were tents of various hue : by some were herds
Of cattle grazing : others whence the sound
Of instruments that made melodious chime
Was heard, of harp and organ, and who moved
Their stops and chords was seen : his volant touch
Instinct through all proportions low and high
Fled and pursued transverse the resonant fugue.
In other part stood one who, at the forge
Labouring, two massy clods of iron and brass
Had melted (whether found where casual fire
Had wasted woods, on mountain or in vale,
Down to the veins of earth, thence gliding hot
To some cave's mouth, or whether washed by stream
From underground) ; the liquid ore he drained

194

Into fit moulds prepared ; from which he formed
First his own tools, then what might else be wrought
Fusil or graven in metal.   After these,
But on the hither side, a different sort
From the high neighbouring hills, which was their seat,
Down to the plain descended : by their guise
Just men they seemed, and all their study bent
To worship God aright, and know His works
Not hid ; nor those things last which might preserve
Freedom and peace to men.   They on the plain
Long had not walked when from the tents behold
A bevy of fair women, richly gay
In gems and wanton dress ! to the harp they sung
Soft amorous ditties, and in dance came on.
The men, though grave, eyed them, and let their eyes
Rove without rein, till, in the amorous net
Fast caught, they liked, and each his liking chose.
And now of love they treat, till the evening-star,
Love's harbinger, appeared ; then, all in heat,
They light the nuptial torch, and bid invoke
Hymen, then first to marriage rites invoked :
With feast and music all the tents resound.
Such happy interview, and fair event
Of love and youth not lost, songs, garlands, flowers,
And charming symphonies, attached the heart
Of Adam, soon inclined to admit delight,
The bent of Nature ; which he thus expressed :—
"True opener of mine eyes, prime Angel blest,
Much better seems this vision, and more hope
Of peaceful days portends, than those two past :
Those were of hate and death, or pain much worse ;
Here Nature seems fulfilled in all her ends."
    To whom thus Michael :—"Judge not what is best
By pleasure, though to Nature seeming meet,
Created, as thou art, to nobler end,
Holy and pure, conformity divine.
Those tents thou saw'st so pleasant were the tents
Of wickedness, wherein shall dwell his race
Who slew his brother : studious they appear
Of arts that polish life, inventors rare ;
Unmindful of their Maker, though His Spirit
Taught them ; but they His gifts acknowledged none.
Yet they a beauteous offspring shall beget ;
For that fair female troop thou saw'st, that seemed
Of goddesses, so blithe, so smooth, so gay,
Yet empty of all good wherein consists
Woman's domestic honour and chief praise ;
Bred only and completed to the taste
Of lustful appetence, to sing, to dance,
To dress, and troll the tongue, and roll the eye ;—
To these that sober race of men, whose lives
Religious titled them the Sons of God,
Shall yield up all their virtue, all their fame,
Ignobly, to the trains and to the smiles

Of these fair atheists, and now swim in joy
(Erelong to swim at large) and laugh ; for which
The world erelong a world of tears must weep."
   To whom thus Adam, of short joy bereft :—
"O pity and shame, that they who to live well
Entered so fair should turn aside to tread
Paths indirect, or in the midway faint !
But still I see the tenor of Man's woe
Holds on the same, from Woman to begin."
   "From Man's effeminate slackness it begins,"
Said the Angel, "who should better hold his place
By wisdom, and superior gifts received.
But now prepare thee for another scene."
   He looked, and saw wide territory spread
Before him—towns, and rural works between,
Cities of men with lofty gates and towers,
Concourse in arms, fierce faces threatening war,
Giants of mighty bone and bold emprise.
Part wield their arms, part curb the foaming steed,
Single or in array of battle ranged
Both horse and foot, nor idly mustering stood.
One way a band select from forage drives
A herd of beeves, fair oxen and fair kine,
From a fat meadow-ground, or fleecy flock,
Ewes and their bleating lambs, over the plain,
Their booty ; scarce with life the shepherds fly,
But call in aid, which makes a bloody fray :
With cruel tournament the squadrons join ;
Where cattle pastured late, now scattered lies
With carcases and arms the ensanguined field
Deserted.   Others to a city strong
Lay siege, encamped, by battery, scale, and mine,
Assaulting ; others from the wall defend
With dart and javelin, stones and sulphurous fire ;
On each hand slaughter and gigantic deeds.
In other part the sceptred haralds call
To council in the city-gates : anon
Grey-headed men and grave, with warriors mixed,
Assemble, and harangues are heard ; but soon
In factious opposition, till at last
Of middle age one rising, eminent
In wise deport, spake much of right and wrong,
Of justice, of religion, truth, and peace,
And judgment from above : him old and young
Exploded, and had seized with violent hands,
Had not a cloud descending snatched him thence,
Unseen amid the throng.   So violence
Proceeded, and oppression, and sword-law,
Through all the plain, and refuge none was found.
Adam was all in tears, and to his guide
Lamenting turned full sad :—"Oh, what are these ?
Death's ministers, not men ! who thus deal death
Inhumanly to men, and multiply
Ten thousandfold the sin of him who slew

His brother ; for of whom such massacre
Make they but of their brethren, men of men ?
But who was that just man, whom had not Heaven
Rescued, had in his righteousness been lost ? "
　　To whom thus Michael :—" These are the product
Of those ill-mated marriages thou saw'st,
Where good with bad were matched ; who of themselves
Abhor to join, and, by imprudence mixed,
Produce prodigious births of body or mind.
Such were these Giants, men of high renown ;
For in those days might only shall be admired,
And valour and heroic virtue called.
To overcome in battle, and subdue
Nations, and bring home spoils with infinite
Manslaughter, shall be held the highest pitch
Of human glory, and, for glory done,
Of triumph to be styled great conquerors,
Patrons of mankind, gods, and sons of gods—
Destroyers rightlier called, and plagues of men.
Thus fame shall be achieved, renown on earth,
And what most merits fame in silence hid.
But he, the seventh from thee, whom thou beheld'st
The only righteous in a world perverse,
And therefore hated, therefore so beset
With foes, for daring single to be just,
And utter odious truth, that God would come
To judge them with His Saints—Him the Most High,
Rapt in a balmy cloud, with winged steeds,
Did, as thou saw'st, receive, to walk with God
High in salvation and the climes of bliss,
Exempt from death, to show thee what reward
Awaits the good, the rest what punishment ;
Which now direct thine eyes and soon behold."
　　He looked, and saw the face of things quite changed.
The brazen throat of war had ceased to roar ;
All now was turned to jollity and game,
To luxury and riot, feast and dance,
Marrying or prostituting, as befell,
Rape or adultery, where passing fair
Allured them ; thence from cups to civil broils.
At length a reverend sire among them came,
And of their doings great dislike declared,
And testified against their ways. He oft
Frequented their assemblies, whereso met,
Triumphs or festivals, and to them preached
Conversion and repentance, as to souls
In prison, under judgments imminent ;
But all in vain. Which, when he saw, he ceased
Contending, and removed his tents far off ;
Then, from the mountain hewing timber tall,
Began to build a vessel of huge bulk,
Measured by cubit, length, and breadth, and highth,
Smeared round with pitch, and in the side a door
Contrived, and of provisions laid in large

For man and beast: when lo! a wonder strange!
Of every beast, and bird, and insect small,
Came sevens and pairs, and entered in, as taught
Their order; last, the sire and his three sons,
With their four wives; and God made fast the door.
Meanwhile the South-wind rose, and, with black wings
Wide-hovering, all the clouds together drove
From under heaven; the hills to their supply
Vapour, and exhalation dusk and moist,
Sent up amain; and now the thickened sky
Like a dark ceiling stood: down rushed the rain
Impetuous, and continued till the earth
No more was seen. The floating vessel swum
Uplifted, and secure with beaked prow
Rode tilting o'er the waves; all dwellings else
Flood overwhelmed, and them with all their pomp
Deep under water rolled; sea covered sea,
Sea without shore: and in their palaces,
Where luxury late reigned, sea-monsters whelped
And stabled: of mankind, so numerous late,
All left in one small bottom swum embarked.
How didst thou grieve then, Adam, to behold
The end of all thy offspring, end so sad,
Depopulation! Thee another flood,
Of tears and sorrow a flood thee also drowned,
And sunk thee as thy sons; till, gently reared
By the Angel, on thy feet thou stood'st at last,
Though comfortless, as when a father mourns
His children, all in view destroyed at once,
And scarce to the Angel utter'dst thus thy plaint:—
  "O visions ill foreseen! Better had I
Lived ignorant of future—so had borne
My part of evil only, each day's lot
Enough to bear. Those now that were dispensed
The burden of many ages on me light
At once, by my foreknowledge gaining birth
Abortive, to torment me, ere their being,
With thought that they must be. Let no man seek
Henceforth to be foretold what shall befall
Him or his children—evil, he may be sure,
Which neither his foreknowing can prevent,
And he the future evil shall no less
In apprehension than in substance feel
Grievous to bear. But that care now is past;
Man is not whom to warn; those few escaped
Famine and anguish will at last consume,
Wandering that watery desert. I had hope,
When violence was ceased and war on Earth,
All would have then gone well, peace would have crowned
With length of happy days the race of Man;
But I was far deceived, for now I see
Peace to corrupt no less than war to waste.
How comes it thus? Unfold, Celestial Guide,
And whether here the race of Man will end."

To whom thus Michael:—"Those whom last thou saw'st
In triumph and luxurious wealth are they
First seen in acts of prowess eminent
And great exploits, but of true virtue void;
Who, having spilt much blood, and done much waste,
Subduing nations, and achieved thereby
Fame in the world, high titles, and rich prey,
Shall change their course to pleasure, ease, and sloth,
Surfeit, and lust, till wantonness and pride
Raise out of friendship hostile deeds in peace.
The conquered, also, and enslaved by war,
Shall, with their freedom lost, all virtue lose,
And fear of God—from whom their piety feigned
In sharp contest of battle found no aid
Against invaders; therefore, cooled in zeal,
Thenceforth shall practise how to live secure,
Worldly or dissolute, on what their lords
Shall leave them to enjoy; for the Earth shall bear
More than enough, that temperance may be tried.
So all shall turn degenerate, all depraved,
Justice and temperance, truth and faith, forgot;
One man except, the only son of light
In a dark age, against example good,
Against allurement, custom, and a world
Offended.   Fearless of reproach and scorn,
Or violence, he of their wicked ways
Shall them admonish, and before them set
The paths of righteousness, how much more safe
And full of peace, denouncing wrath to come
On their impenitence, and shall return
Of them derided, but of God observed
The one just man alive: by his command
Shall build a wondrous ark, as thou beheld'st,
To save himself and household from amidst
A world devote to universal wrack.
No sooner he, with them of man and beast
Select for life, shall in the ark be lodged
And sheltered round, but all the cataracts
Of Heaven set open on the Earth shall pour
Rain day and night; all fountains of the deep,
Broke up, shall heave the ocean to usurp
Beyond all bounds, till inundation rise
Above the highest hills.   Then shall this Mount
Of Paradise by might of waves be moved
Out of his place, pushed by the horned flood,
With all his verdure spoiled, and trees adrift,
Down the great river to the opening Gulf,
And there take root, an island salt and bare,
The haunt of seals, and orcs, and sea-mews' clang—
To teach thee that God attributes to place
No sanctity, if none be thither brought
By men who there frequent or therein dwell.
And now what further shall ensue behold."
   He looked, and saw the ark hull on the flood,

Which now abated; for the clouds were fled,
Driven by a keen North-wind, that, blowing dry,
Wrinkled the face of deluge, as decayed;
And the clear sun on his wide watery glass
Gazed hot, and of the fresh wave largely drew,
As after thirst; which made their flowing shrink
From standing lake to tripping ebb, that stole
With soft foot towards the deep, who now had stopt
His sluices, as the heaven his windows shut.
The ark no more now floats, but seems on ground,
Fast on the top of some high mountain fixed.
And now the tops of hills as rocks appear;
With clamour thence the rapid currents drive
Towards the retreating sea their furious tide.
Forthwith from out the ark a raven flies,
And, after him, the surer messenger,
A dove, sent forth once and again to spy
Green tree or ground whereon his foot may light;
The second time returning, in his bill
An olive-leaf he brings, pacific sign.
Anon dry ground appears, and from his ark
The ancient sire descends, with all his train;
Then, with uplifted hands and eyes devout,
Grateful to Heaven, over his head beholds
A dewy cloud, and in the cloud a bow
Conspicuous with three listed colours gay,
Betokening peace from God, and covenant new.
Whereat the heart of Adam, erst so sad,
Greatly rejoiced; and thus his joy broke forth:—
  "O thou, who future things canst represent
As present, Heavenly Instructor, I revive
At this last sight, assured that Man shall live,
With all the creatures, and their seed preserve.
Far less I now lament for one whole world
Of wicked sons destroyed than I rejoice
For one man found so perfect and so just
That God vouchsafes to raise another world
From him, and all his anger to forget.
But say, what mean those coloured streaks in Heaven:
Distended as the brow of God appeased?
Or serve they as a flowery verge to bind
The fluid skirts of that same watery cloud,
Lest it again dissolve and shower the Earth?"
  To whom the Archangel:—"Dextrously thou aim'st.
So willingly doth God remit His ire:
Though late repenting Him of Man depraved,
Grieved at His heart, when, looking down, He saw
The whole Earth filled with violence, and all flesh
Corrupting each their way; yet, those removed,
Such grace shall one just man find in His sight
That He relents, not to blot out mankind,
And makes a covenant never to destroy
The Earth again by flood, nor let the sea
Surpass His bounds, nor rain to drown the world

200

With man therein or beast; but, when He brings
Over the Earth a cloud, will therein set
His triple-coloured bow, whereon to look
And call to mind His covenant.   Day and night,
Seed-time and harvest, heat and hoary frost,
Shall hold their course, till fire purge all things new,
Both Heaven and Earth, wherein the just shall dwell.

THE END OF THE ELEVENTH BOOK.

PARADISE LOST.

BOOK XII.

THE ARGUMENT.

The Angel Michael continues, from the Flood, to relate what shall succeed; then, in the mention of Abraham, comes by degrees to explain who that Seed of the Woman shall be which was promised Adam and Eve in the Fall: His incarnation, death, resurrection, and ascension ; the state of the Church till His second coming. Adam, greatly satisfied and recomforted by these relations and promises, descends the hill with Michael ; wakens Eve, who all this while had slept, but with gentle dreams composed to quietness of mind and submission. Michael in either hand leads them out of Paradise, the fiery sword waving behind them, and the Cherubim taking their stations to guard the place.

As one who, in his journey, bates at noon,
Though bent on speed, so here the Archangel paused
Betwixt the world destroyed and world restored,
If Adam aught perhaps might interpose;
Then, with transition sweet, new speech resumes:—
"Thus thou hast seen one world begin and end,
And Man as from a second stock proceed.
Much thou hast yet to see; but I perceive
Thy mortal sight to fail; objects divine
Must needs impair and weary human sense.
Henceforth what is to come I will relate;
Thou, therefore, give due audience, and attend.
"This second source of men, while yet but few,
And while the dread of judgment past remains
Fresh in their minds, fearing the Deity,
With some regard to what is just and right
Shall lead their lives and multiply apace,
Labouring the soil, and reaping plenteous crop,
Corn, wine, and oil; and, from the herd or flock
Oft sacrificing bullock, lamb, or kid,
With large wine-offerings poured, and sacred feast,
Shall spend their days in joy unblamed, and dwell
Long time in peace, by families and tribes,
Under paternal rule, till one shall rise,
Of proud, ambitious heart, who, not content
With fair equality, fraternal state,
Will arrogate dominion undeserved
Over his brethren, and quite dispossess

Concord and law of Nature from the Earth—
Hunting (and men, not beasts, shall be his game)
With war and hostile snare such as refuse
Subjection to his empire tyrannous.
A mighty hunter thence he shall be styled
Before the Lord, as in despite of Heaven,
Or from Heaven claiming second sovranty,
And from rebellion shall derive his name,
Though of rebellion others he accuse.
He, with a crew, whom like ambition joins
With him or under him to tyrannize,
Marching from Eden towards the west, shall find
The plain, wherein a black bituminous gurge
Boils out from under ground, the mouth of Hell.
Of brick, and of that stuff, they cast to build
A city and tower, whose top may reach to Heaven;
And get themselves a name, lest, far dispersed
In foreign lands, their memory be lost—
Regardless whether good or evil fame.
But God, who oft descends to visit men
Unseen, and through their habitations walks,
To mark their doings, them beholding soon,
Comes down to see their city, ere the tower
Obstruct Heaven-towers, and in derision sets
Upon their tongues a various spirit, to rase
Quite out their native language, and, instead,
To sow a jangling noise of words unknown.
Forthwith a hideous gabble rises loud
Among the builders; each to other calls,
Not understood—till, hoarse and all in rage,
As mocked they storm. Great laughter was in Heaven,
And looking down to see the hubbub strange
And hear the din. Thus was the building left
Ridiculous, and the work *Confusion* named."
    Whereto thus Adam, fatherly displeased :—
"O execrable son, so to aspire
Above his brethren, to himself assuming
Authority usurped, from God not given!
He gave us only over beast, fish, fowl,
Dominion absolute; that right we hold
By His donation: but man over men
He made not lord—such title to Himself
Reserving, human left from human free.
But this usurper his encroachment proud
Stays not on Man; to God his tower intends
Siege and defiance. Wretched man! what food
Will he convey up thither, to sustain
Himself and his rash army, where thin air
Above the clouds will pine his entrails gross,
And famish him of breath, if not of bread?"
    To whom thus Michael :—"Justly thou abhorr'st
That son, who on the quiet state of men
Such trouble brought, affecting to subdue
Rational liberty; yet know withal,

Since thy original lapse, true liberty
Is lost, which always with right reason dwells
Twinned, and from her hath no dividual being.
Reason in Man obscured, or not obeyed,
Immediately inordinate desires
And upstart passions catch the government
From Reason, and to servitude reduce
Man, till then free. Therefore, since he permits
Within himself unworthy powers to reign
Over free reason, God, in judgment just,
Subjects him from without to violent lords,
Who oft as undeservedly enthral
His outward freedom. Tyranny must be,
Though to the tyrant thereby no excuse.
Yet sometimes nations will decline so low
From virtue, which is reason, that no wrong,
But justice and some fatal curse annexed,
Deprives them of their outward liberty,
Their inward lost: witness the irreverent son
Of him who built the ark, who, for the shame
Done to his father, heard this heavy curse,
Servant of servants, on his vicious race.
Thus will this latter, as the former world,
Still tend from bad to worse, till God at last,
Wearied with their iniquities, withdraw
His presence from among them, and avert
His holy eyes, resolving from thenceforth
To leave them to their own polluted ways,
And one peculiar nation to select
From all the rest, of whom to be invoked—
A nation from one faithful man to spring.
Him on this side Euphrates yet residing,
Bred up in idol-worship—Oh, that men
(Canst thou believe?) should be so stupid grown,
While yet the patriarch lived who 'scaped the Flood,
As to forsake the living God, and fall
To worship their own work in wood and stone
For gods!—yet him God the Most High vouchsafes
To call by vision from his father's house,
His kindred, and false gods, into a land
Which he will show him, and from him will raise
A mighty nation, and upon him shower
His benediction so that in his seed
All nations shall be blest. He straight obeys;
Not knowing to what land, yet firm believes.
I see him, but thou canst not, with what faith
He leaves his gods, his friends, and native soil,
Ur of Chaldæa, passing now the ford
To Haran—after him a cumbrous train
Of herds and flocks, and numerous servitude—
Not wandering poor, but trusting all his wealth
With God, who called him, in a land unknown.
Canaan he now attains; I see his tents
Pitched about Sechem, and the neighbouring plain

Of Moreh.   There, by promise, he receives
Gift to his progeny of all that land,
From Hamath northward to the Desert south
(Things by their names I call, though yet unnamed),
From Hermon east to the great western sea;
Mount Hermon, yonder sea, each place behold
In prospect, as I point them: on the shore,
Mount Carmel; here, the double-founted stream,
Jordan, true limit eastward; but his sons
Shall dwell to Senir, that long ridge of hills.
This ponder, that all nations of the Earth
Shall in his seed be blessed.   By that seed
Is meant thy great Deliverer, who shall bruise
The Serpent's head; whereof to thee anon
Plainlier shall be revealed.   This patriarch blest,
Whom *faithful Abraham* due time shall call,
A son, and of his son a grandchild, leaves,
Like him in faith, in wisdom, and renown.
The grandchild, with twelve sons increased, departs
From Canaan to a land hereafter called
Egypt, divided by the river Nile;
See where it flows, disgorging at seven mouths
Into the sea.   To sojourn in that land
He comes, invited by a younger son
In time of dearth—a son whose worthy deeds
Raise him to be the second in that realm
Of Pharaoh.   There he dies, and leaves his race
Growing into a nation, and now grown
Suspected to a sequent king, who seeks
To stop their overgrowth, as inmate guests
Too numerous; whence of guests he makes them slaves
Inhospitably, and kills their infant males:
Till, by two brethren (those two brethren call
Moses and Aaron) sent from God to claim
His people from enthralment, they return,
With glory and spoil, back to their promised land.
But first the lawless tyrant, who denies
To know their God, or message to regard,
Must be compelled by signs and judgments dire:
To blood unshed the rivers must be turned;
Frogs, lice, and flies must all his palace fill
With loathed intrusion, and fill all the land;
His cattle must of rot and murrain die;
Botches and blains must all his flesh emboss,
And all his people; thunder mixed with hail,
Hail mixed with fire, must rend the Egyptian sky,
And wheel on the earth, devouring where it rolls;
What it devours not, herb, or fruit, or grain,
A darksome cloud of locusts swarming down
Must eat, and on the ground leave nothing green;
Darkness must overshadow all his bounds,
Palpable darkness, and blot out three days;
Last, with one midnight-stroke, all the first-born
Of Egypt must lie dead.   Thus with ten wounds

The river-dragon tamed at length submits
To let his sojourners depart, and oft
Humbles his stubborn heart, but still as ice
More hardened after thaw; till, in his rage
Pursuing whom he late dismissed, the sea
Swallows him with his host, but them lets pass,
As on dry land, between two crystal walls,
Awed by the rod of Moses so to stand
Divided till his rescued gain their shore :
Such wondrous power God to his Saint will lend,
Though present in His Angel, who shall go
Before them in a cloud, and pillar of fire—
By day a cloud, by night a pillar of fire—
To guide them in their journey, and remove
Behind them, while the obdurate king pursues.
All night he will pursue, but his approach
Darkness defends between till morning-watch;
Then through the fiery pillar and the cloud
God looking forth will trouble all His host,
And craze their chariot-wheels : when, by command,
Moses once more his potent rod extends
Over the sea; the sea his rod obeys;
On their embattled ranks the waves return,
And overwhelm their war. The race elect
Safe towards Canaan, from the shore, advance
Through the wild Desert—not the readiest way,
Lest, entering on the Canaanite alarmed,
War terrify them inexpert, and fear
Return them back to Egypt, choosing rather
Inglorious life with servitude; for life
To noble and ignoble is more sweet
Untrained in arms, where rashness leads not on.
This also shall they gain by their delay
In the wide wilderness : there they shall found
Their government, and their great Senate choose
Through the twelve tribes, to rule by laws ordained.
God, from the Mount of Sinai, whose grey top
Shall tremble, He descending, will Himself,
In thunder, lightning, and loud trumpet's sound,
Ordain them laws—part, such as appertain
To civil justice; part, religious rites
Of sacrifice, informing them, by types
And shadows, of that destined Seed to bruise
The Serpent, by what means he shall achieve
Mankind's deliverance. But the voice of God
To mortal ear is dreadful : they beseech
That Moses might report to them His will,
And terror cease; he grants what they besought,
Instructed that to God is no access
Without Mediator, whose high office now
Moses in figure bears, to introduce
One greater, of whose day he shall foretell,
And all the Prophets, in their age, the times
Of great Messiah shall sing. Thus laws and rites

Established, such delight hath God in men
Obedient to His will that He vouchsafes
Among them to set up His tabernacle—
The Holy One with mortal men to dwell.
By His prescript a sanctuary is framed
Of cedar, overlaid with gold; therein
An ark, and in the ark His testimony,
The records of His covenant; over these
A mercy-seat of gold, between the wings
Of two bright Cherubim; before Him burn
Seven lamps, as in a zodiac representing
The heavenly fires.   Over the tent a cloud
Shall rest by day, a fiery gleam by night,
Save when they journey; and at length they come,
Conducted by His Angel, to the land
Promised to Abraham and his seed.   The rest
Were long to tell—how many battles fought;
How many kings destroyed, and kingdoms won;
Or how the sun shall in mid-heaven stand still
A day entire, and night's due course adjourn,
Man's voice commanding, 'Sun, in Gibeon stand,
And, thou, Moon, in the vale of Aialon,
Till *Israel* overcome!'—so call the third
From Abraham, son of Isaac, and from him
His whole descent, who thus shall Canaan win."

     Here Adam interposed :—"O sent from Heaven,
Enlightener of my darkness, gracious things
Thou hast revealed, those chiefly which concern
Just Abraham and his seed.   Now first I find
Mine eyes true opening, and my heart much eased,
Erewhile perplexed with thoughts what would become
Of me and all mankind; but now I see
His day, in whom all nations shall be blest—
Favour unmerited by me, who sought
Forbidden knowledge by forbidden means.
This yet I apprehend not—why to those
Among whom God will deign to dwell on Earth
So many and so various laws are given.
So many laws argue so many sins
Among them; how can God with such reside?"

     To whom thus Michael :—"Doubt not but that sin
Will reign among them, as of thee begot;
And therefore was law given them, to evince
Their natural pravity, by stirring up
Sin against Law to fight, that, when they see
Law can discover sin, but not remove,
Save by those shadowy expiations weak,
The blood of bulls and goats, they may conclude
Some blood more precious must be paid for Man,
Just for unjust, that in such righteousness,
To them by faith imputed, they may find
Justification towards God, and peace
Of conscience, which the law by ceremonies
Cannot appease, nor man the moral part

Perform, and not performing cannot live.
So Law appears imperfect, and but given
With purpose to resign them, in full time,
Up to a better covenant, disciplined
From shadowy types to truth, from flesh to spirit,
From imposition of strict laws to free
Acceptance of large grace, from servile fear
To filial, works of law to works of faith.
And therefore shall not Moses, though of God
Highly beloved, being but the minister
Of Law, his people into Canaan lead;
But Joshua, whom the Gentiles Jesus call,
His name and office bearing who shall quell
The adversary Serpent, and bring back
Through the world's wilderness long-wandered Man
Safe to eternal Paradise of rest.
Meanwhile they, in their earthly Canaan placed,
Long time shall dwell and prosper, but when sins
National interrupt their public peace,
Provoking God to raise them enemies—
From whom as oft He saves them penitent,
By Judges first, then under Kings; of whom
The second, both for piety renowned
And puissant deeds, a promise shall receive
Irrevocable, that his regal throne
For ever shall endure. The like shall sing
All Prophecy—that of the royal stock
Of David (so I name this king) shall rise
A son, the Woman's Seed to thee foretold,
Foretold to Abraham as in whom shall trust
All nations, and to kings foretold of kings
The last, for of His reign shall be no end.
But first a long succession must ensue;
And his next son, for wealth and wisdom famed,
The clouded ark of God, till then in tents
Wandering, shall in a glorious temple enshrine.
Such follow him as shall be registered
Part good, part bad; of bad the longer scroll:
Whose foul idolatries and other faults,
Heaped to the popular sum, will so incense
God, as to leave them, and expose their land,
Their city, His temple, and His holy ark,
With all His sacred things, a scorn and prey
To that proud city whose high walls thou saw'st
Left in confusion, Babylon thence called.
There in captivity He lets them dwell
The space of seventy years; then brings them back,
Remembering mercy, and His covenant sworn
To David, stablished as the days of Heaven.
Returned from Babylon by leave of kings,
Their lords, whom God disposed, the house of God
They first re-edify, and for a while
In mean estate live moderate, till, grown
In wealth and multitude, factious they grow.

But first among the priests dissension springs—
Men who attend the altar, and should most
Endeavour peace: their strife pollution brings
Upon the temple itself; at last they seize
The sceptre, and regard not David's sons;
Then lose it to a stranger, that the true
Anointed King Messiah might be born
Barred of His right. Yet at His birth a star,
Unseen before in heaven, proclaims Him come,
And guides the eastern sages, who inquire
His place, to offer incense, myrrh, and gold:
His place of birth a solemn Angel tells
To simple shepherds, keeping watch by night;
They gladly thither haste, and by a quire
Of squadroned Angels hear His carol sung.
A Virgin is His mother, but His Sire
The Power of the Most High. He shall ascend
The throne hereditary, and bound His reign
With Earth's wide bounds, His glory with the Heavens."
    He ceased, discerning Adam with such joy
Surcharged as had, like grief, been dewed in tears,
Without the vent of words; which these He breathed:—
    "O prophet of glad tidings, finisher
Of utmost hope! now clear I understand
What oft my steadiest thoughts have searched in vain—
Why our great Expectation should be called
The Seed of Woman. Virgin Mother, hail!
High in the love of Heaven, yet from my loins
Thou shalt proceed, and from thy womb the Son
Of God Most High; so God with Man unites.
Needs must the Serpent now his capital bruise
Expect with mortal pain. Say where and when
Their fight, what stroke shall bruise the Victor's heel."
    To whom thus Michael:—"Dream not of their fight
As of a duel, or the local wounds
Of head or heel. Not therefore joins the Son
Manhood to Godhead, with more strength to foil
Thy enemy; nor so is overcome
Satan, whose fall from Heaven, a deadlier bruise,
Disabled not to give thee thy death's wound;
Which He who comes thy Saviour shall recure,
Not by destroying Satan, but his works
In thee and in thy seed. Nor can this be,
But by fulfilling that which thou didst want,
Obedience to the law of God, imposed
On penalty of death, and suffering death,
The penalty to thy transgression due,
And due to theirs which out of thine will grow:
So only can high justice rest appaid.
The Law of God exact He shall fulfil
Both by obedience and by love, though love
Alone fulfil the Law; thy punishment
He shall endure, by coming in the flesh
To a reproachful life and cursed death,

M.—P

Proclaiming life to all who shall believe
In His redemption, and that His obedience
Imputed becomes theirs by faith—His merits
To save them, not their own, though legal, works.
For this He shall live hated, be blasphemed,
Seized on by force, judged, and to death condemned
A shameful and accursed, nailed to the cross
By His own nation, slain for bringing life;
But to the cross He nails thy enemies—
The Law that is against thee, and the sins
Of all mankind, with Him there crucified,
Never to hurt them more who rightly trust
In this His satisfaction. So He dies,
But soon revives; Death over Him no power
Shall long usurp. Ere the third dawning light
Return, the stars of morn shall see Him rise
Out of His grave, fresh as the dawning light,
Thy ransom paid, which Man from Death redeems—
His death for Man, as many as offered life
Neglect not, and the benefit embrace
By faith not void of works. This godlike act
Annuls thy doom, the death thou shouldst have died,
In sin for ever lost from life; this act
Shall bruise the head of Satan, crush his strength,
Defeating Sin and Death, his two main arms,
And fix far deeper in his head their stings
Than temporal death shall bruise the Victor's heel,
Or theirs whom He redeems—a death like sleep,
A gentle wafting to immortal life.
Nor after resurrection shall He stay
Longer on Earth than certain times to appear
To His disciples—men who in His life
Still followed Him; to them shall leave in charge
To teach all nations what of Him they learned
And His salvation, them who shall believe
Baptizing in the profluent stream—the sign
Of washing them from guilt of sin to life
Pure, and in mind prepared, if so befall,
For death like that which the Redeemer died.
All nations they shall teach; for from that day
Not only to the sons of Abraham's loins
Salvation shall be preached, but to the sons
Of Abraham's faith wherever through the world;
So in His seed all nations shall be blest.
Then to the Heaven of Heavens He shall ascend
With victory, triumphing through the air
Over His foes and thine ; there shall surprise
The Serpent, Prince of Air, and drag in chains
Through all his realm, and there confounded leave;
Then enter into glory, and resume
His seat at God's right hand, exalted high
Above all names in Heaven ; and thence shall come,
When this World's dissolution shall be ripe,
With glory and power, to judge both quick and dead—

To judge the unfaithful dead, but to reward
His faithful, and receive them into bliss,
Whether in Heaven or Earth; for then the Earth
Shall be all Paradise, far happier place
Than this of Eden, and far happier days."
　So spake the Archangel Michael; then paused,
As at the World's great period; and our Sire,
Replete with joy and wonder, thus replied:—
　"O Goodness infinite, Goodness immense,
That all this good of evil shall produce,
And evil turn to good—more wonderful
Than that which by creation first brought forth
Light out of darkness! Full of doubt I stand,
Whether I should repent me now of sin
By me done and occasioned, or rejoice
Much more that much more good thereof shall spring—
To God more glory, more good-will to men
From God—and over wrath grace shall abound.
But say, if our Deliverer up to Heaven
Must reascend, what will betide the few,
His faithful, left among the unfaithful herd,
The enemies of Truth. Who then shall guide
His people, who defend? Will they not deal
Worse with His followers than with Him they dealt"?
　"Be sure they will," said the Angel; "but from Heaven
He to His own a Comforter will send,
The promise of the Father, who shall dwell,
His Spirit, within them, and the law of faith
Working through love upon their hearts shall write,
To guide them in all Truth, and also arm
With spiritual armour, able to resist
Satan's assaults, and quench his fiery darts—
What man can do against them not afraid,
Though to the death; against such cruelties
With inward consolations recompensed,
And oft supported so as shall amaze
Their proudest persecutors. For the Spirit,
Poured first on His Apostles, whom He sends
To evangelize the nations, then on all
Baptized, shall them with wondrous gifts endue
To speak all tongues, and do all miracles,
As did their Lord before them. Thus they win
Great numbers of each nation to receive
With joy the tidings brought from Heaven: at length,
Their ministry performed, and race well run,
Their doctrine and their story written left,
They die; but in their room, as they forewarn,
Wolves shall succeed for teachers, grievous wolves,
Who all the sacred mysteries of Heaven
To their own vile advantages shall turn
Of lucre and ambition, and the truth
With superstitions and traditions taint,
Left only in those written records pure,
Though not but by the Spirit understood.

211

Then shall they seek to avail themselves of names,
Places, and titles, and with these to join
Secular power, though feigning still to act
By spiritual; to themselves appropriating
The Spirit of God, promised alike and given
To all believers; and, from that pretence,
Spiritual laws by carnal power shall force
On every conscience—laws which none shall find
Left them enrolled, or what the Spirit within
Shall on the heart engrave.   What will they then
But force the Spirit of Grace itself, and bind
His consort, Liberty? what but unbuild
His living temples, built by faith to stand—
Their own faith, not another's? for, on Earth,
Who against faith and conscience can be heard
Infallible? Yet many will presume:
Whence heavy persecution shall arise
On all who in the worship persevere
Of Spirit and Truth; the rest, far greater part,
Will deem in outward rites and specious forms
Religion satisfied; Truth shall retire
Bestuck with slanderous darts, and works of Faith
Rarely be found.   So shall the World go on,
To good malignant, to bad men benign,
Under her own weight groaning, till the day
Appear of respiration to the just
And vengeance to the wicked, at return
Of Him so lately promised to thy aid,
The Woman's Seed—obscurely then foretold,
Now amplier known thy Saviour and thy Lord;
Last in the clouds from Heaven to be revealed
In glory of the Father, to dissolve
Satan with his perverted World; then raise
From the conflagrant mass, purged and refined,
New Heavens, new Earth, Ages of endless date
Founded in righteousness and peace and love,
To bring forth fruits, joy and eternal bliss."
    He ended; and thus Adam last replied:—
"How soon hath thy prediction, Seer blest,
Measured this transient World, the race of Time,
Till Time stand fixed!   Beyond is all abyss—
Eternity, whose end no eye can reach.
Greatly instructed I shall hence depart,
Greatly in peace of thought, and have my fill
Of knowledge, what this vessel can contain;
Beyond which was my folly to aspire.
Henceforth I learn that to obey is best,
And love with fear the only God, to walk
As in His presence, ever to observe
His providence, and on Him sole depend,
Merciful over all His works, with good
Still overcoming evil, and by small
Accomplishing great things—by things deemed weak
Subverting worldly-strong, and worldly-wise

By simply meek; that suffering for Truth's sake
Is fortitude to highest victory,
And to the faithful death the gate of life—
Taught this by His example whom I now
Acknowledge my Redeemer ever blest."
 To whom thus also the Angel last replied :—
"This having learned, thou hast attained the sum
Of wisdom; hope no higher, though all the stars
Thou knew'st by name, and all the ethereal powers,
All secrets of the Deep, all Nature's works,
Or works of God in heaven, air, earth, or sea,
And all the riches of this world enjoy'dst,
And all the rule, one empire. Only add
Deeds to thy knowledge answerable; add faith;
Add virtue, patience, temperance; add love,
By name to come called Charity, the soul
Of all the rest : then wilt thou not be loth
To leave this Paradise, but shalt possess
A Paradise within thee, happier far.
Let us descend now, therefore, from this top
Of speculation ; for the hour precise
Exacts our parting hence ; and, see ! the guards,
By me encamped on yonder hill, expect
Their motion, at whose front a flaming sword,
In signal of remove, waves fiercely round.
We may no longer stay. Go, waken Eve ;
Her also I with gentle dreams have calmed,
Portending good, and all her spirits composed
To meek submission : thou, at season fit,
Let her with thee partake what thou hast heard—
Chiefly what may concern her faith to know,
The great deliverance by her seed to come
(For by the Woman's Seed) on all mankind—
That ye may live, which will be many days,
Both in one faith unanimous ; though sad
With cause for evils past, yet much more cheered
With meditation on the happy end."
 He ended, and they both descend the hill.
Descended, Adam to the bower where Eve
Lay sleeping ran before, but found her waked ;
And thus with words not sad she him received :—
 "Whence thou return'st and whither went'st I know ;
For God is also in sleep, and dreams advise,
Which He hath sent propitious, some great good
Presaging, since, with sorrow and heart's distress
Wearied, I fell asleep. But now lead on ;
In me is no delay ; with thee to go
Is to stay here ; without thee here to stay
Is to go hence unwilling ; thou to me
Art all things under Heaven, all places thou,
Who for my wilful crime art banished hence.
This further consolation yet secure
I carry hence : though all by me is lost,
Such favour I unworthy am vouchsafed,

By me the Promised Seed shall all restore."
  So spake our mother Eve ; and Adam heard
Well pleased, but answered not ; for now too nigh
The Archangel stood, and from the other hill
To their fixed station, all in bright array,
The Cherubim descended, on the ground
Gliding meteorous, as evening mist
Risen from a river o'er the marish glides,
And gathers ground fast at the labourer's heel
Homeward returning. High in front advanced,
The brandished sword of God before them blazed,
Fierce as a comet ; which as with torrid heat,
And vapour as the Libyan air adust,
Began to parch that temperate clime ; whereat
In either hand the hastening Angel caught
Our lingering parents, and to the eastern gate
Led them direct, and down the cliff as fast
To the subjected plain—then disappeared.
They, looking back, all the eastern side beheld
Of Paradise, so late their happy seat,
Waved over by that flaming brand ; the gate
With dreadful faces thronged and fiery arms.
Some natural tears they dropped, but wiped them soon ;
The world was all before them, where to choose
Their place of rest, and Providence their guide.
They, hand in hand, with wandering steps and slow,
Through Eden took their solitary way.

THE END.

PARADISE REGAINED:

A POEM IN FOUR BOOKS.

THE AUTHOR
JOHN MILTON.

PARADISE REGAINED.

THE FIRST BOOK.

I, WHO erewhile the happy Garden sung
By one man's disobedience lost, now sing
Recovered Paradise to all mankind,
By one man's firm obedience fully tried
Through all temptation, and the Tempter foiled
In all his wiles, defeated and repulsed,
And Eden raised in the waste Wilderness.
  Thou Spirit, who led'st this glorious Eremite
Into the desert, His victorious field
Against the spiritual foe, and brought'st Him thence
By proof the undoubted Son of God, inspire,
As thou art wont, my prompted song, else mute,
And bear through highth or depth of Nature's bounds,
With prosperous wing full summed, to tell of deeds
Above heroic, though in secret done,
And unrecorded left through many an age:
Worthy to have not remained so long unsung.
  Now had the great Proclaimer, with a voice
More awful than the sound of trumpet, cried
Repentance, and Heaven's kingdom nigh at hand
To all baptized.   To his great baptism flocked
With awe the regions round, and with them came
From Nazareth the Son of Joseph deemed
To the flood Jordan—came as then obscure,
Unmarked, unknown.   But Him the Baptist soon
Descried, divinely warned, and witness bore
As to his worthier, and would have resigned
To Him his heavenly office.   Nor was long
His witness unconfirmed: on Him baptized
Heaven opened, and in likeness of a dove
The Spirit descended, while the Father's voice
From Heaven pronounced Him His beloved Son.
That heard the Adversary, who, roving still
About the world, at that assembly famed
Would not be last, and, with the voice divine
Nigh thunder-struck, the exalted Man to whom
Such high attest was given a while surveyed
With wonder; then, with envy fraught and rage,
Flies to his place, nor rests, but in mid air
To council summons all his mighty peers,

Within thick clouds and dark tenfold involved,
A gloomy consistory; and then amidst,
With looks aghast and sad, he thus bespake :—
    "O ancient Powers of Air and this wide World
(For much more willingly I mention Air,
This our old conquest, than remember Hell,
Our hated habitation), well ye know
How many ages, as the years of men,
This Universe we have possessed, and ruled
In manner at our will the affairs of Earth,
Since Adam and his facile consort Eve
Lost Paradise, deceived by me, though since
With dread attending when that fatal wound
Shall be inflicted by the Seed of Eve
Upon my head.   Long the decrees of Heaven
Delay, for longest time to Him is short;
And now, too soon for us, the circling hours
This dreaded time have compassed, wherein we
Must bide the stroke of that long-threatened wound
(At least, if so we can, and by the head
Broken be not intended all our power
To be infringed, our freedom and our being
In this fair empire won of Earth and Air)—
For this ill news I bring :   The Woman's Seed,
Destined to this, is late of woman born.
His birth to our just fear gave no small cause;
But His growth now to youth's full flower, displaying
All virtue, grace and wisdom to achieve
Things highest, greatest, multiplies my fear.
Before Him a great Prophet, to proclaim
His coming, is sent harbinger, who all
Invites, and in the consecrated stream
Pretends to wash off sin, and fit them so
Purified to receive Him pure, or rather
To do Him honour as their King.   All come,
And He Himself among them was baptized—
Not thence to be more pure, but to receive
The testimony of Heaven, that who He is
Thenceforth the nations may not doubt.   I saw
The Prophet do Him reverence ; on Him, rising
Out of the water, Heaven above the clouds
Unfold her crystal doors; thence on His head
A perfect dove descend (whate'er it meant);
And out of Heaven the sovran voice I heard,
'This is My Son beloved,—in Him am pleased.'
His mother, then, is mortal, but His Sire
He who obtains the monarchy of Heaven;
And what will He not do to advance His Son?
His first-begot we know, and sore have felt,
When His fierce thunder drove us to the Deep;
Who this is we must learn, for Man He seems
In all His lineaments, though in His face
The glimpses of His Father's glory shine.
Ye see our danger on the utmost edge

Of hazard, which admits no long debate,
But must with something sudden be opposed—
(Not force, but well-couched fraud, well-woven snares),
Ere in the head of nations He appear,
Their King, their Leader, and supreme on Earth.
I, when no other durst, sole undertook
The dismal expedition to find out
And ruin Adam, and the exploit performed
Successfully: a calmer voyage now
Will waft me; and the way found prosperous once
Induces best to hope of like success."
  He ended, and his words impression left
Of much amazement to the infernal crew,
Distracted and surprised with deep dismay
At these sad tidings. But no time was then
For long indulgence to their fears or grief :
Unanimous they all commit the care
And management of this main enterprise
To him, their great Dictator, whose attempt
At first against mankind so well had thrived
In Adam's overthrow, and led their march
From Hell's deep-vaulted den to dwell in light,
Regents, and potentates, and kings, yea gods,
Of many a pleasant realm and province wide.
So to the coast of Jordan he directs
His easy steps, girded with snaky wiles,
Where he might likeliest find this new-declared,
This Man of men, attested Son of God,
Temptation and all guile on Him to try—
So to subvert whom he suspected raised
To end his reign on Earth so long enjoyed :
But, contrary, unweeting he fulfilled
The purposed counsel, pre-ordained and fixed,
Of the Most High, who, in full frequence bright
Of Angels, thus to Gabriel smiling spake :—
  " Gabriel, this day, by proof, thou shalt behold,
Thou and all Angels conversant on Earth
With Man or men's affairs, how I begin
To verify that solemn message late,
On which I sent thee to the Virgin pure
In Galilee, that she should bear a Son,
Great in renown, and called the Son of God.
Then told'st her, doubting how these things could be
To her a virgin, that on her should come
The Holy Ghost, and the power of the Highest
O'ershadow her. This Man, born and now upgrown,
To show Him worthy of His birth divine
And high prediction, henceforth I expose
To Satan ; let him tempt, and now assay
His utmost subtlety, because he boasts
And vaunts of his great cunning to the throng
Of his apostasy. He might have learnt
Less overweening, since he failed in Job,
Whose constant perseverance overcame

Whate'er his cruel malice could invent.
He now shall know I can produce a man,
Of female seed, far abler to resist
All his solicitations, and at length
All his vast force, and drive him back to Hell—
Winning by conquest what the first man lost
By fallacy surprised.   But first I mean
To exercise Him in the Wilderness;
There He shall first lay down the rudiments
Of His great warfare, ere I send Him forth
To conquer Sin and Death, the two grand foes.
By humiliation and strong sufferance
His weakness shall o'ercome Satanic strength,
And all the world, and mass of sinful flesh;
That all the Angels and ethereal Powers—
They now, and men hereafter—may discern
From what consummate virtue I have chose
This perfect Man, by merit called My Son,
To earn salvation for the sons of men."
    So spake the Eternal Father, and all Heaven
Admiring stood a space; then into hymns
Burst forth, and in celestial measures moved,
Circling the throne and singing, while the hand
Sung with the voice, and this the argument:—
    "Victory and triumph to the Son of God,
Now entering His great duel, not of arms,
But to vanquish by wisdom hellish wiles!
The Father knows the Son; therefore secure
Ventures His filial virtue, though untried,
Against whate'er may tempt, whate'er seduce,
Allure, or terrify, or undermine.
Be frustrate, all ye stratagems of Hell,
And, devilish machinations, come to nought!"
    So they in Heaven their odes and vigils tuned.
Meanwhile the Son of God, who yet some days
Lodged in Bethabara, where John baptized,
Musing and much revolving in His breast
How best the mighty work He might begin
Of Saviour to mankind, and which way first
Publish His godlike office now mature,
One day forth walked alone, the Spirit leading
And His deep thoughts, the better to converse
With solitude, till, far from track of men,
Thought following thought, and step by step led on,
He entered now the bordering Desert wild,
And, with dark shades and rocks environed round,
His holy meditations thus pursued:—
    "O what a multitude of thoughts at once
Awakened in Me swarm, while I consider
What from within I feel Myself, and hear
What from without comes often to My ears,
Ill sorting with My present state compared!
When I was yet a child, no childish play
To Me was pleasing; all My mind was set

Serious to learn and know, and thence to do,
What might be public good ; Myself I thought
Born to that end, born to promote all truth,
All righteous things.   Therefore, above My years,
The Law of God I read, and found it sweet ;
Made it My whole delight, and in it grew
To such perfection that, ere yet My age
Had measured twice six years, at our great Feast
I went into the Temple, there to hear
The teachers of our Law, and to propose
What might improve My knowledge or their own,
And was admired by all.   Yet this not all
To which My spirit aspired.   Victorious deeds
Flamed in My heart, heroic acts—one while
To rescue Israel from the Roman yoke ;
Then to subdue and quell, o'er all the earth,
Brute violence and proud tyrannic power,
Till truth were freed, and equity restored :
Yet held it more humane, more heavenly, first
By winning words to conquer willing hearts,
And make persuasion do the work of fear ;
At least to try, and teach the erring soul,
Not wilfully misdoing, but unware
Misled ; the stubborn only to subdue.
These growing thoughts My mother soon perceiving,
By words at times cast forth, inly rejoiced,
And said to Me apart, 'High are Thy thoughts,
O Son! but nourish them, and let them soar
To what highth sacred virtue and true worth
Can raise them, though above example high ;
By matchless deeds express Thy matchless Sire.
For know, Thou art no son of mortal man ;
Though men esteem Thee low of parentage,
Thy Father is the Eternal King who rules
All Heaven and Earth, Angels and sons of men.
A messenger from God foretold Thy birth
Conceived in me a virgin ; he foretold
Thou shouldst be great, and sit on David's throne,
And of Thy kingdom there should be no end.
At Thy nativity a glorious quire
Of Angels, in the fields of Bethlehem, sung
To shepherds, watching at their folds by night
And told them the Messiah now was born,
Where they might see Him ; and to Thee they came,
Directed to the manger where Thou lay'st ;
For in the inn was left no better room.
A star, not seen before, in heaven appearing,
Guided the wise men thither from the East,
To honour Thee with incense, myrrh, and gold ;
By whose bright course led on they found the place,
Affirming it Thy star, new-graven in heaven,
By which they knew Thee King of Israel born.
Just Simeon and prophetic Anna, warned
By vision, found Thee in the Temple, and spake,

Before the altar and the vested priest,
Like things of Thee to all that present stood.'
This having heard, straight I again revolved
The Law and Prophets, searching what was writ
Concerning the Messiah, to our scribes
Known partly, and soon found of whom they spake
I am—this chiefly, that My way must lie
Through many a hard assay, even to the death,
Ere I the promised Kingdom can attain,
Or work redemption for mankind, whose sins'
Full weight must be transferred upon My head.
Yet, neither thus disheartened or dismayed,
The time prefixed I waited; when behold
The Baptist (of whose birth I oft had heard,
Not knew by sight) now come, who was to come
Before Messiah, and His way prepare!
I, as all others, to his baptism came,
Which I believed was from above; but he
Straight knew Me, and with loudest voice proclaimed
Me Him (for it was shown him so from heaven)—
Me Him whose harbinger he was; and first
Refused on Me his baptism to confer,
As much his greater, and was hardly won.
But, as I rose out of the laving stream,
Heaven opened her eternal doors, from whence
The Spirit descended on Me like a dove;
And last, the sum of all, My Father's voice,
Audibly heard from Heaven, pronounced Me His,
Me His beloved Son, in whom alone
He was well pleased: by which I knew the time
Now full, that I no more should live obscure,
But openly begin, as best becomes
The authority which I derived from Heaven.
And now by some strong motion I am led
Into this wilderness; to what intent
I learn not yet. Perhaps I need not know;
For what concerns My knowledge God reveals."

So spake our Morning Star, then in His rise,
And, looking round, on every side beheld
A pathless desert, dusk with horrid shades.
The way He came, not having marked return,
Was difficult, by human steps untrod;
And He still on was led, but with such thoughts
Accompanied of things past and to come
Lodged in His breast as well might recommend
Such solitude before choicest society.

Full forty days He passed—whether on hill
Sometimes, anon in shady vale, each night
Under the covert of some ancient oak
Or cedar to defend Him from the dew,
Or harboured in one cave, is not revealed;
Nor tasted human food, nor hunger felt,
Till those days ended; hungered then at last
Among wild beasts. They at His sight grew mild,

Nor sleeping Him nor waking harmed ; His walk
The fiery serpent fled and noxious worm ;
The lion and fierce tiger glared aloof.
But now an aged man in rural weeds,
Following, as seemed, the quest of some stray ewe,
Or withered sticks to gather, which might serve
Against a winter's day, when winds blow keen,
To warm him wet returned from field at eve,
He saw approach ; who first with curious eye
Perused Him, then with words thus uttered spake :—
"Sir, what ill chance hath brought Thee to this place,
So far from path or road of men, who pass
In troop or caravan ? for single none
Durst ever, who returned, and dropt not here
His carcass, pined with hunger and with droughth.
I ask the rather, and the more admire,
For that to me Thou seem'st the man whom late
Our new baptizing Prophet at the ford
Of Jordan honoured so, and called Thee Son
Of God. I saw and heard, for we sometimes
Who dwell this wild, constrained by want, come forth
To town or village nigh (nighest is far),
Where aught we hear, and curious are to hear,
What happens new ; fame also finds us out."
To whom the Son of God :—"Who brought Me hither
Will bring Me hence ; no other guide I seek."
"By miracle He may," replied the swain ;
"What other way I see not ; for we here
Live on tough roots and stubs, to thirst inured
More than the camel, and to drink go far—
Men to much misery and hardship born.
But, if Thou be the Son of God, command
That out of these hard stones be made Thee bread ;
So shalt Thou save Thyself, and us relieve
With food, whereof we wretched seldom taste."
He ended, and the Son of God replied :—
"Think'st thou such force in bread ? Is it not written
(For I discern thee other than thou seem'st),
Man lives not by bread only, but each word
Proceeding from the mouth of God, who fed
Our fathers here with manna ? In the Mount
Moses was forty days, nor eat nor drank ;
And forty days Eliah without food
Wandered this barren waste ; the same I now.
Why dost thou, then, suggest to me distrust,
Knowing who I am, as I know who *thou* art ?"
Whom thus answered the Arch-Fiend, now undisguised :—
"'T is true, I am that Spirit unfortunate
Who, leagued with millions more in rash revolt,
Kept not my happy station, but was driven
With them from bliss to the bottomless Deep—
Yet to that hideous place not so confined
By rigour unconniving but that oft,
Leaving my dolorous prison, I enjoy

Large liberty to round this globe of Earth,
Or range in the Air ; nor from the Heaven of Heavens
Hath He excluded my resort sometimes.
I came, among the Sons of God, when He
Gave up into my hands Uzzean Job,
To prove him, and illustrate his high worth ;
And, when to all His Angels He proposed
To draw the proud king Ahab into fraud,
That he might fall in Ramoth, they demurring,
I undertook that office, and the tongues
Of all his flattering prophets glibbed with lies
To his destruction, as I had in charge :
For what He bids I do. Though I have lost
Much lustre of my native brightness, lost
To be beloved of God, I have not lost
To love, at least contemplate and admire,
What I see excellent in good, or fair,
Or virtuous ; I should so have lost all sense.
What can be then less in me than desire
To see Thee and approach Thee, whom I know
Declared the Son of God, to hear attent
Thy wisdom, and behold Thy godlike deeds ?
Men generally think me much a foe
To all mankind. Why should I ? they to me
Never did wrong or violence. By them
I lost not what I lost ; rather by them
I gained what I have gained, and with them dwell
Co-partner in these regions of the World,
If not disposer—lend them oft my aid,
Oft my advice by presages and signs,
And answers, oracles, portents, and dreams,
Whereby they may direct their future life.
Envy, they say, excites me, thus to gain
Companions of my misery and woe !
At first it may be ; but, long since with woe
Nearer acquainted, now I feel by proof
That fellowship in pain divides not smart,
Nor lightens aught each man's peculiar load ;
Small consolation, then, were Man adjoined.
This wounds me most (what can it less ?) that Man,
Man fallen, shall be restored, I never more."
  To whom our Saviour sternly thus replied :—
" Deservedly thou griev'st, composed of lies
From the beginning, and in lies wilt end,
Who boast'st release from Hell, and leave to come
Into the Heaven of Heavens. Thou com'st, indeed
As a poor miserable captive thrall
Comes to the place where he before had sat
Among the prime in splendour, now deposed,
Ejected, emptied, gazed, unpitied, shunned,
A spectacle of ruin, or of scorn,
To all the host of Heaven. The happy place
Imparts to thee no happiness, no joy—
Rather inflames thy torment, representing

Lost bliss, to thee no more communicable ;
So never more in Hell than when in Heaven.
But thou art serviceable to Heaven's King !
Wilt thou impute to obedience what thy fear
Extorts, or pleasure to do ill excites ?
What but thy malice moved thee to misdeem
Of righteous Job, then cruelly to afflict him
With all inflictions ? but his patience won.
The other service was thy chosen task,
To be a liar in four hundred mouths ;
For lying is thy sustenance, thy food.
Yet thou pretend'st to truth ! all oracles
By thee are given, and what confessed more true
Among the nations ?   That hath been thy craft,
By mixing somewhat true to vent more lies.
But what have been thy answers ? what but dark,
Ambiguous, and with double sense deluding,
Which they who asked have seldom understood,
And, not well understood, as good not known ?
Who ever, by consulting at thy shrine,
Returned the wiser, or the more instruct
To fly or follow what concerned him most,
And run not sooner to his fatal snare ?
For God hath justly given the nations up
To thy delusions ; justly, since they fell
Idolatrous,   But, when His purpose is
Among them to declare His providence,
To thee not known, whence hast thou then thy truth,
But from Him, or His Angels president
In every province, who, themselves disdaining
To approach thy temples, give thee in command
What, to the smallest tittle, thou shalt say
To thy adorers ?   Thou, with trembling fear,
Or like a fawning parasite, obey'st ;
Then to thyself ascrib'st the truth foretold.
But this thy glory shall be soon retrenched ;
No more shalt thou by oracling abuse
The Gentiles ; henceforth oracles are ceased,
And thou no more with pomp and sacrifice
Shalt be inquired at Delphos or elsewhere—
At least in vain, for they shall find thee mute.
God hath now sent His living Oracle
Into the world to teach His final will,
And sends His Spirit of Truth henceforth to dwell
In pious hearts, an inward oracle
To all truth requisite for men to know."
  So spake our Saviour ; but the subtle Fiend,
Though inly stung with anger and disdain,
Dissembled, and this answer smooth returned :—
  "Sharply Thou hast insisted on rebuke,
And urged me hard with doings which not will,
But misery, hath wrested from me.   Where
Easily canst Thou find one miserable,
And not enforced oft-times to part from truth,

If it may stand him more in stead to lie,
Say and unsay, feign, flatter, or abjure?
But Thou art placed above me ; Thou art Lord ;
From Thee I can, and must, submiss, endure
Check or reproof, and glad to 'scape so quit.
Hard are the ways of truth, and rough to walk,
Smooth on the tongue discoursed, pleasing to the ear,
And tunable as sylvan pipe or song ;
What wonder, then, if I delight to hear
Her dictates from Thy mouth ? most men admire
Virtue who follow not her lore.   Permit me
To hear Thee when I come (since no man comes),
And talk at least, though I despair to attain.
Thy Father, who is holy, wise, and pure,
Suffers the hypocrite or atheous priest
To tread His sacred courts, and minister
About His altar, handling holy things,
Praying or vowing, and vouchsafed His voice
To Balaam reprobate, a prophet yet
Inspired : disdain not such access to me."
    To whom our Saviour, with unaltered brow :—
"Thy coming hither, though I know thy scope,
I bid not, or forbid.   Do as thou find'st
Permission from above ; thou canst not more."
    He added not ; and Satan, bowing low
His gray dissimulation, disappeared,
Into thin air diffused : for now began
Night with her sullen wing to double-shade
The desert ; fowls in their clay nests were couched ;
And now wild beasts came forth the woods to roam.

THE END OF THE FIRST BOOK.

PARADISE REGAINED.

THE SECOND BOOK.

MEANWHILE the new-baptized, who yet remained
At Jordan with the Baptist, and had seen
Him whom they heard so late expressly called
Jesus Messiah, Son of God, declared,
And on that high authority had believed,
And with Him talked, and with Him lodged—I mean
Andrew and Simon, famous after known,
With others, though in Holy Writ not named—
Now missing Him, their joy so lately found,
So lately found and so abruptly gone,
Began to doubt, and doubted many days,
And, as the days increased, increased their doubt.
Sometimes they thought He might be only shown,
And for a time caught up to God, as once
Moses was in the Mount and missing long,
And the great Tishbite, who on fiery wheels
Rode up to Heaven, yet once again to come.
Therefore, as those young prophets then with care
Sought lost Eliah, so in each place these
Nigh to Bethabara—in Jericho
The city of palms, Ænon, and Salem old,
Machærus, and each town or city walled
On this side the broad lake Genezaret,
Or in Peræa—but returned in vain.
Then on the bank of Jordan, by a creek,
Where winds with reeds and osiers whispering play,
Plain fishermen (no greater men them call),
Close in a cottage low together got,
Their unexpected loss and plaints outbreathed :—
    "Alas, from what high hope to what relapse
Unlooked for are we fallen ! Our eyes beheld
Messiah certainly now come, so long
Expected of our fathers ; we have heard
His words, His wisdom full of grace and truth.
'Now, now, for sure, deliverance is at hand ;
The kingdom shall to Israel be restored ' :
Thus we rejoiced, but soon our joy is turned
Into perplexity and new amaze.
For whither is He gone ? what accident
Hath rapt Him from us ? will He now retire
After appearance, and again prolong

Our expectation? God of Israel,
Send Thy Messiah forth ; the time is come.
Behold the kings of the earth, how they oppress
Thy Chosen, to what highth their power unjust
They have exalted, and behind them cast
All fear of Thee ; arise, and vindicate
Thy glory ; free Thy people from their yoke !
But let us wait ; thus far He hath performed—
Sent His Anointed, and to us revealed Him,
By His great Prophet pointed at and shown
In public, and with Him we have conversed.
Let us be glad of this, and all our fears
Lay on His providence ; He will not fail,
Nor will withdraw Him now, nor will recall—
Mock us with His blest sight, then snatch Him hence :
Soon we shall see our hope, our joy, return."
    Thus they out of their plaints new hope resume
To find whom at the first they found unsought.
But to His mother Mary, when she saw
Others returned from baptism, not her Son,
Nor left at Jordan tidings of Him none,
Within her breast though calm, her breast though pure,
Motherly cares and fears got head, and raised
Some troubled thoughts, which she in sighs thus clad :—
    "Oh, what avails me now that honour high,
To have conceived of God, or that salute,
'Hail, highly favoured, among women blest !'
While I to sorrows am no less advanced,
And fears as eminent above the lot
Of other women, by the birth I bore :
In such a season born, when scarce a shed
Could be obtained to shelter Him or me
From the bleak air ! A stable was our warmth,
A manger His ; yet soon enforced to fly
Thence into Egypt, till the murderous king
Were dead, who sought His life, and, missing, filled
With infant blood the streets of Bethlehem.
From Egypt home returned, in Nazareth
Hath been our dwelling many years ; His life
Private, unactive, calm, contemplative,
Little suspicious to any king. But now,
Full grown to man, acknowledged, as I hear,
By John the Baptist, and in public shown,
Son owned from Heaven by His Father's voice,
I looked for some great change. To honour ? no ;
But trouble, as old Simeon plain foretold,
That to the fall and rising He should be
Of many in Israel, and to a sign
Spoken against—that through my very soul
A sword shall pierce. This is my favoured lot,
My exaltation to afflictions high !
Afflicted I may be, it seems, and blest !
I will not argue that, nor will repine.
But where delays He now ? Some great intent

228

Conceals Him. When twelve years He scarce had seen,
I lost Him, but so found as well I saw
He could not lose Himself, but went about
His Father's business. What He meant I mused—
Since understand ; much more His absence now
Thus long to some great purpose He obscures.
But I to wait with patience am inured ;
My heart hath been a storehouse long of things
And sayings laid up, portending strange events."
    Thus Mary, pondering oft, and oft to mind
Recalling what remarkably had passed
Since first her salutation heard, with thoughts
Meekly composed awaited the fulfilling :
The while her Son, tracing the desert wild,
Sole, but with holiest meditations fed,
Into Himself descended, and at once
All His great work to come before Him set—
How to begin, how to accomplish best
His end of being on Earth, and mission high.
For Satan, with sly preface to return,
Had left Him vacant, and with speed was gone
Up to the middle region of thick air,
Where all his Potentates in council sat.
There, without sign of boast, or sign of joy,
Solicitous and blank, he thus began :—
    " Princes, Heaven's ancient Sons, Ethereal Thrones—
Demonian Spirits now, from the element
Each of his reign allotted, rightlier called
Powers of Fire, Air, Water, and Earth beneath
(So may we hold our place and these mild seats
Without new trouble)—such an enemy
Is risen to invade us, who no less
Threatens than our expulsion down to Hell.
I, as I undertook, and with the vote
Consenting in full frequence was empowered,
Have found Him, viewed Him, tasted Him ; but find
Far other labour to be undergone
Than when I dealt with Adam, first of men,
Though Adam by his wife's allurement fell,
However to this Man inferior far—
If He be Man by mother's side, at least
With more than human gifts from Heaven adorned,
Perfections absolute, graces divine,
And amplitude of mind to greatest deeds.
Therefore I am returned, lest confidence
Of my success with Eve in Paradise
Deceive ye to persuasion over-sure
Of like succeeding here. I summon all
Rather to be in readiness with hand
Or counsel to assist, lest I, who erst
Thought none my equal, now be overmatched."
    So spake the old Serpent, doubting, and from all
With clamour was assured their utmost aid
At his command ; when from amidst them rose

229

Belial, the dissolutest Spirit that fell,
The sensualest, and, after Asmodai,
The fleshliest Incubus, and thus advised :—
  "Set women in His eye and in His walk,
Among daughters of men the fairest found.
Many are in each region passing fair
As the noon sky, more like to goddesses
Than mortal creatures, graceful and discreet,
Expert in amorous arts, enchanting tongues
Persuasive, virgin majesty with mild
And sweet allayed, yet terrible to approach,
Skilled to retire, and in retiring draw
Hearts after them tangled in amorous nets.
Such object hath the power to soften and tame
Severest temper, smooth the rugged'st brow,
Enerve, and with voluptuous hope dissolve,
Draw out with credulous desire, and lead
At will the manliest, resolutest breast,
As the magnetic hardest iron draws.
Women, when nothing else, beguiled the heart
Of wisest Solomon, and made him build,
And made him bow, to the gods of his wives."
  To whom quick answer Satan thus returned :—
"Belial, in much uneven scale thou weigh'st
All others by thyself.   Because of old
Thou thyself doat'st on womankind, admiring
Their shape, their colour, and attractive grace,
None are, thou think'st, but taken with such toys.
Before the Flood, thou, with thy lusty crew,
False titled Sons of God, roaming the Earth,
Cast wanton eyes on the daughters of men,
And coupled with them, and begot a race.
Have we not seen, or by relation heard,
In courts and regal chambers how thou lurk'st,
In wood or grove, by mossy fountain-side,
In valley or green meadow, to waylay
Some beauty rare, Calisto, Clymene,
Daphne, or Semele, Antiopa,
Or Amymone, Syrinx, many more
Too long—then lay'st thy scapes on names adored,
Apollo, Neptune, Jupiter, or Pan,
Satyr, or Faun, or Silvan?   But these haunts
Delight not all.   Among the sons of men
How many have with a smile made small account
Of beauty and her lures, easily scorned
All her assaults, on worthier things intent!
Remember that Pellean conqueror,
A youth, how all the beauties of the East
He slightly viewed, and slightly overpassed ;
How he surnamed of Africa dismissed,
In his prime youth, the fair Iberian maid.
For Solomon, he lived at ease, and, full
Of honour, wealth, high fare, aimed not beyond
Higher design than to enjoy his state ;

Thence to the bait of women lay exposed.
But He whom we attempt is wiser far
Than Solomon, of more exalted mind,
Made and set wholly on the accomplishment
Of greatest things.   What woman will you find,
Though of this age the wonder and the fame,
On whom His leisure will vouchsafe an eye
Of fond desire ?   Or should she, confident,
As sitting queen adored on Beauty's throne,
Descend with all her winning charms begirt
To enamour, as the zone of Venus once
Wrought that effect on Jove (so fables tell),
How would one look from his majestic brow,
Seated as on the top of Virtue's hill,
Discountenance her despised, and put to rout
All her array, her female pride deject,
Or turn to reverent awe!   For Beauty stands
In the admiration only of weak minds
Led captive; cease to admire, and all her plumes
Fall flat, and shrink into a trivial toy,
At every sudden slighting quite abashed.
Therefore with manlier objects we must try
His constancy—with such as have more show
Of worth, of honour, glory, and popular praise
(Rocks whereon greatest men have oftest wrecked);
Or that which only seems to satisfy
Lawful desires of nature, not beyond.
And now I know he hungers, where no food
Is to be found, in the wild Wilderness :
The rest commit to me; I shall let pass
No advantage, and his strength as oft assay."
   He ceased, and heard their grant in loud acclaim ;
Then forthwith to him takes a chosen band
Of Spirits likest to himself in guile,
To be at hand and at his beck appear.
If cause were to unfold some active scene
Of various persons, each to know his part ;
Then to the desert takes with these his flight,
Where still, from shade to shade, the Son of God,
After forty days' fasting, had remained,
Now hungering first, and to himself thus said :—
   "Where will this end ?   Four times ten days I have passed
Wandering this woody maze, and human food
Nor tasted, nor had appetite.   That fast
To virtue I impute not, or count part
Of what I suffer here.   If nature need not,
Or God support nature without repast,
Though needing, what praise is it to endure ?
But now I feel I hunger ; which declares
Nature hath need of what she asks.   Yet God
Can satisfy that need some other way,
Though hunger still remain.   So it remain
Without this body's wasting, I content Me,
And from the sting of famine fear no harm ;

Nor mind it, fed with better thoughts, that feed
Me hungering more to do My Father's will."
   It was the hour of night, when thus the Son
Communed in silent walk, then laid Him down
Under the hospitable covert nigh
Of trees thick interwoven.   There He slept,
And dreamed, as appetite is wont to dream,
Of meats and drinks, nature's refreshment sweet.
Him thought He by the brook of Cherith stood,
And saw the ravens with their horny beaks
Food to Elijah bringing even and morn—
Though ravenous, taught to abstain from what they brought;
He saw the Prophet also, how he fled
Into the desert, and how there he slept
Under a juniper—then how, awaked,
He found his supper on the coals prepared,
And by the Angel was bid rise and eat,
And eat the second time after repose,
The strength whereof sufficed him forty days:
Sometimes that with Elijah He partook,
Or as a guest with Daniel at his pulse.
Thus wore out night; and now the herald lark
Left his ground-nest, high towering to descry
The Morn's approach, and greet her with his song.
As lightly from His grassy couch up rose
Our Saviour, and found all was but a dream;
Fasting He went to sleep, and fasting waked.
Up to a hill anon His steps He reared,
From whose high top to ken the prospect round,
If cottage were in view, sheep-cote, or herd;
But cottage, herd, or sheep-cote, none He saw—
Only in a bottom saw a pleasant grove,
With chant of tuneful birds resounding loud.
Thither He bent His way, determined there
To rest at noon, and entered soon the shade
High-roofed, and walks beneath, and alleys brown,
That opened in the midst a woody scene;
Nature's own work it seemed (Nature taught Art),
And to a superstitious eye the haunt
Of wood-gods and wood-nymphs.   He viewed it round;
When suddenly a man before Him stood,
Not rustic as before, but seemlier clad,
As one in city or court, or palace bred,
And with fair speech these words to Him addressed :—
   "With granted leave officious I return,
But much more wonder that the Son of God
In this wild solitude so long should bide,
Of all things destitute, and, well I know,
Not without hunger.   Others of some note,
As story tells, have trod this wilderness :
The fugitive bond-woman, with her son,
Outcast Nebaioth, yet found here relief
By a providing Angel; all the race
Of Israel here had famished, had not God

232

Rained from heaven manna; and that Prophet bold,
Native of Thebez, wandering here, was fed
Twice by a voice inviting him to eat.
Of Thee these forty days none hath regard,
Forty and more deserted here indeed."
    To whom thus Jesus :—" What conclud'st thou hence?
They all had need; I, as Thou seest, have none."
    " How hast Thou hunger then?" Satan replied.
" Tell me, if food were now before Thee set,
Wouldst Thou not eat?" " Thereafter as I like
The giver," answered Jesus. " Why should that
Cause Thy refusal?" said the subtle Fiend.
" Hast Thou not right to all created things?
Owe not all creatures, by just right, to Thee
Duty and service, nor to stay till bid,
But tender all their power? Nor mention I
Meats by the law unclean, or offered first
To idols—those young Daniel could refuse;
Nor proffered by an enemy—though who
Would scruple that, with want oppressed? Behold,
Nature ashamed, or, better to express,
Troubled, that Thou shouldst hunger, hath purveyed
From all the elements her choicest store,
To treat Thee as beseems, and as her Lord
With honour. Only deign to sit and eat."
    He spake no dream; for, as his words had end,
Our Saviour, lifting up His eyes, beheld,
In ample space under the broadest shade,
A table richly spread in regal mode,
With dishes piled and meats of noblest sort
And savour—beasts of chase, or fowl of game,
In pastry built, or from the spit, or boiled,
Grisamber-steamed; all fish, from sea or shore,
Freshet or purling brook, of shell or fin,
And exquisitest name, for which was drained
Pontus, and Lucrine bay, and Afric coast.
Alas! how simple, to these cates compared,
Was that crude apple that diverted Eve!
And at a stately sideboard, by the wine,
That fragrant smell diffused, in order stood
Tall stripling youths rich-clad, of fairer hue
Than Ganymed or Hylas; distant more,
Under the trees now tripped, now solemn stood,
Nymphs of Diana's train, and Naiades
With fruits and flowers from Amalthea's horn,
And ladies of the Hesperides, that seemed
Fairer than feigned of old, or fabled since
Of faery damsels met in forest wide
By knights of Logres, or of Lyones,
Lancelot, or Pelleas, or Pellenore.
And all the while harmonious airs were heard
Of chiming strings or charming pipes; and winds
Of gentlest gale Arabian odours fanned
From their soft wings, and Flora's earliest smells.

233

Such was the splendour; and the Tempter now
His invitation earnestly renewed :—
  "What doubts the Son of God to sit and eat?
These are not fruits forbidden; no interdict
Defends the touching of these viands pure;
Their taste no knowledge works, at least of evil,
But life preserves, destroys life's enemy,
Hunger, with sweet restorative delight.
All these are Spirits of air, and woods, and springs,
Thy gentle ministers, who come to pay
Thee homage, and acknowledge Thee their Lord.
What doubt'st Thou, Son of God? Sit down and eat."
  To whom thus Jesus temperately replied :—
"Said'st thou not that to all things I had right?
And who withholds My power that right to use?
Shall I receive by gift what of My own,
When and where likes Me best, I can command?
I can at will, doubt not, as soon as thou,
Command a table in this wilderness,
And call swift flights of Angels ministrant,
Arrayed in glory, on My cup to attend:
Why shouldst thou, then, obtrude this diligence
In vain, where no acceptance it can find?
And with My hunger what hast thou to do?
Thy pompous delicacies I contemn,
And count thy specious gifts no gifts, but guiles."
  To whom thus answered Satan, malecontent :—
"That I have also power to give Thou seest;
If of that power I bring Thee voluntary
What I might have bestowed on whom I pleased,
And rather opportunely in this place
Chose to impart to Thy apparent need,
Why shouldst Thou not accept it? But I see
What I can do or offer is suspect.
Of these things others quickly will dispose,
Whose pains have earned the far-fet spoil."   With that
Both table and provision vanished quite,
With sound of harpies' wings and talons heard;
Only the importune Tempter still remained,
And with these words his temptation pursued :—
  "By hunger, that each other creature tames,
Thou art not to be harmed, therefore not moved;
Thy temperance, invincible besides,
For no allurement yields to appetite;
And all Thy heart is set on high designs,
High actions. But wherewith to be achieved?
Great acts require great means of enterprise;
Thou art unknown, unfriended, low of birth,
A carpenter Thy father known, Thyself
Bred up in poverty and straits at home,
Lost in a desert here and hunger-bit.
Which way, or from what hope, dost Thou aspire
To greatness? whence authority deriv'st?
What followers, what retinue canst Thou gain,

Or at Thy heels the dizzy multitude,
Longer than Thou canst feed them on Thy cost?
Money brings honour, friends, conquest, and realms.
What raised Antipater the Edomite,
And his son Herod placed on Judah's throne,
Thy throne, but gold, that got him puissant friends?
Therefore, if at great things Thou wouldst arrive,
Get riches first, get wealth, and treasure heap—
Not difficult, if Thou hearken to me.
Riches are mine, fortune is in my hand;
They whom I favour thrive in wealth amain,
While virtue, valour, wisdom, sit in want."
    To whom thus Jesus patiently replied:—
"Yet wealth without these three is impotent
To gain dominion, or to keep it gained—
Witness those ancient empires of the earth,
In highth of all their flowing wealth dissolved;
But men endued with these have oft attained,
In lowest poverty, to highest deeds—
Gideon, and Jephtha, and the shepherd lad
Whose offspring on the throne of Judah sat
So many ages, and shall yet regain
That seat, and reign in Israel without end.
Among the Heathen (for throughout the world
To Me is not unknown what hath been done
Worthy of memorial) canst thou not remember
Quintius, Fabricius, Curius, Regulus?
For I esteem those names of men so poor,
Who could do mighty things, and could contemn
Riches, though offered from the hand of kings.
And what in Me seems wanting but that I
May also in this poverty as soon
Accomplish what they did, perhaps. and more?
Extol not riches, then, the toil of fools,
The wise man's cumbrance, if not snare; more apt
To slacken virtue and abate her edge
Than prompt her to do aught may merit praise.
What if with like aversion I reject
Riches and realms! Yet not for that a crown,
Golden in show, is but a wreath of thorns,
Brings dangers, troubles, cares, and sleepless nights,
To him who wears the regal diadem,
When on his shoulders each man's burden lies;
For therein stands the office of a king,
His honour, virtue, merit, and chief praise,
That for the public all this weight he bears.
Yet he who reigns within himself, and rules
Passions, desires, and fears, is more a king—
Which every wise and virtuous man attains;
And who attains not ill aspires to rule
Cities of men, or headstrong multitudes,
Subject himself to anarchy within,
Or lawless passions in him, which he serves.
But to guide nations in the way of truth

By saving doctrine, and from error lead
To know, and, knowing, worship God aright,
Is yet more kingly. This attracts the soul,
Governs the inner man, the nobler part;
That other o'er the body only reigns,
And oft by force—which to a generous mind
So reigning can be no sincere delight.
Besides, to give a kingdom hath been thought
Greater and nobler done, and to lay down
Far more magnanimous, than to assume.
Riches are needless, then, both for themselves,
And for thy reason why they should be sought—
To gain a sceptre, oftest better missed."

THE END OF THE SECOND BOOK.

PARADISE REGAINED.

THE THIRD BOOK.

So spake the Son of God; and Satan stood
A while as mute, confounded what to say,
What to reply, confuted and convinced
Of his weak arguing and fallacious drift;
At length, collecting all his serpent wiles,
With soothing words renewed, Him thus accosts:—
"I see Thou know'st what is of use to know,
What best to say canst say, to do canst do;
Thy actions to Thy words accord; Thy words
To Thy large heart give utterance due; Thy heart
Contains of good, wise, just, the perfect shape.
Should kings and nations from Thy mouth consult,
Thy counsel would be as the oracle
Urim and Thummim, those oraculous gems
On Aaron's breast, or tongue of Seers old
Infallible; or, wert Thou sought to deeds
That might require the array of war, Thy skill
Of conduct would be such that all the world
Could not sustain Thy prowess, or subsist
In battle, though against Thy few in arms.
These godlike virtues wherefore dost Thou hide?
Affecting private life, or more obscure
In savage wilderness, wherefore deprive
All Earth her wonder at Thy acts, Thyself
The fame and glory—glory, the reward
That sole excites to high attempts the flame
Of most erected spirits, most tempered pure
Ethereal, who all pleasures else despise,
All treasures and all gain esteem as dross,
And dignities and powers, all but the highest?
Thy years are ripe and over-ripe.   The son
Of Macedonian Philip had ere these
Won Asia, and the throne of Cyrus held
At his dispose; young Scipio had brought down
The Carthaginian pride; young Pompey quelled
The Pontic king, and in triumph had rode.
Yet years, and to ripe years judgment mature,
Quench not the thirst of glory, but augment.
Great Julius, whom now all the world admires,
The more he grew in years, the more inflamed
With glory, wept that he had lived so long

237

Inglorious.   But Thou yet art not too late."
   To whom our Saviour calmly thus replied:—
"Thou neither dost persuade Me to seek wealth
For empire's sake, nor empire to affect
For glory's sake, by all thy argument.
For what is glory but the blaze of fame,
The people's praise, if always praise unmixed?
And what the people but a herd confused,
A miscellaneous rabble, who extol
Things vulgar, and, well weighed, scarce worth the praise?
They praise and they admire they know not what,
And know not whom, but as one leads the other;
And what delight to be by such extolled,
To live upon their tongues, and be their talk?
Of whom to be dispraised were no small praise—
His lot who dares be singularly good.
The intelligent among them and the wise
Are few, and glory scarce of few is raised.
This is true glory and renown—when God,
Looking on the Earth, with approbation marks
The just man, and divulges him through Heaven
To all His Angels, who with true applause
Recount his praises.   Thus He did to Job,
When, to extend his fame through Heaven and Earth,
As thou to thy reproach may'st well remember,
He asked thee, ' Hast thou seen My servant Job?'
Famous he was in Heaven; on Earth less known,
Where glory is false glory, attributed
To things not glorious, men not worthy of fame.
They err who count it glorious to subdue
By conquest far and wide, to overrun
Large countries, and in field great battles win,
Great cities by assault.   What do these worthies
But rob and spoil, burn, slaughter, and enslave
Peaceable nations, neighbouring or remote,
Made captive, yet deserving freedom more
Than those their conquerors, who leave behind
Nothing but ruin wheresoe'er they rove,
And all the flourishing works of peace destroy;
Then swell with pride, and must be titled Gods,
Great Benefactors of mankind, Deliverers,
Worshipped with temple, priest, and sacrifice?
One is the son of Jove, of Mars the other;
Till conqueror Death discover them scarce men,
Rolling in brutish vices, and deformed,
Violent or shameful death their due reward.
But, if there be in glory aught of good,
It may by means far different be attained,
Without ambition, war, or violence—
By deeds of peace, by wisdom eminent,
By patience, temperance.   I mention still
Him whom thy wrongs, with saintly patience borne,
Made famous in a land and times obscure;
Who names not now with honour patient Job?

Poor Socrates (who next more memorable?)
By what he taught and suffered for so doing,
For truth's sake suffering death unjust, lives now
Equal in fame to proudest conquerors.
Yet, if for fame and glory aught be done,
Aught suffered—if young African for fame
His wasted country freed from Punic rage—
The deed becomes unpraised, the man at least,
And loses, though but verbal, his reward.
Shall I seek glory, then, as vain men seek,
Oft not deserved?   I seek not Mine, but His
Who sent Me, and thereby witness whence I am."

   To whom the Tempter, murmuring, thus replied:—
"Think not so slight of glory, therein least
Resembling Thy great Father.   He seeks glory,
And for His glory all things made, all things
Orders and governs; nor content in Heaven,
By all His Angels glorified, requires
Glory from men, from all men, good or bad,
Wise or unwise, no difference, no exemption.
Above all sacrifice, or hallowed gift,
Glory He requires, and glory He receives,
Promiscuous from all nations, Jew, or Greek,
Or Barbarous, nor exception hath declared;
From us, His foes pronounced, glory He exacts."

   To whom our Saviour fervently replied:—
"And reason; since His Word all things produced,
Though chiefly not for glory as prime end,
But to show forth His goodness, and impart
His good communicable to every soul
Freely; of whom what could He less expect
Than glory and benediction—that is, thanks—
The slightest, easiest, readiest recompense
From them who could return Him nothing else,
And, not returning that, would likeliest render
Contempt instead, dishonour, obloquy?
Hard recompense, unsuitable return
For so much good, so much beneficence!
But why should man seek glory, who of his own
Hath nothing, and to whom nothing belongs
But condemnation, ignominy, and shame—
Who, for so many benefits received,
Turned recreant to God, ingrate and false,
And so of all true good himself despoiled;
Yet, sacrilegious, to himself would take
That which to God alone of right belongs?
Yet so much bounty is in God, such grace,
That who advance His glory, not their own,
Them He Himself to glory will advance."

   So spake the Son of God; and here again
Satan had not to answer, but stood struck
With guilt of his own sin—for he himself,
Insatiable of glory, had lost all;
Yet of another plea bethought him soon:—

" Of glory, as Thou wilt," said he, "so deem;
Worth or not worth the seeking, let it pass.
But to a Kingdom Thou art born—ordained
To sit upon Thy father David's throne,
By mother's side Thy father, though Thy right
Be now in powerful hands, that will not part
Easily from possession won with arms.
Judæa now and all the Promised Land,
Reduced a province under Roman yoke,
Obeys Tiberius, nor is always ruled
With temperate sway: oft have they violated
The Temple, oft the Law, with foul affronts,
Abominations rather, as did once
Antiochus.   And think'st Thou to regain
Thy right in sitting still, or thus retiring?
So did not Machabeus.   He indeed
Retired unto the Desert, but with arms;
And o'er a mighty king so oft prevailed
That by strong hand his family obtained,
Though priests, the crown, and David's throne usurped,
With Modin and her suburbs once content.
If kingdom move Thee not, let move Thee zeal
And duty—zeal and duty are not slow,
But on Occasion's forelock watchful wait:
They themselves rather are occasion best—
Zeal of Thy Father's house, duty to free
Thy country from her heathen servitude.
So shalt Thou best fulfil, best verify,
The Prophets old, who sung Thy endless reign—
The happier reign the sooner it begins.
Reign then; what canst Thou better do the while?"
      To whom our Saviour answer thus returned:—
" All things are best fulfilled in their due time;
And time there is for all things, Truth hath said.
If of My reign Prophetic Writ hath told
That it shall never end, so, when begin
The Father in His purpose hath decreed—
He in whose hand all times and seasons roll.
What if He hath decreed that I shall first
Be tried in humble state, and things adverse,
By tribulations, injuries, insults,
Contempts, and scorns, and snares, and violence,
Suffering, abstaining, quietly expecting
Without distrust or doubt, that He may know
What I can suffer, how obey?   Who best
Can suffer best can do, best reign who first
Well hath obeyed—just trial ere I merit
My exaltation without change or end.
But what concerns it *thee* when I begin
My everlasting Kingdom?   Why art *thou*
Solicitous?   What moves *thy* inquisition?
Know'st thou not that My rising is thy fall,
And My promotion will be thy destruction?"
      To whom the Tempter, inly racked, replied:—

" Let that come when it comes.   All hope is lost
Of my reception into grace ; what worse?
For where no hope is left is left no fear.
If there be worse, the expectation more
Of worse torments me than the feeling can.
I would be at the worst; worst is my port,
My harbour, and my ultimate repose,
The end I would attain, my final good.
My error was my error, and my crime
My crime; whatever, for itself condemned,
And will alike be punished, whether Thou
Reign or reign not—though to that gentle brow
Willingly I could fly, and hope Thy reign,
From that placid aspect and meek regard,
Rather than aggravate my evil state,
Would stand between me and Thy Father's ire
(Whose ire I dread more than the fire of Hell)
A shelter and a kind of shading cool
Interposition, as a summer's cloud.
If I, then, to the worst that can be haste,
Why move Thy feet so slow to what is best ?
Happiest, both to Thyself and all the world,
That Thou, who worthiest art, shouldst be their King!
Perhaps Thou linger'st in deep thoughts detained
Of the enterprise so hazardous and high!
No wonder; for, though in Thee be united
What of perfection can in Man be found,
Or human nature can receive, consider
Thy life hath yet been private, most part spent
At home, scarce viewed the Galilean towns,
And once a year Jerusalem few days'
Short sojourn; and what thence couldst Thou observe ?
The world Thou hast not seen, much less her glory,
Empires, and monarchs, and their radiant courts—
Best school of best experience, quickest in sight
In all things that to greatest actions lead.
The wisest, unexperienced, will be ever
Timorous, and loth, with novice modesty
(As he who, seeking asses, found a kingdom)
Irresolute, unhardy, unadventurous.
But I will bring Thee where Thou soon shalt quit
Those rudiments, and see before Thine eyes
The monarchies of the Earth, their pomp and state—
Sufficient introduction to inform
Thee, of Thyself so apt, in regal arts,
And regal mysteries; that Thou may'st know
How best their opposition to withstand."
    With that (such power was given him then), he took
The Son of God up to a mountain high.
It was a mountain at whose verdant feet
A spacious plain outstretched in circuit wide
Lay pleasant; from his side two rivers flowed,
The one winding, the other straight, and left between
Fair champaign, with less rivers interveined

Then meeting joined their tribute to the sea.
Fertile of corn the glebe, of oil, and wine;
With herds the pasture thronged, with flocks the hills;
Huge cities and high-towered, that well might seem
The seats of mightiest monarchs; and so large
The prospect was that here and there was room
For barren desert, fountainless and dry.
To this high mountain-top the Tempter brought
Our Saviour, and new train of words began:—
    " Well have we speeded, and o'er hill and dale,
Forest, and field, and flood, temples and towers,
Cut shorter many a league.   Here thou behold'st
Assyria, and her empire's ancient bounds,
Araxes and the Caspian lake; thence on
As far as Indus east, Euphrates west,
And oft beyond; to south the Persian bay,
And, inaccessible, the Arabian drouth:
Here, Nineveh, of length within her wall
Several days' journey, built by Ninus old,
Of that first golden monarchy the seat,
And seat of Salmanassar, whose success
Israel in long captivity still mourns;
There Babylon, the wonder of all tongues,
As ancient, but rebuilt by him who twice
Judah and all Thy father David's house
Led captive, and Jerusalem laid waste,
Till Cyrus set them free; Persepolis,
His city, there Thou seest, and Bactra there;
Ecbatana her structure vast there shows,
And Hecatompylos her hundred gates;
There Susa by Choaspes, amber stream,
The drink of none but kings; of later fame,
Built by Emathian or by Parthian hands,
The great Seleucia, Nisibis, and there
Artaxata, Teredon, Ctesiphon,
Turning with easy eye, Thou may'st behold.
All these the Parthian (now some ages past
By great Arsaces led, who founded first
That empire) under his dominion holds,
From the luxurious kings of Antioch won.
And just in time thou com'st to have a view
Of his great power; for now the Parthian king
In Ctesiphon hath gathered all his host
Against the Scythian, whose incursions wild
Have wasted Sogdiana; to her aid
He marches now in haste.   See, though from far,
His thousands, in what martial equipage
They issue forth, steel bows and shafts their arms,
Of equal dread in flight or in pursuit—
All horsemen, in which fight they most excel;
See how in warlike muster they appear,
In rhombs, and wedges, and half-moons, and wings."
    He looked, and saw what numbers numberless
The city gates outpoured, light-armed troops

In coats of mail and military pride.
In mail their horses clad, yet fleet and strong,
Prancing their riders bore, the flower and choice
Of many provinces from bound to bound—
From Arachosia, from Candaor east,
And Margiana, to the Hyrcanian cliffs
Of Caucasus, and dark Iberian dales;
From Atropatia, and the neighbouring plains
Of Adiabene, Media, and the south
Of Susiana, to Balsara's haven.
He saw them in their forms of battle ranged,
How quick they wheeled, and flying behind them shot
Sharp sleet of arrowy showers against the face
Of their pursuers, and overcame by flight;
The field all iron cast a gleaming brown.
Nor wanted clouds of foot, nor, on each horn,
Cuirassiers all in steel for standing fight,
Chariots, or elephants indorsed with towers
Of archers; nor of labouring pioneers
A multitude, with spades and axes armed,
To lay hills plain, fell woods, or valleys fill,
Or where plain was raise hill, or overlay
With bridges rivers proud, as with a yoke:
Mules after these, camels and dromedaries,
And waggons fraught with utensils of war.
Such forces met not, nor so wide a camp,
When Agrican, with all his northern powers,
Besieged Albracca, as romances tell,
The city of Gallaphrone, from thence to win
The fairest of her sex, Angelica,
His daughter, sought by many prowest knights,
Both Paynim and the peers of Charlemain.
Such and so numerous was their chivalry;
At sight whereof the Fiend yet more presumed,
And to our Saviour thus his words renewed:—
   "That Thou may'st know I seek not to engage
Thy virtue, and not every way secure
On no slight grounds Thy safety, hear and mark
To what end I have brought Thee hither, and show
All this fair sight.   Thy kingdom, though foretold
By Prophet or by Angel, unless Thou
Endeavour, as Thy father David did,
Thou never shalt obtain: prediction still
In all things, and all men, supposes means;
Without means used, what it predicts revokes.
But say Thou wert possessed of David's throne
By free consent of all, none opposite,
Samaritan or Jew; how couldst Thou hope
Long to enjoy it quiet and secure
Between two such enclosing enemies,
Roman and Parthian?   Therefore one of these
Thou must make sure Thy own: the Parthian first,
By my advice, as nearer, and of late
Found able by invasion to annoy

Thy country, and captive lead away her kings,
Antigonus and old Hyrcanus, bound,
Maugre the Roman.   It shall be my task
To render Thee the Parthian at dispose,
Choose which Thou wilt, by conquest or by league.
By him Thou shalt regain, without him not,
That which alone can truly reinstall Thee
In David's royal seat, his true successor—
Deliverance of Thy brethren, those Ten Tribes
Whose offspring in his territory yet serve
In Habor, and among the Medes dispersed:
Ten sons of Jacob, two of Joseph, lost
Thus long from Israel, serving, as of old
Their fathers in the land of Egypt served,
This offer sets before Thee to deliver.
These if from servitude Thou shalt restore
To their inheritance, then, nor till then,
Thou on the throne of David in full glory,
From Egypt to Euphrates and beyond,
Shalt reign, and Rome or Cæsar not need fear."
    To whom our Saviour answered thus, unmoved:—
"Much ostentation vain of fleshly arm
And fragile arms, much instrument of war,
Long in preparing, soon to nothing brought,
Before Mine eyes thou hast set, and in My ear
Vented much policy, and projects deep
Of enemies, of aids, battles, and leagues,
Plausible to the world, to Me worth naught.
Means I must use, thou say'st; prediction else
Will unpredict, and fail Me of the throne!
My time, I told thee (and that time for thee
Were better farthest off), is not yet come.
When that comes, think not thou to find Me slack
On My part aught endeavouring, or to need
Thy politic maxims, or that cumbersome
Luggage of war there shown Me—argument
Of human weakness rather than of strength.
My brethren, as thou call'st them, those Ten Tribes,
I must deliver, if I mean to reign
David's true heir, and his full sceptre sway
To just extent over all Israel's sons!
But whence to *thee* this zeal?   Where was it then
For Israel, or for David, or his throne,
When thou stood'st up his tempter to the pride
Of numbering Israel—which cost the lives
Of threescore and ten thousand Israelites
By three days' pestilence?   Such was thy zeal
To Israel then, the same that now to Me.
As for those captive tribes, themselves were they
Who wrought their own captivity, fell off
From God to worship calves, the deities
Of Egypt, Baal next and Ashtaroth,
And all the idolatries of heathen round,
Besides their other worse than heathenish crimes;

244

Nor in the land of their captivity
Humbled themselves, or penitent besought
The God of their forefathers, but so died
Impenitent, and left a race behind
Like to themselves, distinguishable scarce
From Gentiles, but by circumcision vain,
And God with idols in their worship joined.
Should I of these the liberty regard,
Who, freed, as to their ancient patrimony,
Unhumbled, unrepentant, unreformed,
Headlong would follow, and to their gods perhaps
Of Bethel and of Dan? No; let them serve
Their enemies who serve idols with God.
Yet He at length, time to Himself best known,
Remembering Abraham, by some wondrous call
May bring them back, repentant and sincere,
And at their passing cleave the Assyrian flood,
While to their native land with joy they haste,
As the Red Sea and Jordan once he cleft,
When to the Promised Land their fathers passed.
To His due time and providence I leave them."
  So spake Israel's true King, and to the Fiend
Made answer meet, that made void all his wiles.
So fares it when with truth falsehood contends.

THE END OF THE THIRD BOOK.

PARADISE REGAINED.

THE FOURTH BOOK.

PERPLEXED and troubled at his bad success
The Tempter stood, nor had what to reply,
Discovered in his fraud, thrown from his hope
So oft, and the persuasive rhetoric
That sleeked his tongue, and won so much on Eve,
So little here, nay lost.   But Eve was Eve;
This far his over-match, who, self-deceived
And rash, beforehand had no better weighed
The strength he was to cope with, or his own.
But—as a man who had been matchless held
In cunning, over-reached where least he thought,
To salve his credit, and for very spite,
Still will be tempting Him who foils him still,
And never cease, though to his shame the more;
Or as a swarm of flies in vintage-time,
About the wine-press where sweet must is poured,
Beat off, returns as oft with humming sound;
Or surging waves against a solid rock,
Though all to shivers dashed, the assault renew,
(Vain battery!) and in froth or bubbles end—
So Satan, whom repulse upon repulse
Met ever, and to shameful silence brought,
Yet gives not o'er, though desperate of success,
And his vain importunity pursues.
He brought our Saviour to the western side
Of that high mountain, whence He might behold
Another plain, long, but in breadth not wide,
Washed by the southern sea, and on the north
To equal length backed with a ridge of hills
That screened the fruits of the earth and seats of men
From cold Septentrion blasts; thence in the midst
Divided by a river, off whose banks
On each side an imperial city stood,
With towers and temples proudly elevate
On seven small hills, with palaces adorned,
Porches and theatres, baths, aqueducts,
Statues and trophies, and triumphal arcs,
Gardens and groves, presented to His eyes
Above the highth of mountains interposed—
By what strange parallax, or optic skill
Of vision, multiplied through air, or glass

Of telescope, were curious to inquire.
And now the Tempter thus his silence broke :—
  "The city which Thou seest no other deem
Than great and glorious Rome, Queen of the Earth
So far renowned, and with the spoils enriched
Of nations.   There the Capitol Thou seest,
Above the rest lifting his stately head
On the Tarpeian rock, her citadel
Impregnable ; and there Mount Palatine,
The imperial palace, compass huge, and high
The structure, skill of noblest architects,   .
With gilded battlements, conspicuous far,
Turrets, and terraces, and glittering spires.
Many a fair edifice besides, more like
Houses of gods—so well I have disposed
My aery microscope—Thou may'st behold,
Outside and inside both, pillars and roofs
Carved work, the hand of famed artificers
In cedar, marble, ivory, or gold.
Thence to the gates cast round Thine eye, and see
What conflux issuing forth, or entering in :
Prætors, proconsuls to their provinces
Hasting, or on return, in robes of state ;
Lictors and rods, the ensigns of their power ;
Legions and cohorts, turms of horse and wings ;
Or embassies from regions far remote,
In various habits, on the Appian road,
Or on the Æmilian—some from farthest south,
Syene, and where the shadow both way falls,
Meroë, Nilotic isle, and, more to west,
The realm of Bocchus to the Blackmoor sea ;
From the Asian kings (and Parthian among these),
From India and the Golden Chersoness,
And utmost Indian isle Taprobane,
Dusk faces with white silken turbants wreathed ;
From Gallia, Gades, and the British west ;
Germans, and Scythians, and Sarmatians north
Beyond Danubius to the Tauric pool.
All nations now to Rome obedience pay—
To Rome's great Emperor, whose wide domain,
In ample territory, wealth and power,
Civility of manners, arts and arms,
And long renown, Thou justly may'st prefer
Before the Parthian.   These two thrones except,
The rest are barbarous, and scarce worth the sight,
Shared among petty kings too far removed ;
These having shown Thee, I have shown Thee all
The kingdoms of the world, and all their glory.
This Emperor hath no son, and now is old,
Old and lascivious, and from Rome retired
To Capreæ, an island small but strong
On the Campanian shore, with purpose there
His horrid lusts in private to enjoy ;
Committing to a wicked favourite

All public cares, and yet of him suspicious;
Hated of all, and hating. With what ease,
Endued with regal virtues as Thou art,
Appearing, and beginning noble deeds,
Might'st Thou expel this monster from his throne,
Now made a sty, and, in his place ascending,
A victor-people free from servile yoke !
And with my help Thou may'st ; to me the power
Is given, and by that right I give it Thee.
Aim, therefore, at no less than all the world ;
Aim at the highest ; without the highest attained,
Will be for Thee no sitting, or not long,
On David's throne, be prophesied what will."
    To whom the Son of God, unmoved, replied :—
" Nor doth this grandeur and majestic show
Of luxury, though called magnificence,
More than of arms before, allure Mine eye,
Much less My mind ; though thou shouldst add to tell
Their sumptuous gluttonies, and gorgeous feasts
On citron tables or Atlantic stone
(For I have also heard, perhaps have read),
Their wines of Setia, Cales, and Falerne,
Chios and Crete, and how they quaff in gold,
Crystal, and myrrhine cups, embossed with gems
And studs of pearl—to me shouldst tell, who thirst
And hunger still.   Then embassies thou show'st
From nations far and nigh ! What honour that,
But tedious waste of time, to sit and hear
So many hollow compliments and lies,
Outlandish flatteries ? Then proceed'st to talk
Of the Emperor, how easily subdued,
How gloriously.   I shall, thou say'st, expel
A brutish monster : what if I withal
Expel a Devil who first made him such ?
Let his tormentor, Conscience, find him out ;
For him I was not sent, nor yet to free
That people, victor once, now vile and base,
Deservedly made vassal—who, once just,
Frugal, and mild, and temperate, conquered well,
But govern ill the nations under yoke,
Peeling their provinces, exhausted all
By lust and rapine ; first ambitious grown
Of triumph, that insulting vanity ;
Then cruel, by their sports to blood inured
Of fighting beasts, and men to beasts exposed ;
Luxurious by their wealth, and greedier still,
And from the daily scene effeminate.
What wise and valiant man would seek to free
These, thus degenerate, by themselves enslaved,
Or could of inward slaves make outward free ?
Know, therefore, when My season comes to sit
On David's throne, it shall be like a tree
Spreading and overshadowing all the Earth,
Or as a stone that shall to pieces dash

All monarchies besides throughout the world ;
And of My kingdom there shall be no end.
Means there shall be to this ; but what the means
Is not for thee to know, nor Me to tell."
   To whom the Tempter, impudent, replied :—
" I see all offers made by me how slight
Thou valuest, because offered, and reject'st.
Nothing will please the difficult and nice,
Or nothing more than still to contradict.
On the other side know also Thou that I
On what I offer set as high esteem,
Nor what I part with mean to give for naught.
All these, which in a moment Thou behold'st,
The kingdoms of the world, to Thee I give
(For, given to me, I give to whom I please),
No trifle ; yet with this reserve, not else—
On this condition, if Thou wilt fall down,
And worship me as Thy superior lord
(Easily done), and hold them all of me ;
For what can less so great a gift deserve ?"
   Whom thus our Saviour answered with disdain :—
" I never liked thy talk, thy offers less ;
Now both abhor, since thou hast dared to utter
The abominable terms, impious condition.
But I endure the time, till which expired
Thou hast permission on me. It is written,
The first of all commandments, ' Thou shalt worship
The Lord thy God, and only Him shalt serve ' ;
And dar'st thou to the Son of God propound
To worship thee, accursed ? now more accursed
For this attempt, bolder than that on Eve,
And more blasphemous ; which expect to rue.
The kingdoms of the world to thee were given !
Permitted rather, and by thee usurped ;
Other donation none thou canst produce.
If given, by whom but by the King of kings,
God over all supreme ? If given to thee,
By thee how fairly is the Giver now
Repaid ! But gratitude in thee is lost
Long since. Wert thou so void of fear or shame
As offer them to Me, the Son of God—
To Me My own, on such abhorred pact,
That I fall down and worship thee as God ?
Get thee behind Me ! Plain thou now appear'st
That Evil One, Satan for ever damned."
   To whom the Fiend, with fear abashed, replied :—
" Be not so sore offended, Son of God—
Though sons of God both Angels are and Men—
If I, to try whether in higher sort
Than these Thou bear'st that title, have proposed
What both from Men and Angels I receive,
Tetrarchs of Fire, Air, Flood, and on the Earth
Nations besides from all the quartered winds—
God of this World invoked, and World beneath.

Who then Thou art, whose coming is foretold
To me most fatal, me it most concerns.
The trial hath indamaged Thee no way,
Rather more honour left and more esteem ;
Me naught advantaged, missing what I aimed.
Therefore let pass, as they are transitory,
The kingdoms of this world ; I shall no more
Advise Thee ; gain them as Thou canst, or not.
And Thou Thyself seem'st otherwise inclined
Than to a worldly crown, addicted more
To contemplation and profound dispute ;
As by that early action may be judged,
When, slipping from Thy mother's eye, Thou went'st
Alone into the Temple, there wast found
Among the gravest Rabbies, disputant
On points and questions fitting Moses' chair,
Teaching, not taught. The childhood shows the man,
As morning shows the day. Be famous, then,
By wisdom ; as Thy empire must extend,
So let extend Thy mind o'er all the world
In knowledge ; all things in it comprehend.
All knowledge is not couched in Moses' law,
The Pentateuch, or what the Prophets wrote ;
The Gentiles also know, and write, and teach
To admiration, led by Nature's light ;
And with the Gentiles much Thou must converse,
Ruling them by persuasion, as Thou mean'st.
Without their learning, how wilt Thou with them,
Or they with Thee, hold conversation meet ?
How wilt Thou reason with them, how refute
Their idolisms, traditions, paradoxes ?
Error by his own arms is best evinced.
Look once more, ere we leave this specular mount,
Westward, much nearer by south-west ; behold
Where on the Ægean shore a city stands,
Built nobly, pure the air and light the soil—
Athens, the eye of Greece, mother of arts
And eloquence, native to famous wits
Or hospitable, in her sweet recess,
City or suburban, studious walks and shades.
See there the olive-grove of Academe,
Plato's retirement, where the Attic bird
Trills her thick-warbled notes the summer long ,
There, flowery hill, Hymettus, with the sound
Of bees' industrious murmur, oft invites
To studious musing ; there Ilissus rolls
His whispering stream. Within the walls then view
The schools of ancient sages—his who bred
Great Alexander to subdue the world,
Lyceum there ; and painted Stoa next.
There Thou shalt hear and learn the secret power
Of harmony, in tones and numbers hit
By voice or hand, and various-measured verse,
Æolian charms and Dorian lyric odes,

And his who gave them breath, but higher sung,
Blind Melesigenes, thence Homer called,
Whose poem Phœbus challenged for his own.
Thence what the lofty grave Tragedians taught
In chorus or iambic, teachers best
Of moral prudence, with delight received
In brief sententious precepts, while they treat
Of fate, and chance, and change in human life,
High actions and high passions best describing.
Thence to the famous Orators repair,
Those ancient whose resistless eloquence
Wielded at will that fierce democraty,
Shook the Arsenal, and fulmined over Greece
To Macedon and Artaxerxes' throne.
To sage Philosopy next lend thine ear,
From heaven descended to the low-roofed house
Of Socrates—see there his tenement—
Whom, well inspired, the oracle pronounced
Wisest of men ; from whose mouth issued forth
Mellifluous streams, that watered all the schools
Of Academics old and new, with those
Surnamed Peripatetics, and the sect
Epicurean, and the Stoic severe.
These here revolve, or, as thou likest, at home,
Till time mature Thee to a kingdom's weight ;
These rules will render Thee a king complete
Within Thyself, much more with empire joined."
    To whom our Saviour sagely thus replied :—
" Think not but that I know these things ; or, think
I know them not, not therefore am I short
Of knowing what I ought.   He who receives
Light from above, from the Fountain of Light,
No other doctrine needs, though granted true ;
But these are false, or little else but dreams,
Conjectures, fancies, built on nothing firm.
The first and wisest of them all professed
To know this only, that he nothing knew ;
The next to fabling fell and smooth conceits ;
A third sort doubted all things, though plain sense ;
Others in virtue placed felicity,
But virtue joined with riches and long life ;
In corporal pleasure he, and careless ease ;
The Stoic last in philosophic pride,
By him called virtue, and his virtuous man,
Wise, perfect in himself, and all possessing,
Equal to God, oft shames not to prefer,
As fearing God nor man, contemning all
Wealth, pleasure, pain or torment, death and life—
Which, when he lists, he leaves, or boasts he can ;
For all his tedious talk is but vain boast,
Or subtle shifts conviction to evade.
Alas ! what can they teach, and not mislead,
Ignorant of themselves, of God much more,
And how the World began, and how Man fell,

Degraded by himself, on grace depending?
Much of the Soul they talk, but all awry;
And in themselves seek virtue; and to themselves
All glory arrogate, to God give none;
Rather accuse Him under usual names,
Fortune and Fate, as one regardless quite
Of mortal things.   Who, therefore, seeks in these
True wisdom finds her not, or, by delusion
Far worse, her false resemblance only meets,
An empty cloud.   However, many books,
Wise men have said, are wearisome; who reads
Incessantly, and to his reading brings not
A spirit and judgment equal or superior,
(And what he brings what needs he elsewhere seek?)
Uncertain and unsettled still remains,
Deep-versed in books and shallow in himself,
Crude or intoxicate, collecting toys
And trifles for choice matters, worth a sponge,
As children gathering pebbles on the shore.
Or, if I would delight my private hours
With music or with poem, where so soon
As in our native language can I find
That solace?   All our Law and Story strewed
With hymns, our Psalms with artful terms inscribed,
Our Hebrew songs and harps, in Babylon
That pleased so well our victor's ear, declare
That rather Greece from us these arts derived—
Ill imitated while they loudest sing
The vices of their deities, and their own,
In fable, hymn, or song, so personating
Their gods ridiculous, and themselves past shame.
Remove their swelling epithets, thick-laid
As varnish on a harlot's cheek, the rest,
Thin-sown with aught of profit or delight,
Will far be found unworthy to compare
With Sion's songs, to all true tastes excelling,
Where God is praised aright and godlike men,
The Holiest of Holies and His Saints
(Such are from God inspired, not such from thee);
Unless where moral virtue is expressed
By light of Nature, not in all quite lost.
Their orators thou then extoll'st as those
The top of eloquence—statists indeed,
And lovers of their country, as may seem;
But herein to our Prophets far beneath,
As men divinely taught, and better teaching
The solid rules of civil government,
In their majestic, unaffected style,
Than all the oratory of Greece and Rome.
In them is plainest taught, and easiest learnt,
What makes a nation happy, and keeps it so,
What ruins kingdoms, and lays cities flat;
These only, with our Law, best form a king."
    So spake the Son of God; but Satan, now

Quite at a loss (for all his darts were spent),
Thus to our Saviour, with stern brow, replied :—
  "Since neither wealth nor honour, arms nor arts,
Kingdom nor empire, pleases Thee, nor aught
By me proposed in life contemplative
Or active, tended on by glory or fame,
What dost Thou in this world ?   The Wilderness
For Thee is fittest place : I found Thee there,
And thither will return Thee.   Yet remember
What I foretell Thee ; soon Thou shalt have cause
To wish Thou never hadst rejected, thus
Nicely or cautiously, my offered aid,
Which would have set Thee in short time with ease
On David's throne, or throne of all the world,
Now at full age, fulness of time, Thy season,
When prophecies of Thee are best fulfilled.
Now, contrary—if I read aught in heaven,
Or heaven write aught of fate—by what the stars
Voluminous, or single characters
In their conjunction met, give me to spell,
Sorrows and labours, opposition, hate,
Attends Thee ; scorns, reproaches, injuries,
Violence and stripes, and, lastly, cruel death.
A kingdom they portend Thee, but what kingdom,
Real or allegoric, I discern not ;
Nor when : eternal sure—as without end,
Without beginning ; for no date prefixed
Directs me in the starry rubric set."
  So saying, he took (for still he knew his power
Not yet expired), and to the Wilderness
Brought back, the Son of God, and left Him there,
Feigning to disappear.   Darkness now rose,
As daylight sunk, and brought in louring Night,
Her shadowy offspring, unsubstantial both,
Privation mere of light and absent day.
Our Saviour, meek, and with untroubled mind
After His aery jaunt, though hurried sore,
Hungry and cold, betook Him to His rest,
Wherever, under some concourse of shades,
Whose branching arms thick intertwined might shield
From dews and damps of night His sheltered head ;
But, sheltered, slept in vain ; for at His head
The Tempter watched, and soon with ugly dreams
Disturbed His sleep.   And either tropic now
'Gan thunder, and both ends of heaven ; the clouds
From many a horrid rift abortive poured
Fierce rain with lightning mixed, water with fire
In ruin reconciled ; nor slept the winds
Within their stony caves, but rushed abroad
From the four hinges of the world, and fell
On the vexed wilderness, whose tallest pines,
Though rooted deep as high, and sturdiest oaks,
Bowed their stiff necks, loaden with stormy blasts,
Or torn up sheer.   Ill wast Thou shrouded then,

O patient Son of God, yet only stood'st
Unshaken ! Nor yet staid the terror there :
Infernal ghosts and hellish furies round
Environed Thee; some howled, some yelled, some shrieked,
Some bent at Thee their fiery darts, while Thou
Sat'st unappalled in calm and sinless peace.
Thus passed the night so foul, till Morning fair
Came forth with pilgrim steps, in amice gray,
Who with her radiant finger stilled the roar
Of thunder, chased the clouds, and laid the winds,
And grisly spectres, which the Fiend had raised
To tempt the Son of God with terrors dire.
And now the sun with more effectual beams
Had cheered the face of earth, and dried the wet
From drooping plant, or dropping tree ; the birds,
Who all things now behold more fresh and green,
After a night of storm so ruinous,
Cleared up their choicest notes in bush and spray,
To gratulate the sweet return of morn.
Nor yet, amidst this joy and brightest morn,
Was absent, after all his mischief done,
The Prince of Darkness ; glad would also seem
Of this fair change, and to our Saviour came ;
Yet with no new device (they all were spent),
Rather by this his last affront resolved,
Desperate of better course, to vent his rage
And mad despite to be so oft repelled.
Him walking on a sunny hill he found,
Backed on the north and west by a thick wood ;
Out of the wood he starts in wonted shape,
And in a careless mood thus to Him said :—
   " Fair morning yet betides Thee, Son of God,
After a dismal night. I heard the wrack,
As earth and sky would mingle ; but myself
Was distant ; and these flaws, though mortals fear them,
As dangerous to the pillared frame of Heaven,
Or to the Earth's dark basis underneath,
Are to the main as inconsiderable
And harmless, if not wholesome, as a sneeze
To man's less universe, and soon are gone.
Yet, as being oft-times noxious where they light
On man, beast, plant, wasteful and turbulent,
Like turbulencies in the affairs of men,
Over whose heads they roar, and seem to point,
They oft fore-signify and threaten ill.
This tempest at this desert most was bent ;
Of men at Thee, for only Thou here dwell'st.
Did I not tell Thee, if Thou didst reject
The perfect season offered with my aid
To win Thy destined seat, but wilt prolong
All to the push of fate, pursue Thy way
Of gaining David's throne no man knows when
(For both the when and how is nowhere told),
Thou shalt be what Thou art ordained, no doubt ;

For Angels have proclaimed it, but concealing
The time and means? Each act is rightliest done
Not when it must, but when it may be best.
If Thou observe not this, be sure to find
What I foretold Thee—many a hard assay
Of dangers, and adversities, and pains,
Ere Thou of Israel's sceptre get fast hold ;
Whereof this ominous night that closed Thee round,
So many terrors, voices, prodigies,
May warn Thee, as a sure foregoing sign."
 So talked he, while the Son of God went on,
And staid not, but in brief him answered thus :—
 " Me worse than wet thou find'st not ; other harm
Those terrors which thou speak'st of did Me none.
I never feared they could, though noising loud
And threatening nigh : what they can do as signs
Betokening or ill-boding I contemn
As false portents, not sent from God, but thee ;
Who, knowing I shall reign past thy preventing,
Obtrud'st thy offered aid, that I, accepting,
At least might seem to hold all power of thee,
Ambitious Spirit ! and would'st be thought My God ;
And storm'st, refused, thinking to terrify
Me to thy will ? Desist (thou art discerned,
And toil'st in vain), nor Me in vain molest."
 To whom the Fiend, now swoln with rage, replied :—
" Then hear, O Son of David, virgin-born !
For Son of God to me is yet in doubt.
Of the Messiah I have heard foretold
By all the Prophets ; of Thy birth, at length
Announced by Gabriel, with the first I knew,
And of the angelic song in Bethlehem field,
On Thy birth-night, that sung Thee Saviour born.
From that time seldom have I ceased to eye
Thy infancy, Thy childhood, and Thy youth,
Thy manhood last, though yet in private bred ;
Till, at the ford of Jordan, whither all
Flocked to the Baptist, I among the rest
(Though not to be baptized) by voice from Heaven
Heard Thee pronounced the Son of God beloved.
Thenceforth I thought Thee worth my nearer view
And narrower scrutiny, that I might learn
In what degree or meaning Thou art called
The Son of God, which bears no single sense.
The Son of God I also am, or was ;
And, if I was, I am ; relation stands ;
All men are Sons of God ; yet Thee I thought
In some respect far higher so declared.
Therefore I watched Thy footsteps from that hour,
And followed Thee still on to this waste wild,
Where, by all best conjectures, I collect
Thou art to be my fatal enemy.
Good reason, then, if I beforehand seek
To understand my adversary, who

And what He is ; His wisdom, power, intent ;
By parle or composition, truce or league,
To win Him, or win from Him what I can.
And opportunity I here have had
To try Thee, sift Thee, and confess have found Thee
Proof against all temptation, as a rock
Of adamant and as a centre, firm
To the utmost of mere man both wise and good,
Not more ; for honours, riches, kingdoms, glory,
Have been before contemned, and may again.
Therefore, to know what more Thou art than man,
Worth naming Son of God by voice from Heaven,
Another method I must now begin."
   So saying, he caught Him up, and, without wing
Of hippogrif, bore through the air sublime,
Over the wilderness and o'er the plain,
Till underneath them fair Jerusalem,
The Holy City, lifted high her towers,
And higher yet the glorious Temple reared
Her pile, far off appearing like a mount
Of alabaster, topt with golden spires :
There, on the highest pinnacle, he set
The Son of God, and added thus in scorn :—
   "There stand, if Thou wilt stand ; to stand upright
Will ask Thee skill.   I to Thy Father's house
Have brought Thee, and highest placed : highest is best.
Now show Thy progeny ; if not to stand,
Cast Thyself down.   Safely, if Son of God ;
For it is written, 'He will give command
Concerning Thee to His Angels ; in their hands
They shall uplift Thee, lest at any time
Thou chance to dash Thy foot against a stone.'"
   To whom thus Jesus : "Also it is written,
'Tempt not the Lord thy God.'"   He said, and stood ;
But Satan, smitten with amazement, fell.
As when Earth's son, Antæus (to compare
Small things with greatest), in Irassa strove
With Jove's Alcides, and, oft foiled, still rose,
Receiving from his mother Earth new strength,
Fresh from his fall, and fiercer grapple joined,
Throttled at length in the air expired and fell,
So, after many a foil, the Tempter proud,
Renewing fresh assaults, amidst his pride
Fell whence he stood to see his victor fall ;
And, as that Theban monster that proposed
Her riddle, and him who solved it not devoured,
That once found out and solved, for grief and spite
Cast herself headlong from the Ismenian steep,
So, strook with dread and anguish, fell the Fiend,
And to his crew, that sat consulting, brought
Joyless triumphals of his hoped success,
Ruin, and desperation, and dismay,
Who durst so proudly tempt the Son of God.
So Satan fell ; and straight a fiery globe

Of Angels on full sail of wing flew nigh,
Who on their plumy vans received Him soft
From His uneasy station, and upbore,
As on a floating couch, through the blithe air ;
Then, in a flowery valley, set Him down
On a green bank, and set before Him spread
A table of celestial food, divine
Ambrosial fruits fetched from the Tree of Life,
And from the Fount of Life ambrosial drink,
That soon refreshed Him wearied, and repaired
What hunger, if aught hunger, had impaired,
Or thirst ; and, as He fed, Angelic quires
Sung heavenly anthems of His victory
Over temptation and the Tempter proud :—
  "True Image of the Father, whether throned
In the bosom of bliss, and light of light
Conceiving, or, remote from Heaven, enshrined
In fleshly tabernacle and human form,
Wandering the wilderness—whatever place,
Habit, or state, or motion, still expressing
The Son of God, with Godlike force endued
Against the attempter of Thy Father's throne
And thief of Paradise ! Him long of old
Thou didst debel, and down from Heaven cast
With all his army ; now Thou hast avenged
Supplanted Adam, and, by vanquishing
Temptation, hast regained lost Paradise,
And frustrated the conquest fraudulent.
He never more henceforth will dare set foot
In Paradise to tempt ; his snares are broke.
For, though that seat of earthly bliss be failed,
A fairer Paradise is founded now
For Adam and his chosen sons, whom Thou,
A Saviour, art come down to reinstall ;
Where they shall dwell secure, when time shall be,
Of tempter and temptation without fear.
But thou, Infernal Serpent ! shalt not long
Rule in the clouds. Like an autumnal star,
Or lightning, thou shalt fall from Heaven, trod down
Under His feet. For proof, ere this thou feel'st
Thy wound (yet not thy last and deadliest wound)
By this repulse received, and hold'st in Hell
No triumph ; in all her gates Abaddon rues
Thy bold attempt. Hereafter learn with awe
To dread the Son of God. He, all unarmed,
Shall chase thee, with the terror of His voice,
From thy demoniac holds, possession foul—
Thee and thy legions ; yelling they shall fly,
And beg to hide them in a herd of swine,
Lest He command them down into the Deep,
Bound, and to torment sent before their time.
Hail, Son of the Most High, heir of both Worlds,
Queller of Satan ! On Thy glorious work
Now enter, and begin to save Mankind."

Thus they the Son of God, our Saviour meek,
Sung victor, and, from heavenly feast refreshed,
Brought on His way with joy.   He, unobserved,
Home to His mother's house private returned.

THE END.

SAMSON AGONISTES.

A DRAMATIC POEM.

THE AUTHOR
JOHN MILTON.

Aristot. Poet. cap. 6. Τραγῳδία μίμησις πράξεως σπουδαίας, &c.—
Tragœdia est imitatio actionis seriæ, &c., per misericordiam et metum
perficiens talium affectuum lustrationem.

OF THAT SORT OF DRAMATIC POEM
CALLED TRAGEDY.

TRAGEDY, as it was anciently composed, hath been ever held the gravest, moralest, and most profitable of all other poems ; therefore said by Aristotle to be of power, by raising pity and fear, or terror, to purge the mind of those and such-like passions—that is, to temper and reduce them to just measure with a kind of delight, stirred up by reading or seeing those passions well imitated. Nor is Nature wanting in her own effects to make good his assertion ; for so, in physic, things of melancholic hue and quality are used against melancholy, sour against sour, salt to remove salt humours. Hence philosophers and other gravest writers, as Cicero, Plutarch, and others, frequently cite out of tragic poets, both to adorn and illustrate their discourse. The Apostle Paul himself thought it not unworthy to insert a verse of Euripides into the text of Holy Scripture, 1 Cor. xv. 33 ; and Paræus, commenting on the *Revelation*, divides the whole book, as a tragedy, into acts, distinguished each by a Chorus of heavenly harpings and song between. Heretofore men in highest dignity have laboured not a little to be thought able to compose a tragedy. Of that honour Dionysius the elder was no less ambitious than before of his attaining to the tyranny. Augustus Cæsar also had begun his *Ajax*, but, unable to please his own judgment with what he had begun, left it unfinished. Seneca, the philosopher, is by some thought the author of those tragedies (at least, the best of them) that go under that name. Gregory Nazianzen, a Father of the Church, thought it not unbeseeming the sanctity of his person to write a tragedy, which he entitled *Christ Suffering*. This is mentioned to vindicate Tragedy from the small esteem, or rather infamy, which in the account of many it undergoes at this day, with other common interludes ; happening through the poet's error of intermixing comic stuff with tragic sadness and gravity, or introducing trivial and vulgar persons : which by all judicious hath been counted absurd, and brought in, without discretion, corruptly to gratify the people. And, though ancient Tragedy use no Prologue, yet using sometimes, in case of self-defence or explanation, that which Martial calls an Epistle, in behalf of this tragedy, coming forth after the ancient manner, much different from what among us passes for best, thus much beforehand may be *epistled*—that Chorus is here introduced after the Greek manner, not ancient only, but modern, and still in use among the Italians. In the modelling therefore of this poem, with good reason, the Ancients and Italians are rather followed, as of much more authority and fame. The measure of verse used in the Chorus is of all sorts, called by the Greeks *Monostrophic*, or rather *Apolelymenon*, without regard had to Strophe, Antistrophe, or Epode,—which were a kind of stanzas framed only for the music, then used with the Chorus that sung ; not essential to the poem, and therefore not material ; or, being divided into stanzas or pauses, they may be called *Allæostropha*. Division into act and scene, referring chiefly to the stage (to which this work never was intended), is here omitted.

It suffices if the whole drama be found not produced beyond the fifth act. Of the style and uniformity, and that commonly called the plot, whether intricate or explicit—which is nothing indeed but such economy, or disposition of the fable, as may stand best with verisimilitude and decorum—they only will best judge who are not unacquainted with Æschylus, Sophocles, and Euripides, the three tragic poets unequalled yet by any, and the best rule to all who endeavour to write Tragedy. The circumscription of time, wherein the whole drama begins and ends, is, according to ancient rule and best example, within the space of twenty-four hours.

THE PERSONS.

SAMSON.

MANOA, the father of Samson.	Public Officer.
DALILA, his wife.	Messenger.
HARAPHA of Gath.	Chorus of Danites.

The Scene, before the Prison in Gaza.

SAMSON AGONISTES.

THE ARGUMENT.

SAMSON, made captive, blind, and now in the prison at Gaza, there to labour as in a common workhouse, on a festival day, in the general cessation from labour, comes forth into the open air, to a place nigh, somewhat retired, there to sit a while and bemoan his condition. Where he happens at length to be visited by certain friends and equals of his tribe, which make the Chorus, who seek to comfort him what they can; then by his old father, Manoa, who endeavours the like, and withal tells him his purpose to procure his liberty by ransom; lastly, that this feast was proclaimed by the Philistines as a day of thanksgiving for their deliverance from the hands of Samson—which yet more troubles him. Manoa then departs to prosecute his endeavour with the Philistian lords for Samson's redemption; who, in the meanwhile, is visited by other persons, and, lastly, by a public officer to require his coming to the feast before the lords and people, to play or show his strength in their presence. He at first refuses, dismissing the public officer with absolute denial to come; at length, persuaded inwardly that this was from God, he yields to go along with him, who came now the second time with great threatenings to fetch him. The Chorus yet remaining on the place, Manoa returns full of joyful hope to procure ere long his son's deliverance; in the midst of which discourse an Ebrew comes in haste, confusedly at first, and afterwards more distinctly, relating the catastrophe—what Samson had done to the Philistines, and by accident to himself; wherewith the Tragedy ends.

> *Sams.* A little onward lend thy guiding hand
> To these dark steps, a little further on;
> For yonder bank hath choice of sun or shade.
> There I am wont to sit when any chance
> Relieves me from my task of servile toil,
> Daily in the common prison else enjoined me,
> Where I, a prisoner chained, scarce freely draw
> The air, imprisoned also, close and damp,
> Unwholesome draught. But here I feel amends—
> The breath of Heaven, fresh blowing, pure and sweet,
> With day-spring born; here leave me to respire.
> This day a solemn feast the people hold
> To Dagon, their sea-idol, and forbid
> Laborious works. Unwillingly this rest
> Their superstition yields me; hence, with leave
> Retiring from the popular noise, I seek
> This unfrequented place to find some ease—
> Ease to the body some, none to the mind
> From restless thoughts, that, like a deadly swarm
> Of hornets armed, no sooner found alone

But rush upon me thronging, and present
Times past, what once I was, and what am now.
Oh, wherefore was my birth from Heaven foretold
Twice by an Angel, who at last, in sight
Of both my parents, all in flames ascended
From off the altar where an offering burned,
As in a fiery column charioting
His godlike presence, and from some great act
Or benefit revealed to Abraham's race?
Why was my breeding ordered and prescribed
As of a person separate to God,
Designed for great exploits, if I must die
Betrayed, captived, and both my eyes put out,
Made of my enemies the scorn and gaze,
To grind in brazen fetters under task
With this heaven-gifted strength? O glorious strength,
Put to the labour of a beast, debased
Lower than bond-slave! Promise was that I
Should Israel from Philistian yoke deliver!
Ask for this great deliverer now, and find him
Eyeless in Gaza, at the mill with slaves,
Himself in bonds under Philistian yoke.
Yet stay; let me not rashly call in doubt
Divine prediction. What if all foretold
Had been fulfilled but through mine own default?
Whom have I to complain of but myself,
Who this high gift of strength committed to me,
In what part lodged, how easily bereft me,
Under the seal of silence could not keep,
But weakly to a woman must reveal it,
O'ercome with importunity and tears?
O impotence of mind in body strong!
But what is strength without a double share
Of wisdom? Vast, unwieldy, burdensome,
Proudly secure, yet liable to fall
By weakest subtleties; not made to rule,
But to subserve where wisdom bears command.
God, when He gave me strength, to show withal
How slight the gift was, hung it in my hair.
But peace! I must not quarrel with the will
Of highest dispensation, which herein
Haply had ends above my reach to know.
Suffices that to me strength is my bane,
And proves the source of all my miseries—
So many, and so huge, that each apart
Would ask a life to wail. But, chief of all,
O loss of sight, of thee I most complain!
Blind among enemies! O worse than chains,
Dungeon, or beggary, or decrepit age!
Light, the prime work of God, to me is extinct,
And all her various objects of delight
Annulled, which might in part my grief have eased.
Inferior to the vilest now become
Of man or worm, the vilest here excel me:

They creep, yet see; I, dark in light, exposed
To daily fraud, contempt, abuse, and wrong,
Within doors, or without, still as a fool,
In power of others, never in my own—
Scarce half I seem to live, dead more than half.
O dark, dark, dark, amid the blaze of noon,
Irrecoverably dark, total eclipse
Without all hope of day!
O first-created beam, and thou great Word,
"Let there be light, and light was over all,"
Why am I thus bereaved thy prime decree?
The Sun to me is dark
And silent as the Moon,
When she deserts the night,
Hid in her vacant interlunar cave.
Since light so necessary is to life,
And almost life itself, if it be true
That light is in the soul,
She all in every part, why was the sight
To such a tender ball as the eye confined,
So obvious and so easy to be quenched,
And not, as feeling, through all parts diffused,
That she might look at will through every pore?
Then had I not been thus exiled from light,
As in the land of darkness, yet in light,
To live a life half dead, a living death,
And buried; but, O yet more miserable!
Myself my sepulchre, a moving grave;
Buried, yet not exempt,
By privilege of death and burial,
From worst of other evils, pains, and wrongs;
But made hereby obnoxious more
To all the miseries of life,
Life in captivity
Among inhuman foes.
But who are these? for with joint pace I hear
The tread of many feet steering this way;
Perhaps my enemies, who come to stare
At my affliction, and perhaps to insult—
Their daily practice to afflict me more.
   Chor. This, this is he; softly a while;
Let us not break in upon him.
O change beyond report, thought, or belief!
See how he lies at random, carelessly diffused,
With languished head unpropt,
As one past hope, abandoned,
And by himself given over,
In slavish habit, ill-fitted weeds
O'er-worn and soiled.
Or do my eyes misrepresent? Can this be he,
That heroic, that renowned,
Irresistible Samson? whom, unarmed,
No strength of man, or fiercest wild beast, could withstand;
Who tore the lion as the lion tears the kid;

Ran on embattled armies clad in iron,
And, weaponless himself,
Made arms ridiculous, useless the forgery
Of brazen shield and spear the hammered cuirass,
Chalybean-tempered steel, and frock of mail
Adamantean proof :
But safest he who stood aloof,
When insupportably his foot advanced,
In scorn of their proud arms and warlike tools,
Spurned them to death by troops.   The bold Ascalonite
Fled from his lion ramp ; old warriors turned
Their plated backs under his heel,
Or grovelling soiled their crested helmets in the dust.
Then with what trivial weapon came to hand,
The jaw of a dead ass, his sword of bone,
A thousand foreskins fell, the flower of Palestine,
In Ramath-lechi, famous to this day :
Then by main force pulled up, and on his shoulders bore,
The gates of Azza, post and massy bar,
Up to the hill by Hebron, seat of giants old—
No journey of a Sabbath-day, and loaded so—
Like whom the Gentiles feign to bear up Heaven.
Which shall I first bewail—
Thy bondage or lost sight,
Prison within prison
Inseparably dark ?
Thou art become (O worst imprisonment !)
The dungeon of thyself ; thy soul
(Which men enjoying sight oft without cause complain)
Imprisoned now indeed,
In real darkness of the body dwells,
Shut up from outward light
To incorporate with gloomy night ;
For inward light, alas !
Puts forth no visual beam.
O mirror of our fickle state,
Since man on earth, unparalleled,
The rarer thy example stands,
By how much from the top of wondrous glory,
Strongest of mortal men,
To lowest pitch of abject fortune thou art fallen.
For him I reckon not in high estate
Whom long descent of birth,
Or the sphere of fortune, raises ;
But thee, whose strength, while virtue was her mate,
Might have subdued the Earth,
Universally crowned with highest praises.
  Sams. I hear the sound of words ; their sense the air
Dissolves unjointed ere it reach my ear.
  Chor. He speaks : let us draw nigh.   Matchless in might,
The glory late of Israel, now the grief !
We come, thy friends and neighbours not unknown,
From Eshtaol and Zora's fruitful vale,
To visit or bewail thee ; or, if better,

Counsel or consolation we may bring,
Salve to thy sores: apt words have power to swage
The tumours of a troubled mind,
And are as balm to festered wounds.
  Sams. Your coming, friends, revives me; for I learn
Now of my own experience, not by talk,
How counterfeit a coin they are who 'friends'
Bear in their superscription (of the most
I would be understood). In prosperous days
They swarm, but in adverse withdraw their head,
Not to be found, though sought. Ye see, O friends,
How many evils have enclosed me round:
Yet that which was the worst now least afflicts me,
Blindness; for, had I sight, confused with shame,
How could I once look up, or heave the head,
Who, like a foolish pilot, have shipwracked
My vessel trusted to me from above,
Gloriously rigged, and for a word, a tear,
Fool! have divulged the secret gift of God
To a deceitful woman? Tell me, friends,
Am I not sung and proverbed for a fool
In every street? Do they not say, 'How well
Are come upon him his deserts'? Yet why?
Immeasurable strength they might behold
In me; of wisdom nothing more than mean.
This with the other should at least have paired;
These two, proportioned ill, drove me transverse.
  Chor. Tax not divine disposal. Wisest men
Have erred, and by bad women been deceived;
And shall again, pretend they ne'er so wise.
Deject not, then, so overmuch thyself,
Who hast of sorrow thy full load besides.
Yet, truth to say, I oft have heard men wonder
Why thou shouldst wed Philistian women rather
Than of thine own tribe fairer, or as fair,
At least of thy own nation, and as noble.
  Sams. The first I saw at Timna, and she pleased
Me, not my parents, that I sought to wed
The daughter of an infidel. They knew not
That what I motioned was of God; I knew
From intimate impulse, and therefore urged
The marriage on, that, by occasion hence,
I might begin Israel's deliverance—
The work to which I was divinely called.
She proving false, the next I took to wife
(O that I never had! fond wish too late!)
Was in the vale of Sorec, Dalila,
That specious monster, my accomplished snare.
I thought it lawful from my former act,
And the same end, still watching to oppress
Israel's oppressors. Of what now I suffer
She was not the prime cause, but I myself,
Who, vanquished with a peal of words, (O weakness!)
Gave up my fort of silence to a woman,

Chor. In seeking just occasion to provoke
The Philistine, thy country's enemy,
Thou never wast remiss, I bear thee witness;
Yet Israel still serves with all his sons.
　　Sams. That fault I take not on me, but transfer
On Israel's governors and heads of tribes,
Who, seeing those great acts which God had done
Singly by me against their conquerors,
Acknowledged not, or not at all considered,
Deliverance offered. I, on the other side,
Used no ambition to commend my deeds;
The deeds themselves, though mute, spoke loud the doer.
But they persisted deaf, and would not seem
To count them things worth notice, till at length
Their lords, the Philistines, with gathered powers,
Entered Judea, seeking me, who then
Safe to the rock of Etham was retired—
Not flying, but forecasting in what place
To set upon them, what advantaged best.
Meanwhile the men of Judah, to prevent
The harass of their land, beset me round;
I willingly on some conditions came
Into their hands, and they as gladly yield me
To the Uncircumcised a welcome prey,
Bound with two cords. But cords to me were threads
Touched with the flame: on their whole host I flew
Unarmed, and with a trivial weapon felled
Their choicest youth; they only lived who fled.
Had Judah that day joined, or one whole tribe,
They had by this possessed the towers of Gath,
And lorded over them whom now they serve.
But what more oft, in nations grown corrupt,
And by their vices brought to servitude,
Than to love bondage more than liberty—
Bondage with ease than strenuous liberty—
And to despise, or envy, or suspect,
Whom God hath of His special favour raised
As their deliverer? If he aught begin,
How frequent to desert him, and at last
To heap ingratitude on worthiest deeds !
　　Chor. Thy words to my remembrance bring
How Succoth and the fort of Penuel
Their great deliverer contemned,
The matchless Gideon, in pursuit
Of Madian, and her vanquished kings;
And how ingrateful Ephraim
Had dealt with Jephtha, who by argument,
Not worse than by his shield and spear,
Defended Israel from the Ammonite,
Had not his prowess quelled their pride
In that sore battle when so many died
Without reprieve, adjudged to death
For want of well pronouncing *Shibboleth.*
　　Sams. Of such examples add me to the roll.

Me easily indeed mine may neglect,
But God's proposed deliverance not so.
   Chor. Just are the ways of God,
And justifiable to men,
Unless there be who think not God at all.
If any be, they walk obscure;
For of such doctrine never was there school,
But the heart of the fool,
And no man therein doctor but himself.

   Yet more there be who doubt His ways not just,
And to His own edicts found contradicting;
Then give the reins to wandering thought,
Regardless of His glory's diminution,
Till, by their own perplexities involved,
They ravel more, still less resolved,
But never find self-satisfying solution.

   As if they would confine the Interminable,
And tie Him to His own prescript,
Who made our laws to bind us, not Himself,
And hath full right to exempt
Whomso it pleases Him by choice
From national obstriction, without taint
Of sin, or legal debt;
For with His own laws He can best dispense.

   He would not else, who never wanted means,
Nor in respect of the enemy just cause,
To set His people free,
Have prompted this heroic Nazarite,
Against his vow of strictest purity,
To seek in marriage that fallacious bride,
Unclean, unchaste.

   Down, Reason, then; at least, vain reasonings down;
Though Reason here aver
That moral verdict quits her of unclean:
Unchaste was subsequent; her stain, not his.

   But see! here comes thy reverend sire,
With careful step, locks white as down,
Old Manoa: advise
Forthwith how thou ought'st to receive him.

   Sams. Ay me! another inward grief, awaked
With mention of that name, renews the assault.

   Man. Brethren and men of Dan (for such ye seem
Though in this uncouth place), if old respect,
As I suppose, towards your once gloried friend,
My son, now captive, hither hath informed
Your younger feet, while mine, cast back with age,
Came lagging after, say if he be here.

   Chor. As signal now in low dejected state
As erst in highest, behold him where he lies.

   Man. O miserable change! Is this the man,
That invincible Samson, far renowned,
The dread of Israel's foes, who with a strength
Equivalent to Angels' walked their streets,
None offering fight; who, single combatant,

Duelled their armies ranked in proud array,
Himself an army—now unequal match
To save himself against a coward armed
At one spear's length ?   O ever-failing trust
In mortal strength ! and, oh, what not in man
Deceivable and vain ?   Nay, what thing good
Prayed for, but often proves our woe, our bane ?
I prayed for children, and thought barrenness
In wedlock a reproach ; I gained a son,
And such a son as all men hailed me happy :
Who would be now a father in my stead ?
Oh, wherefore did God grant me my request,
And as a blessing with such pomp adorned ?
Why are His gifts desirable, to tempt
Our earnest prayers, then, given with solemn hand
As graces, draw a scorpion's tail behind ?
For this did the Angel twice descend ? for this
Ordained thy nurture holy, as of a plant
Select and sacred ? glorious for a while,
The miracle of men ; then in an hour
Ensnared, assaulted, overcome, led bound,
Thy foes' derision, captive, poor and blind,
Into a dungeon thrust, to work with slaves !
Alas ! methinks whom God hath chosen once
To worthiest deeds, if he through frailty err,
He should not so o'erwhelm, and as a thrall
Subject him to so foul indignities,
Be it but for honour's sake of former deeds.
    Sams. Appoint not heavenly disposition, father.
Nothing of all these evils hath befallen me
But justly ; I myself have brought them on ;
Sole author I, sole cause.   If aught seem vile,
As vile hath been my folly, who have profaned
The mystery of God, given me under pledge
Of vow, and have betrayed it to a woman,
A Canaanite, my faithless enemy.
This well I knew, nor was at all surprised,
But warned by oft experience.   Did not she
Of Timna first betray me, and reveal
The secret wrested from me in her highth
Of nuptial love professed, carrying it straight
To them who had corrupted her, my spies
And rivals ?   In this other was there found
More faith, who, also in her prime of love,
Spousal embraces, vitiated with gold,
Though offered only, by the scent conceived,
Her spurious first-born, Treason against me ?
Thrice she assayed, with flattering prayers and sighs,
And amorous reproaches, to win from me
My capital secret, in what part my strength
Lay stored, in what part summed, that she might know ;
Thrice I deluded her, and turned to sport
Her importunity, each time perceiving
How openly and with what impudence

She purposed to betray me, and (which was worse
Than undissembled hate) with what contempt
She sought to make me traitor to myself.
Yet, the fourth time, when, mustering all her wiles,
With blandished parleys, feminine assaults,
Tongue-batteries, she surceased not day nor night
To storm me, over-watched and wearied out,
At times when men seek most repose and rest,
I yielded, and unlocked her all my heart,
Who, with a grain of manhood well resolved,
Might easily have shook off all her snares ;
But foul effeminacy held me yoked
Her bond-slave.   O indignity, O blot
To honour and religion ! servile mind
Rewarded well with servile punishment !
The base degree to which I now am fallen,
These rags, this grinding, is not yet so base
As was my former servitude, ignoble,
Unmanly, ignominious, infamous,
True slavery ; and that blindness worse than this,
That saw not how degenerately I served.
    Man. I cannot praise thy marriage-choices, son—
Rather approved them not ; but thou didst plead
Divine impulsion prompting how thou might'st
Find some occasion to infest our foes.
I state not that ; this I am sure—our foes
Found soon occasion thereby to make thee
Their captive, and their triumph ; thou the sooner
Temptation found'st, or over-potent charms,
To violate the sacred trust of silence
Deposited within thee—which to have kept
Tacit was in thy power.   True ; and thou bear'st
Enough, and more, the burden of that fault ;
Bitterly hast thou paid, and still art paying,
That rigid score.   A worse thing yet remains :
This day the Philistines a popular feast
Here celebrate in Gaza, and proclaim
Great pomp, and sacrifice, and praises loud,
To Dagon, as their god who hath delivered
Thee, Samson, bound and blind, into their hands—
Them out of thine, who slew'st them many a slain.
So Dagon shall be magnified, and God,
Besides whom is no god, compared with idols,
Disglorified, blasphemed, and had in scorn
By the idolatrous rout amidst their wine ;
Which to have come to pass by means of thee,
Samson, of all thy sufferings think the heaviest,
Of all reproach the most with shame that ever
Could have befallen thee and thy father's house.
    Sams. Father, I do acknowledge and confess
That I this honour, I this pomp, have brought
To Dagon, and advanced his praises high
Among the Heathen round—to God have brought
Dishonour, obloquy, and oped the mouths

Of idolists and atheists ; have brought scandal
To Israel, diffidence of God, and doubt
In feeble hearts, propense enough before
To waver, or fall off and join with idols :
Which is my chief affliction, shame, and sorrow,
The anguish of my soul, that suffers not
Mine eye to harbour sleep, or thoughts to rest.
This only hope relieves me, that the strife
With me hath end.   All the contest is now
'Twixt God and Dagon.   Dagon hath presumed,
Me overthrown, to enter lists with God,
His deity comparing and preferring
Before the God of Abraham.   He, be sure,
Will not connive, or linger, thus provoked,
But will arise, and His great name assert.
Dagon must stoop, and shall ere long receive
Such a discomfit as shall quite despoil him
Of all these boasted trophies won on me,
And with confusion blank his worshippers.
   Man. With cause this hope relieves thee ; and these words
I as a prophecy receive ; for God
(Nothing more certain) will not long defer
To vindicate the glory of His name
Against all competition, nor will long
Endure it doubtful whether God be Lord
Or Dagon.   But for thee what shall be done ?
Thou must not in the meanwhile, here forgot,
Lie in this miserable loathsome plight
Neglected.   I already have made way
To some Philistian lords, with whom to treat
About thy ransom.   Well they may by this
Have satisfied their utmost of revenge,
By pains and slaveries, worse than death, inflicted
On thee, who now no more canst do them harm.
   Sams. Spare that proposal, father ; spare the trouble
Of that solicitation.   Let me here,
As I deserve, pay on my punishment,
And expiate, if possible, my crime,
Shameful garrulity.   To have revealed
Secrets of *men*, the secrets of a friend,
How heinous had the fact been, how deserving
Contempt and scorn of all—to be excluded
All friendship, and avoided as a blab,
The mark of fool set on his front !
But I *God's* counsel have not kept, His holy secret
Presumptuously have published, impiously,
Weakly at least and shamefully—a sin
That Gentiles in their parables condemn
To their Abyss and horrid pains confined.
   Man. Be penitent, and for thy fault contrite ;
But act not in thy own affliction, son.
Repent the sin ; but, if the punishment
Thou canst avoid, self-preservation bids ;
Or the execution leave to high disposal,

And let another hand, not thine, exact
Thy penal forfeit from thyself.   Perhaps
God will relent, and quit thee all His debt;
Who ever more approves and more accepts
(Best pleased with humble and filial submission)
Him who, imploring mercy, sues for life,
Than who, self-rigorous, chooses death as due;
Which argues over-just, and self-displeased
For self-offence more than for God offended.
Reject not, then, what offered means who knows
But God hath set before us to return thee
Home to thy country and His sacred house,
Where thou may'st bring thy offerings, to avert
His further ire, with prayers and vows renewed.

    Sams. His pardon I implore; but, as for life,
To what end should I seek it?   When in strength
All mortals I excelled, and great in hopes,
With youthful courage, and magnanimous thoughts
Of birth from Heaven foretold and high exploits,
Full of divine instinct, after some proof
Of acts indeed heroic, far beyond
The sons of Anak, famous now and blazed,
Fearless of danger, like a petty god
I walked about, admired of all, and dreaded
On hostile ground, none daring my affront—
Then, swollen with pride, into the snare I fell
Of fair fallacious looks, venereal trains,
Softened with pleasure and voluptuous life,
At length to lay my head and hallowed pledge
Of all my strength in the lascivious lap
Of a deceitful concubine, who shore me,
Like a tame wether, all my precious fleece,
Then turned me out ridiculous, despoiled,
Shaven, and disarmed among my enemies.

    Chor. Desire of wine and all delicious drinks,
Which many a famous warrior overturns,
Thou couldst repress; nor did the dancing ruby,
Sparkling out-poured, the flavour or the smell,
Or taste, that cheers the heart of gods and men,
Allure thee from the cool crystalline stream.

    Sams. Wherever fountain or fresh current flowed
Against the eastern ray, translucent, pure
With touch ethereal of Heaven's fiery rod,
I drank, from the clear milky juice allaying
Thirst, and refreshed; nor envied them the grape
Whose heads that turbulent liquor fills with fumes.

    Chor. O madness! to think use of strongest wines
And strongest drinks our chief support of health,
When God with these forbidden made choice to rear
His mighty champion, strong above compare,
Whose drink was only from the liquid brook!

    Sams. But what availed this temperance, not complete
Against another object more enticing?
What boots it at one gate to make defence,

M.—T

And at another to let in the foe,
Effeminately vanquished? by which means,
Now blind, disheartened, shamed, dishonoured, quelled,
To what can I be useful? wherein serve
My nation, and the work from Heaven imposed?
But to sit idle on the household hearth,
A burdenous drone; to visitants a gaze,
Or pitied object; these redundant locks,
Robustious to no purpose, clustering down,
Vain monument of strength; till length of years
And sedentary numbness craze my limbs
To a contemptible old age obscure.
Here rather let me drudge, and earn my bread,
Till vermin, or the draff of servile food,
Consume me, and oft-invocated death
Hasten the welcome end of all my pains.
Man. Wilt thou then serve the Philistines with that gift
Which was expressly given thee to annoy them?
Better at home lie bed-rid, not only idle,
Inglorious, unemployed, with age outworn.
But God, who caused a fountain at thy prayer
From the dry ground to spring, thy thirst to allay
After the brunt of battle, can as easy
Cause light again within thy eyes to spring,
Wherewith to serve Him better than thou hast.
And I persuade me so. Why else this strength
Miraculous yet remaining in those locks?
His might continues in thee not for naught,
Nor shall His wondrous gifts be frustrate thus.
Sams. All otherwise to me my thoughts portend—
That these dark orbs no more shall treat with light,
Nor the other light of life continue long,
But yield to double darkness nigh at hand;
So much I feel my genial spirits droop,
My hopes all flat; Nature within me seems
In all her functions weary of herself;
My race of glory run, and race of shame,
And I shall shortly be with them that rest.
Man. Believe not these suggestions, which proceed
From anguish of the mind, and humours black
That mingle with thy fancy. I, however,
Must not omit a father's timely care
To prosecute the means of thy deliverance
By ransom or how else: meanwhile be calm,
And healing words from these thy friends admit.
Sams. Oh, that torment should not be confined
To the body's wounds and sores,
With maladies innumerable
In heart, head, breast, and reins,
But must secret passage find
To the inmost mind,
There exercise all his fierce accidents,
And on her purest spirits prey,
As on entrails, joints, and limbs,

With answerable pains, but more intense,
Though void of corporal sense !
  My griefs not only pain me
As a lingering disease,
But, finding no redress, ferment and rage ;
Nor less than wounds immedicable
Rankle, and fester, and gangrene,
To black mortification.
Thoughts, my tormentors, armed with deadly stings,
Mangle my apprehensive tenderest parts,
Exasperate, exulcerate, and raise
Dire inflammation, which no cooling herb
Or medicinal liquor can assuage,
Nor breath of vernal air from snowy Alp.
Sleep hath forsook and given me o'er
To death's benumbing opium as my only cure ;
Thence faintings, swoonings of despair,
And sense of Heaven's desertion.
  I was His nursling once and choice delight,
His destined from the womb,
Promised by heavenly message twice descending.
Under His special eye
Abstemious I grew up and thrived amain ;
He led me on to mightiest deeds,
Above the nerve of mortal arm,
Against the Uncircumcised, our enemies :
But now hath cast me off as never known,
And to those cruel enemies,
Whom I by His appointment had provoked,
Left me all helpless, with the irreparable loss
Of sight, reserved alive to be repeated,
The subject of their cruelty or scorn.
Nor am I in the list of them that hope ;
Hopeless are all my evils, all remediless.
This one prayer yet remains, might I be heard,
No long petition—speedy death,
The close of all my miseries and the balm.
  Chor. Many are the sayings of the wise,
In ancient and in modern books enrolled,
Extolling patience as the truest fortitude,
And to the bearing well of all calamities,
All chances incident to man's frail life,
Consolatories writ
With studied argument, and much persuasion sought,
Lenient of grief and anxious thought.
But with the afflicted in his pangs their sound
Little prevails, or rather seems a tune
Harsh, and of dissonant mood from his complaint,
Unless he feel within
Some source of consolation from above,
Secret refreshings that repair his strength
And fainting spirits uphold.
  God of our fathers ! what is Man,
That Thou towards him with hand so various—

Or might I say contrarious?—
Temper'st Thy providence through his short course:
Not evenly, as Thou rul'st
The angelic orders, and inferior creatures mute,
Irrational and brute?
Nor do I name of men the common rout,
That, wandering loose about,
Grow up and perish as the summer fly,
Heads without name, no more remembered;
But such as Thou hast solemnly elected,
With gifts and graces eminently adorned,
To some great work, Thy glory,
And people's safety, which in part they effect.
Yet toward these, thus dignified, Thou oft,
Amidst their highth of noon,
Changest Thy countenance and Thy hand, with no regard
Of highest favours past
From Thee on them, or them to Thee of service.
 Nor only dost degrade them, or remit
To life obscured, which were a fair dismission,
But throw'st them lower than Thou didst exalt them high—
Unseemly falls in human eye,
Too grievous for the trespass or omission;
Oft leav'st them to the hostile sword
Of heathen and profane, their carcasses
To dogs and fowls a prey, or else captived,
Or to the unjust tribunals, under change of times,
And condemnation of the ungrateful multitude.
If these they 'scape, perhaps in poverty
With sickness and disease Thou bow'st them down,
Painful diseases and deformed,
In crude old age;
Though not disordinate, yet causeless suffering
The punishment of dissolute days. In fine,
Just or unjust alike seem miserable,
For oft alike both come to evil end.
 So deal not with this once Thy glorious champion,
The image of Thy strength, and mighty minister.
What do I beg? how hast Thou dealt already!
Behold him in this state calamitous, and turn
His labours, for Thou canst, to peaceful end.
 But who is this? what thing of sea or land—
Female of sex it seems—
That, so bedecked, ornate, and gay,
Comes this way sailing,
Like a stately ship
Of Tarsus, bound for the isles
Of Javan or Gadire,
With all her bravery on, and tackle trim,
Sails filled, and streamers waving,
Courted by all the winds that hold them play;
An amber scent of odorous perfume
Her harbinger, a damsel train behind?
Some rich Philistian matron she may seem;

And now, at nearer view, no other certain
Than Dalila, thy wife.
   Sams. My wife! my traitress! let her not come near me.
   Chor. Yet on she moves; now stands and eyes thee fixed,
About to have spoke, but now, with head declined,
Like a fair flower surcharged with dew, she weeps,
And words addressed seem into tears dissolved,
Wetting the borders of her silken veil.
But now again she makes address to speak.
   Dal. With doubtful feet and wavering resolution
I came, still dreading thy displeasure, Samson;
Which to have merited, without excuse,
I cannot but acknowledge. Yet, if tears
May expiate (though the fact more evil drew
In the perverse event than I foresaw),
My penance hath not slackened, though my pardon
No way assured. But conjugal affection,
Prevailing over fear and timorous doubt,
Hath led me on, desirous to behold
Once more thy face, and know of thy estate,
If aught in my ability may serve
To lighten what thou suffer'st, and appease
Thy mind with what amends is in my power—
Though late, yet in some part to recompense
My rash but more unfortunate misdeed.
   Sams. Out, out, hyæna! These are thy wonted arts,
And arts of every woman false like thee—
To break all faith, all vows, deceive, betray;
Then, as repentant, to submit, beseech,
And reconcilement move with feigned remorse,
Confess and promise wonders in her change—
Not truly penitent, but chief to try
Her husband, how far urged his patience bears,
His virtue or weakness which way to assail:
Then, with more cautious and instructed skill,
Again transgresses, and again submits;
That wisest and best men, full oft beguiled,
With goodness principled not to reject
The penitent, but ever to forgive,
Are drawn to wear out miserable days,
Entangled with a poisonous bosom-snake,
If not by quick destruction soon cut off,
As I by thee, to ages an example.
   Dal. Yet hear me, Samson; not that I endeavour
To lessen or extenuate my offence,
But that, on the other side, if it be weighed
By itself, with aggravations not surcharged,
Or else with just allowance counterpoised,
I may, if possible, thy pardon find,
The easier towards me, or thy hatred less.
First granting, as I do, it was a weakness
In me, but incident to all our sex,
Curiosity, inquisitive, importune
Of secrets, then with like infirmity

To publish them—both common female faults—
Was it not weakness also to make known
For importunity, that is, for naught,
Wherein consisted all thy strength and safety?
To what I did thou show'dst me first the way.
But I to enemies revealed, and should not!
Nor shouldst thou have trusted that to woman's frailty:
Ere I to thee, thou to thyself wast cruel.
Let weakness, then, with weakness come to parle,
So near related, or the same of kind ;
Thine forgive mine, that men may censure thine
The gentler, if severely thou exact not
More strength from me than in thyself was found.
And what if love, which thou interpret'st hate,
The jealousy of love, powerful of sway
In human hearts, not less in mine towards thee,
Caused what I did ? I saw thee mutable
Of fancy ; feared lest one day thou wouldst leave me
As her at Timna ; sought by all means, therefore,
How to endear, and hold thee to me firmest:
No better way I saw than by importuning
To learn thy secrets, get into my power
Thy key of strength and safety. Thou wilt say,
'Why, then, revealed?' I was assured by those
Who tempted me that nothing was designed
Against thee but safe custody and hold.
That made for me ; I knew that liberty
Would draw thee forth to perilous enterprises,
While I at home sat full of cares and fears,
Wailing thy absence in my widowed bed ;
Here I should still enjoy thee, day and night,
Mine and love's prisoner, not the Philistines',
Whole to myself, unhazarded abroad,
Fearless at home of partners in my love.
These reasons in Love's law have passed for good,
Though fond and reasonless to some perhaps ;
And love hath oft, well meaning, wrought much woe,
Yet always pity or pardon hath obtained.
Be not unlike all others, not austere
As thou art strong, inflexible as steel.
If thou in strength all mortals dost exceed,
In uncompassionate anger do not so.
   Sams. How cunningly the sorceress displays
Her own transgressions to upbraid me mine!
That malice, not repentance, brought thee hither
By this appears. I gave, thou say'st, the example,
I led the way—bitter reproach, but true ;
I to myself was false ere thou to me.
Such pardon, therefore, as I give my folly
Take to thy wicked deed ; which when thou seest
Impartial, self-severe, inexorable,
Thou wilt renounce thy seeking, and much rather
Confess it feigned. Weakness is thy excuse,
And I believe it—weakness to resist

Philistian gold. If weakness may excuse,
What murtherer, what traitor, parricide,
Incestuous, sacrilegious, but may plead it?
All wickedness is weakness; that plea, therefore,
With God or man will gain thee no remission.
But love constrained thee! Call it furious rage
To satisfy thy lust. Love seeks to have love;
My love how couldst thou hope, who took'st the way
To raise in me inexpiable hate,
Knowing, as needs I must, by thee betrayed?
In vain thou striv'st to cover shame with shame,
Or by evasions thy crime uncover'st more.
   Dal. Since thou determin'st weakness for no plea
In man or woman, though to thy own condemning,
Hear what assaults I had, what snares besides,
What sieges girt me round, ere I consented;
Which might have awed the best-resolved of men,
The constantest, to have yielded without blame.
It was not gold, as to my charge thou lay'st,
That wrought with me. Thou know'st the magistrates
And princes of my country came in person,
Solicited, commanded, threatened, urged,
Adjured by all the bonds of civil duty
And of religion—pressed how just it was,
How honourable, how glorious, to entrap
A common enemy, who had destroyed
Such numbers of our nation: and the priest
Was not behind, but ever at my ear,
Preaching how meritorious with the gods
It would be to ensnare an irreligious
Dishonourer of Dagon. What had I
To oppose against such powerful arguments?
Only my love of thee held long debate,
And combated in silence all these reasons
With hard contest. At length, that grounded maxim,
So rife and celebrated in the mouths
Of wisest men, that to the public good
Private respects must yield, with grave authority
Took full possession of me, and prevailed;
Virtue, as I thought, truth, duty, so enjoining.
   Sams. I thought where all thy circling wiles would end—
In feigned religion, smooth hypocrisy!
But, had thy love, still odiously pretended,
Been, as it ought, sincere, it would have taught thee
Far other reasonings, brought forth other deeds.
I, before all the daughters of my tribe
And of my nation, chose thee from among
My enemies, loved thee, as too well thou knew'st;
Too well; unbosomed all my secrets to thee,
Not out of levity, but overpowered
By thy request, who could deny thee nothing;
Yet now am judged an enemy. Why, then,
Didst thou at first receive me for thy husband—
Then, as since then, thy country's foe professed?

Being once a wife, for me thou wast to leave
Parents and country; nor was I their subject,
Nor under their protection, but my own;
Thou mine, not theirs. If aught against my life
Thy country sought of thee, it sought unjustly,
Against the law of nature, law of nations;
No more thy country, but an impious crew
Of men conspiring to uphold their state
By worse than hostile deeds, violating the ends
For which our country is a name so dear;
Not therefore to be obeyed. But zeal moved thee;
To please thy gods thou didst it! Gods unable
To acquit themselves and prosecute their foes
But by ungodly deeds, the contradiction
Of their own deity, Gods cannot be—
Less therefore to be pleased, obeyed, or feared.
These false pretexts and varnished colours failing,
Bare in thy guilt, how foul must thou appear!
    Dal. In argument with men a woman ever
Goes by the worse, whatever be her cause.
    Sams. For want of words, no doubt, or lack of breath!
Witness when I was worried with thy peals.
    Dal. I was a fool, too rash, and quite mistaken
In what I thought would have succeeded best.
Let me obtain forgiveness of thee, Samson;
Afford me place to show what recompense
Towards thee I intend for what I have misdone,
Misguided. Only what remains past cure
Bear not too sensibly, nor still insist
To afflict thyself in vain. Though sight be lost,
Life yet hath many solaces, enjoyed
Where other senses want not their delights—
At home, in leisure and domestic ease,
Exempt from many a care and chance to which
Eyesight exposes, daily, men abroad.
I to the lords will intercede, not doubting
Their favourable ear, that I may fetch thee
From forth this loathsome prison-house, to abide
With me, where my redoubled love and care,
With nursing diligence, to me glad office,
May ever tend about thee to old age,
With all things grateful cheered, and so supplied
That what by me thou hast lost thou least shalt miss.
    Sams. No, no; of my condition take no care;
It fits not; thou and I long since are twain;
Nor think me so unwary or accursed
To bring my feet again into the snare
Where once I have been caught. I know thy trains,
Though dearly to my cost, thy gins, and toils.
Thy fair enchanted cup, and warbling charms,
No more on me have power; their force is nulled;
So much of adder's wisdom I have learned,
To fence my ear against thy sorceries.
If in my flower of youth and strength, when all men

280

Loved, honoured, feared me, thou alone could hate me,
Thy husband, slight me, sell me, and forego me,
How wouldst thou use me now, blind, and thereby
Deceivable, in most things as a child
Helpless, thence easily contemned and scorned,
And last neglected! How wouldst thou insult,
When I must live uxorious to thy will
In perfect thraldom! how again betray me,
Bearing my words and doings to the lords
To gloss upon, and, censuring, frown or smile!
This jail I count the house of liberty
To thine, whose doors my feet shall never enter.
   Dal. Let me approach, at least, and touch thy hand.
   Sams. Not for thy life, lest fierce remembrance wake
My sudden rage to tear thee joint by joint.
At distance I forgive thee; go with that;
Bewail thy falsehood, and the pious works
It hath brought forth to make thee memorable
Among illustrious women, faithful wives;
Cherish thy hastened widowhood with the gold
Of matrimonial treason: so farewell.
   Dal. I see thou art implacable, more deaf
To prayers than winds and seas. Yet winds to seas
Are reconciled at length, and sea to shore:
Thy anger, unappeasable, still rages,
Eternal tempest never to be calmed.
Why do I humble thus myself, and, suing
For peace, reap nothing but repulse and hate,
Bid go with evil omen, and the brand
Of infamy upon my name denounced?
To mix with thy concernments I desist
Henceforth, nor too much disapprove my own.
Fame, if not double-faced, is double-mouthed,
And with contrary blast proclaims most deeds;
On both his wings, one black, the other white,
Bears greatest names in his wild aery flight.
My name, perhaps, among the Circumcised
In Dan, in Judah, and the bordering tribes,
To all posterity may stand defamed,
With malediction mentioned, and the blot
Of falsehood most unconjugal traduced.
But in my country, where I most desire,
In Ecron, Gaza, Asdod, and in Gath,
I shall be named among the famousest
Of women, sung at solemn festivals,
Living and dead recorded, who, to save
Her country from a fierce destroyer, chose
Above the faith of wedlock bands; my tomb
With odours visited and annual flowers;
Not less renowned than in Mount Ephraim
Jael, who, with inhospitable guile,
Smote Sisera sleeping, through the temples nailed.
Nor shall I count it heinous to enjoy
The public marks of honour and reward

Conferred upon me for the piety
Which to my country I was judged to have shown.
At this whoever envies or repines,
I leave him to his lot, and like my own.
   Chor. She's gone—a manifest serpent by her sting
Discovered in the end, till now concealed.
   Sams. So let her go.   God sent her to debase me,
And aggravate my folly, who committed
To such a viper His most sacred trust
Of secrecy, my safety, and my life.
   Chor. Yet beauty, though injurious, hath strange power,
After offence returning, to regain
Love once possessed, nor can be easily
Repulsed, without much inward passion felt,
And secret sting of amorous remorse.
   Sams. Love-quarrels oft in pleasing concord end;
Not wedlock-treachery endangering life.
   Chor. It is not virtue, wisdom, valour, wit,
Strength, comeliness of shape, or amplest merit,
That woman's love can win, or long inherit;
But what it is, hard is to say,
Harder to hit,
Which way soever men refer it,
(Much like thy riddle, Samson) in one day
Or seven though one should musing sit.
   If any of these, or all, the Timnian bride
Had not so soon preferred
Thy paranymph, worthless to thee compared,
Successor in thy bed,
Nor both so loosely disallied
Their nuptials, nor this last so treacherously
Had shorn the fatal harvest of thy head.
Is it for that such outward ornament
Was lavished on their sex, that inward gifts
Were left for haste unfinished, judgment scant,
Capacity not raised to apprehend
Or value what is best,
In choice, but oftest to affect the wrong?
Or was too much of self-love mixed,
Of constancy no root infixed,
That either they love nothing, or not long?
   Whate'er it be, to wisest men and best,
Seeming at first all heavenly under virgin veil,
Soft, modest, meek, demure,
Once joined, the contrary she proves—a thorn
Intestine, far within defensive arms
A cleaving mischief, in his way to virtue
Adverse and turbulent; or by her charms
Draws him awry, enslaved
With dotage, and his sense depraved
To folly and shameful deeds, which ruin ends.
What pilot so expert but needs must wreck,
Embarked with such a steers-mate at the helm?
   Favoured of Heaven who finds

282

One virtuous, rarely found,
That in domestic good combines!
Happy that house; his way to peace is smooth:
But virtue which breaks through all opposition,
And all temptation can remove,
Most shines and most is acceptable above.

   Therefore God's universal law
Gave to the man despotic power
Over his female in due awe,
Nor from that right to part an hour,
Smile she or lour:
So shall he least confusion draw
On his whole life, not swayed
By female usurpation, nor dismayed.

   But had we best retire? I see a storm.

   Sams. Fair days have oft contracted wind and rain.

   Chor. But this another kind of tempest brings.

   Sams. Be less abstruse; my riddling days are past.

   Chor. Look now for no enchanting voice, nor fear
The bait of honeyed words; a rougher tongue
Draws hitherward: I know him by his stride,
The giant Harapha of Gath, his look
Haughty, as is his pile high-built and proud.
Comes he in peace? What wind hath blown him hither
I less conjecture than when first I saw
The sumptuous Dalila floating this way:
His habit carries peace, his brow defiance.

   Sams. Or peace or not, alike to me he comes.

   Chor. His fraught we soon shall know: he now arrives.

   Har. I come not, Samson, to condole thy chance,
As these perhaps, yet wish it had not been,
Though for no friendly intent. I am of Gath;
Men call me Harapha, of stock renowned
As Og, or Anak, and the Emims old
That Kiriathaim held. Thou know'st me now,
If thou at all art known. Much I have heard
Of thy prodigious might and feats performed,
Incredible to me, in this displeased,
That I was never present on the place
Of those encounters, where we might have tried
Each other's force in camp or listed field;
And now am come to see of whom such noise
Hath walked about, and each limb to survey,
If thy appearance answer loud report.

   Sams. The way to know were not to see, but taste.

   Har. Dost thou already single me? I thought
Gyves and the mill had tamed thee. O that fortune
Had brought me to the field where thou art famed
To have wrought such wonders with an ass's jaw!
I should have forced thee soon wish other arms,
Or left thy carcass where the ass lay thrown;
So had the glory of prowess been recovered
To Palestine, won by a Philistine
From the unforeskinned race, of whom thou bear'st

The highest name for valiant acts.   That honour,
Certain to have won by mortal duel from thee,
I lose, prevented by thy eyes put out.
  Sams. Boast not of what thou wouldst have done, but do
What then thou wouldst ; thou seest it in thy hand.
  Har. To combat with a blind man I disdain,
And thou hast need much washing to be touched.
  Sams. Such usage as your honourable lords
Afford me, assassinated and betrayed ;
Who durst not with their whole united powers
In fight withstand me single and unarmed,
Nor in the house with chamber-ambushes
Close-banded durst attack me, no, not sleeping,
Till they had hired a woman with their gold,
Breaking her marriage-faith, to circumvent me.
Therefore, without feign'd shifts, let be assigned
Some narrow place enclosed, where sight may give thee,
Or rather flight, no great advantage on me ;
Then put on all thy gorgeous arms, thy helmet
And brigandine of brass, thy broad habergeon,
Vant-brace and greaves and gauntlet ; add thy spear,
A weaver's beam, and seven-times-folded shield :
I only with an oaken staff will meet thee,
And raise such outcries on thy clattered iron,
Which long shall not withhold me from thy head,
That in a little time, while breath remains thee,
Thou oft shalt wish thyself at Gath, to boast
Again in safety what thou wouldst have done
To Samson, but shalt never see Gath more.
  Har. Thou durst not thus disparage glorious arms
Which greatest heroes have in battle worn,
Their ornament and safety, had not spells
And black enchantments, some magician's art,
Armed thee or charmed thee strong, which thou from **Heaven**
Feign'dst at thy birth was given thee in thy hair,
Where strength can least abide, though all thy hairs
Were bristles ranged like those that ridge the back
Of chafed wild boars or ruffled porcupines.
  Sams. I know no spells, use no forbidden arts ;
My trust is in the Living God, who gave me,
At my nativity, this strength, diffused
No less through all my sinews, joints, and bones,
Than thine, while I preserved these locks unshorn,
The pledge of my unviolated vow.
For proof hereof, if Dagon be thy god,
Go to his temple, invocate his aid
With solemnest devotion, spread before him
How highly it concerns his glory now
To frustrate and dissolve these magic spells,
Which I to be the power of Israel's God
Avow, and challenge Dagon to the test,
Offering to combat thee, his champion bold,
With the utmost of his godhead seconded :
Then thou shalt see, or rather to thy sorrow

Soon feel, whose God is strongest, thine or mine.
   Har. Presume not on thy God. Whate'er He be,
Thee He regards not, owns not, hath cut off
Quite from His people, and delivered up
Into thy enemies' hand ; permitted them
To put out both thine eyes, and fettered send thee
Into the common prison, there to grind
Among the slaves and asses, thy comrades,
As good for nothing else, no better service
With those thy boisterous locks ; no worthy match
For valour to assail, nor by the sword
Of noble warrior, so to stain his honour,
But by the barber's razor best subdued.
   Sams. All these indignities, for such they are
From thine, these evils I deserve and more,
Acknowledge them from God inflicted on me
Justly, yet despair not of His final pardon,
Whose ear is ever open, and His eye
Gracious to re-admit the suppliant ;
In confidence whereof I once again
Defy thee to the trial of mortal fight,
By combat to decide whose god is God,
Thine, or whom I with Israel's sons adore.
   Har. Fair honour that thou dost thy God, in trusting
He will accept thee to defend his cause,
A murtherer, a revolter, and a robber !
   Sams. Tongue-doughty giant, how dost thou prove me these ?
   Har. Is not thy nation subject to our lords ?
Their magistrates confessed it when they took thee
As a league-breaker, and delivered bound
Into our hands ; for hadst thou not committed
Notorious murder on those thirty men
At Ascalon, who never did thee harm,
Then, like a robber, stripp'dst them of their robes ?
The Philistines, when thou hadst broke the league,
Went up with armed powers thee only seeking,
To others did no violence or spoil.
   Sams. Among the daughters of the Philistines
I chose a wife, which argued me no foe,
And in your city held my nuptial feast ;
But your ill-meaning politician lords,
Under pretence of bridal friends and guests,
Appointed to await me thirty spies,
Who, threatening cruel death, constrained the bride
To wring from me, and tell to them, my secret,
That solved the riddle which I had proposed.
When I perceived all set on enmity,
As on my enemies, wherever chanced,
I used hostility, and took their spoil,
To pay my underminers in their coin.
My nation was subjected to your lords !
It was the force of conquest ; force with force
Is well ejected when the conquered can.
But I, a private person, whom my country

As a league-breaker gave up bound, presumed
Single rebellion, and did hostile acts !
I was no private, but a person raised,
With strength sufficient, and command from Heaven,
To free my country.   If their servile minds
Me, their deliverer sent, would not receive,
But to their masters gave me up for nought,
The unworthier they ; whence to this day they serve.
I was to do my part from Heaven assigned,
And had performed it if my known offence
Had not disabled me, not all your force.
These shifts refuted, answer thy appellant,
Though by his blindness maimed for high attempts,
Who now defies thee thrice to single fight,
As a petty enterprise of small enforce.
  Har. With thee, a man condemned, a slave enrolled,
Due by the law to capital punishment ?
To fight with thee no man of arms will deign.
  Sams. Cam'st thou for this, vain boaster, to survey me,
To descant on my strength, and give thy verdict ?
Come nearer ; part not hence so slight informed ;
But take good heed my hand survey not thee.
  Har. O Baal-zebub ! can my ears unused
Hear these dishonours, and not render death ?
  Sams. No man withholds thee ; nothing from thy hand
Fear I incurable ; bring up thy van ;
My heels are fettered, but my fist is free.
  Har. This insolence other kind of answer fits.
  Sams. Go, baffled coward, lest I run upon thee,
Though in these chains, bulk without spirit vast,
And with one buffet lay thy structure low,
Or swing thee in the air, then dash thee down,
To the hazard of thy brains and shattered sides.
  Har. By Astaroth, ere long thou shalt lament
These braveries, in irons loaden on thee.
  Chor. His giantship is gone somewhat crest-fallen,
Stalking with less unconscionable strides,
And lower looks, but in a sultry chafe.
  Sams. I dread him not, nor all his giant brood,
Though fame divulge him father of five sons,
All of gigantic size, Goliah chief.
  Chor. He will directly to the lords, I fear,
And with malicious counsel stir them up
Some way or other yet further to afflict thee.
  Sams. He must allege some cause, and offered fight
Will not dare mention, lest a question rise
Whether he durst accept the offer or not ;
And that he durst not plain enough appeared.
Much more affliction than already felt
They cannot well impose, nor I sustain,
If they intend advantage of my labours,
The work of many hands, which earns my keeping,
With no small profit daily to my owners.
But come what will ; my deadliest foe will prove

286

My speediest friend, by death to rid me hence;
The worst that he can give to me the best.
Yet so it may fall out, because their end
Is hate, not help to me, it may with mine
Draw their own ruin who attempt the deed.
  Chor. O, how comely it is, and how reviving
To the spirits of just men long oppressed,
When God into the hands of their deliverer
Puts invincible might,
To quell the mighty of the earth, the oppressor,
The brute and boisterous force of violent men,
Hardy and industrious to support
Tyrannic power, but raging to pursue
The righteous, and all such as honour truth !
He all their ammunition
And feats of war defeats,
With plain heroic magnitude of mind
And celestial vigour armed ;
Their armouries and magazines contemns,
Renders them useless, while
With winged expedition
Swift as the lightning glance he executes
His errand on the wicked, who, surprised,
Lose their defence, distracted and amazed.
  But patience is more oft the exercise
Of saints, the trial of their fortitude,
Making them each his own deliverer,
And victor over all
That tyranny or fortune can inflict.
Either of these is in thy lot,
Samson, with might endued
Above the sons of men ; but sight bereaved
May chance to number thee with those
Whom patience finally must crown.
  This Idol's day hath been to thee no day of rest,
Labouring thy mind
More than the working day thy hands.
And yet, perhaps, more trouble is behind ;
For I descry this way
Some other tending ; in his hand
A sceptre or quaint staff he bears,
Comes on amain, speed in his look.
By his habit I discern him now
A public officer, and now at hand.
His message will be short and voluble.
  Off. Ebrews, the prisoner Samson here I seek.
  Chor. His manacles remark him ; there he sits.
  Off. Samson, to thee our lords thus bid me say :
This day to Dagon is a solemn feast,
With sacrifices, triumph, pomp, and games ;
Thy strength they know surpassing human rate,
And now some public proof thereof require
To honour this great feast, and great assembly.
Rise, therefore, with all speed, and come along,

287

Where I will see thee heartened and fresh clad,
To appear as fits before the illustrious lords.
   Sams. Thou know'st I am an Ebrew; therefore tell them
Our law forbids at their religious rites
My presence; for that cause I cannot come.
   Off. This answer, be assured, will not content them.
   Sams. Have they not sword-players, and every sort
Of gymnic artists, wrestlers, riders, runners,
Jugglers and dancers, antics, mummers, mimics,
But they must pick me out, with shackles tired,
And over-laboured at their public mill,
To make them sport with blind activity?
Do they not seek occasion of new quarrels,
On my refusal, to distress me more,
Or make a game of my calamities?
Return the way thou cam'st; I will not come.
   Off. Regard thyself; this will offend them highly.
   Sams. Myself! my conscience, and internal peace.
Can they think me so broken, so debased
With corporal servitude, that my mind ever
Will condescend to such absurd commands?
Although their drudge, to be their fool or jester,
And, in my midst of sorrow and heart-grief,
To show them feats, and play before their god—
The worst of all indignities, yet on me
Joined with extreme contempt! I will not come.
   Off. My message was imposed on me with speed,
Brooks no delay: is this thy resolution?
   Sams. So take it with what speed thy message needs.
   Off. I am sorry what this stoutness will produce.
   Sams. Perhaps thou shalt have cause to sorrow indeed.
   Chor. Consider, Samson; matters now are strained
Up to the highth, whether to hold or break.
He's gone, and who knows how he may report
Thy words by adding fuel to the flame?
Expect another message, more imperious,
More lordly thundering than thou well wilt bear.
   Sams. Shall I abuse this consecrated gift
Of strength, again returning with my hair
After my great transgression—so requite
Favour renewed, and add a greater sin
By prostituting holy things to idols,
A Nazarite, in place abominable,
Vaunting my strength in honour to their Dagon?
Besides how vile, contemptible, ridiculous,
What act more execrably unclean, profane?
   Chor. Yet with this strength thou serv'st the Philistines,
Idolatrous, uncircumcised, unclean.
   Sams. Not in their idol-worship, but by labour
Honest and lawful to deserve my food
Of those who have me in their civil power.
   Chor. Where the heart joins not, outward acts defile not.
   Sams. Where outward force constrains, the sentence holds:
But who constrains me to the temple of Dagon,

288

Not dragging? The Philistian lords command:
Commands are no constraints. If I obey them,
I do it freely, venturing to displease
God for the fear of man, and man prefer,
Set God behind; which, in His jealousy,
Shall never, unrepented, find forgiveness.
Yet that He may dispense with me, or thee,
Present in temples at idolatrous rites
For some important cause, thou need'st not doubt.
   Chor. How thou wilt here come off surmounts my reach.
   Sams. Be of good courage; I begin to feel
Some rousing motions in me, which dispose
To something extraordinary my thoughts.
I with this messenger will go along—
Nothing to do, be sure, that may dishonour
Our Law, or stain my vow of Nazarite.
If there be aught of presage in the mind,
This day will be remarkable in my life
By some great act, or of my days the last.
   Chor. In time thou hast resolved: the man returns.
   Off. Samson, this second message from our lords
To thee I am bid say: Art thou our slave,
Our captive, at the public mill our drudge,
And dar'st thou, at our sending and command,
Dispute thy coming? Come without delay;
Or we shall find such engines to assail
And hamper thee, as thou shalt come of force,
Though thou wert firmlier fastened than a rock.
   Sams. I could be well content to try their art,
Which to no few of them would prove pernicious;
Yet, knowing their advantages too many,
Because they shall not trail me through their streets
Like a wild beast, I am content to go.
Masters' commands come with a power resistless
To such as owe them absolute subjection;
And for a life who will not change his purpose?
(So mutable are all the ways of men!)
Yet this be sure, in nothing to comply
Scandalous or forbidden in our Law.
   Off. I praise thy resolution. Doff these links:
By this compliance thou wilt win the lords
To favour, and perhaps to set thee free.
   Sams. Brethren, farewell. Your company along
I will not wish, lest it perhaps offend them
To see me girt with friends; and how the sight
Of me, as of a common enemy,
So dreaded once, may now exasperate them
I know not. Lords are lordliest in their wine;
And the well-feasted priest then soonest fired
With zeal, if aught religion seem concerned;
No less the people, on their holy-days,
Impetuous, insolent, unquenchable.
Happen what may, of me expect to hear
Nothing dishonourable, impure, unworthy

M.—U

Our God, our Law, my nation, or myself;
The last of me or no I cannot warrant.
   Chor. Go, and the Holy One
Of Israel be thy guide
To what may serve His glory best, and spread His name
Great among the Heathen round;
Send thee the Angel of thy birth, to stand
Fast by thy side, who from thy father's field
Rode up in flames after his message told
Of thy conception, and be now a shield
Of fire; that Spirit that first rushed on thee
In the camp of Dan,
Be efficacious in thee now at need!
For never was from Heaven imparted
Measure of strength so great to mortal seed,
As in thy wondrous actions hath been seen.
But wherefore comes old Manoa in such haste
With youthful steps? Much livelier than erewhile
He seems: supposing here to find his son,
Or of him bringing to us some glad news?
   Man. Peace with you, brethren! My inducement hither
Was not at present here to find my son,
By order of the lords new parted hence
To come and play before them at their feast.
I heard all as I came; the city rings,
And numbers thither flock: I had no will,
Lest I should see him forced to things unseemly.
But that which moved my coming now was chiefly
To give ye part with me what hope I have
With good success to work his liberty.
   Chor. That hope would much rejoice us to partake
With thee. Say, reverend sire; we thirst to hear.
   Man. I have attempted, one by one, the lords,
Either at home, or through the high street passing,
With supplication prone and father's tears,
To accept of ransom for my son, their prisoner.
Some much averse I found, and wondrous harsh,
Contemptuous, proud, set on revenge and spite;
That part most reverenced Dagon and his priests:
Others more moderate seeming, but their aim
Private reward, for which both God and State
They easily would set to sale: a third
More generous far and civil, who confessed
They had enough revenged, having reduced
Their foe to misery beneath their fears;
The rest was magnanimity to remit,
If some convenient ransom were proposed.
What noise or shout was that? It tore the sky.
   Chor. Doubtless the people shouting to behold
Their once great dread, captive and blind before them,
Or at some proof of strength before them shown.
   Man. His ransom, if my whole inheritance
May compass it, shall willingly be paid
And numbered down. Much rather I shall choose

To live the poorest in my tribe, than richest
And he in that calamitous prison left.
No, I am fixed not to part hence without him.
For his redemption all my patrimony,
If need be, I am ready to forego
And quit.   Not wanting him, I shall want nothing.
   Chor. Fathers are wont to lay up for their sons ;
Thou for thy son art bent to lay out all :
Sons wont to nurse their parents in old age ;
Thou in old age car'st how to nurse thy son,
Made older than thy age through eye-sight lost.
   Man. It shall be my delight to tend his eyes,
And view him sitting in his house, ennobled
With all those high exploits by him achieved,
And on his shoulders waving down those locks
That of a nation armed the strength contained.
And I persuade me God hath not permitted
His strength again to grow up with his hair
Garrisoned round about him like a camp
Of faithful soldiery, were not His purpose
To use him further yet in some great service—
Not to sit idle with so great a gift
Useless, and thence ridiculous, about him.
And, since his strength with eye-sight was not lost,
God will restore him eye-sight to his strength.
   Chor. Thy hopes are not ill founded, nor seem vain,
Of his delivery, and thy joy thereon
Conceived, agreeable to a father's love ;
In both which we, as next, participate.
   Man. I know your friendly minds, and . . . O, what noise !
Mercy of Heaven ! what hideous noise was that ?
Horribly loud, unlike the former shout.
   Chor. Noise call you it, or universal groan,
As if the whole inhabitation perished ?
Blood, death, and deathful deeds, are in that noise,
Ruin, destruction at the utmost point.
   Man. Of ruin indeed methought I heard the noise.
Oh ! it continues ; they have slain my son.
   Chor. Thy son is rather slaying them : that outcry
From slaughter of one foe could not ascend.
   Man. Some dismal accident it needs must be.
What shall we do—stay here, or run and see ?
   Chor. Best keep together here, lest, running thither,
We unawares run into danger's mouth.
This evil on the Philistines is fallen :
From whom could else a general cry be heard ?
The sufferers, then, will scarce molest us here ;
From other hands we need not much to fear.
What if, his eye-sight (for to Israel's God
Nothing is hard) by miracle restored,
He now be dealing dole among his foes,
And over heaps of slaughtered walks his way ?
   Man. That were a joy presumptuous to be thought.
   Chor. Yet God hath wrought things as incredible

For His people of old ; what hinders now ?
   Man. He can, I know, but doubt to think He will ;
Yet hope would fain subscribe, and tempts belief,
A little stay will bring some notice hither.
   Chor. Of good or bad so great, of bad the sooner ;
For evil news rides post, while good news baits.
And to our wish I see one hither speeding—
An Ebrew, as I guess, and of our tribe.
   Messenger. O, whither shall I run, or which way fly
The sight of this so horrid spectacle,
Which erst my eyes beheld, and yet behold ?
For dire imagination still pursues me.
But providence or instinct of nature seems,
Or reason, though disturbed and scarce consulted,
To have guided me aright, I know not how,
To thee first, reverend Manoa, and to these
My countrymen, whom here I knew remaining,
As at some distance from the place of horror,
So in the sad event too much concerned.
   Man. The accident was loud, and here before thee
With rueful cry ; yet what it was we hear not.
No preface needs ; thou seest we long to know.
   Mess. It would burst forth ; but I recover breath,
And sense distract, to know well what I utter.
   Man. Tell us the sum ; the circumstance defer.
   Mess. Gaza yet stands ; but all her sons are fallen,
All in a moment overwhelmed and fallen.
   Man. Sad ! but thou know'st to Israelites not saddest
The desolation of a hostile city.
   Mess. Feed on that first ; there may in grief be surfeit.
   Man. Relate by whom.
   Mess.   By Samson.
   Man.   That still lessens
The sorrow, and converts it nigh to joy.
   Mess. Ah ! Manoa, I refrain too suddenly
To utter what will come at last too soon,
Lest evil tidings, with too rude irruption
Hitting thy aged ear, should pierce too deep.
   Man. Suspense in news is torture ; speak them out.
   Mess. Then take the worst in brief : Samson is dead.
   Man. The worst indeed ! O, all my hopes defeated
To free him hence ! but Death, who sets all free,
Hath paid his ransom now and full discharge.
What windy joy this day had I conceived,
Hopeful of his delivery, which now proves
Abortive as the first-born bloom of spring
Nipt with the lagging rear of winter's frost !
Yet, ere I give the reins to grief, say first
How died he ; death to life is crown or shame.
All by him fell, thou say'st ; by whom fell he ?
What glorious hand gave Samson his death's wound ?
   Mess. Unwounded of his enemies he fell.
   Man. Wearied with slaughter, then, or how ? explain.
   Mess. By his own hands.

Man.   Self-violence! What cause
Brought him so soon at variance with himself
Among his foes?
   Mess.   Inevitable cause—
At once both to destroy and be destroyed.
The edifice, where all were met to see him,
Upon their heads and on his own he pulled.
   Man. O lastly over-strong against thyself!
A dreadful way thou took'st to thy revenge.
More than enough we know; but, while things yet
Are in confusion, give us, if thou canst,
Eye-witness of what first or last was done,
Relation more particular and distinct.
   Mess. Occasions drew me early to this city;
And, as the gates I entered with sun-rise,
The morning trumpets festival proclaimed
Through each high street. Little I had dispatched,
When all abroad was rumoured that this day
Samson should be brought forth, to show the people
Proof of his mighty strength in feats and games.
I sorrowed at his captive state, but minded
Not to be absent at that spectacle.
The building was a spacious theatre,
Half round on two main pillars vaulted high,
With seats where all the lords, and each degree
Of sort, might sit in order to behold;
The other side was open, where the throng
On banks and scaffolds under sky might stand:
I among these aloof obscurely stood.
The feast and noon grew high, and sacrifice
Had filled their hearts with mirth, high cheer, and wine,
When to their sports they turned. Immediately
Was Samson as a public servant brought,
In their state livery clad: before him pipes
And timbrels; on each side went armed guards;
Both horse and foot before him and behind,
Archers and slingers, cataphracts, and spears.
At sight of him the people with a shout
Rifted the air, clamouring their god with praise,
Who had made their dreadful enemy their thrall.
He patient, but undaunted, where they led him,
Came to the place; and what was set before him,
Which without help of eye might be assayed,
To heave, pull, draw, or break, he still performed
All with incredible, stupendious force,
None daring to appear antagonist.
At length, for intermission sake, they led him
Between the pillars; he his guide requested
(For so from such as nearer stood we heard),
As over-tired, to let him lean a while
With both his arms on those two massy pillars,
That to the arched roof gave main support.
He unsuspicious led him; which when Samson
Felt in his arms, with head a while inclined,

And eyes fast fixed, he stood, as one who prayed,
Or some great matter in his mind revolved:
At last, with head erect, thus cried aloud:—
" Hitherto, lords, what your commands imposed
I have performed, as reason was, obeying,
Not without wonder or delight beheld;
Now, of my own accord, such other trial
I mean to show you of my strength yet greater
As with amaze shall strike all who behold."
This uttered, straining all his nerves, he bowed;
As with the force of winds and waters pent
When mountains tremble, those two massy pillars
With horrible convulsion to and fro
He tugged, he shook, till down they came, and drew
The whole roof after them with burst of thunder
Upon the heads of all who sat beneath,
Lords, ladies, captains, counsellors, or priests,
Their choice nobility and flower, not only
Of this, but each Philistian city round,
Met from all parts to solemnize this feast.
Samson, with these immixed, inevitably
Pulled down the same destruction on himself;
The vulgar only 'scaped, who stood without.

   Chor. O dearly bought revenge, yet glorious!
Living or dying thou hast fulfilled
The work for which thou wast foretold
To Israel, and now liest victorious
Among thy slain self-killed;
Not willingly, but tangled in the fold
Of dire Necessity, whose law in death conjoined
Thee with thy slaughtered foes, in number more
Than all thy life had slain before.

   Semichor. While their hearts were jocund and sublime,
Drunk with idolatry, drunk with wine
And fat regorged of bulls and goats,
Chaunting their idol, and preferring
Before our living Dread, who dwells
In Silo, His bright sanctuary,
Among them He a spirit of phrenzy sent,
Who hurt their minds,
And urged them on with mad desire
To call in haste for their destroyer.
They, only set on sport and play,
Unweetingly importuned
Their own destruction to come speedy upon them.
So fond are mortal men,
Fallen into wrath divine,
As their own ruin on themselves to invite,
Insensate left, or to sense reprobate,
And with blindness internal struck.
But he, though blind of sight,
Despised, and thought extinguished quite,
With inward eyes illuminated,
His fiery virtue roused

294

From under ashes into sudden flame,
And as an evening dragon came,
Assailant on the perched roosts
And nests in order ranged
Of tame villatic fowl, but as an eagle
His cloudless thunder bolted on their heads.
So Virtue, given for lost,
Depressed and overthrown, as seemed,
Like that self-begotten bird
In the Arabian woods embost,
That no second knows nor third,
And lay erewhile a holocaust,
From out her ashy womb now teemed,
Revives, reflourishes, then vigorous most
When most unactive deemed;
And, though her body die, her fame survives,
A secular bird, ages of lives.
    Man. Come, come; no time for lamentation now,
Nor much more cause. Samson hath quit himself
Like Samson, and heroicly hath finished
A life heroic, on his enemies
Fully revenged—hath left them years of mourning,
And lamentation to the sons of Caphtor
Through all Philistian bounds; to Israel
Honour hath left and freedom, let but them
Find courage to lay hold on this occasion;
To himself and father's house eternal fame;
And, which is best and happiest yet, all this
With God not parted from him, as was feared,
But favouring and assisting to the end.
Nothing is here for tears, nothing to wail
Or knock the breast; no weakness, no contempt,
Dispraise, or blame; nothing but well and fair,
And what may quiet us in a death so noble.
Let us go find the body where it lies
Soaked in his enemies' blood, and from the stream
With lavers pure, and cleansing herbs, wash off
The clotted gore. I, with what speed the while
(Gaza is not in plight to say us nay),
Will send for all my kindred, all my friends,
To fetch him hence, and solemnly attend,
With silent obsequy and funeral train,
Home to his father's house. There will I build him
A monument, and plant it round with shade
Of laurel ever green and branching palm,
With all his trophies hung, and acts enrolled
In copious legend, or sweet lyric song.
Thither shall all the valiant youth resort,
And from his memory inflame their breasts
To matchless valour and adventures high;
The virgins also shall, on feastful days,
Visit his tomb with flowers, only bewailing
His lot unfortunate in nuptial choice,
From whence captivity and loss of eyes.

Chor. All is best, though we oft doubt
What the unsearchable dispose
Of Highest Wisdom brings about,
And ever best found in the close.
Oft He seems to hide His face,
But unexpectedly returns,
And to His faithful champion hath in place
Bore witness gloriously; whence Gaza mourns,
And all that band them to resist
His uncontrollable intent.
His servants He, with new acquist
Of true experience from this great event,
With peace and consolation hath dismissed,
And calm of mind, all passion spent.

THE END.

POEMS:

ENGLISH AND LATIN,

WITH A FEW IN ITALIAN AND GREEK.

COMPOSED AT SEVERAL TIMES.

ENGLISH POEMS.

A PARAPHRASE ON PSALM CXIV.

This and the following Psalm were done by the Author at fifteen years old.

WHEN the blest seed of Terah's faithful son
After long toil their liberty had won,
And passed from Pharian fields to Canaan-land,
Led by the strength of the Almighty's hand,
Jehovah's wonders were in Israel shown,
His praise and glory was in Israel known.
That saw the troubled sea, and shivering fled,
And sought to hide his froth-becurlèd head
Low in the earth; Jordan's clear streams recoil,
As a faint host that hath received the foil.
The high huge-bellied mountains skip like rams
Amongst their ewes, the little hills like lambs.
Why fled the ocean? and why skipped the mountains?
Why turnèd Jordan toward his crystal fountains?
Shake, Earth, and at the presence be aghast
Of Him that ever was and aye shall last,
That glassy floods from rugged rocks can crush,
And make soft rills from fiery flint-stones gush.

PSALM CXXXVI.

LET us with a gladsome mind
Praise the Lord for He is kind;
    For His mercies aye endure,
    Ever faithful, ever sure.

Let us blaze His name abroad,
For of gods He is the God;
    For His, &c.

O let us His praises tell,
Who doth the wrathful tyrants quell;
    For His, &c.

Who with His miracles doth make
Amazed heaven and earth to shake;
    For His, &c.

Who by His wisdom did create
The painted heavens so full of state;
    For His, &c.

299

Who did the solid earth ordain
To rise above the watery plain ;
   For His, &c.

Who, by His all-commanding might,
Did fill the new-made world with light ;
   For His, &c.

And caused the golden-tressèd sun
All the day long his course to run ;
   For His, &c.

The hornèd moon to shine by night
Amongst her spangled sisters bright ;
   For His, &c.

He, with His thunder-clasping hand,
Smote the first-born of Egypt land ;
   For His, &c.

And, in despite of Pharao fell,
He brought from thence His Israel ;
   For His, &c.

The ruddy waves He cleft in twain
Of the Erythræan main ;
   For His, &c.

The floods stood still, like walls of glass,
While the Hebrew bands did pass ;
   For His, &c.

But full soon they did devour
The tawny king with all his power ;
   For His, &c.

His chosen people He did bless
In the wasteful wilderness ;
   For His, &c.

In bloody battle He brought down
Kings of prowess and renown ;
   For His, &c.

He foiled bold Seon and his host,
That ruled the Amorrean coast ;
   For His, &c.

And large-limbed Og He did subdue,
With all his over-hardy crew ;
   For His, &c.

And to His servant Israel
He gave their land, therein to dwell ;
   For His, &c.

He hath, with a piteous eye,
Beheld us in our misery ;
   For His, &c.

And freed us from the slavery
Of the invading enemy ;
   For His, &c.

All living creatures He doth feed,
And with full hand supplies their need ;
   For His, &c.

Let us, therefore, warble forth
His mighty majesty and worth ;
   For His, &c.

That His mansion hath on high,
Above the reach of mortal eye ;
   For His mercies aye endure,
   Ever faithful, ever sure.

ON THE DEATH OF A FAIR INFANT DYING OF A COUGH.

Anno ætatis 17.

I.

O FAIREST flower, no sooner blown but blasted,
Soft silken primrose fading timelessly,
Summer's chief honour, if thou hadst outlasted
Bleak Winter's force that made thy blossom dry ;
For he, being amorous on that lovely dye
   That did thy cheek envermeil, thought to kiss,
But killed, alas ! and then bewailed his fatal bliss.

II.

For, since grim Aquilo, his charioteer,
By boisterous rape the Athenian damsel got,
He thought it touched his deity full near,
If likewise he some fair one wedded not,
Thereby to wipe away the infámous blot
   Of long uncoupled bed and childless eld,
Which 'mongst the wanton gods a foul reproach was held.

III.

So, mounting up in icy-pearlèd car,
Through middle empire of the freezing air
He wandered long, till thee he spied from far ;
There ended was his quest, there ceased his care ;
Down he descended from his snow-soft chair,
   But, all unwares, with his cold-kind embrace,
Unhoused thy virgin soul from her fair biding-place.

IV.

Yet art thou not inglorious in thy fate ;
For so Apollo, with unweeting hand,
Whilom did slay his dearly-lovèd mate,
Young Hyacinth, born on Eurotas' strand,
Young Hyacinth, the pride of Spartan land ;
   But then transformed him to a purple flower :
Alack, that so to change thee Winter had no power !

V.

Yet can I not persuade me thou art dead,
Or that thy corse corrupts in earth's dark womb,
Or that thy beauties lie in wormy bed
Hid from the world in a low-delvèd tomb;
Could Heaven, for pity, thee so strictly doom?
    Oh no! for something in thy face did shine
Above mortality, that showed thou wast divine.

VI.

Resolve me, then, O Soul most surely blest
(If so it be that thou these plaints dost hear)!
Tell me, bright Spirit, where'er thou hoverest,
Whether above that high first-moving sphere,
Or in the Elysian fields (if such there were),
    Oh, say me true if thou wert mortal wight,
And why from us so quickly thou didst take thy flight.

VII.

Wert thou some star, which from the ruined roof
Of shaked Olympus by mischance didst fall;
Which careful Jove in nature's true behoof
Took up, and in fit place did reinstal?
Or did of late Earth's sons besiege the wall
    Of sheeny Heaven, and thou some goddess fled
Amongst us here below to hide thy nectared head?

VIII.

Or wert thou that just Maid who once before
Forsook the hated earth, oh! tell me sooth,
And camest again to visit me once more?
Or wert thou [Mercy], that sweet smiling Youth?
Or that crowned Matron, sage white-robèd Truth?
    Or any other of that heavenly brood
Let down in cloudy throne to do the world some good?

IX.

Or wert thou of the golden-wingèd host,
Who, having clad thyself in human weed,
To Earth from thy prefixèd seat didst post,
And after short abode fly back with speed,
As if to show what creatures Heaven doth breed;
    Thereby to set the hearts of men on fire
To scorn the sordid world, and unto Heaven aspire?

X.

But oh! why didst thou not stay here below
To bless us with thy heaven-loved innocence,
To slake his wrath whom sin hath made our foe,
To turn swift-rushing black perdition hence,
Or drive away the slaughtering pestilence,
    To stand 'twixt us and our deservèd smart?
But thou canst best perform that office where thou art.

XI.

Then thou, the mother of so sweet a child,
Her false-imagined loss cease to lament,
And wisely learn to curb thy sorrows wild;
Think what a present thou to God hast sent,
And render Him with patience what He lent:
   This if thou do, He will an offspring give
That till the world's last end shall make thy name to live.

AT A VACATION EXERCISE IN THE COLLEGE, PART LATIN, PART ENGLISH.

Anno ætatis 19.

The Latin Speeches ended, the English thus began :—

HAIL, Native Language, that by sinews weak
Didst move my first endeavouring tongue to speak,
And mad'st imperfect words with childish trips,
Half unpronounced, slide through my infant lips,
Driving dumb Silence from the portal door,
Where he had mutely sat two years before :
Here I salute thee, and thy pardon ask
That now I use thee in my latter task !
Small loss it is that thence can come unto thee;
I know my tongue but little grace can do thee.
Thou need'st not be ambitious to be first;
Believe me, I have thither packed the worst;
And, if it happen as I did forecast,
The daintiest dishes shall be served up last.
I pray thee then deny me not thy aid,
For this same small neglect that I have made;
But haste thee straight to do me once a pleasure,
And from thy wardrobe bring thy chiefest treasure;
Not those new-fangled toys, and trimming slight
Which takes our late fantastics with delight;
But cull those richest robes and gayest attire,
Which deepest spirits and choicest wits desire.
I have some naked thoughts that rove about,
And loudly knock to have their passage out,
And, weary of their place, do only stay
Till thou hast decked them in thy best array;
That so they may, without suspect or fears,
Fly swiftly to this fair assembly's ears.
Yet I had rather, if I were to choose,
Thy service in some graver subject use,
Such as may make thee search thy coffers round,
Before thou clothe my fancy in fit sound:
Such where the deep transported mind may soar
Above the wheeling poles, and at Heaven's door
Look in, and see each blissful deity
How he before the thunderous throne doth lie,
Listening to what unshorn Apollo sings
To the touch of golden wires, while Hebe brings

303

Immortal nectar to her kingly sire;
Then, passing through the spheres of watchful fire,
And misty regions of wide air next under,
And hills of snow and lofts of pilèd thunder,
May tell at length how green-eyed Neptune raves,
In heaven's defiance mustering all his waves;
Then sing of secret things that came to pass
When beldam Nature in her cradle was;
And last of kings and queens and heroes old,
Such as the wise Demodocus once told
In solemn songs at king Alcinous' feast,
While sad Ulysses' soul and all the rest
Are held, with his melodious harmony,
In willing chains and sweet captivity.
But fie, my wandering Muse, how thou dost stray!
Expectance calls thee now another way.
Thou know'st it must be now thy only bent
To keep in compass of thy Predicament.
Then quick about thy purposed business come,
That to the next I may resign my room.

Then ENS *is represented as Father of the Predicaments, his
ten Sons; whereof the eldest stood for* SUBSTANCE *with his
Canons; which* ENS, *thus speaking, explains:—*

Good luck befriend thee, Son; for at thy birth
The faery ladies danced upon the hearth.
The drowsy nurse hath sworn she did them spy
Come tripping to the room where thou didst lie,
And sweetly singing round about thy bed,
Strew all their blessings on thy sleeping head.
She heard them give thee this, that thou shouldst still
From eyes of mortals walk invisible.
Yet there is something that doth force my fear;
For once it was my dismal hap to hear
A sibyl old, bow-bent with crooked age,
That far events full wisely could presage,
And, in Time's long and dark prospective-glass,
Foresaw what future days should bring to pass.
"Your son," said she, "(nor can you it prevent,)
Shall subject be to many an *Accident.*
O'er all his brethren he shall reign as king;
Yet every one shall make him underling,
And those that cannot live from him asunder
Ungratefully shall strive to keep him under.
In worth and excellence he shall outgo them;
Yet, being above them, he shall be below them.
From others he shall stand in need of nothing,
Yet on his brothers shall depend for clothing.
To find a foe it shall not be his hap,
And peace shall lull him in her flowery lap;
Yet shall he live in strife, and at his door
Devouring war shall never cease to roar;
Yea, it shall be his natural property

304

To harbour those that are at enmity."
What power, what force, what mighty spell, if not
Your learned hands, can loose this Gordian knot?

The next, QUANTITY and QUALITY, spake in prose: then
RELATION was called by his name.

Rivers, arise: whether thou be the son
Of utmost Tweed, or Ouse, or gulfy Dun,
Or Trent, who, like some earth-born giant, spreads
His thirty arms along the indented meads,
Or sullen Mole, that runneth underneath,
Or Severn swift, guilty of maiden's death,
Or rocky Avon, or of sedgy Lea,
Or coaly Tyne, or ancient hallowed Dee,
Or Humber loud, that keeps the Scythian's name,
Or Medway smooth, or royal-towered Thame.

The rest was prose.

ON THE MORNING OF CHRIST'S NATIVITY.

Composed 1629.

I.

THIS is the month, and this the happy morn,
Wherein the Son of Heaven's eternal King,
Of wedded maid and virgin mother born,
Our great redemption from above did bring;
For so the holy sages once did sing,
   That He our deadly forfeit should release,
And with His Father work us a perpetual peace.

II.

That glorious form, that light unsufferable,
And that far-beaming blaze of majesty,
Wherewith He wont at Heaven's high council-table
To sit the midst of Trinal Unity,
He laid aside, and, here with us to be,
   Forsook the courts of everlasting day,
And chose with us a darksome house of mortal clay.

III.

Say, Heavenly Muse, shall not thy sacred vein
Afford a present to the Infant God?
Hast thou no verse, no hymn, or solemn strain,
To welcome Him to this His new abode,
Now while the heaven, by the Sun's team untrod,
   Hath took no print of the approaching light,
And all the spangled host keep watch in squadrons bright?

IV.

See how from far upon the eastern road
The star-led wizards haste with odours sweet!
Oh! run; prevent them with thy humble ode
And lay it lowly at His blessed feet;

M.—X

Have thou the honour first thy Lord to greet,
    And join thy voice unto the Angel Quire,
From out His secret altar touched with hallowed fire.

THE HYMN.

I.

It was the winter wild,
    While the heaven-born child
All meanly wrapt in the rude manger lies;
    Nature, in awe to Him,
    Had doffed her gaudy trim,
With her great Master so to sympathize:
It was no season then for her
To wanton with the Sun, her lusty paramour.

II.

Only with speeches fair
    She woos the gentle air
To hide her guilty front with innocent snow,
    And on her naked shame,
    Pollute with sinful blame,
The saintly veil of maiden white to throw;
Confounded, that her Maker's eyes
Should look so near upon her foul deformities.

III.

But He, her fears to cease,
    Sent down the meek-eyed Peace:
She, crowned with olive green, came softly sliding
    Down through the turning sphere,
    His ready harbinger,
With turtle wing the amorous clouds dividing;
And, waving wide her myrtle wand,
She strikes a universal peace through sea and land.

IV.

No war, or battle's sound,
    Was heard the world around;
The idle spear and shield were high uphung;
    The hooked chariot stood,
    Unstained with hostile blood;
The trumpet spake not to the armèd throng;
And kings sat still with awful eye,
As if they surely knew their sovran Lord was by.

V.

But peaceful was the night
    Wherein the Prince of Light
His reign of peace upon the earth began.
    The winds, with wonder whist,
    Smoothly the waters kissed,
Whispering new joys to the mild Ocean,
Who now hath quite forgot to rave,
While birds of calm sit brooding on the charmèd wave.

306

VI.

The stars, with deep amaze,
Stand fixed in steadfast gaze,
Bending one way their precious influence,
And will not take their flight,
For all the morning light,
Or Lucifer that often warned them thence;
But in their glimmering orbs did glow,
Until their Lord Himself bespake, and bid them go.

VII.

And, though the shady gloom
Had given day her room,
The Sun himself withheld his wonted speed,
And hid his head for shame,
As his inferior flame
The new-enlightened world no more should need:
He saw a greater Sun appear
Than his bright throne or burning axletree could bear.

VIII.

The shepherds on the lawn,
Or ere the point of dawn,
Sat simply chatting in a rustic row;
Full little thought they than
That the mighty Pan
Was kindly come to live with them below:
Perhaps their loves, or else their sheep,
Was all that did their silly thoughts so busy keep.

IX.

When such music sweet
Their hearts and ears did greet
As never was by mortal finger strook,
Divinely-warbled voice
Answering the stringed noise,
As all their souls in blissful rapture took:
The air, such pleasure loth to lose,
With thousand echoes still prolongs each heavenly close.

X.

Nature, that heard such sound
Beneath the hollow round
Of Cynthia's seat the Airy region thrilling,
Now was almost won
To think her part was done,
And that her reign had here its last fulfilling:
She knew such harmony alone
Could hold all Heaven and Earth in happier union.

XI.

At last surrounds their sight
A globe of circular light,
That with long beams the shamefaced Night arrayed;

The helmèd cherubim
And sworded seraphim
Are seen in glittering ranks with wings displayed,
Harping in loud and solemn quire,
With unexpressive notes, to Heaven's new-born Heir.

XII.

Such music (as 't is said)
Before was never made,
But when of old the Sons of Morning sung,
While the Creator great
His constellations set,
And the well-balanced World on hinges hung,
And cast the dark foundations deep,
And bid the weltering waves their oozy channel keep.

XIII.

Ring out, ye crystal spheres !
Once bless our human ears,
If ye have power to touch our senses so ;
And let your silver chime
Move in melodious time ;
And let the bass of heaven's deep organ blow ;
And with your ninefold harmony
Make up full consort to the angelic symphony.

XIV.

For, if such holy song
Enwrap our fancy long,
Time will run back and fetch the Age of Gold ;
And speckled Vanity
Will sicken soon and die,
And leprous Sin will melt from earthly mould ;
And Hell itself will pass away,
And leave her dolorous mansions to the peering day.

XV.

Yea, Truth and Justice then
Will down return to men,
Orbed in a rainbow ; and, like glories wearing,
Mercy will sit between,
Throned in celestial sheen,
With radiant feet the tissued clouds down steering ;
And Heaven, as at some festival,
Will open wide the gates of her high palace-hall.

XVI.

But wisest Fate says No,
This must not yet be so ;
The Babe yet lies in smiling infancy
That on the bitter cross
Must redeem our loss,
So both Himself and us to glorify :
Yet first, to those ychained in sleep,
The wakeful trump of doom must thunder through the deep.

XVII.

With such a horrid clang
  As on Mount Sinai rang,
While the red fire and smouldering clouds outbrake,
  The aged Earth, aghast
  With terror of that blast,
Shall from the surface to the centre shake,
When, at the world's last session,
The dreadful Judge in middle air shall spread His throne.

XVIII.

And then at last our bliss
  Full and perfect is,
But now begins; for from this happy day
  The Old Dragon under ground,
  In straiter limits bound,
Not half so far casts his usurpèd sway,
And, wroth to see his kingdom fail,
Swinges the scaly horror of his folded tail.

XIX.

The Oracles are dumb;
  No voice or hideous hum
Runs through the archèd roof in words deceiving.
  Apollo from his shrine
  Can no more divine,
With hollow shriek the steep of Delphos leaving.
No nightly trance, or breathèd spell,
Inspires the pale-eyed priest from the prophetic cell.

XX.

The lonely mountains o'er,
  And the resounding shore,
A voice of weeping heard and loud lament;
  From haunted spring, and dale
  Edged with poplar pale,
The parting Genius is with sighing sent;
With flower-inwoven tresses torn
The Nymphs in twilight shade of tangled thickets mourn.

XXI.

In consecrated earth,
  And on the holy hearth,
The Lars and Lemures moan with midnight plaint;
  In urns, and altars round,
  A drear and dying sound
Affrights the flamens at their service quaint;
And the chill marble seems to sweat,
While each peculiar power foregoes his wonted seat.

XXII.

Peor and Baälim
  Forsake their temples dim,
With that twice-battered god of Palestine;

And moonèd Ashtaroth,
  Heaven's queen and mother both,
Now sits not girt with tapers' holy shine:
The Libyc Hammon shrinks his horn;
In vain the Tyrian maids their wounded Thammuz mourn.

XXIII.

And sullen Moloch, fled,
  Hath left in shadows dread
His burning idol all of blackest hue;
  In vain with cymbals' ring
  They call the grisly king,
In dismal dance about the furnace blue;
The brutish gods of Nile as fast,
Isis, and Orus, and the dog Anubis, haste.

XXIV.

Nor is Osiris seen
  In Memphian grove or green,
Trampling the unshowered grass with lowings loud;
  Nor can he be at rest
  Within his sacred chest;
Nought but profoundest Hell can be his shroud;
In vain, with timbreled anthems dark,
The sable-stolèd sorcerers bear his worshipped ark.

XXV.

He feels from Juda's land
  The dreaded Infant's hand;
The rays of Bethlehem blind his dusky eyn;
  Nor all the gods beside
  Longer dare abide,
Not Typhon huge ending in snaky twine:
Our Babe, to show His Godhead true,
Can in His swaddling bands control the damnèd crew.

XXVI.

So, when the sun in bed,
  Curtained with cloudy red,
Pillows his chin upon an orient wave,
  The flocking shadows pale
  Troop to the infernal jail,
Each fettered ghost slips to his several grave,
And the yellow-skirted fays
Fly after the night-steeds, leaving their moon-loved maze.

XXVII.

But, see! the Virgin blest
  Hath laid her Babe to rest.
Time is our tedious song should here have ending:
  Heaven's youngest-teemèd star
  Hath fixed her polished car,
Her sleeping Lord with handmaid lamp attending;
And all about the courtly stable
Bright-harnessed Angels sit in order serviceable.

UPON THE CIRCUMCISION.

Ye flaming Powers, and wingèd Warriors bright,
That erst with music, and triumphant song,
First heard by happy watchful shepherds' ear,
So sweetly sung your joy the clouds along,
Through the soft silence of the listening night,
Now mourn; and, if sad share with us to bear
Your fiery essence can distil no tear,
Burn in your sighs, and borrow
Seas wept from our deep sorrow.
He who with all Heaven's heraldry whilere
Entered the world now bleeds to give us ease.
Alas! how soon our sin
  Sore doth begin
    His infancy to seize!

O more exceeding love, or law more just!
Just law, indeed, but more exceeding love!
For we, by rightful doom remediless,
Were lost in death, till He, that dwelt above
High-throned in secret bliss, for us frail dust
Emptied His glory, even to nakedness;
And that great covenant which we still transgress
Entirely satisfied,
And the full wrath beside
Of vengeful justice bore for our excess,
And seals obedience first with wounding smart
This day; but oh! ere long,
  Huge pangs and strong
    Will pierce more near His heart.

THE PASSION.

I.

Erewhile of music, and ethereal mirth,
Wherewith the stage of Air and Earth did ring,
And joyous news of heavenly Infant's birth,
My muse with Angels did divide to sing;
But headlong joy is ever on the wing,
  In wintry solstice like the shortened light
Soon swallowed up in dark and long outliving night.

II.

For now to sorrow must I tune my song,
And set my harp to notes of saddest woe,
Which on our dearest Lord did seize ere long,
Dangers, and snares, and wrongs, and worse than so,
Which He for us did freely undergo;
  Most perfect Hero, tried in heaviest plight
Of labours huge and hard, too hard for human wight!

III.

He, sovran Priest, stooping His regal head,
That dropt with odorous oil down His fair eyes,
Poor fleshly tabernacle enterèd,

His starry front low-roofed beneath the skies:
Oh, what a mask was there, what a disguise!
   Yet more: the stroke of death He must abide;
Then lies Him meekly down fast by His brethren's side.

IV.

These latest scenes confine my roving verse;
To this horizon is my Phœbus bound.
His godlike acts, and His temptations fierce,
And former sufferings, otherwhere are found;
Loud o'er the rest Cremona's trump doth sound;
   Me softer airs befit, and softer strings
Of lute, or viol still, more apt for mournful things.

V.

Befriend me, Night, best patroness of grief!
Over the pole thy thickest mantle throw,
And work my flattered fancy to belief
That Heaven and Earth are coloured with my woe;
My sorrows are too dark for day to know;
   The leaves should all be black whereon I write,
And letters, where my tears have washed, a wannish white.

VI.

See, see the chariot, and those rushing wheels,
That whirled the prophet up at Chebar flood;
My spirit some transporting cherub feels
To bear me where the towers of Salem stood,
Once glorious towers, now sunk in guiltless blood.
   There doth my soul in holy vision sit,
In pensive trance, and anguish, and ecstatic fit.

VII.

Mine eye hath found that sad sepulchral rock
That was the casket of Heaven's richest store,
And here, though grief my feeble hands up-lock,
Yet on the softened quarry would I score
My plaining verse as lively as before;
   For sure so well instructed are my tears
That they would fitly fall in ordered characters.

VIII.

Or, should I thence, hurried on viewless wing,
Take up a weeping on the mountains wild,
The gentle neighbourhood of grove and spring
Would soon unbosom all their echoes mild;
And I (for grief is easily beguiled)
   Might think the infection of my sorrows loud
Had got a race of mourners on some pregnant cloud.

*This Subject the Author finding to be above the years he had
  when he wrote it, and nothing satisfied with what was
  begun, left it unfinished.*

ON TIME.

FLY, envious Time, till thou run out thy race:
Call on the lazy, leaden-stepping Hours,
Whose speed is but the heavy plummet's pace;
And glut thyself with what thy womb devours,
Which is no more than what is false and vain,
And merely mortal dross;
So little is our loss,
So little is thy gain!
For, whenas each thing bad thou hast entombed,
And, last of all, thy greedy self consumed,
Then long Eternity shall greet our bliss
With an individual kiss,
And Joy shall overtake us as a flood;
When every thing that is sincerely good
And perfectly divine,
With Truth, and Peace, and Love shall ever shine
About the supreme throne
Of Him, to whose happy-making sight alone
When once our heavenly-guided soul shall climb,
Then, all this earthy grossness quit,
Attired with stars we shall for ever sit,
    Triumphing over Death, and Chance, and thee, O Time!

AT A SOLEMN MUSIC.

BLEST pair of Sirens, pledges of Heaven's joy,
Sphere-born harmonious sisters, Voice and Verse,
Wed your divine sounds, and mixed power employ,
Dead things with inbreathed sense able to pierce;
And to our high-raised phantasy present
That undisturbèd song of pure concent,
Aye sung before the sapphire-coloured throne
To Him that sits thereon,
With saintly shout and solemn jubilee;
Where the bright Seraphim in burning row
Their loud uplifted angel-trumpets blow,
And the Cherubic host in thousand quires
Touch their immortal harps of golden wires,
With those just Spirits that wear victorious palms,
Hymns devout and holy psalms
Singing everlastingly:
That we on Earth with undiscording voice,
May rightly answer that melodious noise;
As once we did, till disproportioned sin
Jarred against nature's chime, and with harsh din
Broke the fair music that all creatures made
To their great Lord, whose love their motion swayed
In perfect diapason, whilst they stood
In first obedience, and their state of good.
O, may we soon again renew that song,
And keep in tune with Heaven, till God ere long
To His celestial consort us unite,
To live with Him, and sing in endless morn of light!

313

SONG ON MAY MORNING.

Now the bright morning-star, Day's harbinger,
Comes dancing from the east, and leads with her
The flowery May, who from her green lap throws
The yellow cowslip and the pale primrose.
 Hail, bounteous May, that dost inspire
 Mirth, and youth, and warm desire!
 Woods and groves are of thy dressing;
 Hill and dale doth boast thy blessing.
Thus we salute thee with our early song,
And welcome thee, and wish thee long.

ON SHAKESPEARE. 1630.

What needs my Shakespeare for his honoured bones
The labour of an age in pilèd stones?
Or that his hallowed reliques should be hid
Under a stary-pointing pyramid?
Dear son of memory, great heir of fame,
What need'st thou such weak witness of thy name?
Thou in our wonder and astonishment
Hast built thyself a livelong monument.
For whilst, to the shame of slow-endeavouring art,
Thy easy numbers flow, and that each heart
Hath from the leaves of thy unvalued book
Those Delphic lines with deep impression took,
Then thou, our fancy of itself bereaving,
Dost make *us* marble with too much conceiving,
And so sepúlchred in such pomp dost lie
That kings for such a tomb would wish to die.

ON THE UNIVERSITY CARRIER,

WHO SICKENED IN THE TIME OF HIS VACANCY, BEING FORBID TO GO TO LONDON BY REASON OF THE PLAGUE.

Here lies old Hobson. Death hath broke his girt,
And here, alas! hath laid him in the dirt;
Or else, the ways being foul, twenty to one
He's here stuck in a slough, and overthrown.
'T was such a shifter that, if truth were known,
Death was half glad when he had got him down;
For he had any time this ten years full
Dodged with him betwixt Cambridge and *The Bull*.
And surely Death could never have prevailed,
Had not his weekly course of carriage failed;
But lately, finding him so long at home,
And thinking now his journey's end was come,
And that he had ta'en up his latest inn,
In the kind office of a chamberlin
Showed him his room where he must lodge that night,
Pulled off his boots, and took away the light.
If any ask for him, it shall be said,
"Hobson has supped, and's newly gone to bed."

314

ANOTHER ON THE SAME.

HERE lieth one who did most truly prove
That he could never die while he could move;
So hung his destiny, never to rot
While he might still jog on and keep his trot;
Made of sphere-metal, never to decay
Until his revolution was at stay.
Time numbers motion, yet (without a crime
'Gainst old Truth) motion numbered out his time;
And, like an engine moved with wheel and weight,
His principles being ceased, he ended straight.
Rest, that gives all men life, gave him his death,
And too much breathing put him out of breath;
Nor were it contradiction to affirm
Too long vacation hastened on his term.
Merely to drive the time away he sickened,
Fainted, and died, nor would with ale be quickened.
"Nay," quoth he, on his swooning bed outstretched,
"If I mayn't carry, sure I 'll ne'er be fetched,
But vow, though the cross doctors all stood hearers,
For one carrier put down to make six bearers."
Ease was his chief disease; and, to judge right,
He died for heaviness that his cart went light.
His leisure told him that his time was come,
And lack of load made his life burdensome,
That even to his last breath (there be that say 't),
As he were pressed to death, he cried, "More weight!"
But, had his doings lasted as they were,
He had been an immortal carrier.
Obedient to the moon he spent his date
In course reciprocal, and had his fate
Linked to the mutual flowing of the seas;
Yet (strange to think) his wain was his increase.
His letters are delivered all and gone;
Only remains this superscription.

AN EPITAPH ON THE MARCHIONESS OF WINCHESTER.

THIS rich marble doth inter
The honoured wife of Winchester,
A Viscount's daughter, an Earl's heir,
Besides what her virtues fair
Added to her noble birth,
More than she could own from Earth.
Summers three times eight save one
She had told; alas! too soon,
After so short time of breath,
To house with darkness and with death!
Yet, had the number of her days
Been as complete as was her praise,
Nature and Fate had had no strife
In giving limit to her life.

Her high birth and her graces sweet
Quickly found a lover meet ;
The virgin quire for her request
The god that sits at marriage-feast ;
He at their invoking came,
But with a scarce well-lighted flame ;
And in his garland, as he stood,
Ye might discern a cypress-bud.
Once had the early matrons run
To greet her of a lovely son,
And now with second hope she goes,
And calls Lucina to her throes ;
But, whether by mischance or blame,
Atropos for Lucina came,
And with remorseless cruelty
Spoiled at once both fruit and tree.
The hapless babe before his birth
Had burial, not yet laid in earth ;
And the languished mother's womb
Was not long a living tomb.
So have I seen some tender slip,
Saved with care from winter's nip,
The pride of her carnation train,
Plucked up by some unheedy swain,
Who only thought to crop the flower
New shot up from vernal shower ;
But the fair blossom hangs the head
Sideways, as on a dying bed,
And those pearls of dew she wears
Prove to be presaging tears
Which the sad morn had let fall
On her hastening funeral.
Gentle Lady, may thy grave
Peace and quiet ever have !
After this thy travail sore,
Sweet rest seize thee evermore,
That, to give the world increase,
Shortened hast thy own life's lease !
Here, besides the sorrowing
That thy noble house doth bring,
Here be tears of perfect moan
Weept for thee in Helicon ;
And some flowers and some bays
For thy hearse, to strew the ways,
Sent thee from the banks of Came,
Devoted to thy virtuous name ;
Whilst thou, bright Saint, high sitt'st in glory,
Next her, much like to thee in story,
That fair Syrian shepherdess,
Who, after years of barrenness,
The highly-favoured Joseph bore
To him that served for her before,
And at her next birth, much like thee,
Through pangs fled to felicity,

Far within the bosom bright
Of blazing Majesty and Light :
There with thee, new-welcome Saint,
Like fortunes may her soul acquaint,
With thee there clad in radiant sheen,
No Marchioness, but now a Queen.

L' ALLEGRO.

HENCE, loathed Melancholy,
    Of Cerberus and blackest Midnight born
In Stygian cave forlorn
    'Mongst horrid shapes, and shrieks, and sights unholy!
Find out some uncouth cell,
    Where brooding Darkness spreads his jealous wings,
And the night-raven sings ;
    There, under ebon shades and low-browed rocks,
As ragged as thy locks,
    In dark Cimmerian desert ever dwell.
But come, thou Goddess fair and free,
In heaven yclept Euphrosyne,
And by men heart-easing Mirth ;
Whom lovely Venus, at a birth,
With two sister Graces more,
To ivy-crownèd Bacchus bore :
Or whether (as some sager sing)
The frolic wind that breathes the spring,
Zephyr, with Aurora playing,
As he met her once a-Maying,
There, on beds of violets blue,
And fresh-blown roses washed in dew,
Filled her with thee, a daughter fair,
So buxom, blithe, and debonair.
Haste thee, Nymph, and bring with thee
Jest, and youthful Jollity,
Quips and Cranks and wanton Wiles,
Nods and Becks and wreathèd Smiles,
Such as hang on Hebe's cheek,
And love to live in dimple sleek ;
Sport that wrinkled Care derides,
And Laughter holding both his sides.
Come, and trip it, as you go,
On the light fantastic toe ;
And in thy right hand lead with thee
The mountain-nymph, sweet Liberty ;
And, if I give thee honour due,
Mirth, admit me of thy crew,
To live with her, and live with thee,
In unreproved pleasures free ;
To hear the lark begin his flight,
And, singing, startle the dull night,
From his watch-tower in the skies,
Till the dappled dawn doth rise ;

Then to come, in spite of sorrow,
And at my window bid good-morrow,
Through the sweet-briar or the vine,
Or the twisted eglantine;
While the cock, with lively din,
Scatters the rear of darkness thin;
And to the stack, or the barn-door,
Stoutly struts his dames before:
Oft listening how the hounds and horn
Cheerily rouse the slumbering morn,
From the side of some hoar hill,
Through the high wood echoing shrill:
Sometime walking, not unseen,
By hedgerow elms, on hillocks green,
Right against the eastern gate
Where the great Sun begins his state,
Robed in flames and amber light,
The clouds in thousand liveries dight;
While the ploughman, near at hand,
Whistles o'er the furrowed land,
And the milkmaid singeth blithe,
And the mower whets his scythe,
And every shepherd tells his tale
Under the hawthorn in the dale.
Straight mine eye hath caught new pleasures,
Whilst the landskip round it measures:
Russet lawns, and fallows grey,
Where the nibbling flocks do stray;
Mountains on whose barren breast
The labouring clouds do often rest;
Meadows trim, with daisies pied;
Shallow brooks, and rivers wide;
Towers and battlements it sees
Bosomed high in tufted trees,
Where perhaps some beauty lies,
The cynosure of neighbouring eyes.
Hard by a cottage chimney smokes
From betwixt two aged oaks,
Where Corydon and Thyrsis met
Are at their savoury dinner set
Of herbs and other country messes,
Which the neat-handed Phillis dresses;
And then in haste her bower she leaves,
With Thestylis to bind the sheaves;
Or, if the earlier season lead,
To the tanned haycock in the mead.
Sometimes, with secure delight,
The upland hamlets will invite,
When the merry bells ring round,
And jocund rebecks sound
To many a youth and many a maid
Dancing in the chequered shade,
And young and old come forth to play
On a sunshine holiday,

Till the livelong daylight fail:
Then to the spicy nut-brown ale,
With stories told of many a feat,
How Faery Mab the junkets eat.
She was pinched and pulled, she said;
And he, by Friar's lantern led,
Tells how the drudging goblin sweat
To earn his cream-bowl duly set,
When in one night, ere glimpse of morn,
His shadowy flail hath threshed the corn
That ten day-labourers could not end;
Then lies him down, the lubber fiend,
And, stretched out all the chimney's length,
Basks at the fire his hairy strength,
And crop-full out of doors he flings,
Ere the first cock his matin rings.
Thus done the tales, to bed they creep,
By whispering winds soon lulled asleep.
Towered cities please us then,
And the busy hum of men,
Where throngs of knights and barons bold,
In weeds of peace, high triumphs hold,
With store of ladies, whose bright eyes
Rain influence, and judge the prize
Of wit or arms, while both contend
To win her grace whom all commend.
There let Hymen oft appear
In saffron robe, with taper clear,
And pomp, and feast, and revelry,
With mask, and antique pageantry;
Such sights as youthful poets dream
On summer eves by haunted stream.
Then to the well-trod stage anon,
If Jonson's learned sock be on,
Or sweetest Shakespeare, Fancy's child,
Warble his native wood-notes wild,
And ever, against eating cares,
Lap me in soft Lydian airs,
Married to immortal verse,
Such as the meeting soul may pierce,
In notes with many a winding bout
Of linkèd sweetness long drawn out
With wanton heed and giddy cunning,
The melting voice through mazes running,
Untwisting all the chains that tie
The hidden soul of harmony;
That Orpheus' self may heave his head
From golden slumber on a bed
Of heaped Elysian flowers, and hear
Such strains as would have won the ear
Of Pluto to have quite set free
His half-regained Eurydice.
These delights if thou canst give,
Mirth, with thee I mean to live.

319

IL PENSEROSO.

HENCE, vain deluding Joys,
  The brood of Folly without father bred!
How little you bested,
  Or fill the fixèd mind with all your toys!
Dwell in some idle brain,
  And fancies fond with gaudy shapes possess,
As thick and numberless
  As the gay motes that people the sunbeams,
Or likest hovering dreams,
  The fickle pensioners of Morpheus' train.
But, hail! thou Goddess sage and holy!
Hail, divinest Melancholy!
Whose saintly visage is too bright
To hit the sense of human sight,
And therefore to our weaker view
O'erlaid with black, staid Wisdom's hue;
Black, but such as in esteem
Prince Memnon's sister might beseem,
Or that starred Ethiop queen that strove
To set her beauty's praise above
The Sea-Nymphs, and their powers offended.
Yet thou art higher far descended:
Thee bright-haired Vesta long of yore
To solitary Saturn bore;
His daughter she; in Saturn's reign
Such mixture was not held a stain.
Oft in glimmering bowers and glades
He met her, and in secret shades
Of woody Ida's inmost grove,
Whilst yet there was no fear of Jove.
Come, pensive Nun, devout and pure,
Sober, steadfast, and demure,
All in a robe of darkest grain,
Flowing with majestic train,
And sable stole of cypress lawn
Over thy decent shoulders drawn.
Come; but keep thy wonted state,
With even step, and musing gait,
And looks commercing with the skies,
Thy wrapt soul sitting in thine eyes:
There, held in holy passion still,
Forget thyself to marble, till
With a sad leaden downward cast
Thou fix them on the earth as fast.
And join with thee calm Peace and Quiet,
Spare Fast, that oft with gods doth diet,
And hears the Muses in a ring
Aye round about Jove's altar sing;
And add to these retired Leisure,
That in trim gardens takes his pleasure;
But, first and chiefest, with thee bring
Him that yon soars on golden wing,

Guiding the fiery-wheelèd throne,
The Cherub Contemplation;
And the mute Silence hist along,
'Less Philomel will deign a song,
In her sweetest, saddest plight,
Smoothing the rugged brow of Night,
While Cynthia checks her dragon yoke
Gently o'er the accustomed oak.
Sweet bird, that shunn'st the noise of folly,
Most musical, most melancholy!
Thee, chauntress, oft the woods among
I woo, to hear thy even-song;
And, missing thee, I walk unseen
On the dry smooth-shaven green,
To behold the wandering moon,
Riding near her highest noon,
Like one that had been led astray
Through the heaven's wide pathless way,
And oft, as if her head she bowed,
Stooping through a fleecy cloud.
Oft, on a plat of rising ground,
I hear the far-off curfew sound,
Over some wide-watered shore,
Swinging slow with sullen roar;
Or, if the air will not permit,
Some still removèd place will fit,
Where glowing embers through the room
Teach light to counterfeit a gloom,
Far from all resort of mirth,
Save the cricket on the hearth,
Or the bellman's drowsy charm
To bless the doors from nightly harm.
Or let my lamp, at midnight hour,
Be seen in some high lonely tower,
Where I may oft outwatch the Bear,
With thrice great Hermes, or unsphere
The spirit of Plato, to unfold
What worlds or what vast regions hold
The immortal mind that hath forsook
Her mansion in this fleshy nook;
And of those demons that are found
In fire, air, flood, or underground,
Whose power hath a true consent
With planet or with element.
Sometime let gorgeous Tragedy
In sceptred pall come sweeping by,
Presenting Thebe's, or Pelops' line,
Or the tale of Troy divine,
Or what (though rare) of later age
Ennobled hath the buskined stage.
But, O sad Virgin! that thy power
Might raise Musæus from his bower;
Or bid the soul of Orpheus sing
Such notes as, warbled to the string,

Drew iron tears down Pluto's cheek,
And made Hell grant what love did seek;
Or call up him that left half-told
The story of Cambuscan bold,
Of Camball, and of Algarsife,
And who had Canace to wife,
That owned the virtuous ring and glass,
And of the wondrous horse of brass
On which the Tartar king did ride;
And if aught else great bards beside
In sage and solemn tunes have sung,
Of turneys, and of trophies hung,
Of forests, and enchantments drear,
Where more is meant than meets the ear.
Thus, Night, oft see me in thy pale career,
Till civil-suited Morn appear,
Not tricked and frounced, as she was wont
With the Attic boy to hunt,
But kerchieft in a comely cloud,
While rocking winds are piping loud,
Or ushered with a shower still,
When the gust hath blown his fill,
Ending on the rustling leaves,
With minute-drops from off the eaves.
And, when the sun begins to fling
His flaring beams, me, Goddess, bring
To archèd walks of twilight groves,
And shadows brown, that Sylvan loves,
Of pine, or monumental oak,
Where the rude axe with heavèd stroke
Was never heard the nymphs to daunt,
Or fright them from their hallowed haunt.
There, in close covert, by some brook,
Where no profaner eye may look,
Hide me from day's garish eye,
While the bee with honeyed thigh,
That at her flowery work doth sing,
And the waters murmuring,
With such consort as they keep,
Entice the dewy-feathered Sleep.
And let some strange mysterious dream
Wave at his wings, in airy stream
Of lively portraiture displayed,
Softly on my eyelids laid;
And, as I wake, sweet music breathe
Above, about, or underneath,
Sent by some Spirit to mortals good,
Or the unseen Genius of the wood.
But let my due feet never fail
To walk the studious cloister's pale,
And love the high embowèd roof,
With antique pillars massy-proof,
And storied windows richly dight,
Casting a dim religious light.

There let the pealing organ blow,
To the full-voiced quire below,
In service high and anthems clear,
As may with sweetness, through mine ear,
Dissolve me into ecstasies,
And bring all Heaven before mine eyes.
And may at last my weary age
Find out the peaceful hermitage,
The hairy gown and mossy cell,
Where I may sit and rightly spell
Of every star that heaven doth shew,
And every herb that sips the dew,
Till old experience do attain
To something like prophetic strain.
These pleasures, Melancholy, give,
And I with thee will choose to live.

ARCADES.

*Part of an Entertainment presented to the Countess Dowager of Derby at
Harefield by some Noble Persons of her Family; who appear on the
Scene in pastoral habit, moving toward the seat of state, with this song:*

I. Song.

Look, Nymphs and Shepherds, look!
What sudden blaze of majesty
Is that which we from hence descry,
Too divine to be mistook?
    This, this is she
To whom our vows and wishes bend:
Here our solemn search hath end.
Fame, that her high worth to raise
Seemed erst so lavish and profuse,
We may justly now accuse
Of detraction from her praise:
    Less than half we find expressed;
    Envy bid conceal the rest.

Mark what radiant state she spreads,
In circle round her shining throne
Shooting her beams like silver threads:
This, this is she alone,
    Sitting like a goddess bright
    In the centre of her light.

Might she the wise Latona be,
Or the towered Cybele,
Mother of a hundred gods?
Juno dares not give her odds:
    Who had thought this clime had held
    A deity so unparalleled?

323

As they come forward, THE GENIUS OF THE WOOD *appears, and, turning toward them, speaks.*

Gen. Stay, gentle Swains, for, though in this disguise,
I see bright honour sparkle through your eyes;
Of famous Arcady ye are, and sprung
Of that renownèd flood, so often sung,
Divine Alpheus, who, by secret sluice,
Stole under seas to meet his Arethuse;
And ye, the breathing roses of the wood,
Fair silver-buskined Nymphs, as great and good.
I know this quest of yours and free intent
Was all in honour and devotion meant
To the great mistress of yon princely shrine,
Whom with low reverence I adore as mine,
And with all helpful service will comply
To further this night's glad solemnity,
And lead ye where ye may more near behold
What shallow-searching Fame hath left untold;
Which I full oft, amidst these shades alone,
Have sat to wonder at, and gaze upon.
For know, by lot from Jove, I am the Power
Of this fair wood, and live in oaken bower,
To nurse the saplings tall, and curl the grove
With ringlets quaint and wanton windings wove;
And all my plants I save from nightly ill
Of noisome winds and blasting vapours chill;
And from the boughs brush off the evil dew,
And heal the harms of thwarting thunder blue,
Or what the cross dire-looking planet smites,
Or hurtful worm with cankered venom bites.
When evening grey doth rise, I fetch my round
Over the mount, and all this hallowed ground;
And early, ere the odorous breath of morn
Awakes the slumbering leaves, or tasselled horn
Shakes the high thicket, haste I all about,
Number my ranks, and visit every sprout
With puissant words and murmurs made to bless.
But else, in deep of night, when drowsiness
Hath locked up mortal sense, then listen I
To the celestial Sirens' harmony,
That sit upon the nine infolded spheres,
And sing to those that hold the vital shears,
And turn the adamantine spindle round
On which the fate of gods and men is wound.
Such sweet compulsion doth in music lie,
To lull the daughters of Necessity,
And keep unsteady Nature to her law,
And the low world in measured motion draw
After the heavenly tune, which none can hear
Of human mould with gross unpurgèd ear.
And yet such music worthiest were to blaze
The peerless height of her immortal praise
Whose lustre leads us, and for her most fit,

If my inferior hand or voice could hit
Inimitable sounds. Yet, as we go,
Whate'er the skill of lesser gods can show
I will assay, her worth to celebrate,
And so attend ye toward her glittering state;
Where ye may all, that are of noble stem,
Approach, and kiss her sacred vesture's hem.

II. Song.

O'er the smooth enamelled green,
Where no print of step hath been,
   Follow me, as I sing
   And touch the warbled string:
Under the shady roof
Of branching elm star-proof
    Follow me.
I will bring you where she sits,
Clad in splendour as befits
    Her deity.
Such a rural Queen
All Arcadia hath not seen.

III. Song.

Nymphs and Shepherds, dance no more
   By sandy Ladon's lilied banks;
On old Lycæus, or Cyllene hoar,
   Trip no more in twilight ranks;
Though Erymanth your loss deplore,
   A better soil shall give ye thanks.
From the stony Mænalus
Bring your flocks, and live with us;
Here ye shall have greater grace,
To serve the Lady of this place.
Though Syrinx your Pan's mistress were,
Yet Syrinx well might wait on her.
   Such a rural Queen
   All Arcadia hath not seen.

COMUS.

A MASQUE PRESENTED AT LUDLOW CASTLE, 1634,
BEFORE THE EARL OF BRIDGEWATER,
LORD PRESIDENT OF WALES.

THE PERSONS.

The ATTENDANT SPIRIT, afterwards in the habit of THYRSIS.
COMUS, with his Crew.
THE LADY.
FIRST BROTHER.
SECOND BROTHER.
SABRINA, the Nymph.

The Chief Persons which presented were :—

> The Lord Brackley ;
> Mr. Thomas Egerton, his Brother ;
> The Lady Alice Egerton.

COMUS.

The first Scene discovers a wild wood.

The ATTENDANT SPIRIT *descends or enters.*

BEFORE the starry threshold of Jove's court
My mansion is, where those immortal shapes
Of bright aerial spirits live insphered
In regions mild of calm and serene air,
Above the smoke and stir of this dim spot
Which men call Earth, and, with low-thoughted care,
Confined and pestered in this pinfold here,
Strive to keep up a frail and feverish being,
Unmindful of the crown that Virtue gives,
After this mortal change, to her true servants
Amongst the enthroned gods on sainted seats.
Yet some there be that by due steps aspire
To lay their just hands on that golden key
That opes the palace of eternity.
To such my errand is; and, but for such,
I would not soil these pure ambrosial weeds
With the rank vapours of this sin-worn mould.
    But to my task.   Neptune, besides the sway
Of every salt flood and each ebbing stream,
Took in, by lot 'twixt high and nether Jove,
Imperial rule of all the sea-girt isles
That, like to rich and various gems, inlay
The unadornèd bosom of the deep;
Which he, to grace his tributary gods,
By course commits to several government,
And gives them leave to wear their sapphire crowns
And wield their little tridents.   But this Isle,
The greatest and the best of all the main,
He quarters to his blue-haired deities;
And all this tract that fronts the falling sun
A noble Peer of mickle trust and power
Has in his charge, with tempered awe to guide
An old and haughty nation, proud in arms:
Where his fair offspring, nursed in princely lore,
Are coming to attend their father's state,
And new-intrusted sceptre.   But their way
Lies through the perplexed paths of this drear wood,
The nodding horror of whose shady brows

Threats the forlorn and wandering passenger;
And here their tender age might suffer peril,
But that, by quick command from sovran Jove,
I was despatched for their defence and guard!
And listen why; for I will tell you now
What never yet was heard in tale or song,
From old or modern bard, in hall or bower.
  Bacchus, that first from out the purple grape
Crushed the sweet poison of misusèd wine,
After the Tuscan mariners transformed,
Coasting the Tyrrhene shore, as the winds listed,
On Circe's island fell. (Who knows not Circe,
The daughter of the Sun, whose charmèd cup
Whoever tasted lost his upright shape,
And downward fell into a grovelling swine?)
This Nymph, that gazed upon his clustering locks,
With ivy berries wreathed, and his blithe youth,
Had by him, ere he parted thence, a son
Much like his father, but his mother more,
Whom therefore she brought up, and Comus named:
Who, ripe and frolic of his full-grown age,
Roving the Celtic and Iberian fields,
At last betakes him to this ominous wood,
And, in thick shelter of black shades imbowered,
Excels his mother at her mighty art;
Offering to every weary traveller
His orient liquor in a crystal glass,
To quench the drouth of Phœbus; which as they taste
(For most do taste through fond intemperate thirst),
Soon as the potion works, their human count'nance,
The express resemblance of the gods, is changed
Into some brutish form of wolf or bear,
Or ounce or tiger, hog or bearded goat,
All other parts remaining as they were.
And they, so perfect is their misery,
Not once perceive their foul disfigurement,
But boast themselves more comely than before,
And all their friends and native home forget,
To roll with pleasure in a sensual sty.
Therefore, when any favoured of high Jove
Chances to pass through this adventurous glade,
Swift as the sparkle of a glancing star
I shoot from heaven, to give him safe convoy,
As now I do. But first I must put off
These my sky-robes, spun out of Iris' woof,
And take the weeds and likeness of a swain
That to the service of this house belongs,
Who, with his soft pipe and smooth-dittied song,
Well knows to still the wild winds when they roar,
And hush the waving woods; nor of less faith,
And in this office of his mountain watch
Likeliest, and nearest to the present aid
Of this occasion. But I hear the tread
Of hateful steps; I must be viewless now.

330

COMUS

Comus enters, with a charming-rod in one hand, his glass in the other; with him a rout of monsters, headed like sundry sorts of wild beasts, but otherwise like men and women, their apparel glistering. They come in making a riotous and unruly noise, with torches in their hands.

    Comus. The star that bids the shepherd fold
Now the top of heaven doth hold;
And the gilded car of day
His glowing axle doth allay
In the steep Atlantic stream:
And the slope sun his upward beam
Shoots against the dusky pole,
Pacing toward the other goal
Of his chamber in the east.
Meanwhile, welcome joy and feast,
Midnight shout and revelry,
Tipsy dance and jollity.
Braid your locks with rosy twine,
Dropping odours, dropping wine.
Rigour now is gone to bed;
And Advice with scrupulous head,
Strict Age, and sour Severity,
With their grave saws, in slumber lie.
We, that are of purer fire,
Imitate the starry quire,
Who, in their nightly watchful spheres,
Lead in swift round the months and years.
The sounds and seas, with all their finny drove,
Now to the moon in wavering morrice move;
And on the tawny sands and shelves
Trip the pert fairies and the dapper elves.
By dimpled brook and fountain-brim,
The wood-nymphs, decked with daisies trim,
Their merry wakes and pastimes keep:
What hath night to do with sleep?
Night hath better sweets to prove;
Venus now wakes, and wakens Love.
Come, let us our rites begin;
'Tis only daylight that makes sin,
Which these dun shades will ne'er report.
Hail, goddess of nocturnal sport,
Dark-veiled Cotytto, to whom the secret flame
Of midnight torches burns! mysterious dame,
That ne'er art called but when the dragon womb
Of Stygian darkness spets her thickest gloom,
And makes one blot of all the air!
Stay thy cloudy ebon chair,
Wherein thou ridest with Hecat', and befriend
Us thy vowed priests, till utmost end
Of all thy dues be done, and none left out
Ere the blabbing eastern scout,
The nice Morn on the Indian steep,
From her cabined loop-hole peep,
And to the tell-tale Sun descry

331

Our concealed solemnity.
Come, knit hands, and beat the ground
In a light fantastic round.

The Measure.

Break off, break off ! I feel the different pace
Of some chaste footing near about this ground.
Run to your shrouds within these brakes and trees ;
Our number may affright.   Some virgin sure
(For so I can distinguish by mine art)
Benighted in these woods ! Now to my charms,
And to my wily trains : I shall ere long
Be well stocked with as fair a herd as grazed
About my mother Circe.   Thus I hurl
My dazzling spells into the spongy air,
Of power to cheat the eye with blear illusion,
And give it false presentments, lest the place
And my quaint habits breed astonishment,
And put the damsel to suspicious flight,
Which must not be, for that's against my course.
I, under fair pretence of friendly ends,
And well-placed words of glozing courtesy,
Baited with reasons not unplausible,
Wind me into the easy-hearted man,
And hug him into snares.   When once her eye
Hath met the virtue of this magic dust
I shall appear some harmless villager,
Whom thrift keeps up about his country gear.
But here she comes ; I fairly step aside,
And hearken, if I may her business hear.

The LADY enters.

Lady. This way the noise was, if mine ear be true,
My best guide now.   Methought it was the sound
Of riot and ill-managed merriment,
Such as the jocund flute or gamesome pipe
Stirs up among the loose unlettered hinds,
When, for their teeming flocks and granges full,
In wanton dance they praise the bounteous Pan,
And thank the gods amiss.   I should be loth
To meet the rudeness and swilled insolence
Of such late wassailers ; yet, oh ! where else
Shall I inform my unacquainted feet
In the blind mazes of this tangled wood ?
My brothers, when they saw me wearied out
With this long way, resolving here to lodge
Under the spreading favour of these pines,
Stepped, as they said, to the next thicket-side
To bring me berries, or such cooling fruit
As the kind hospitable woods provide.
They left me then when the grey-hooded Even,
Like a sad votarist in palmer's weed,

Rose from the hindmost wheels of Phœbus' wain.
But where they are, and why they came not back,
Is now the labour of my thoughts.   'T is likeliest
They had engaged their wandering steps too far ;
And envious darkness, ere they could return,
Had stole them from me.   Else, O thievish Night,
Why shouldst thou, but for some felonious end,
In thy dark lantern thus close up the stars
That Nature hung in heaven, and filled their lamps
With everlasting oil, to give due light
To the misled and lonely traveller ?
This is the place, as well as I may guess,
Whence even now the tumult of loud mirth
Was rife, and perfect in my listening ear ;
Yet nought but single darkness do I find.
What might this be ?   A thousand fantasies
Begin to throng into my memory,
Of calling shapes, and beckoning shadows dire,
And airy tongues that syllable men's names
On sands and shores and desert wildernesses.
These thoughts may startle well, but not astound
The virtuous mind, that ever walks attended
By a strong siding champion, Conscience.
O, welcome, pure-eyed Faith, white-handed Hope,
Thou hovering angel girt with golden wings,
And thou unblemished form of Chastity !
I see ye visibly, and now believe
That He, the Supreme Good, to whom all things ill
Are but as slavish officers of vengeance,
Would send a glistering guardian, if need were,
To keep my life and honour unassailed. . . . .
Was I deceived, or did a sable cloud
Turn forth her silver lining on the night ?
I did not err : there does a sable cloud
Turn forth her silver lining on the night,
And casts a gleam over this tufted grove.
I cannot hallo to my brothers, but
Such noise as I can make to be heard farthest
I 'll venture ; for my new-enlivened spirits
Prompt me, and they perhaps are not far off.

Song.

Sweet Echo, sweetest nymph, that liv'st unseen
     Within thy airy shell
     By slow Meander's margent green,
And in the violet-embroidered vale
     Where the love-lorn nightingale
Nightly to thee her sad song mourneth well :
Canst thou not tell me of a gentle pair
     That likest thy Narcissus are ?
       Oh, if thou have
     Hid them in some flowery cave,
      Tell me but where,

Sweet Queen of Parley, Daughter of the Sphere !
So may'st thou be translated to the skies,
And give resounding grace to all Heaven's harmonies !

Comus. Can any mortal mixture of earth's mould
Breathe such divine enchanting ravishment ?
Sure something holy lodges in that breast,
And with these raptures moves the vocal air
To testify his hidden residence.
How sweetly did they float upon the wings
Of silence, through the empty-vaulted night,
At every fall smoothing the raven down
Of darkness till it smiled !   I have oft heard
My mother Circe with the Sirens three,
Amidst the flowery-kirtled Naiades,
Culling their potent herbs and baleful drugs,
Who, as they sung, would take the prisoned soul,
And lap it in Elysium : Scylla wept,
And chid her barking waves into attention,
And fell Charybdis murmured soft applause.
Yet they in pleasing slumber lulled the sense,
And in sweet madness robbed it of itself ;
But such a sacred and home-felt delight,
Such sober certainty of waking bliss,
I never heard till now.   I 'll speak to her,
And she shall be my queen.—Hail, foreign wonder !
Whom certain these rough shades did never breed,
Unless the goddess that in rural shrine
Dwell'st here with Pan or Sylvan, by blest song
Forbidding every bleak unkindly fog
To touch the prosperous growth of this tall wood.
    Lady. Nay, gentle shepherd, ill is lost that praise
That is addressed to unattending ears.
Not any boast of skill, but extreme shift
How to regain my severed company,
Compelled me to awake the courteous Echo
To give me answer from her mossy couch.
    Comus. What chance, good Lady, has bereft you thus ?
    Lady. Dim darkness and this leavy labyrinth.
    Comus. Could that divide you from near-ushering guides ?
    Lady. They left me weary on a grassy turf.
    Comus. By falsehood, or discourtesy, or why ?
    Lady. To seek i' the valley some cool friendly spring.
    Comus. And left your fair side all unguarded, Lady ?
    Lady. They were but twain, and purposed quick return.
    Comus. Perhaps forestalling night prevented them.
    Lady. How easy my misfortune is to hit !
    Comus. Imports their loss, beside the present need ?
    Lady. No less than if I should my brothers lose.
    Comus. Were they of manly prime, or youthful bloom ?
    Lady. As smooth as Hebe's their unrazored lips.
    Comus. Two such I saw, what time the laboured ox
In his loose traces from the furrow came,
And the swinked hedger at his supper sat.

I saw them under a green mantling vine,
That crawls along the side of yon small hill,
Plucking ripe clusters from the tender shoots;
Their port was more than human, as they stood.
I took it for a faery vision
Of some gay creatures of the element,
That in the colours of the rainbow live,
And play i' the plighted clouds. I was awe-strook,
And, as I passed, I worshipped. If those you seek,
It were a journey like the path to Heaven
To help you find them.
    Lady.   Gentle villager,
What readiest way would bring me to that place?
   Comus. Due west it rises from this shrubby point.
   Lady. To find out that, good shepherd, I suppose,
In such a scant allowance of star-light,
Would overtask the best land-pilot's art,
Without the sure guess of well-practised feet.
   Comus. I know each lane, and every alley green,
Dingle, or bushy dell, of this wild wood,
And every bosky bourn from side to side,
My daily walks and ancient neighbourhood;
And, if your stray attendants be yet lodged,
Or shroud within these limits, I shall know
Ere morrow wake, or the low-roosted lark
From her thatched pallet rouse. If otherwise,
I can conduct you, Lady, to a low
But loyal cottage, where you may be safe
Till further quest.
    Lady.   Shepherd, I take thy word,
And trust thy honest-offered courtesy,
Which oft is sooner found in lowly sheds,
With smoky rafters, than in tapestry halls
And courts of princes, where it first was named,
And yet is most pretended. In a place
Less warranted than this, or less secure,
I cannot be, that I should fear to change it.
Eye me, blest Providence, and square my trial
To my proportioned strength! Shepherd, lead on. . . .

The Two Brothers.

   Eld. Bro. Unmuffle, ye faint stars; and thou, fair moon,
That wont'st to love the traveller's benison,
Stoop thy pale visage through an amber cloud,
And disinherit Chaos, that reigns here
In double night of darkness and of shades;
Or, if your influence be quite dammed up
With black usurping mists, some gentle taper,
Though a rush candle from the wicker hole
Of some clay habitation, visit us
With thy long levelled rule of streaming light,
And thou shalt be our star of Arcady,
Or Tyrian Cynosure.

Sec. Bro.   Or, if our eyes
Be barred that happiness, might we but hear
The folded flocks, penned in their wattled cotes,
Or sound of pastoral reed with oaten stops,
Or whistle from the lodge, or village cock
Count the night-watches to his feathery dames,
'T would be some solace yet, some little cheering,
In this close dungeon of innumerous boughs.
But, oh, that hapless virgin, our lost sister!
Where may she wander now, whither betake her
From the chill dew, amongst rude burs and thistles?
Perhaps some cold bank is her bolster now,
Or 'gainst the rugged bark of some broad elm
Leans her unpillowed head, fraught with sad fears.
What if in wild amazement and affright,
Or, while we speak, within the direful grasp
Of savage hunger, or of savage heat!
    Eld. Bro. Peace, brother: be not over-exquisite
To cast the fashion of uncertain evils;
For, grant they be so, while they rest unknown,
What need a man forestall his date of grief,
And run to meet what he would most avoid?
Or, if they be but false alarms of fear,
How bitter is such self-delusion!
I do not think my sister so to seek,
Or so unprincipled in virtue's book,
And the sweet peace that goodness bosoms ever,
As that the single want of light and noise
(Not being in danger, as I trust she is not)
Could stir the constant mood of her calm thoughts,
And put them into misbecoming plight.
Virtue could see to do what Virtue would
By her own radiant light, though sun and moon
Were in the flat sea sunk.   And Wisdom's self
Oft seeks to sweet retired solitude,
Where, with her best nurse, Contemplation,
She plumes her feathers, and lets grow her wings,
That, in the various bustle of resort,
Were all to-ruffled, and sometimes impaired.
He that has light within his own clear breast
May sit i' the centre, and enjoy bright day:
But he that hides a dark soul and foul thoughts
Benighted walks under the mid-day sun;
Himself is his own dungeon.
    Sec. Bro.   'T is most true
That musing Meditation most affects
The pensive secrecy of desert cell,
Far from the cheerful haunt of men and herds,
And sits as safe as in a senate-house;
For who would rob a hermit of his weeds,
His few books, or his beads, or maple dish,
Or do his grey hairs any violence?
But Beauty, like the fair Hesperian tree
Laden with blooming gold, had need the guard

Of dragon-watch with unenchanted eye
To save her blossoms, and defend her fruit,
From the rash hand of bold Incontinence.
You may as well spread out the unsunned heaps
Of miser's treasure by an outlaw's den,
And tell me it is safe, as bid me hope
Danger will wink on Opportunity,
And let a single helpless maiden pass
Uninjured in this wild surrounding waste.
Of night or loneliness it recks me not;
I fear the dread events that dog them both,
Lest some ill-greeting touch attempt the person
Of our unowned sister.

    Eld. Bro.   I do not, brother,
Infer as if I thought my sister's state
Secure without all doubt or controversy;
Yet, where an equal poise of hope and fear
Does arbitrate the event, my nature is
That I incline to hope rather than fear,
And gladly banish squint suspicion.
My sister is not so defenceless left
As you imagine; she has a hidden strength,
Which you remember not.

    Sec. Bro.   What hidden strength,
Unless the strength of Heaven, if you mean that?

    Eld. Bro. I mean that too, but yet a hidden strength,
Which, if Heaven gave it, may be termed her own.
'T is chastity, my brother, chastity:
She that has that is clad in complete steel,
And, like a quivered nymph with arrows keen,
May trace huge forests, and unharboured heaths,
Infamous hills, and sandy perilous wilds;
Where, through the sacred rays of chastity,
No savage fierce, bandite, or mountaineer,
Will dare to soil her virgin purity.
Yea, there where very desolation dwells,
By grots and caverns shagged with horrid shades,
She may pass on with unblenched majesty,
Be it not done in pride, or in presumption.
Some say no evil thing that walks by night,
In fog or fire, by lake or moorish fen,
Blue meagre hag, or stubborn unlaid ghost,
That breaks his magic chains at curfew time,
No goblin or swart faery of the mine,
Hath hurtful power o'er true virginity.
Do ye believe me yet, or shall I call
Antiquity from the old schools of Greece
To testify the arms of chastity?
Hence had the huntress Dian her dread bow,
Fair silver-shafted queen for ever chaste,
Wherewith she tamed the brinded lioness
And spotted mountain-pard, but set at nought
The frivolous bolt of Cupid; gods and men
Feared her stern frown, and she was queen o' the woods.

M.—Z

What was that snaky-headed Gorgon shield
That wise Minerva wore, unconquered virgin,
Wherewith she freezed her foes to congealed stone,
But rigid looks of chaste austerity,
And noble grace that dashed brute violence
With sudden adoration and blank awe?
So dear to Heaven is saintly chastity
That, when a soul is found sincerely so,
A thousand liveried angels lackey her,
Driving far off each thing of sin and guilt,
And in clear dream and solemn vision
Tell her of things that no gross ear can hear;
Till oft converse with heavenly habitants
Begin to cast a beam on the outward shape,
The unpolluted temple of the mind,
And turns it by degrees to the soul's essence,
Till all be made immortal. But, when lust,
By unchaste looks, loose gestures, and foul talk,
But most by lewd and lavish act of sin,
Lets in defilement to the inward parts,
The soul grows clotted by contagion,
Imbodies, and imbrutes, till she quite lose
The divine property of her first being.
Such are those thick and gloomy shadows damp
Oft seen in charnel-vaults and sepulchres,
Lingering and sitting by a new-made grave,
As loth to leave the body that it loved,
And linked itself by carnal sensualty
To a degenerate and degraded state.
  Sec. Bro. How charming is divine Philosophy!
Not harsh and crabbed, as dull fools suppose,
But musical as is Apollo's lute,
And a perpetual feast of nectared sweets,
Where no crude surfeit reigns.
  Eld. Bro.   List! list! I hear
Some far-off hallo break the silent air.
  Sec. Bro. Methought so too; what should it be?
  Eld. Bro.   For certain,
Either some one, like us, night-foundered here,
Or else some neighbour woodman, or, at worst,
Some roving robber calling to his fellows.
  Sec. Bro. Heaven keep my sister! Again, again, and near!
Best draw, and stand upon our guard.
  Eld. Bro.   I'll hallo.
If he be friendly, he comes well: if not,
Defence is a good cause, and Heaven be for us!

The ATTENDANT SPIRIT, *habited like a shepherd.*

That hallo I should know. What are you? speak.
Come not too near; you fall on iron stakes else.
  Spir. What voice is that? my young Lord? speak again.
  Sec. Bro. O brother, 't is my father's Shepherd, sure.
  Eld. Bro. Thyrsis! whose artful strains have oft delayed
338

COMUS

The huddling brook to hear his madrigal,
And sweetened every musk-rose of the dale.
How camest thou here, good swain? Hath any ram
Slipped from the fold, or young kid lost his dam,
Or straggling wether the pent flock forsook?
How couldst thou find this dark sequestered nook?
   Spir. O my loved master's heir, and his next joy,
I came not here on such a trivial toy
As a strayed ewe, or to pursue the stealth
Of pilfering wolf; not all the fleecy wealth
That doth enrich these downs is worth a thought
To this my errand, and the care it brought.
But, oh! my virgin Lady, where is she?
How chance she is not in your company?
   Eld. Bro. To tell thee sadly, Shepherd, without blame
Or our neglect, we lost her as we came.
   Spir. Ay me unhappy! then my fears are true.
   Eld. Bro. What fears, good Thyrsis? Prithee briefly shew.
   Spir. I'll tell ye. 'T is not vain or fabulous
(Though so esteemed by shallow ignorance)
What the sage poets, taught by the heavenly Muse,
Storied of old in high immortal verse
Of dire Chimeras and enchanted isles,
And rifted rocks whose entrance leads to Hell;
For such there be, but unbelief is blind.
   Within the navel of this hideous wood,
Immured in cypress shades, a sorcerer dwells,
Of Bacchus and of Circe born, great Comus,
Deep skilled in all his mother's witcheries,
And here to every thirsty wanderer
By sly enticement gives his baneful cup,
With many murmurs mixed, whose pleasing poison
The visage quite transforms of him that drinks,
And the inglorious likeness of a beast
Fixes instead, unmoulding reason's mintage
Charactered in the face. This have I learnt
Tending my flocks hard by i' the hilly crofts
That brow this bottom glade; whence night by night
He and his monstrous rout are heard to howl
Like stabled wolves, or tigers at their prey,
Doing abhorred rites to Hecate
In their obscurèd haunts of inmost bowers.
Yet have they many baits and guileful spells
To inveigle and invite the unwary sense
Of them that pass unweeting by the way.
This evening late, by then the chewing flocks
Had ta'en their supper on the savoury herb
Of knot-grass dew-besprent, and were in fold,
I sat me down to watch upon a bank
With ivy canopied, and interwove
With flaunting honeysuckle, and began,
Wrapt in a pleasing fit of melancholy,
To meditate my rural minstrelsy,
Till fancy had her fill. But ere a close

339

The wonted roar was up amidst the woods,
And filled the air with barbarous dissonance;
At which I ceased, and listened them a while,
Till an unusual stop of sudden silence
Gave respite to the drowsy-flighted steeds
That draw the litter of close-curtained Sleep.
At last a soft and solemn-breathing sound
Rose like a steam of rich distilled perfumes,
And stole upon the air, that even Silence
Was took ere she was ware, and wished she might
Deny her nature, and be never more,
Still to be so displaced. I was all ear,
And took in strains that might create a soul
Under the ribs of Death. But, oh! ere long
Too well I did perceive it was the voice
Of my most honoured Lady, your dear sister.
Amazed I stood, harrowed with grief and fear;
And 'O poor hapless nightingale,' thought I,
'How sweet thou sing'st, how near the deadly snare!'
Then down the lawns I ran with headlong haste,
Through paths and turnings often trod by day,
Till, guided by mine ear, I found the place
Where that damned wizard, hid in sly disguise
(For so by certain signs I knew), had met
Already, ere my best speed could prevent,
The aidless innocent Lady, his wished prey;
Who gently asked if he had seen such two,
Supposing him some neighbour villager.
Longer I durst not stay, but soon I guessed
Ye were the two she meant; with that I sprung
Into swift flight, till I had found you here;
But further know I not.
   Sec. Bro.   O night and shades,
How are ye joined with Hell in triple knot
Against the unarmed weakness of one virgin,
Alone and helpless! Is this the confidence
You gave me, brother?
   Eld. Bro.   Yes, and keep it still;
Lean on it safely; not a period
Shall be unsaid for me. Against the threats
Of malice or of sorcery, or that power
Which erring men call Chance, this I hold firm:
Virtue may be assailed, but never hurt,
Surprised by unjust force, but not enthralled;
Yea, even that which Mischief meant most harm
Shall in the happy trial prove most glory.
But evil on itself shall back recoil,
And mix no more with goodness, when at last,
Gathered like scum, and settled to itself,
It shall be in eternal restless change
Self-fed and self-consumed. If this fail,
The pillared firmament is rottenness,
And earth's base built on stubble. But come, let's on!
Against the opposing will and arm of Heaven

May never this just sword be lifted up;
But, for that damned magician, let him be girt
With all the griesly legions that troop
Under the sooty flag of Acheron,
Harpies and Hydras, or all the monstrous forms
'Twixt Africa and Ind, I'll find him out,
And force him to return his purchase back,
Or drag him by the curls to a foul death,
Cursed as his life.

 Spir.   Alas! good venturous youth,
I love thy courage yet, and bold emprise;
But here thy sword can do thee little stead.
Far other arms and other weapons must
Be those that quell the might of hellish charms.
He with his bare wand can unthread thy joints,
And crumble all thy sinews.

 Eld. Bro.   Why, prithee, Shepherd,
How durst thou then thyself approach so near
As to make this relation?

 Spir.   Care and utmost shifts
How to secure the Lady from surprisal
Brought to my mind a certain shepherd lad,
Of small regard to see to, yet well skilled
In every virtuous plant and healing herb
That spreads her verdant leaf to the morning ray.
He loved me well, and oft would beg me sing;
Which when I did, he on the tender grass
Would sit, and hearken even to ecstasy,
And in requital ope his leathern scrip,
And show me simples of a thousand names,
Telling their strange and vigorous faculties.
Amongst the rest a small unsightly root,
But of divine effect, he culled me out.
The leaf was darkish, and had prickles on it,
But in another country, as he said,
Bore a bright golden flower, but not in this soil:
Unknown, and like esteemed, and the dull swain
Treads on it daily with his clouted shoon;
And yet more med'cinal is it than that Moly
That Hermes once to wise Ulysses gave.
He called it Hæmony, and gave it me,
And bade me keep it as of sovran use
'Gainst all enchantments, mildew blast, or damp,
Or ghastly Furies' apparition.
I pursed it up, but little reckoning made,
Till now that this extremity compelled.
But now I find it true; for by this means
I knew the foul enchanter, though disguised,
Entered the very lime-twigs of his spells,
And yet came off. If you have this about you
(As I will give you when we go) you may
Boldly assault the necromancer's hall;
Where if he be, with dauntless hardihood
And brandished blade rush on him: break his glass,

And shed the luscious liquor on the ground;
But seize his wand.   Though he and his curst crew
Fierce sign of battle make, and menace high,
Or, like the sons of Vulcan, vomit smoke,
Yet will they soon retire, if he but shrink.
 Eld. Bro. Thyrsis, lead on apace; I'll follow thee;
And some good angel bear a shield before us!

*The Scene changes to a stately palace, set out with all manner of delicious-
ness: soft music, tables spread with all dainties.* COMUS *appears with
his rabble, and* THE LADY *set in an enchanted chair: to whom he offers
his glass; which she puts by, and goes about to rise.*

 Comus. Nay, Lady, sit.   If I but wave this wand,
Your nerves are all chained up in alabaster,
And you a statue, or as Daphne was,
Root-bound, that fled Apollo.
 Lady.   Fool, do not boast.
Thou canst not touch the freedom of my mind
With all thy charms, although this corporal rind
Thou hast immanacled while Heaven sees good.
 Comus. Why are you vexed, Lady? why do you frown?
Here dwell no frowns, nor anger; from these gates
Sorrow flies far.   See, here be all the pleasures
That fancy can beget on youthful thoughts,
When the fresh blood grows lively, and returns
Brisk as the April buds in primrose season.
And first behold this cordial julep here,
That flames and dances in his crystal bounds,
With spirits of balm and fragrant syrups mixed.
Not that Nepenthes which the wife of Thone
In Egypt gave to Jove-born Helena
Is of such power to stir up joy as this,
To life so friendly, or so cool to thirst.
Why should you be so cruel to yourself,
And to those dainty limbs, which Nature lent
For gentle usage and soft delicacy?
But you invert the covenants of her trust,
And harshly deal, like an ill borrower,
With that which you received on other terms,
Scorning the unexempt condition
By which all mortal frailty must subsist,
Refreshment after toil, ease after pain,
That have been tired all day without repast,
And timely rest have wanted.   But, fair virgin,
This will restore all soon.
 Lady.   'T will not, false traitor!
'T will not restore the truth and honesty
That thou hast banished from thy tongue with lies.
Was this the cottage and the safe abode
Thou told'st me of?   What grim aspects are these,
These ugly-headed monsters?   Mercy guard me!
Hence with thy brewed enchantments, foul deceiver!
Hast thou betrayed my credulous innocence

With vizored falsehood and base forgery?
And wouldst thou seek again to trap me here
With liquorish baits, fit to ensnare a brute?
Were it a draught for Juno when she banquets,
I would not taste thy treasonous offer.   None
But such as are good men can give good things;
And that which is not good is not delicious
To a well-governed and wise appetite.
   Comus. O foolishness of men! that lend their ears
To those budge doctors of the Stoic fur,
And fetch their precepts from the Cynic tub,
Praising the lean and sallow Abstinence!
Wherefore did Nature pour her bounties forth
With such a full and unwithdrawing hand,
Covering the earth with odours, fruits, and flocks,
Thronging the seas with spawn innumerable,
But all to please and sate the curious taste?
And set to work millions of spinning worms,
That in their green shops weave the smooth-haired silk,
To deck her sons; and, that no corner might
Be vacant of her plenty, in her own loins
She hutched the all-worshipped ore and precious gems,
To store her children with.   If all the world
Should, in a pet of temperance, feed on pulse,
Drink the clear stream, and nothing wear but frieze,
The All-giver would be unthanked, would be unpraised,
Not half His riches known, and yet despised;
And we should serve Him as a grudging Master,
As a penurious niggard of His wealth,
And live like Nature's bastards, not her sons,
Who would be quite surcharged with her own weight,
And strangled with her waste fertility:
The earth cumbered, and the winged air darked with plumes,
The herds would over-multitude their lords;
The sea o'erfraught would swell, and the unsought diamonds
Would so emblaze the forehead of the deep,
And so bestud with stars, that they below
Would grow inured to light, and come at last
To gaze upon the sun with shameless brows.
List, Lady; be not coy, and be not cozened
With that same vaunted name, Virginity.
Beauty is Nature's coin; must not be hoarded,
But must be current; and the good thereof
Consists in mutual and partaken bliss,
Unsavoury in the enjoyment of itself.
If you let slip time, like a neglected rose
It withers on the stalk with languished head.
Beauty is Nature's brag, and must be shown
In courts, at feasts, and high solemnities,
Where most may wonder at the workmanship.
It is for homely features to keep home;
They had their name thence: coarse complexions
And cheeks of sorry grain will serve to ply
The sampler, and to tease the huswife's wool.

What need a vermeil-tinctured lip for that,
Love-darting eyes, or tresses like the morn?
There was another meaning in these gifts;
Think what, and be advised; you are but young yet.

Lady. I had not thought to have unlocked my lips
In this unhallowed air, but that this juggler
Would think to charm my judgment, as mine eyes,
Obtruding false rules pranked in reason's garb.
I hate when vice can bolt her arguments
And virtue has no tongue to check her pride.
Impostor! do not charge most innocent Nature,
As if she would her children should be riotous
With her abundance. She, good cateress,
Means her provision only to the good,
That live according to her sober laws,
And holy dictate of spare Temperance.
If every just man that now pines with want
Had but a moderate and beseeming share
Of that which lewdly-pampered Luxury
Now heaps upon some few with vast excess,
Nature's full blessings would be well-dispensed
In unsuperfluous even proportion,
And she no whit encumbered with her store;
And then the Giver would be better thanked,
His praise due paid: for swinish gluttony
Ne'er looks to Heaven amidst his gorgeous feast,
But with besotted base ingratitude
Crams, and blasphemes his Feeder. Shall I go on?
Or have I said enow? To him that dares
Arm his profane tongue with contemptuous words
Against the sun-clad power of chastity
Fain would I something say;—yet to what end?
Thou hast nor ear, nor soul, to apprehend
The sublime notion and high mystery
That must be uttered to unfold the sage
And serious doctrine of Virginity;
And thou art worthy that thou shouldst not know
More happiness than this thy present lot.
Enjoy your dear wit, and gay rhetoric,
That hath so well been taught her dazzling fence;
Thou art not fit to hear thyself convinced.
Yet, should I try, the uncontrollèd worth
Of this pure cause would kindle my rapt spirits
To such a flame of sacred vehemence
That dumb things would be moved to sympathize,
And the brute Earth would lend her nerves, and shake,
Till all thy magic structures, reared so high,
Were shattered into heaps o'er thy false head.

Comus. She fables not. I feel that I do fear
Her words set off by some superior power;
And, though not mortal, yet a cold shuddering dew
Dips me all o'er, as when the wrath of Jove
Speaks thunder and the chains of Erebus
To some of Saturn's crew. I must dissemble,

And try her yet more strongly.—Come, no more!
This is mere moral babble, and direct
Against the canon laws of our foundation.
I must not suffer this; yet 't is but the lees
And settlings of a melancholy blood.
But this will cure all straight; one sip of this
Will bathe the drooping spirits in delight
Beyond the bliss of dreams.   Be wise, and taste . . .

The BROTHERS *rush in with swords drawn, wrest his glass out of his hand, and break it against the ground: his rout make sign of resistance, but are all driven in.   The* ATTENDANT SPIRIT *comes in.*

   Spir. What! have you let the false enchanter 'scape?
O ye mistook; ye should have snatched his wand,
And bound him fast.   Without his rod reversed,
And backward mutters of dissevering power,
We cannot free the Lady that sits here
In stony fetters fixed and motionless.
Yet stay: be not disturbed; now I bethink me,
Some other means I have which may be used,
Which once of Melibœus old I learnt,
The soothest shepherd that e'er piped on plains.
   There is a gentle Nymph not far from hence,
That with moist curb sways the smooth Severn stream:
Sabrina is her name: a virgin pure;
Whilom she was the daughter of Locrine,
That had the sceptre from his father Brute.
She, guiltless damsel, flying the mad pursuit
Of her enragèd stepdame, Guendolen,
Commended her fair innocence to the flood
That stayed her flight with his cross-flowing course.
The water-nymphs, that in the bottom played,
Held up their pearled wrists, and took her in,
Bearing her straight to agèd Nereus' hall;
Who, piteous of her woes, reared her lank head,
And gave her to his daughters to imbathe
In nectared lavers strewed with asphodel,
And through the porch and inlet of each sense
Dropt in ambrosial oils, till she revived,
And underwent a quick immortal change,
Made Goddess of the river.   Still she retains
Her maiden gentleness, and oft at eve
Visits the herds along the twilight meadows,
Helping all urchin blasts, and ill-luck signs
That the shrewd meddling elf delights to make,
Which she with precious vialed liquors heals;
For which the shepherds, at their festivals,
Carol her goodness loud in rustic lays,
And throw sweet garland wreaths into her stream
Of pansies, pinks, and gaudy daffodils.
And, as the old swain said, she can unlock
The clasping charm, and thaw the numbing spell,
If she be right invoked in warbled song;

For maidenhood she loves, and will be swift
To aid a virgin, such as was herself,
In hard-besetting need.   This will I try,
And add the power of some adjuring verse.

Song.

Sabrina fair,
Listen where thou art sitting
Under the glassy, cool, translucent wave,
In twisted braids of lilies knitting
The loose train of thy amber-dropping hair ;
Listen for dear honour's sake,
Goddess of the silver lake,
Listen and save !

Listen, and appear to us,
In name of great Oceanus,
By the earth-shaking Neptune's mace,
And Tethys' grave majestic pace ;
By hoary Nereus' wrinkled look,
And the Carpathian wizard's hook ;
By scaly Triton's winding shell,
And old soothsaying Glaucus' spell ;
By Leucothea's lovely hands,
And her son that rules the strands ;
By Thetis' tinsel-slippered feet,
And the songs of Sirens sweet ;
By dead Parthenope's dear tomb,
And fair Ligea's golden comb,
Wherewith she sits on diamond rocks
Sleeking her soft alluring locks ;
By all the nymphs that nightly dance
Upon thy streams with wily glance ;
Rise, rise, and heave thy rosy head
From thy coral-paven bed,
And bridle in thy headlong wave,
Till thou our summons answered have.
Listen and save !

Sabrina *rises, attended by Water-nymphs, and sings.*

By the rushy-fringèd bank,
Where grows the willow and the osier dank,
My sliding chariot stays,
Thick set with agate, and the azure sheen
Of turkis blue, and emerald green,
That in the channel strays :
Whilst from off the waters fleet
Thus I set my printless feet
O'er the cowslip's velvet head,
That bends not as I tread.
Gentle swain, at thy request
I am here !

Spir. Goddess dear,
We implore thy powerful hand
To undo the charmèd band
Of true virgin here distressed
Through the force and through the wile
Of unblessed enchanter vile.
    Sabr. Shepherd, 't is my office best
To help ensnared chastity.
Brightest Lady, look on me.
Thus I sprinkle on thy breast
Drops that from my fountain pure
I have kept of precious cure ;
Thrice upon thy finger's tip,
Thrice upon thy rubied lip ;
Next this marble venomed seat,
Smeared with gums of glutinous heat,
I touch with chaste palms moist and cold.
Now the spell hath lost his hold ;
And I must haste ere morning hour
To wait in Amphitrite's bower.

SABRINA *descends, and* THE LADY *rises out of her seat.*

    Spir. Virgin, daughter of Locrine,
Sprung of old Anchises' line,
May thy brimmed waves for this
Their full tribute never miss
From a thousand petty rills,
That tumble down the snowy hills :
Summer drouth or singèd air
Never scorch thy tresses fair,
Nor wet October's torrent flood
Thy molten crystal fill with mud ;
May thy billows roll ashore
The beryl and the golden ore ;
May thy lofty head be crowned
With many a tower and terrace round,
And here and there thy banks upon
With groves of myrrh and cinnamon.
    Come, Lady ; while Heaven lends us grace,
Let us fly this cursed place,
Lest the sorcerer us entice
With some other new device.
Not a waste or needless sound
Till we come to holier ground.
I shall be your faithful guide
Through this gloomy covert wide ;
And not many furlongs thence
Is your father's residence,
Where this night are met in state
Many a friend to gratulate
His wished presence, and beside
All the swains that there abide
With jigs and rural dance resort.

We shall catch them at their sport,
And our sudden coming there
Will double all their mirth and cheer.
Come, let us haste ; the stars grow high,
But Night sits monarch yet in the mid sky.

*The Scene changes, presenting Ludlow Town, and the President's Castle:
then come in Country Dancers: after them the* ATTENDANT SPIRIT,
with the TWO BROTHERS *and* THE LADY.

SONG.

Spir. Back, shepherds, back ! Enough your play
Till next sunshine holiday.
Here be, without duck or nod,
Other trippings to be trod
Of lighter toes, and such court guise
As Mercury did first disguise
With the mincing Dryades
On the lawns and on the leas.

This second Song presents them to their Father and Mother.

Noble Lord and Lady bright,
I have brought ye new delight.
Here behold so goodly grown
Three fair branches of your own.
Heaven hath timely tried their youth,
Their faith, their patience, and their truth,
And sent them here through hard assays
With a crown of deathless praise,
To triumph in victorious dance
O'er sensual folly and intemperance.

The dances ended, the SPIRIT *epiloguizes.*

Spir. To the ocean now I fly,
And those happy climes that lie
Where day never shuts his eye,
Up in the broad fields of the sky.
There I suck the liquid air,
All amidst the gardens fair
Of Hesperus, and his daughters three
That sing about the golden tree.
Along the crisped shades and bowers
Revels the spruce and jocund Spring ;
The Graces and the rosy-bosomed Hours
Thither all their bounties bring.
There eternal Summer dwells,
And west winds with musky wing
About the cedarn alleys fling
Nard and cassia's balmy smells.
Iris there with humid bow
Waters the odorous banks, that blow
Flowers of more mingled hue

348

Than her purfled scarf can shew,
And drenches with Elysian dew
(List, mortals, if your ears be true)
Beds of hyacinth and roses,
Where young Adonis now reposes,
Waxing well of his deep wound,
In slumber soft, and on the ground
Sadly sits the Assyrian queen.
But far above, in spangled sheen,
Celestial Cupid, her famed son, advanced
Holds his dear Psyche, sweet entranced
After her wandering labours long,
Till free consent the gods among
Make her his eternal bride,
And from her fair unspotted side
Two blissful twins are to be born,
Youth and Joy; so Jove hath sworn.

   But now my task is smoothly done:
I can fly, or I can run
Quickly to the green earth's end,
Where the bowed welkin slow doth bend,
And from thence can soar as soon
To the corners of the moon.
Mortals, that would follow me,
Love Virtue; she alone is free.
She can teach ye how to climb
Higher than the sphery chime;
Or, if Virtue feeble were,
Heaven itself would stoop to her.

LYCIDAS.

IN THIS MONODY THE AUTHOR BEWAILS A LEARNED FRIEND, UNFOR-
TUNATELY DROWNED IN HIS PASSAGE FROM CHESTER ON THE IRISH
SEAS, 1637; AND, BY OCCASION, FORETELLS THE RUIN OF OUR
CORRUPTED CLERGY, THEN IN THEIR HEIGHT.

YET once more, O ye laurels, and once more,
Ye myrtles brown, with ivy never sere,
I come to pluck your berries harsh and crude,
And with forced fingers rude
Shatter your leaves before the mellowing year.
Bitter constraint and sad occasion dear
Compels me to disturb your season due;
For Lycidas is dead, dead ere his prime,
Young Lycidas, and hath not left his peer.
Who would not sing for Lycidas? he knew
Himself to sing, and build the lofty rhyme.
He must not float upon his watery bier
Unwept, and welter to the parching wind,
Without the meed of some melodious tear.
 Begin, then, Sisters of the sacred well
That from beneath the seat of Jove doth spring;
Begin, and somewhat loudly sweep the string.
Hence with denial vain and coy excuse:
So may some gentle Muse
With lucky words favour *my* destined urn,
And as he passes turn,
And bid fair peace be to my sable shroud!
 For we were nursed upon the self-same hill,
Fed the same flock, by fountain, shade, and rill;
Together both, ere the high lawns appeared
Under the opening eyelids of the Morn,
We drove a-field, and both together heard
What time the grey-fly winds her sultry horn,
Battening our flocks with the fresh dews of night,
Oft till the star that rose at evening bright
Toward heaven's descent had sloped his westering wheel.
Meanwhile the rural ditties were not mute;
Tempered to the oaten flute
Rough Satyrs danced, and Fauns with cloven heel
From the glad sound would not be absent long;
And old Damœtas loved to hear our song.
 But, oh! the heavy change, now thou art gone,
Now thou art gone and never must return!
350

Thee, Shepherd, thee the woods and desert caves,
With wild thyme and the gadding vine o'ergrown,
And all their echoes, mourn.
The willows, and the hazel copses green,
Shall now no more be seen
Fanning their joyous leaves to thy soft lays.
As killing as the canker to the rose,
Or taint-worm to the weanling herds that graze,
Or frost to flowers, that their gay wardrobe wear,
When first the white-thorn blows;
Such, Lycidas, thy loss to shepherd's ear.
   Where were ye, Nymphs, when the remorseless deep
Closed o'er the head of your loved Lycidas?
For neither were ye playing on the steep
Where your old bards, the famous Druids, lie,
Nor on the shaggy top of Mona high,
Nor yet where Deva spreads her wizard stream.
Ay me! I fondly dream
"Had ye been there," . . . for what could that have done?
What could the Muse herself that Orpheus bore,
The Muse herself, for her enchanting son,
Whom universal nature did lament,
When, by the rout that made the hideous roar,
His gory visage down the stream was sent,
Down the swift Hebrus to the Lesbian shore?
   Alas! what boots it with incessant care
To tend the homely, slighted, shepherd's trade,
And strictly meditate the thankless Muse?
Were it not better done, as others use,
To sport with Amaryllis in the shade,
Or with the tangles of Neæra's hair?
Fame is the spur that the clear spirit doth raise
(That last infirmity of noble mind)
To scorn delights and live laborious days;
But the fair guerdon when we hope to find,
And think to burst out into sudden blaze,
Comes the blind Fury with the abhorred shears,
And slits the thin-spun life. "But not the praise,"
Phœbus replied, and touched my trembling ears:
"Fame is no plant that grows on mortal soil,
Nor in the glistering foil
Set off to the world, nor in broad rumour lies,
But lives and spreads aloft by those pure eyes
And perfect witness of all-judging Jove;
As he pronounces lastly on each deed,
Of so much fame in Heaven expect thy meed."
   O fountain Arethuse, and thou honoured flood,
Smooth-sliding Mincius, crowned with vocal reeds,
That strain I heard was of a higher mood.
But now my oat proceeds,
And listens to the Herald of the Sea,
That came in Neptune's plea.
He asked the waves, and asked the felon winds,
What hard mishap hath doomed this gentle swain?

And questioned every gust of rugged wings
That blows from off each beaked promontory.
They knew not of his story;
And sage Hippotades their answer brings,
That not a blast was from his dungeon strayed:
The air was calm, and on the level brine
Sleek Panope with all her sisters played.
It was that fatal and perfidious bark,
Built in the eclipse, and rigged with curses dark,
That sunk so low that sacred head of thine.

Next, Camus, reverend sire, went footing slow,
His mantle hairy, and his bonnet sedge,
Inwrought with figures dim, and on the edge
Like to that sanguine flower inscribed with woe.
"Ah! who hath reft," quoth he, "my dearest pledge?"
Last came, and last did go,
The Pilot of the Galilean Lake;
Two massy keys he bore of metals twain
(The golden opes, the iron shuts amain).
He shook his mitred locks, and stern bespake :—
"How well could I have spared for thee, young swain,
Enow of such as, for their bellies' sake,
Creep, and intrude, and climb into the fold!
Of other care they little reckoning make
Than how to scramble at the shearers' feast,
And shove away the worthy bidden guest.
Blind mouths! that scarce themselves know how to hold
A sheep-hook, or have learnt aught else the least
That to the faithful herdsman's art belongs!
What recks it them? What need they? They are sped;
And, when they list, their lean and flashy songs
Grate on their scrannel pipes of wretched straw;
The hungry sheep look up, and are not fed,
But, swoln with wind and the rank mist they draw,
Rot inwardly, and foul contagion spread;
Besides what the grim wolf with privy paw
Daily devours apace, and nothing said.
But that two-handed engine at the door
Stands ready to smite once, and smite no more."

Return, Alpheus; the dread voice is past
That shrunk thy streams; return, Sicilian Muse,
And call the vales, and bid them hither cast
Their bells and flowerets of a thousand hues.
Ye valleys low, where the mild whispers use
Of shades, and wanton winds, and gushing brooks,
On whose fresh lap the swart star sparely looks,
Throw hither all your quaint enamelled eyes,
That on the green turf suck the honeyed showers,
And purple all the ground with vernal flowers.
Bring the rathe primrose that forsaken dies,
The tufted crow-toe, and pale jessamine,
The white pink, and the pansy freaked with jet,
The glowing violet,
The musk-rose, and the well-attired woodbine,

With cowslips wan that hang the pensive head,
And every flower that sad embroidery wears;
Bid amaranthus all his beauty shed,
And daffadillies fill their cups with tears,
To strew the laureate hearse where Lycid lies.
For so, to interpose a little ease,
Let our frail thoughts dally with false surmise.
Ay me! whilst thee the shores and sounding seas
Wash far away, where'er thy bones are hurled;
Whether beyond the stormy Hebrides,
Where thou perhaps under the whelming tide
Visit'st the bottom of the monstrous world;
Or whether thou, to our moist vows denied,
Sleep'st by the fable of Bellerus old,
Where the great Vision of the guarded mount
Looks toward Namancos and Bayona's hold.
Look homeward, Angel, now, and melt with ruth:
And, O ye dolphins, waft the hapless youth.

    Weep no more, woeful shepherds, weep no more,
For Lycidas, your sorrow, is not dead,
Sunk though he be beneath the watery floor.
So sinks the day-star in the ocean bed,
And yet anon repairs his drooping head,
And tricks his beams, and with new-spangled ore
Flames in the forehead of the morning sky:
So Lycidas sunk low, but mounted high,
Through the dear might of Him that walked the waves,
Where, other groves and other streams along,
With nectar pure his oozy locks he laves,
And hears the unexpressive nuptial song,
In the blest kingdoms meek of joy and love.
There entertain him all the Saints above,
In solemn troops, and sweet societies,
That sing, and singing in their glory move,
And wipe the tears for ever from his eyes.
Now, Lycidas, the shepherds weep no more;
Henceforth thou art the Genius of the shore,
In thy large recompense, and shalt be good
To all that wander in that perilous flood.

    Thus sang the uncouth swain to the oaks and rills,
While the still morn went out with sandals grey:
He touched the tender stops of various quills,
With eager thought warbling his Doric lay:
And now the sun had stretched out all the hills,
And now was dropt into the western bay.
At last he rose, and twitched his mantle blue:
To-morrow to fresh woods, and pastures new.

SONNETS.

I.

TO THE NIGHTINGALE.

O Nightingale that on yon bloomy spray
    Warblest at eve, when all the woods are still,
    Thou with fresh hope the lover's heart dost fill,
    While the jolly hours lead on propitious May.
Thy liquid notes that close the eye of day,
    First heard before the shallow cuckoo's bill,
    Portend success in love.   Oh, if Jove's will
    Have linked that amorous power to thy soft lay,
Now timely sing, ere the rude bird of hate
    Foretell my hopeless doom, in some grove nigh;
    As thou from year to year hast sung too late
For my relief, yet hadst no reason why.
    Whether the Muse or Love call thee his mate,
    Both them I serve, and of their train am I.

II.

ON HIS BEING ARRIVED TO THE AGE OF TWENTY-THREE.

How soon hath Time, the subtle thief of youth,
    Stolen on his wing my three-and-twentieth year!
    My hasting days fly on with full career,
    But my late spring no bud or blossom shew'th.
Perhaps my semblance might deceive the truth
    That I to manhood am arrived so near;
    And inward ripeness doth much less appear,
    That some more timely-happy spirits endu'th.
Yet, be it less or more, or soon or slow,
    It shall be still in strictest measure even
    To that same lot, however mean or high,
Toward which Time leads me, and the will of Heaven.
    All is, if I have grace to use it so,
    As ever in my great Task-Master's eye.

III.

Donna leggiadra, il cui bel nome onora
    L' erbosa val di Reno e il nobil varco,
    Bene è colui d' ogni valore scarco
    Qual tuo spirto gentil non innamora,
    Che dolcemente mostrasi di fuora,

354

De' sui atti soavi giammai parco,
    E i don', che son d' amor saette ed arco,
    Là onde l' alta tua virtù s' infiora.
Quando tu vaga parli, o lieta canti,
    Che mover possa duro alpestre legno,
    Guardi ciascun agli occhi ed agli orecchi
L' entrata chi di te si truova indegno ;
    Grazia sola di sù gli vaglia, innanti
    Che 'l disio amoroso al cuor s' invecchi.

IV.

QUAL in colle aspro, all' imbrunir di sera,
    L' avezza giovinetta pastorella
    Va bagnando l' erbetta strana e bella
    Che mal si spande a disusata spera
Fuor di sua natia alma primavera,
    Così Amor meco insù la lingua snella
    Desta il fior novo di strania favella,
    Mentre io di te, vezzosamente altera,
Canto, dal mio buon popol non inteso,
    E 'l bel Tamigi cangio col bell' Arno.
    Amor lo volse, ed io all' altrui peso
Seppi ch' Amor cosa mai volse indarno.
    Deh ! foss' il mio cuor lento e 'l duro seno
    A chi pianta dal ciel si buon terreno.

CANZONE.

RIDONSI donne e giovani amorosi
M' accostandosi attorno, e ' Perchè scrivi,
Perchè tu scrivi in lingua ignota e strana
Verseggiando d' amor, e come t' osi ?
Dinne, se la tua speme sia mai vana,
E de' pensieri lo miglior t' arrivi !'
Così mi van burlando : 'altri rivi,
Altri lidi t' aspettan, ed altre onde,
Nelle cui verdi sponde
Spuntati ad or ad or alla tua chioma
L' immortal guiderdon d' eterne frondi.
Perchè alle spalle tue soverchia soma ?'
    Canzon, dirotti, e tu per me rispondi :
' Dice mia Donna, e 'l suo dir è il mio cuore,
"Questa è lingua di cui si vanta Amore."'

V.

DIODATI (e te 'l dirò con maraviglia),
    Quel ritroso io, ch' amor spreggiar solea
    E de' suoi lacci spesso mi ridea,
    Già caddi, ov' uom dabben talor s' impiglia.
Nè treccie d' oro nè guancia vermiglia
    M' abbaglian sì, ma sotto nova idea
    Pellegrina bellezza che 'l cuor bea,
    Portamenti alti onesti, e nelle ciglia
Quel sereno fulgor d' amabil nero,
    Parole adorne di lingua più d' una,

E 'l cantar che di mezzo l' emispero
Traviar ben può la faticosa Luna;
   E degli occhi suoi avventa sì gran fuoco
   Che l' incerar gli orecchi mi fia poco.

VI.

PER certo i bei vostr' occhi, Donna mia,
   Esser non può che non sian lo mio sole ;
   Sì mi percuoton forte, come ei suole
   Per l' arene di Libia chi s' invia,
Mentre un caldo vapor (nè sentì pria)
   Da quel lato si spinge ove mi duole,
   Che forse amanti nelle lor parole
   Chiaman sospir; io non so che si sia.
Parte rinchiusa e turbida si cela
   Scossomi il petto, e poi n' uscendo poco
   Quivi d' attorno o s' agghiaccia o s' ingiela ;
Ma quanto agli occhi giunge a trovar loco
   Tutte le notti a me suol far piovose,
   Finchè mia alba rivien colma di rose.

VII.

GIOVANE, piano, e semplicetto amante,
   Poichè fuggir me stesso in dubbio sono,
   Madonna, a voi del mio cuor l' umil dono
   Farò divoto.   Io certo a prove tante
L' ebbi fedele, intrepido, costante,
   Di pensieri leggiadro, accorto, e buono.
   Quando rugge il gran mondo, e scocca il tuono,
   S' arma di se, e d' intero diamante,
Tanto del forse e d' invidia sicuro,
   Di timori, e speranze al popol use,
   Quanto d' ingegno e d' alto valor vago,
E di cetra sonora, e delle Muse.
   Sol troverete in tal parte men duro
   Ove Amor mise l' insanabil ago.

VIII.

WHEN THE ASSAULT WAS INTENDED TO THE CITY.

CAPTAIN, or Colonel, or Knight in Arms,
   Whose chance on these defenceless doors may seize,
   If deed of honour did thee ever please,
   Guard them, and him within protect from harms.
He can requite thee; for he knows the charms
   That call fame on such gentle acts as these,
   And he can spread thy name o'er lands and seas,
   Whatever clime the sun's bright circle warms.
Lift not thy spear against the Muses' bower:
   The great Emathian conqueror bid spare
   The house of Pindarus, when temple and tower
Went to the ground; and the repeated air
   Of sad Electra's poet had the power
   To save the Athenian walls from ruin bare.

IX.

TO A VIRTUOUS YOUNG LADY.

LADY, that in the prime of earliest youth
    Wisely hast shunned the broad way and the green,
    And with those few art eminently seen
    That labour up the hill of heavenly Truth,
The better part with Mary and with Ruth
    Chosen thou hast; and they that overween,
    And at thy growing virtues fret their spleen,
    No anger find in thee, but pity and ruth.
Thy care is fixed, and zealously attends
    To fill thy odorous lamp with deeds of light,
    And hope that reaps not shame. Therefore be sure
Thou, when the Bridegroom with his feastful friends
    Passes to bliss at the mid-hour of night,
    Hast gained thy entrance, Virgin wise and pure.

X.

TO THE LADY MARGARET LEY.

DAUGHTER to that good Earl, once President
    Of England's Council and her Treasury,
    Who lived in both unstained with gold or fee,
    And left them both, more in himself content,
Till the sad breaking of that Parliament
    Broke him, as that dishonest victory
    At Chæronea, fatal to liberty,
    Killed with report that old man eloquent,
Though later born than to have known the days
    Wherein your father flourished, yet by you,
    Madam, methinks I see him living yet:
So well your words his noble virtues praise
    That all both judge you to relate them true
    And to possess them, honoured Margaret.

XI.

ON THE DETRACTION WHICH FOLLOWED UPON MY WRITING CERTAIN TREATISES.

A BOOK was writ of late called *Tetrachordon*,
    And woven close, both matter, form, and style;
    The subject new: it walked the town a while,
    Numbering good intellects; now seldom pored on.
Cries the stall-reader, "Bless us! what a word on
    A title-page is this!": and some in file
    Stand spelling false, while one might walk to Mile-
    End Green. Why, is it harder, sirs, than *Gordon*,
Colkitto, or *Macdonnel*, or *Galasp?*
    Those rugged names to our like mouths grow sleek
    That would have made Quintilian stare and gasp.
Thy age, like ours, O soul of Sir John Cheek,
    Hated not learning worse than toad or asp,
    When thou taught'st Cambridge and King Edward Greek

357

XII.

ON THE SAME.

I DID but prompt the age to quit their clogs
　　By the known rules of ancient liberty,
　　When straight a barbarous noise environs me
　　Of owls and cuckoos, asses, apes, and dogs;
As when those hinds that were transformed to frogs
　　Railed at Latona's twin-born progeny,
　　Which after held the Sun and Moon in fee.
　　But this is got by casting pearl to hogs,
That bawl for freedom in their senseless mood,
　　And still revolt when Truth would set them free.
　　Licence they mean when they cry Liberty;
For who loves that must first be wise and good:
　　But from that mark how far they rove we see,
　　For all this waste of wealth and loss of blood.

ON THE NEW FORCERS OF CONSCIENCE UNDER THE LONG
PARLIAMENT.

BECAUSE you have thrown off your Prelate Lord,
　　And with stiff vows renounced his Liturgy,
　　To seize the widowed whore Plurality
　　From them whose sin ye envied, not abhorred,
Dare ye for this adjure the civil sword
　　To force our consciences that Christ set free,
　　And ride us with a Classic Hierarchy,
　　Taught ye by mere A. S. and Rutherford?
Men whose life, learning, faith, and pure intent,
　　Would have been held in high esteem with Paul
　　Must now be named and printed heretics
By shallow Edwards and Scotch What-d'ye-call!
　　But we do hope to find out all your tricks,
　　Your plots and packing, worse than those of Trent,
　　　　That so the Parliament
May with their wholesome and preventive shears
Clip your phylacteries, though baulk your ears,
　　　　And succour our just fears,
When they shall read this clearly in your charge:
New *Presbyter* is but old *Priest* writ large.

XIII.

TO MR. H. LAWES ON HIS AIRS.

HARRY, whose tuneful and well-measured song
　　First taught our English music how to span
　　Words with just note and accent, not to scan
　　With Midas' ears, committing short and long,
Thy worth and skill exempts thee from the throng,
　　With praise enough for Envy to look wan;
　　To after age thou shalt be writ the man
　　That with smooth air couldst humour best our tongue.
Thou honour'st Verse, and Verse must send her wing
　　To honour thee, the priest of Phœbus' quire,

That tunest their happiest lines in hymn or story.
Dante shall give Fame leave to set thee higher
Than his Casella, whom he wooed to sing,
Met in the milder shades of Purgatory.

XIV.

ON THE RELIGIOUS MEMORY OF MRS. CATHERINE THOMSON,
MY CHRISTIAN FRIEND, DECEASED DEC. 16, 1646.

WHEN Faith and Love, which parted from thee never,
Had ripened thy just soul to dwell with God,
Meekly thou didst resign this earthly load
Of death, called life, which us from life doth sever.
Thy works and alms, and all thy good endeavour,
Stayed not behind, nor in the grave were trod;
But, as Faith pointed with her golden rod,
Followed thee up to joy and bliss for ever.
Love led them on; and Faith, who knew them best
Thy handmaids, clad them o'er with purple beams
And azure wings, that up they flew so drest,
And speak the truth of thee on glorious themes
Before the Judge; who thenceforth bid thee rest,
And drink thy fill of pure immortal streams.

XV.

ON THE LORD GENERAL FAIRFAX, AT THE SIEGE
OF COLCHESTER.

FAIRFAX, whose name in arms through Europe rings,
Filling each mouth with envy or with praise,
And all her jealous monarchs with amaze,
And rumours loud that daunt remotest kings,
Thy firm unshaken virtue ever brings
Victory home, though new rebellions raise
Their Hydra heads, and the false North displays
Her broken league to imp their serpent wings.
O yet a nobler task awaits thy hand
(For what can war but endless war still breed?)
Till truth and right from violence be freed,
And public faith cleared from the shameful brand
Of public fraud. In vain doth Valour bleed,
While Avarice and Rapine share the land.

XVI.

TO THE LORD GENERAL CROMWELL, MAY 1652,

ON THE PROPOSALS OF CERTAIN MINISTERS AT THE COMMITTEE
FOR PROPAGATION OF THE GOSPEL.

CROMWELL, our chief of men, who through a cloud
Not of war only, but detractions rude,
Guided by faith and matchless fortitude,
To peace and truth thy glorious way hast ploughed,
And on the neck of crowned Fortune proud
Hast reared God's trophies, and his work pursued,
While Darwen stream, with blood of Scots imbrued,

And Dunbar field, resounds thy praises loud,
And Worcester's laureate wreath : yet much remains
   To conquer still; Peace hath her victories
   No less renowned than War; new foes arise,
Threatening to bind our souls with secular chains.
   Help us to save free conscience from the paw
   Of hireling wolves, whose Gospel is their maw.

XVII.
TO SIR HENRY VANE THE YOUNGER.

VANE, young in years, but in sage counsel old,
   Than whom a better senator ne'er held
   The helm of Rome, when gowns, not arms, repelled
   The fierce Epirot and the African bold,
Whether to settle peace, or to unfold
   The drift of hollow states hard to be spelled;
   Then to advise how war may best, upheld,
   Move by her two main nerves, iron and gold,
In all her equipage; besides, to know
   Both spiritual power and civil, what each means,
   What severs each, thou hast learned, which few have done.
The bounds of either sword to thee we owe:
   Therefore on thy firm hand Religion leans
   In peace, and reckons thee her eldest son.

XVIII.
ON THE LATE MASSACRE IN PIEDMONT.

AVENGE, O Lord, thy slaughtered saints, whose bones
   Lie scattered on the Alpine mountains cold;
   Even them who kept Thy truth so pure of old,
   When all our fathers worshipped stocks and stones,
Forget not: in Thy book record their groans
   Who were Thy sheep, and in their ancient fold
   Slain by the bloody Piemontese, that rolled
   Mother with infant down the rocks. Their moans
The vales redoubled to the hills, and they
   To heaven. Their martyred blood and ashes sow
   O'er all the Italian fields, where still doth sway
The triple Tyrant; that from these may grow
   A hundredfold, who, having learnt Thy way,
   Early may fly the Babylonian woe.

XIX.
ON HIS BLINDNESS.

WHEN I consider how my light is spent
   Ere half my days in this dark world and wide,
   And that one talent which is death to hide
   Lodged with me useless, though my soul more bent
To serve therewith my Maker, and present
   My true account, lest He returning chide,
   "Doth God exact day-labour, light denied?"
   I fondly ask. But Patience, to prevent

SONNETS

That murmur, soon replies, "God doth not need
    Either man's work or his own gifts. Who best
    Bear His mild yoke, they serve Him best. His state
Is kingly : thousands at His bidding speed,
    And post o'er land and ocean without rest;
    They also serve who only stand and wait."

XX.

TO MR. LAWRENCE.

LAWRENCE, of virtuous father virtuous son,
    Now that the fields are dank, and ways are mire,
    Where shall we sometimes meet, and by the fire
    Help waste a sullen day, what may be won
From the hard season gaining? Time will run
    On smoother, till Favonius reinspire
    The frozen earth, and clothe in fresh attire
    The lily and rose, that neither sowed nor spun.
What neat repast shall feast us, light and choice,
    Of Attic taste, with wine, whence we may rise
    To hear the lute well touched, or artful voice
Warble immortal notes and Tuscan air?
    He who of those delights can judge, and spare
    To interpose them oft, is not unwise.

XXI.

TO CYRIACK SKINNER.

CYRIACK, whose grandsire on the royal bench
    Of British Themis, with no mean applause,
    Pronounced, and in his volumes taught, our laws,
    Which others at their bar so often wrench,
To-day deep thoughts resolve with me to drench
    In mirth that after no repenting draws;
    Let Euclid rest, and Archimedes pause,
    And what the Swede intend, and what the French.
To measure life learn thou betimes, and know
    Toward solid good what leads the nearest way;
    For other things mild Heaven a time ordains,
And disapproves that care, though wise in show,
    That with superfluous burden loads the day,
    And, when God sends a cheerful hour, refrains.

XXII.

TO THE SAME.

CYRIACK, this three years' day, these eyes, though clear,
    To outward view, of blemish or of spot,
    Bereft of light, their seeing hath forgot;
    Nor to their idle orbs doth sight appear
Of sun, or moon, or star throughout the year,
    Or man, or woman. Yet I argue not
    Against Heaven's hand or will, nor bate a jot
    Of heart or hope, but still bear up and steer
Right onward. What supports me, dost thou ask?

361

The conscience, friend, to have lost them overplied
    In Liberty's defence, my noble task,
Of which all Europe rings from side to side.
    This thought might lead me through the world's vain mask
    Content, though blind, had I no better guide.

XXIII.

ON HIS DECEASED WIFE.

METHOUGHT I saw my late espoused saint
    Brought to me like Alcestis from the grave,
    Whom Jove's great son to her glad husband gave,
    Rescued from Death by force, though pale and faint.
Mine, as whom washed from spot of child-bed taint,
    Purification in the Old Law did save,
    And such as yet once more I trust to have
    Full sight of her in Heaven without restraint,
Came vested all in white, pure as her mind.
    Her face was veiled; yet to my fancied sight
    Love, sweetness, goodness, in her person shined
So clear as in no face with more delight.
    But, oh! as to embrace me she inclined,
    I waked, she fled, and day brought back my night.

TRANSLATIONS.

THE FIFTH ODE OF HORACE, LIB. I.,

Quis multâ gracilis te puer in rosâ.

Rendered almost word for word, without rhyme, according to
the Latin measure, as near as the language will permit.

WHAT slender youth, bedewed with liquid odours,
Courts thee on roses in some pleasant cave,
 Pyrrha? For whom bind'st thou
  In wreaths thy golden hair,
Plain in thy neatness? Oh, how oft shall he
On faith and changed gods complain, and seas
 Rough with black winds and storms
  Unwonted shall admire,
Who now enjoys thee credulous, all gold;
Who always vacant, always amiable,
 Hopes thee, of flattering gales
  Unmindful! Hapless they
To whom thou untried seem'st fair! Me, in my vowed
Picture, the sacred wall declares to have hung
 My dank and dropping weeds
  To the stern God of Sea.

Nine of the Psalms done into Metre; wherein all, but what is
in a different character, are the very words of the Text,
translated from the original.

PSALM LXXX.

April, 1648.—J. M.

1 THOU Shepherd that dost Israel *keep*,
  Give ear *in time of need*,
 Who leadest like a flock of sheep
  Thy loved Joseph's seed,
 Thou sitt'st between the Cherubs *bright*,
  Between their wings outspread;
 Shine forth, *and from Thy cloud give light*,
  And on our foes Thy dread.
2 In Ephraim's view and Benjamin's,
  And in Manasseh's sight,
 Awake Thy strength, come, and *be seen*
  To save us *by Thy might.*
3 Turn us again; *Thy grace divine*
  To us, O God, *vouchsafe*;

Cause Thou Thy face on us to shine,
  And then we shall be safe.
4 Lord God of Hosts, how long wilt Thou,
  How long wilt Thou declare,
Thy smoking wrath, *and angry brow,*
  Against Thy people's prayer?
5 Thou feed'st them with the bread of tears;
  Their bread with tears they eat;
And mak'st them largely drink the tears
  Wherewith their cheeks are wet.
6 A strife Thou mak'st us *and a prey*
  To every neighbour foe;
Among themselves they laugh, they play,
  And flouts at us they throw.
7 Return us, *and Thy grace divine,*
  O God of Hosts, *vouchsafe;*
Cause Thou Thy face on us to shine,
  And then we shall be safe.
8 A Vine from Egypt Thou hast brought,
  Thy free love made it Thine,
And drov'st out nations *proud and haut,*
  To plant this *lovely* Vine.
9 Thou didst prepare for it a place,
  And root it deep and fast,
That it *began to grow apace,*
  And filled the land *at last.*
10 With her *green* shade that covered *all*
  The hills were *overspread;*
Her boughs as *high as* cedars tall
  Advanced their lofty head.
11 Her branches *on the western side*
  Down to the sea she sent,
And *upward* to that river *wide*
  Her other branches *went.*
12 Why hast Thou laid her hedges low,
  And broken down her fence,
That all may pluck her, as they go,
  With rudest violence?
13 The *tusked* boar out of the wood
  Upturns it by the roots;
Wild beasts there browse, and make their food
  Her grapes and tender shoots.
14 Return now, God of Hosts; look down
  From Heaven, Thy seat divine;
Behold *us, but without a frown,*
  And visit this *Thy* Vine.
15 Visit this Vine, which Thy right hand
  Hath set, and planted *long,*
And the young branch that for Thyself
  Thou hast made firm and strong.
16 But now it is consumed with fire,
  And cut *with axes* down;
They perish at Thy dreadful ire,
  At Thy rebuke and frown.

17 Upon the Man of Thy right hand
    Let Thy *good* hand be *laid;*
  Upon the Son of Man, whom Thou
    Strong for Thyself hast made.
18 So shall we not go back from Thee
    To ways of sin and shame:
  Quicken us, Thou; then *gladly* we
    Shall call upon Thy Name.
19 Return us, *and Thy grace divine,*
    Lord God of Hosts, *vouchsafe:*
  Cause Thou Thy face on us to shine,
    And then we shall be safe.

PSALM LXXXI.

1 To God our strength sing loud *and clear;*
    Sing loud to God *our King;*
  To Jacob's God, *that all may hear,*
    Loud acclamations ring.
2 Prepare a hymn, prepare a song;
    The timbrel hither bring;
  The *cheerful* psaltery bring along,
    And harp *with* pleasant *string.*
3 Blow, *as is wont,* in the new moon,
    With trumpets' *lofty sound,*
  The appointed time, the day whereon
    Our solemn feast *comes round.*
4 This was a statute *given of old*
    For Israel *to observe,*
  A law of Jacob's God *to hold,*
    From whence they might not swerve.
5 This He a testimony ordained
    In Joseph, *not to change,*
  When as he passed through Egypt-land,
    The tongue I heard was strange.
6 From burden, *and from slavish toil,*
    I set his shoulder free;
  His hands from pots, *and miry soil,*
    Delivered were *by Me.*
7 When trouble did thee sore assail,
    On Me then didst thou call,
  And I to free thee *did not fail,*
    And led thee out of thrall.
  I answered thee in thunder deep,
    With clouds encompassed round;
  I tried thee at the water *steep*
    Of Meriba *renowned.*
8 Hear, O My people, *hearken well:*
    I testify to thee,
  Thou ancient stock of Israel,
    If thou wilt list to Me:
9 Throughout the land of thy abode
    No alien God shall be,

Nor shalt thou to a foreign god
  In honour bend thy knee.
10 I am the Lord thy God, which brought
    Thee out of Egypt-land;
  Ask large enough, and I, *besought,*
    Will grant thy full demand.
11 And yet My people would not *hear,*
    Nor hearken to My voice;
  And Israel, *whom I loved so dear,*
    Misliked Me for his choice.
12 Then did I leave them to their will,
    And to their wandering mind;
  Their own conceits they followed still—
    Their own devices blind.
13 Oh, that My people would *be wise,*
    To serve Me *all their days!*
  And oh, that Israel would *advise*
    To walk My *righteous* ways!
14 Then would I soon bring down their foes,
    That now so proudly rise,
  And turn My hand against *all those*
    That are their enemies.
15 Who hate the Lord should *then be fain*
    To bow to Him and bend;
  But *they, His people, should remain;*
    Their time should have no end.
16 And He would feed them *from the shock*
    With flour of finest wheat,
  And satisfy them from the rock
    With honey *for their meat.*

PSALM LXXXII.

1 GOD in the great assembly stands
    Of kings and lordly states;
  Among the gods on both His hands
    He judges and debates.
2 How long will ye pervert the right
    With judgment false and wrong,
  Favouring the wicked *by your might,*
    Who thence grow bold and strong?
3 Regard the weak and fatherless;
    Despatch the poor man's cause;
  And raise the man in deep distress
    By just and equal laws.
4 Defend the poor and desolate,
    And rescue from the hands
  Of wicked men the low estate
    Of him *that help demands.*
5 They know not, nor will understand;
    In darkness they walk on;
  The earth's foundations all are moved,
    And out of order gone.

6 I said that ye were gods, yea, all
    The sons of God Most High;
7 But ye shall die like men, and fall
    As other princes *die.*
8 Rise, God; judge Thou the earth in might;
    This *wicked* earth redress:
    For Thou art He who shalt by right
    The nations all possess.

PSALM LXXXIII.

1 BE not Thou silent *now at length;*
    O God, hold not Thy peace:
    Sit Thou not still, O God *of strength;*
    We cry and do not cease.
2 For lo! Thy *furious* foes *now* swell,
    And storm outrageously;
    And they that hate Thee, *proud and fell,*
    Exalt their heads full high.
3 Against Thy people they contrive
    Their plots and counsels deep;
    Them to ensnare they chiefly strive
    Whom Thou dost hide and keep.
4 "Come, let us cut them off," say they,
    "Till they no nation be;
    That Israel's name for ever may
    Be lost in memory."
5 For they consult with all their might,
    And all as one in mind
    Themselves against Thee they unite,
    And in firm union bind.
6 The tents of Edom, and the brood
    Of *scornful* Ishmael,
    Moab, with them of Hagar's blood,
    That in the desert dwell,
7 Gebal and Ammon *there conspire,*
    And *hateful* Amalec,
    The Philistines, and they of Tyre,
    Whose bounds the sea doth check.
8 With them *great* Ashur also bands,
    And doth confirm the knot:
    All these have lent their armed hands
    To aid the sons of Lot.
9 Do to them as to Midian *bold,*
    That wasted all the coast;
    To Sisera, and as *is told*
    Thou didst to Jabin's *host,*
    When at the brook of Kishon *old*
    They were repulsed and slain,
10 At Endor quite cut off, and rolled
    As dung upon the plain.
11 As Zeb and Oreb evil sped,
    So let their princes speed;

As Zeba and Zalmunna *bled,*
    So let their princes *bleed.*
12 *For they amidst their pride* have said,
    "By right now shall we seize
God's houses, and *will now invade*
    Their stately palaces."
13 My God, oh, make them as a wheel;
    No quiet let them find;
Giddy and *restless* let *them reel,*
    Like stubble from the wind.
14 *As, when* an *aged* wood takes fire
    Which on a sudden strays,
The *greedy* flame runs higher and higher,
    Till all the mountains blaze;
15 So with Thy whirlwind them pursue,
    And with Thy tempest chase;
16 And till they yield Thee honour due,
    Lord, fill with shame their face.
17 Ashamed and troubled let them be,
    Troubled and shamed for ever,
Ever confounded, and so die
    With shame, *and scape it never.*
18 Then shall they know that Thou, whose name
    Jehovah is, alone
Art the Most High, *and Thou the same*
    O'er all the earth *art One.*

PSALM LXXXIV.

1 How lovely are Thy dwellings fair!
    O Lord of Hosts, how dear
The *pleasant* tabernacles are
    Where Thou dost dwell so near!
2 My soul doth long and almost die
    Thy courts, O Lord, to see;
My heart and flesh aloud do cry,
    O living God, for Thee.
3 There even the sparrow, *freed from wrong,*
    Hath found a house of *rest;*
The swallow there, to lay her young,
    Hath built her *brooding* nest;
Even *by* Thy altars, Lord of Hosts,
    They find their safe abode;
And home they fly from round the coasts
    Toward Thee, my King, my God,
4 Happy who in Thy house reside,
    Where Thee they ever praise!
5 Happy whose strength in Thee doth bide,
    And in their hearts Thy ways!
6 They pass through Baca's *thirsty* vale,
    That dry and barren ground,
As through a fruitful watery dale
    Where springs and showers abound.

7 They journey on from strength to strength
   With joy and gladsome cheer,
Till all before *our* God *at length*
   In Sion do appear.
8 Lord God of Hosts, hear *now* my prayer,
   O Jacob's God, give ear;
9 Thou, God, our shield, look on the face
   Of Thy anointed *dear.*
10 For one day in Thy courts *to be*
   Is better *and more blest*
Than *in the joys of vanity*
   A thousand days *at best.*
I in the temple of my God
   Had rather keep a door
Than dwell in tents *and rich abode*
   With sin *for evermore.*
11 For God, the Lord, both sun and shield,
   Gives grace and glory *bright;*
No good from them shall be withheld
   Whose ways are just and right.
12 Lord *God* of Hosts *that reign'st on high,*
   That man is *truly* blest
Who *only* on Thee doth rely,
   And in Thee only rest.

PSALM LXXXV.

1 THY land to favour graciously
   Thou hast not, Lord, been slack;
Thou hast from *hard* captivity
   Returned Jacob back.
2 The iniquity Thou didst forgive
   That wrought Thy people woe,
And all their sin *that did Thee grieve*
   Hast hid *where none shall know.*
3 Thine anger all Thou hadst removed,
   And *calmly* didst return
From Thy fierce wrath, which we had proved
   Far worse than fire to burn.
4 God of our saving health and peace,
   Turn us, and us restore;
Thine indignation cause to cease
   Toward us, *and chide no more.*
5 Wilt Thou be angry without end,
   For ever angry thus?
Wilt Thou Thy frowning ire extend
   From age to age on us?
6 Wilt Thou not turn and *hear our voice,*
   And thus again revive,
That so Thy people may rejoice,
   By Thee preserved alive?
7 Cause us to see Thy goodness, Lord;
   To us Thy mercy shew;

M.—2 B

Thy saving health to us afford,
   And life in us renew.
8 *And now* what God the Lord will speak
   I will *go straight and* hear,
For to His people He speaks peace,
   And to His saints *full dear;*
To His dear saints He will speak peace:
   But let them never more
Return to folly, *but surcease*
   To trespass as before.

9 Surely to such as do Him fear
   Salvation is at hand,
And glory shall *ere long appear*
   To dwell within our land.

10 Mercy and Truth, *that long were missed,*
   Now *joyfully* are met;
Sweet Peace and Righteousness have kissed,
   And hand in hand are set.

11 Truth from the earth *like to a flower*
   Shall bud and blossom *then;*
And Justice from her heavenly bower
   Look down *on mortal men.*

12 The Lord will also then bestow
   Whatever thing is good;
Our land shall forth in plenty throw
   Her fruits *to be our food.*

13 Before Him Righteousness shall go,
   His royal harbinger:
Then will He come, and not be slow;
   His footsteps cannot err.

PSALM LXXXVI.

1 THY *gracious* ear, O Lord, incline;
   O hear me, *I thee pray;*
For I am poor, and almost pine
   With need *and sad decay.*

2 Preserve my soul; for I have trod
   Thy ways, and love the just;
Save Thou Thy servant, O my God,
   Who *still* in Thee doth trust.

3 Pity me, Lord, for daily Thee
   I call;   4 Oh make rejoice
Thy servant's soul! for, Lord, to Thee
   I lift my soul *and voice.*

5 For Thou art good; Thou, Lord, art prone
   To pardon; Thou to all
Art full of mercy, Thou *alone,*
   To them that on Thee call.

6 Unto my supplication, Lord,
   Give ear, and to the cry
Of my *incessant* prayers afford
   Thy hearing graciously.

7 I in the day of my distress
    Will call on Thee *for aid;*
  For Thou wilt *grant* me *free access,*
    And answer *what I prayed.*
8 Like Thee among the gods is none,
    O Lord; nor any works
  Of all that other gods have done
    Like to Thy *glorious* works.
9 The nations all whom Thou hast made
    Shall come, *and all shall frame*
  To bow them low before Thee, Lord,
    And glorify Thy name.
10 For great Thou art, and wonders great
    By Thy strong hand are done ;
  Thou *in Thy everlasting seat*
    Remainest God alone.
11 Teach me, O Lord, Thy way *most right;*
    I in Thy truth will bide ;
  To fear Thy name my heart unite;
    So shall it never slide.
12 Thee will I praise, O Lord my God,
    Thee honour and adore
  With my whole heart, and blaze abroad
    Thy name for evermore.
13 For great Thy mercy is toward me,
    And Thou hast freed my soul,
  Ev'n from the lowest hell set free,
    From deepest darkness foul.
14 O God, the proud against me rise,
    And violent men are met
  To seek my life, and in their eyes
    No fear of Thee have set.
15 But Thou, Lord, art the God most mild,
    Readiest Thy grace to shew,
  Slow to be angry, and *art styled*
    Most merciful, most true.
16 Oh, turn to me *Thy face at length,*
    And me have mercy on ;
  Unto Thy servant give Thy strength,
    And save Thy handmaid's son.
17 Some sign of good to me afford,
    And let my foes *then* see
  And be ashamed, because Thou, Lord,
    Dost help and comfort me.

PSALM LXXXVII.

1 AMONG the holy mountains *high*
    Is His foundation fast;
  There seated in His sanctuary,
    His temple there is placed.
2 Sion's *fair* gates the Lord loves more
    Than all the dwellings *fair*

Of Jacob's *land, though there be store,*
  And all within his care.
3 City of God, most glorious things
  Of thee *abroad* are spoke.
I mention Egypt, *where proud kings*
  Did our forefathers yoke;
4 I mention Babel to my friends,
  Philistia *full of scorn,*
And Tyre, with Ethiop's *utmost ends:*
  Lo! this man there was born.
5 But *twice that praise shall in our ear*
  Be said of Sion *last:*
This and this man was born in her;
  High God shall fix her fast.
6 The Lord shall write it in a scroll,
  That ne'er shall be out-worn;
When He the nations doth enroll,
  That this man there was born.
7 Both they who sing and they who dance
  With sacred songs are there;
In Thee *fresh brooks and soft streams glance,*
  And all my fountains *clear.*

PSALM LXXXVIII.

1 Lord God, that dost me save and keep,
  All day to Thee I cry,
And all night long before Thee *weep,*
  Before Thee *prostrate lie.*
2 Into Thy presence let my prayer,
  With sighs devout, ascend;
And to my cries that *ceaseless are,*
  Thine ear with favour bend.
3 For, cloyed with woes and trouble store,
  Surcharged my soul doth lie;
My life, *at death's uncheerful door,*
  Unto the grave draws nigh.
4 Reckoned I am with them that pass
  Down to the *dismal* pit;
I am a man but weak, alas!
  And for that name unfit,
5 From life discharged and parted quite
  Among the dead *to sleep,*
And like the slain *in bloody fight*
  That in the grave lie *deep;*
Whom Thou rememberest no more,
  Dost never more regard:
Them from Thy hand delivered o'er,
  Death's hideous house hath barred.
6 Thou, in the lowest pit *profound,*
  Hast set me *all forlorn,*
Where thickest darkness *hovers round,*
  In horrid deeps *to mourn.*

7 Thy wrath, *from which no shelter saves,*
　　Full sore doth press on me ;
　Thou break'st upon me all Thy waves,
　　And all Thy waves break me.
8 Thou dost my friends from me estrange,
　　And mak'st me odious,
　Me to them odious, *for they change,*
　　And I here pent up thus.
9 Through sorrow and affliction great
　　Mine eye grows dim and dead ;
　Lord, all the day I Thee entreat,
　　My hands to Thee I spread.
10 Wilt Thou do wonders on the dead ?
　　Shall the deceased arise
　And praise Thee *from their loathsome bed*
　　With pale and hollow eyes ?
11 Shall they Thy loving kindness tell
　　On whom the grave *hath hold ?*
　Or they *who* in perdition *dwell*
　　Thy faithfulness *unfold ?*
12 In darkness can Thy mighty *hand*
　　Or wondrous acts be known ?
　Thy justice in the *gloomy* land
　　Of *dark* oblivion ?
13 But I to Thee, O Lord, do cry
　　Ere yet my life be spent ;
　And *up to Thee* my prayer *doth hie*
　　Each morn, and Thee prevent.
14 Why wilt Thou, Lord, my soul forsake
　　And hide Thy face from me,
15 That am already bruised, and shake
　　With terror sent from Thee ;
　Bruised and afflicted, and *so low*
　　As ready to expire,
　While I Thy terrors undergo,
　　Astonished with Thine ire ?
16 Thy fierce wrath over me doth flow ;
　　Thy threatenings cut me through :
17 All day they round about me go ;
　　Like waves they me pursue.
18 Lover and friend Thou hast removed,
　　And severed from me far :
　They *fly me now* whom I have loved,
　　And as in darkness are.

PSALM I.

Done into verse 1653.

BLEST is the man who hath not walked astray
In the counsel of the wicked, and i' the way
Of sinners hath not stood, and in the seat
Of scorners hath not sat ; but in the great
Jehovah's Law is ever his delight,
And in His law he studies day and night.

373

He shall be as a tree which planted grows
By watery streams, and in his season knows
To yield his fruit; and his leaf shall not fall;
And what he takes in hand shall prosper all.
Not so the wicked : but, as chaff which fanned
The wind drives, so the wicked shall not stand
In judgment, or abide their trial then,
Nor sinners in the assembly of just men.
For the Lord knows the upright way of the just,
And the way of bad men to ruin must.

PSALM II.

Done August 8, 1653.—Terzetti.

WHY do the Gentiles tumult, and the nations
  Muse a vain thing, the kings of the earth upstand
  With power, and princes in their congregations
Lay deep their plots together through each land
  Against the Lord and His Messiah dear ?
  "Let us break off," say they, "by strength of hand,
Their bonds, and cast from us, no more to wear,
  Their twisted cords." He who in Heaven doth dwell
  Shall laugh ; the Lord shall scoff them, then severe
Speak to them in His wrath, and in His fell
  And fierce ire trouble them. "But I," saith He,
  "Anointed have My King (though ye rebel)
On Sion My holy hill." A firm decree
  I will declare : the Lord to Me hath said,
  "Thou art My Son ; I have begotten thee
This day ; ask of Me, and the grant is made :
  As Thy possession I on Thee bestow
  The Heathen, and, as thy conquest to be swayed,
Earth's utmost bounds : them shalt Thou bring full low
  With iron sceptre bruised, and them disperse
  Like to a potter's vessel shivered so."
And now be wise at length, ye kings averse ;
  Be taught, ye judges of the earth ; with fear
  Jehovah serve, and let your joy converse
With trembling ; kiss the Son, lest He appear
  In anger, and ye perish in the way,
  If once His wrath take fire, like fuel sere.
Happy all those who have in him their stay.

PSALM III.

August 9, 1653.

When he fled from Absalom.

LORD, how many are my foes !
    How many those
  That in arms against me rise !
    Many are they
  That of my life distrustfully thus say,
"No help for him in God there lies."

But thou, Lord, art my shield, my glory;
 Thee, through my story,
 The exalter of my head I count:
  Aloud I cried
 Unto Jehovah; He full soon replied,
And heard me from His holy mount.
I lay and slept; I waked again:
 For my sustain
 Was the Lord. Of many millions
  The populous rout
 I fear not, though, encamping round about,
They pitch against me their pavilions.
Rise, Lord; save me, my God! for Thou
 Hast smote ere now
 On the cheek-bone all my foes,
  Of men abhorred
 Hast broke the teeth. This help was from the Lord;
 Thy blessing on Thy people flows.

PSALM IV.

August 10, 1653.

ANSWER me when I call,
 God of my righteousness;
 In straits and in distress
 Thou didst me disenthrall
  And set at large: now spare,
Now pity me, and hear my earnest prayer.
 Great ones, how long will ye
 My glory have in scorn?
 How long be thus forborne
 Still to love vanity?
  To love, to seek, to prize
Things false and vain, and nothing else but lies?
 Yet know the Lord hath chose,
 Chose to Himself apart,
 The good and meek of heart
 (For whom to choose He knows);
  Jehovah from on high
Will hear my voice what time to Him I cry.
 Be awed, and do not sin;
 Speak to your hearts alone
 Upon your beds, each one,
 And be at peace within.
  Offer the offerings just
Of righteousness, and in Jehovah trust.
 Many there be that say
 "Who yet will show us good?"
 Talking like this world's brood;
 But, Lord, thus let me pray:
  On us lift up the light,
Lift up the favour, of Thy count'nance bright.

Into my heart more joy
And gladness Thou hast put
Than when a year of glut
Their stores doth over-cloy,
    And from their plenteous grounds
With vast increase their corn and wine abounds.
In peace at once will I
Both lay me down and sleep ;
For Thou alone dost keep
Me safe where'er I lie :
    As in a rocky cell
Thou, Lord, alone in safety mak'st me dwell.

PSALM V.

August 12, 1653.

JEHOVAH, to my words give ear,
    My meditation weigh ;
The voice of my complaining hear,
My King and God, for unto Thee I pray.
Jehovah, Thou my early voice
    Shalt in the morning hear ;
I' the morning I to Thee with choice
Will rank my prayers, and watch till Thou appear.
For Thou art not a God that takes
    In wickedness delight ;
Evil with Thee no biding makes ;
Fools or mad men stand not within Thy sight.
All workers of iniquity
    Thou hat'st ; and them unblest
Thou wilt destroy that speak a lie ;
The bloody and guileful man God doth detest.
But I will in Thy mercies dear,
    Thy numerous mercies, go
Into Thy house ; I, in Thy fear,
Will towards Thy holy temple worship low.
Lord, lead me in Thy righteousness,
    Lead me, because of those
That do observe if I transgress ;
Set Thy ways right before where my step goes.
For in his faltering mouth unstable
    No word is firm or sooth ;
Their inside, troubles miserable ;
An open grave their throat, their tongue they smooth.
God, find them guilty ; let them fall
    By their own counsels quelled ;
Push them in their rebellions all
Still on ; for against Thee they have rebelled.
Then all who trust in Thee shall bring
    Their joy, while Thou from blame
Defend'st them : they shall ever sing,
And shall triumph in Thee, who love Thy name.

For Thou, Jehovah, wilt be found
  To bless the just man still :
As with a shield Thou wilt surround
Him with Thy lasting favour and good will.

PSALM VI.

August 13, 1653.

LORD, in Thy anger do not reprehend me,
  Nor in Thy hot displeasure me correct;
  Pity me, Lord, for I am much deject,
And very weak and faint; heal and amend me:
For all my bones, that even with anguish ache,
  Are troubled ; yea, my soul is troubled sore ;
  And Thou, O Lord, how long ? Turn, Lord ; restore
My soul : oh, save me, for Thy goodness' sake !
For in death no remembrance is of Thee ;
  Who in the grave can celebrate Thy praise ?
  Wearied I am with sighing out my days ;
Nightly my couch I make a kind of sea ;
My bed I water with my tears ; mine eye
  Through grief consumes, is waxen old and dark
  I' the midst of all mine enemies that mark.
Depart, all ye that work iniquity,
Depart from me ; for the voice of my weeping
  The Lord hath heard ; the Lord hath heard my prayer ;
  My supplication with acceptance fair
The Lord will own, and have me in His keeping.
Mine enemies shall all be blank, and dashed
  With much confusion ; then, grown red with shame,
  They shall return in haste the way they came,
And in a moment shall be quite abashed.

PSALM VII.

August 14, 1653.

Upon the words of Chush the Benjamite against him.

LORD, my God, to Thee I fly ;
Save me, and secure me under
Thy protection while I cry ;
Lest, as a lion (and no wonder),
He haste to tear my soul asunder,
Tearing and no rescue nigh.

Lord, my God, if I have thought
Or done this ; if wickedness
Be in my hands ; if I have wrought
Ill to him that meant me peace ;
Or to him have rendered less,
And not freed my foe for naught :

Let the enemy pursue my soul,
And overtake it ; let him tread
My life down to the earth, and roll

In the dust my glory dead,
In the dust, and there outspread
Lodge it with dishonour foul.

Rise, Jehovah, in Thine ire ;
Rouse Thyself amidst the rage
Of my foes that urge like fire ;
And wake for me, their fury assuage ;
Judgment here Thou didst engage
And command, which I desire.

So the assemblies of each nation
Will surround Thee, seeking right :
Thence to Thy glorious habitation
Return on high, and in their sight.
Jehovah judgeth most upright
All people from the world's foundation.

Judge me, Lord ; be judge in this
According to my righteousness,
And the innocence which is
Upon me : cause at length to cease
Of evil men the wickedness,
And their power that do amiss.

But the just establish fast,
Since Thou art the just God that tries
Hearts and reins.   On God is cast
My defence, and in Him lies ;
In Him who, both just and wise,
Saves the upright of heart at last.

God is a just judge and severe,
And God is every day offended ;
If the unjust will not forbear,
His sword He whets ; His bow hath bended
Already, and for him intended
The tools of death that waits him near.

(His arrows purposely made He
For them that persecute).   Behold
He travails big with vanity ;
Truth he hath conceived of old
As in a womb, and from that mould
Hath at length brought forth a lie.

He digg'd a pit, and delved it deep,
And fell into the pit he made :
His mischief, that due course doth keep,
Turns on his head : and his ill trade
Of violence will undelayed
Fall on his crown with ruin steep.

Then will I Jehovah's praise
According to His justice raise.
And sing the Name and Deity
Of Jehovah the Most High.

PSALM VIII.

August 14, 1653.

O JEHOVAH our Lord, how wondrous great
  And glorious is Thy name through all the earth,
So as above the heavens Thy praise to set!
  Out of the tender mouths of latest bearth,
Out of the mouths of babes and sucklings Thou
  Hast founded strength, because of all Thy foes,
To stint the enemy, and slack the avenger's brow,
  That bends His rage Thy providence to oppose.

When I behold Thy heavens, Thy fingers' art,
  The moon and stars, which Thou so bright hast set
In the pure firmament, then saith my heart,
  Oh, what is man that Thou rememberest yet
And think'st upon him, or of man begot
  That him Thou visit'st, and of him art found?
Scarce to be less than gods Thou mad'st his lot;
  With honour and with state Thou hast him crowned.

O'er the works of Thy hand Thou mad'st him lord;
  Thou hast put all under his lordly feet,
All flocks and herds, by Thy commanding word,
  All beasts that in the field or forest meet,
Fowl of the heavens, and fish that through the wet
  Sea-paths in shoals do slide, and know no dearth.
O Jehovah our Lord, how wondrous great
  And glorious is Thy name through all the earth!

MISCELLANEOUS TRANSLATIONS

DANTE, *Inferno*, XIX. 115.

AH, Constantine, of how much ill was cause,
Not thy conversion, but those rich domains
That the first wealthy Pope received of thee!

PETRARCH, *Sonnet* 107.

FOUNDED in chaste and humble poverty,
'Gainst them that raised thee dost thou lift thy horn,
Impudent whore? Where hast thou placed thy hope?
In thy adulterers, or thy ill-got wealth?
Another Constantine comes not in haste.

ARIOSTO, *Orl. Fur.* XXXIV. Stanz. 80.

THEN passed he to a flowery mountain green,
Which once smelt sweet, now stinks as odiously:
This was that gift (if you the truth will have)
That Constantine to good Sylvestro gave.

HORACE, *Sat.* i. 1, 24.

LAUGHING to teach the truth
What hinders? as some teachers give to boys
Junkets and knacks, that they may learn apace.

HORACE, *Sat.* i. 10, 14.

JOKING decides great things
Stronglier and better oft than earnest can.

SOPHOCLES, *Electra*, 624.

'T IS you that say it, not I. You do the deeds,
And your ungodly deeds find me the words.

EURIPIDES, *Supplices*, 438.

THIS is true Liberty, when freeborn men,
Having to advise the public, may speak free:
Which he who can and will deserves high praise:
Who neither can nor will may hold his peace.
What can be juster in a state than this?

HORACE, *Epist.* i. 16, 40.

WHOM do we count a good man? Whom but he
Who keeps the laws and statutes of the senate,
Who judges in great suits and controversies,
Whose witness and opinion wins the cause?
But his own house, and the whole neighbourhood,
Sees his foul inside through his whited skin.

SENECA, *Her. Fur.* 922.

THERE can be slain
No sacrifice to God more acceptable
Than an unjust and wicked king.

FROM GEOFFREY OF MONMOUTH.

GODDESS of Shades, and Huntress, who at will
Walk'st on the rolling sphere, and through the deep,
On thy third reign, the Earth, look now, and tell
What land, what seat of rest thou bidd'st me seek,
What certain seat, where I may worship thee
For aye, with temples vowed, and virgin quires.

Brutus, far to the west, in the ocean wide,
Beyond the realm of Gaul, a land there lies,
Sea-girt it lies, where giants dwelt of old;
Now void, it fits thy people. Thither bend
Thy course; there shalt thou find a lasting seat;
There to thy sons another Troy shall rise,
And kings be born of thee whose dreaded might
Shall awe the world, and conquer nations bold.

380

THE LATIN POEMS.

LATIN POEMS.

Hæc quæ sequuntur de Authore testimonia, tametsi ipse intelligebat non tam de se quam supra se esse dicta, eo quod præclaro ingenio viri, nec non amici, ita fere solent laudare ut omnia suis potius virtutibus quam veritati congruentia nimis cupide affingant, noluit tamen horum egregiam in se voluntatem non esse notam, cum alii præsertim ut id faceret magnopere suaderent. Dum enim nimiæ laudis invidiam totis ab se viribus amolitur, sibique quod plus æquo est non attributum esse mavult, judicium interim hominum cordatorum atque illustrium quin summo sibi honori ducat negare non potest.

JOANNES BAPTISTA MANSUS, MARCHIO VILLENSIS NEAPOLITANUS, AD JOANNEM MILTONIUM ANGLUM.

Ut mens, forma, decor, facies, mos, si pietas sic,
  Non Anglus, verùm herclè Angelus ipse, fores.

AD JOANNEM MILTONEM ANGLUM, TRIPLICI POESEOS LAUREÂ CORONANDUM, GRÆCÂ NIMIRUM, LATINÂ, ATQUE HETRUSCÂ, EPIGRAMMA JOANNIS SALSILLI ROMANI.

Cede, Meles ; cedat depressâ Mincius urnâ ;
  Sebetus Tassum desinat usque loqui ;
At Thamesis victor cunctis ferat altior undas ;
  Nam per te, Milto, par tribus unus erit.

AD JOANNEM MILTONUM.

Græcia Mæonidem, jactet sibi Roma Maronem ;
  Anglia Miltonum jactat utrique parem.
                                          SELVAGGI.

AL SIGNOR GIO. MILTONI, NOBILE INGLESE.

ODE.

Ergimi all' Etra o Clio,
Perchè di stelle intreccierò corona !
Non più del biondo Dio
La fronde eterna in Pindo, e in Elicona :
Diensi a merto maggior maggiori i fregi,
A celeste virtù celesti pregi.

Non può del Tempo edace
Rimaner preda eterno alto valore ;
Non può l' obblio rapace
Furar dalle memorie eccelso onore.
Sull' arco di mia cetra un dardo forte
Virtù m' adatti, e ferirò la Morte.

Dell' Ocean profondo
Cinta dagli ampi gorghi Anglia risiede
Separata dal mondo,
Però che il suo valor l' umano eccede :
Questa feconda sa produrre Eroi,
Ch' hanno a ragion del sovruman tra noi.

Alla virtù sbandita
Danno nei petti lor fido ricetto,
Quella gli è sol gradita,
Perchè in lei san trovar gioia e diletto ;
Ridillo tu, Giovanni, e mostra in tanto,
Con tua vera virtù, vero il mio Canto.

Lungi dal patrio lido
Spinse Zeusi l' industre ardente brama ;
Ch' udio d' Elena il grido
Con aurea tromba rimbombar la fama,
E per poterla effigiare al paro
Dalle più belle Idee trasse il più raro.

Così l' ape ingegnosa
Trae con industria il suo liquor pregiato
Dal giglio e dalla rosa,
E quanti vaghi fiori ornano il prato ;
Formano un dolce suon diverse corde,
Fan varie voci melodia concorde.

Di bella gloria amante
Milton, dal Ciel natio, per varie parti
Le peregrine piante
Volgesti a ricercar scienze ed arti ;
Dell Gallo regnator vedesti i Regni,
E dell' Italia ancor gl' Eroi più degni.

Fabro quasi divino,
Sol virtù rintracciando, il tuo pensiero
Vide in ogni confino
Chi di nobil valor calca il sentiero ;
L' ottimo dal miglior dopo scegliea
Per fabbricar d' ogni virtù l' Idea.

Quanti nacquero in Flora,
O in lei del parlar Tosco appreser l' arte,
La cui memoria onora
Il mondo fatta eterna in dotte carte,
Volesti ricercar per tuo tesoro,
E parlasti con lor nell' opre loro.

Nell' altera Babelle
Per te il parlar confuse Giove in vano,
Che per varie favelle
Di se stessa trofeo cadde sul piano :
Ch' ode, oltr' all' Anglia, il suo più degno idioma
Spagna, Francia, Toscana, e Grecia, e Roma.

I più profondi arcani
Ch' occulta la Natura, e in cielo e in terra,
Ch' a Ingegni sovrumani
Troppo avara talor gli chiude, e serra,
Chiaramente conosci, e giungi al fine
Della moral virtude al gran confine.

Non batta il Tempo l' ale,
Fermisi immoto, e in un ferminsi gli anni,
Che di virtù immortale
Scorron di troppo ingiuriosi ai danni;
Che s' opre degne di poema e storia
Furon già, l' hai presenti alla memoria.

Dammi tua dolce Cetra,
Se vuoi ch' io dica del tuo dolce canto,
Ch' inalzandoti all' Etra
Di farti uomo celeste ottiene il vanto;
Il Tamigi il dirà, chè gli è concesso
Per te, suo cigno, pareggiar Permesso.

Io, che in riva dell' Arno
Tento spiegar tuo merto alto e preclaro,
So che fatico indarno,
E ad ammirar, non a lodarlo imparo;
Freno dunque la lingua, e ascolto il core,
Che ti prende a lodar con lo stupore.

Del Sig. Antonio Francini,
Gentiluomo Fiorentino.

JOANNI MILTONI, LONDINENSI.

Juveni patriâ, virtutibus, eximio:
Viro qui multa peregrinatione, studio cuncta, orbis terrarum loca perspexit, ut, novus Ulysses, omnia ubique ab omnibus apprehenderet:
Polyglotto, in cujus ore linguæ jam deperditæ sic reviviscunt ut idiomata omnia sint in ejus laudibus infacunda; et jure ea percallet ut admirationes et plausus populorum ab propriâ sapientiâ excitatos intelligat:
Illi, cujus animi dotes corporisque sensus ad admirationem commovent, et per ipsam motum cuique auferunt; cujus opera ad plausus hortantur, sed venustate vocem laudatoribus adimunt:
Cui in Memoriâ totus orbis; in Intellectu sapientia; in Voluntate ardor gloriæ; in Ore eloquentia; harmonicos cælestium sphærarum sonitus Astronomiâ duce audienti; characteres mirabilium Naturæ per quos Dei magnitudo describitur magistrâ Philosophiâ legenti; antiquitatum latebras, vetustatis excidia, eruditionis ambages, comite assiduâ Autorum lectione, 'exquirenti, restauranti, percurrenti'
(At cur nitor in arduum?):
Illi in cujus virtutibus evulgandis ora Famæ non sufficiant, nec hominum stupor in laudandis satis est, Reverentiæ at Amoris ergo hoc ejus meritis debitum admirationis tributum offert

Carolus Datus, Patricius Florentinus,
Tanto homini servus, tantæ virtutis amator.

ELEGIARUM LIBER.

ELEGIA PRIMA.

Ad Carolum Diodatum.

Tandem, chare, tuæ mihi pervenere tabellæ,
  Pertulit et voces nuncia charta tuas ;
Pertulit occiduâ Devæ Cestrensis ab orâ
  Vergivium prono quà petit amne salum
Multùm, crede, juvat terras aluisse remotas
  Pectus amans nostri, tamque fidele caput
Quòdque mihi lepidum tellus longinqua sodalem
  Debet, at unde brevi reddere jussa velit.
Me tenet urbs refluâ quam Thamesis alluit undâ,
  Meque nec invitum patria dulcis habet.
Jam nec arundiferum mihi cura revisere Camum,
  Nec dudum vetiti me laris angit amor.
Nuda nec arva placent, umbrasque negantia molles ;
  Quàm male Phœbicolis convenit ill locus !
Nec duri libet usque minas perferre Magistri,
  Cæteraque ingenio non subeunda meo.
Si sit hoc exilium, patrios adiisse penates,
  Et vacuum curis otia grata sequi,
Non ego vel profugi nomen sortemve recuso,
  Lætus et exilii conditione fruor.
O utinam vates nunquam graviora tulisset
  Ille Tomitano flebilis exul agro ;
Non tunc Ionio quicquam cessisset Homero,
  Neve foret victo laus tibi prima, Maro.
Tempora nam licet hic placidis dare libera Musis,
  Et totum rapiunt me, mea vita, libri.
Excipit hinc fessum sinuosi pompa theatri,
  Et vocat ad plausus garrula scena suos.
Seu catus auditur senior, seu prodigus hæres,
  Seu procus, aut positâ casside miles adest,
Sive decennali fœcundus lite patronus
  Detonat inculto barbara verba foro ;
Sæpe vafer gnato succurrit servus amanti,
  Et nasum rigidi fallit ubique patris ;
Sæpe novos illic virgo mirata calores
  Quid sit amor nescit, dum quoque nescit amat :
Sive cruentatum furiosa Tragœdia sceptrum
  Quassat, et effusis crinibus ora rotat ;
Et dolet, et specto, juvat et spectasse dolendo ;
  Interdum et lacrymis dulcis amaror inest :
Seu puer infelix indelibata reliquit
  Gaudia, et abrupto flendus amore cadit ;
Seu ferus e tenebris iterat Styga criminis ultor,
  Conscia funereo pectora torre movens ;
Seu mœret Pelopeia domus, seu nobilis Ili,
  Aut luit incestos aula Creontis avos.
Sed neque sub tecto semper nec in urbe latemus,
  Irrita nec nobis tempora veris eunt.

386

Nos quoque lucus habet vicinâ consitus ulmo,
   Atque suburbani nobilis umbra loci.
Sæpius hic, blandas spirantia sidera flammas,
   Virgineos videas præteriisse choros.
Ah quoties dignæ stupui miracula formæ
   Quæ possit senium vel reparare Jovis!
Ah quoties vidi superantia lumina gemmas,
   Atque faces quotquot volvit uterque polus;
Collaque bis vivi Pelopis quæ brachia vincant,
   Quæque fluit puro nectare tincta via,
Et decus eximium frontis, tremulosque capillos,
   Aurea quæ fallax retia tendit Amor;
Pellacesque genas, ad quas hyacinthina sòrdet
   Purpura, et ipse tui floris, Adoni, rubor!
Cedite laudatæ toties Heröides olim,
   Et quæcunque vagum cepit amica Jovem;
Cedite Achæmeniæ turritâ fronte puellæ,
   Et quot Susa colunt, Memnoniamque Ninon;
Vos etiam Danaæ fasces submittite Nymphæ,
   Et vos Iliacæ, Romuleæque nurus;
Nec Pompeianas Tarpëia Musa columnas
   Jactet, et Ausoniis plena theatra stolis.
Gloria virginibus debetur prima Britannis;
   Extera sat tibi sit fœmina posse sequi.
Tuque urbs Dardaniis, Londinum, structa colonis,
   Turrigerum latè conspicienda caput,
Tu nimium felix intra tua mœnia claudis
   Quicquid formosi pendulus orbis habet.
Non tibi tot cælo scintillant astra sereno,
   Endymioneæ turba ministra deæ,
Quot tibi conspicuæ formâque auroque puellæ
   Per medias radiant turba videnda vias.
Creditur huc geminis venisse invecta columbis
   Alma pharetrigero milite cincta Venus,
Huic Cnidon, et riguas Simoentis flumine valles,
   Huic Paphon, et roseam posthabitura Cypron.
Ast ego, dum pueri sinit indulgentia cæci,
   Mœnia quàm subitò linquere fausta paro;
Et vitare procul malefidæ infamia Circes
   Atria, divini Molyos usus ope.
Stat quoque juncosas Cami remeare paludes,
   Atque iterum raucæ murmur adire Scholæ.
Interea fidi parvum cape munus amici,
   Paucaque in alternos verba coacta modos.

ELEGIA SECUNDA.

Anno ætatis 17.

IN OBITUM PRÆCONIS ACADEMICI CANTABRIGIENSIS.

TE, qui conspicuus baculo fulgente solebas
   Palladium toties ore ciere gregem,
Ultima præconum præconem te quoque sæva
   Mors rapit, officio nec favet ipsa suo.

Candidiora licet fuerint tibi tempora plumis
    Sub quibus accipimus delituisse Jovem,
O dignus tamen Hæmonio juvenescere succo,
    Dignus in Æsonios vivere posse dies,
Dignus quem Stygiis medicâ revocaret ab undis
    Arte Coronides, sæpe rogante deâ.
Tu si jussus eras acies accire togatas,
    Et celer a Phœbo nuntius ire tuo,
Talis in Iliacâ stabat Cyllenius aulâ
    Alipes, æthereâ missus ab arce Patris;
Talis et Eurybates ante ora furentis Achillei
    Rettulit Atridæ jussa severa ducis.
Magna sepulchrorum regina, satelles Averni,
    Sæva nimis Musis, Palladi sæva nimis,
Quin illos rapias qui pondus inutile terræ?
    Turba quidem est telis ista petenda tuis.
Vestibus hunc igitur pullis, Academia, luge,
    Et madeant lacrymis nigra feretra tuis.
Fundat et ipsa modos querebunda Elegëia tristes,
    Personet et totis nænia mœsta scholis.

ELEGIA TERTIA.

Anno ætatis 17.

In obitum Præsulis Wintoniensis.

Mœstus eram, et tacitus, nullo comitante, sedebam,
    Hærebantque animo tristia plura meo:
Protinus en subiit funestæ cladis imago
    Fecit in Angliaco quam Libitina solo;
Dum procerum ingressa est splendentes marmore turres
    Dira sepulchrali Mors metuenda face,
Pulsavitque auro gravidos et jaspide muros,
    Nec metuit satrapum sternere falce greges.
Tunc memini clarique ducis, fratrisque verendi,
    Intempestivis ossa cremata rogis;
Et memini Heroum quos vidit ad æthera raptos,
    Flevit et amissos Belgia tota duces.
At te præcipuè luxi, dignissime Præsul,
    Wintoniæque olim gloria magna tuæ;
Delicui fletu, et tristi sic ore querebar:
"Mors fera, Tartareo diva secunda Jovi,
Nonne satis quod sylva tuas persentiat iras,
    Et quod in herbosos jus tibi detur agros,
Quodque afflata tuo marcescant lilia tabo,
    Et crocus, et pulchræ Cypridi sacra rosa?
Nec sinis ut semper fluvio contermina quercus
    Miretur lapsus prætereuntis aquæ;
Et tibi succumbit liquido quæ plurima cælo
    Evehitur pennis, quamlibet augur, avis,
Et quæ mille nigris errant animalia sylvis,
    Et quod alunt mutum Proteos antra pecus.
Invida, tanta tibi cum sit concessa potestas,
    Quid juvat humanâ tingere cæde manus?

388

Nobileque in pectus certas acuisse sagittas,
  Semideamque animam sede fugâsse suâ ?"
Talia dum lacrymans alto sub pectore volvo,
  Roscidus occidius Hesperus exit aquis,
Et Tartessiaco submerserat æquore currum
  Phœbus, ab Eöo littore mensus iter.
Nec mora ; membra cavo posui refovenda cubili ;
  Condiderant oculos noxque soporque meos,
Cum mihi visus eram lato spatiarier agro ;
  Heu ! nequit ingenium visa referre meum.
Illic puniceâ radiabant omnia luce,
  Ut matutino cum juga sole rubent ;
Ac veluti cum pandit opes Thaumantia proles
  Vestitu nituit multicolore solum ;
Non dea tam variis ornavit floribus hortos
  Alcinoi Zephyro Chloris amata levi.
Flumina vernantes lambunt argentea campos ;
  Ditior Hesperio flavet arena Tago ;
Serpit odoriferas per opes levis aura Favoni,
  Aura sub innumeris humida nata rosis :
Talis in extremis terræ Gangetidis oris
  Luciferi regis fingitur esse domus.
Ipse racemiferis dum densas vitibus umbras
  Et pellucentes miror ubique locos,
Ecce mihi subitò Præsul Wintonius astat !
  Sidereum nitido fulsit in ore jubar ;
Vestis ad auratos defluxit candida talos ;
  Infula divinum cinxerat alba caput.
Dumque senex tali incedit venerandus amictu,
  Intremuit læto florea terra sono ;
Agmina gemmatis plaudunt cælestia pennis ;
  Pura triumphali personat æthra tubâ.
Quisque novum amplexu comitem cantuque salutat,
  Hosque aliquis placido misit ab ore sonos :
"Nate, veni, et patrii felix cape gaudia regni ;
  Semper abhinc duro, nate, labore vaca."
Dixit, et aligeræ tetigerunt nablia turmæ ;
  At mihi cum tenebris aurea pulsa quies ;
Flebam turbatos Cephaleiâ pellice somnos.
  Talia contingant somnia sæpe mihi !

ELEGIA QUARTA.

Anno ætatis 18.

Ad THOMAM JUNIUM, Præceptorem suum, apud Mercatores Anglicos Hamburgæ agentes Pastoris munere fungentem.

Curre per immensum subitò, mea littera, pontum ;
  I, pete Teutonicos læve per æquor agros ;
Segnes rumpe moras, et nil, precor, obstet eunti,
  Et festinantis nil remoretur iter.
Ipse ego Sicanio frænantem carcere ventos
  Æolon, et virides sollicitabo Deos,

389

Cæruleamque suis comitatam Dorida Nymphis,
    Ut tibi dent placidam per sua regna viam.
At tu, si poteris, celeres tibi sume jugales,
    Vecta quibus Colchis fugit ab ore viri ;
Aut queis Triptolemus Scythicas devenit in oras,
    Gratus Eleusinâ missus ab urbe puer.
Atque, ubi Germanas flavere videbis arenas,
    Ditis ad Hamburgæ moenia flecte gradum,
Dicitur occiso quæ ducere nomen ab Hamâ,
    Cimbrica quem fertur clava dedisse neci.
Vivit ibi antiquæ clarus pietatis honore
    Præsul Christicolas pascere doctus oves ;
Ille quidem est animæ plusquam pars altera nostræ ;
    Dimidio vitæ vivere cogor ego.
Hei mihi, quot pelagi, quot montes interjecti,
    Me faciunt aliâ parte carere mei !
Charior ille mihi quàm tu, doctissime Graiûm,
    Cliniadi, pronepos qui Telamonis erat ;
Quàmque Stagirites generoso magnus alumno,
    Quem peperit Lybico Chaonis alma Jovi.
Qualis Amyntorides, qualis Philyrëius Heros
    Myrmidonum regi, talis et ille mihi.
Primus ego Aonios illo præeunte recessus
    Lustrabam, et bifidi sacra vireta jugi,
Pieriosque hausi latices, Clioque favente
    Castalio sparsi læta ter ora mero.
Flammeus at signum ter viderat arietis Æthon
    Induxitque auro lanea terga novo,
Bisque novo terram sparsisti, Chlori, senilem
    Gramine, bisque tuas abstulit Auster opes ;
Necdum ejus licuit mihi lumina pascere vultu,
    Aut linguæ dulces aure bibisse sonos.
Vade igitur, cursuque Eurum præverte sonorum ;
    Quàm sit opus monitis res docet, ipsa vides.
Invenies dulci cum conjuge fortè sedentem,
    Mulcentem gremio pignora chara suo ;
Forsitan aut veterum prælarga volumina Patrum
    Versantem, aut veri Biblia sacra Dei,
Cælestive animas saturantem rore tenellas,
    Grande salutiferæ religionis opus.
Utque solet, multam sit dicere cura salutem,
    Dicere quam decuit, si modo adesset, herum.
Hæc quoque, paulùm oculos in humum defixa modestos,
    Verba verecundo sis memor ore loqui :
"Hæc tibi, si teneris vacat inter prælia Musis,
    Mittit ab Angliaco littore fida manus.
Accipe sinceram, quamvis sit sera, salutem ;
    Fiat et hoc ipso gratior illa tibi.
Sera quidem, sed vera fuit, quam casta recepit
    Icaris a lento Penelopeia viro.
Ast ego quid volui manifestum tollere crimen,
    Ipse quod ex omni parte levare nequit ?
Arguitur tardus meritò, noxamque fatetur,
    Et pudet officium deseruisse suum.

Tu modò da veniam fasso, veniamque roganti ;
    Crimina diminui quæ patuere solent.
Non ferus in pavidos rictus diducit hiantes,
    Vulnifico pronos nec rapit ungue leo.
Sæpe sarissiferi crudelia pectora Thracis
    Supplicis ad mœstas delicuere preces ;
Extensæque manus avertunt fulminis ictus,
    Placat et iratos hostia parva Deos.
Jamque diu scripsisse tibi fuit impetus illi,
    Neve moras ultra ducere passus Amor ;
Nam vaga Fama refert, heu nuntia vera malorum !
    In tibi finitimis bella tumere locis,
Teque tuamque urbem truculento milite cingi,
    Et jam Saxonicos arma parâsse duces.
Te circum latè campos populatur Enyo,
    Et sata carne virûm jam cruor arva rigat.
Germanisque suum concessit Thracia Martem ;
    Illuc Odrysios Mars pater egit equos ;
Perpetuòque comans jam deflorescit oliva ;
    Fugit et ærisonam Diva perosa tubam,
Fugit, io ! terris, et jam non ultima Virgo
    Creditur ad superas justa volâsse domos.
Te tamen interea belli circumsonat horror,
    Vivis et ignoto solus inopsque solo ;
Et, tibi quam patrii non exhibuere penates,
    Sede peregrinâ quæris egenus opem.
Patria, dura parens, et saxis sævior albis
    Spumea quæ pulsat littoris unda tui,
Siccine te decet innocuous exponere fœtus,
    Siccine in externam ferrea cogis humum,
Et sinis ut terris quærant alimenta remotis
    Quos tibi prospiciens miserat ipse Deus,
Et qui læta ferunt de cælo nuntia, quique
    Quæ via post cineres ducat ad astra docent ?
Digna quidem Stygiis quæ vivas clausa tenebris,
    Æternâque animæ digna perire fame !
Haud aliter vates terræ Thesbitidis olim
    Pressit inassueto devia tesqua pede,
Desertasque Arabum salebras, dum regis Achabi
    Effugit, atque tuas, Sidoni dira, manus.
Talis et, horrisono laceratus membra flagello,
    Paulus ab Æmathiâ pellitur urbe Cilix ;
Piscosæque ipsum Gergessæ civis Iësum
    Finibus ingratus jussit abire suis.
At tu sume animos, nec spes cadat anxia curis,
    Nec tua concutiat decolor ossa metus.
Sis etenim quamvis fulgentibus obsitus armis,
    Intententque tibi millia tela necem,
At nullis vel inerme latus violabitur armis,
    Deque tuo cuspis nulla cruore bibet.
Namque eris ipse Dei radiante sub ægide tutus ;
    Ille tibi custos, et pugil ille tibi ;
Ille Sionææ qui tot sub mœnibus arcis
    Assyrios fudit nocte silente viros ;

Inque fugam vertit quos in Samaritidas oras
  Misit ab antiquis prisca Damascus agris;
Terruit et densas pavido cum rege cohortes,
  Aëre dum vacuo buccina clara sonat,
Cornea pulvereum dum verberat ungula campum,
  Currus arenosam dum quatit actus humum,
Auditurque hinnitus equorum ad bella ruentûm,
  Et strepitus ferri, murmuraque alta virûm.
Et tu (quod superest miseris) sperare memento,
  Et tua magnanimo pectore vince mala;
Nec dubites quandoque frui melioribus annis,
  Atque iterum patrios posse videre lares."

ELEGIA QUINTA.

Anno ætatis 20.

In Adventum Veris.

In se perpetuo Tempus revolubile gyro
  Jam revocat Zephyros, vere tepente, novos;
Induiturque brevem Tellus reparata juventam,
  Jamque soluta gelu dulcè virescit humus.
Fallor? an et nobis redeunt in carmina vires,
  Ingeniumque mihi munere veris adest?
Munere veris adest, iterumque vigescit ab illo
  (Quis putet?) atque aliquod jam sibi poscit opus.
Castalis ante oculos, bifidumque cacumen oberrat,
  Et mihi Pirenen somnia nocte ferunt;
Concitaque arcano fervent mihi pectora motu,
  Et furor, et sonitus me sacer intùs agit.
Delius ipse venit (video Penëide lauro
  Implicitos crines), Delius ipse venit.
Jam mihi mens liquidi raptatur in ardua cæli,
  Perque vagas nubes corpore liber eo;
Perque umbras, perque antra feror, penetralia vatum;
  Et mihi fana patent interiora Deûm;
Intuiturque animus toto quid agatur Olympo,
  Nec fugiunt oculos Tartara cæca meos.
Quid tam grande sonat distento spiritus ore?
  Quid parit hæc rabies, quid sacer iste furor?
Ver mihi, quod dedit ingenium, cantabitur illo;
  Profuerint isto reddita dona modo.
Jam, Philomela, tuos, foliis adoperta novellis,
  Instituis modulos, dum silet omne nemus:
Urbe ego, tu sylvâ, simul incipiamus utrique.
  Et simul adventum veris uterque canat.
Veris, io! rediere vices; celebremus honores
  Veris, et hoc subeat Musa perennis opus.
Jam sol, Æthiopas fugiens Tithoniaque arva,
  Flectit ad Arctoas aurea lora plagas.
Est breve noctis iter, brevis est mora noctis opacæ,
  Horrida cum tenebris exulat illa suis.

392

Jamque Lycaonius plaustrum cæleste Bootes
  Non longâ sequitur fessus ut ante viâ;
Nunc etiam solitas circum Jovis atria toto
  Excubias agitant sidera rara polo.
Nam dolus, et cædes, et vis cum nocte recessit,
  Neve Giganteum Dii timuere scelus.
Fortè aliquis scopuli recubans in vertice pastor,
  Roscida cum primo sole rubescit humus,
"Hac," ait, "hac certè caruisti nocte puellâ,
  Phœbe, tuâ, celeres quæ retineret equos."
Læta suas repetit sylvas, pharetramque resumit
  Cynthia, luciferas ut videt alta rotas,
Et, tenues ponens radios, gaudere videtur
  Officium fieri tam breve fratris ope.
"Desere," Phœbus ait, "thalamos, Aurora, seniles;
  Quid juvat effœto procubuisse toro?
Te manet Æolides viridi venator in herbâ;
  Surge; tuos ignes altus Hymettus habet."
Flava verecundo dea crimen in ore fatetur,
  Et matutinos ociùs urget equos.
Exuit invisam Tellus rediviva senectam,
  Et cupit amplexus, Phœbe, subire tuos.
Et cupit, et digna est; quid enim formosius illâ,
  Pandit ut omniferos luxuriosa sinus,
Atque Arabum spirat messes, et ab ore venusto
  Mitia cum Paphiis fundit amoma rosis?
Ecce, coronatur sacro frons ardua luco,
  Cingit ut Idæam pinea turris Opim;
Et vario madidos intexit flore capillos,
  Floribus et visa est posse placere suis.
Floribus effusos ut erat redimita capillos,
  Tænario placuit diva Sicana Deo.
Aspice, Phœbe; tibi faciles hortantur amores,
  Mellitasque movent flamina verna preces;
Cinnameâ Zephyrus leve plaudit odorifer alâ;
  Blanditiasque tibi ferre videntur aves.
Nec sine dote tuos temeraria quærit amores
  Terra, nec optatos poscit egena toros;
Alma salutiferum medicos tibi gramen in usus
  Præbet, et hinc titulos adjuvat ipsa tuos.
Quòd si te pretium, si te fulgentia tangunt
  Munera (muneribus sæpe coemptus amor),
Illa tibi ostentat quascunque sub æquore vasto,
  Et superinjectis montibus, abdit opes.
Ah! quoties, cum tu clivoso fessus Olympo
  In vespertinas præcipitaris aquas,
"Cur te," inquit, "cursu languentem, Phœbe, diurno
  Hesperiis recipit cærula mater aquis?
Quid tibi cum Tethy? quid cum Tartesside lymphâ?
  Dia quid immundo perluis ora salo?
Frigora, Phœbe, meâ melius captabis in umbrâ;
  Huc ades; ardentes imbue rore comas.
Mollior egelidâ veniet tibi somnus in herbâ;
  Huc ades, et gremio lumina pone meo.

Quàque jaces circum mulcebit lenè susurrans
    Aura per humentes corpora fusa rosas.
Nec me (crede mihi) terrent Semelëia fata,
    Nec Phaëtonteo fumidus axis equo ;
Cum tu, Phœbe, tuo sapientiùs uteris igni,
    Huc ades, et gremio lumina pone meo."
Sic Tellus lasciva suos suspirat amores ;
    Matris in exemplum cætera turba ruunt.
Nunc etenim toto currit vagus orbe Cupido,
    Languentesque fovet solis ab igne faces.
Insonuere novis lethalia cornua nervis,
    Triste micant ferro tela corusca novo.
Jamque vel invictam tentat superâsse Dianam,
    Quæque sedet sacro Vesta pudica foco.
Ipsa senescentem reparat Venus annua formam,
    Atque iterum tepido creditur orta mari.
Marmoreas juvenes clamant *Hymenæe* per urbes ;
    Littus *io Hymen* et cava saxa sonant.
Cultior ille venit, tunicâque decentior aptâ ;
    Puniceum redolet vestis odora crocum.
Egrediturque frequens ad amœni gaudia veris
    Virgineos auro cincta puella sinus.
Votum est cuique suum ; votum est tamen omnibus unum,
    Ut sibi quem cupiat det Cytherea virum.
Nunc quoque septenâ modulatur arundine pastor,
    Et sua quæ jungat carmina Phyllis habet.
Navita nocturno placat sua sidera cantu,
    Delphinasque leves ad vada summa vocat.
Jupiter ipse alto cum conjuge ludit Olympo,
    Convocat et famulos ad sua festa Deos.
Nunc etiam Satyri, cum sera crepuscula surgunt,
    Pervolitant celeri florea rura choro,
Sylvanusque suâ cyparissi fronde revinctus,
    Semicaperque Deus, semideusque caper.
Quæque sub arboribus Dryades latuere vetustis
    Per juga, per solos expatiantur agros.
Per sata luxuriat fruticetaque Mænalius Pan ;
    Vix Cybele mater, vix sibi tuta Ceres ;
Atque aliquam cupidus prædatur Oreada Faunus,
    Consulit in trepidos dum sibi nympha pedes,
Jamque latet, latitansque cupit malè tecta videri,
    Et fugit, et fugiens pervelit ipsa capi.
Dii quoque non dubitant cælo præponere sylvas,
    Et sua quisque sibi numina lucus habet.
Et sua quisque diu sibi numina lucus habeto,
    Nec vos arboreâ, dii, precor, ite domo.
Te referant, miseris te, Jupiter, aurea terris
    Sæcla ! quid ad nimbos, aspera tela, redis ?
Tu saltem lentè rapidos age, Phœbe, jugales
    Quà potes, et sensim tempora veris eant :
Brumaque productas tardè ferat hispida noctes,
    Ingruat et nostro serior umbra polo !

394

ELEGIA SEXTA.

Ad CAROLUM DIODATUM, ruri commorantem;

Qui, cum Idibus Decemb. scripsisset, et sua carmina excusari
postulâsset si solito minus essent bona, quod inter lautitias
quibus erat ab amicis exceptus haud satis felicem operam
Musis dare se posse affirmabat, hoc habuit responsum.

Mitto tibi sanam non pleno ventre salutem,
  Quâ tu distento fortè carere potes.
At tua quid nostram prolectat Musa camœnam,
  Nec sinit optatas posse sequi tenebras?
Carmine scire velis quàm te redamemque colamque;
  Crede mihi vix hoc carmine scire queas.
Nam neque noster amor modulis includitur arctis,
  Nec venit ad claudos integer ipse pedes.
Quàm bene solennes epulas, hilaremque Decembrim,
  Festaque cælifugam quæ coluere Deum,
Deliciasque refers, hiberni gaudia ruris,
  Haustaque per lepidos Gallica musta focos!
Quid quereris refugam vino dapibusque poesin?
  Carmen amat Bacchum, carmina Bacchus amat.
Nec puduit Phœbum virides gestâsse corymbos,
  Atque hederam lauro præposuisse suæ.
Sæpiùs Aoniis clamavit collibus *Euœ*
  Mista Thyoneo turba novena choro.
Naso Corallæis mala carmina misit ab agris;
  Non illic epulæ, non sata vitis erat.
Quid nisi vina, rosasque, racemiferumque Lyæum,
  Cantavit brevibus Tëia Musa modis?
Pindaricosque inflat numeros Teumesius Euan,
  Et redolet sumptum pagina quæque merum;
Dum gravis everso currus crepat axe supinus,
  Et volat Eleo pulvere fuscus eques.
Quadrimoque madens Lyricen Romanus Iaccho
  Dulcè canit Glyceran, flavicomamque Chloen.
Jam quoque lauta tibi generoso mensa paratu
  Mentis alit vires, ingeniumque fovet.
Massica fœcundam despumant pocula venam,
  Fundis et ex ipso condita metra cado.
Addimus his artes, fusumque per intima Phœbum
  Corda; favent uni Bacchus, Apollo, Ceres.
Scilicet haud mirum tam dulcia carmina per te,
  Numine composito, tres peperisse Deos.
Nunc quoque Thressa tibi cælato barbitos auro
  Insonat argutâ molliter icta manu;
Auditurque chelys suspensa tapetia circum,
  Virgineos tremulâ quæ regat arte pedes.
Illa tuas saltem teneant spectacula Musas,
  Et revocent quantum crapula pellit iners.
Crede mihi, dum psallit ebur, comitataque plectrum
  Implet odoratos festa chorea tholos,
Percipies tacitum per pectora serpere Phœbum,
  Quale repentinus permeat ossa calor;

Perque puellares oculos digitumque sonantem
    Irruet in totos lapsa Thalia sinus.
Namque Elegia levis multorum cura deorum est,
    Et vocat ad numeros quemlibet illa suos ;
Liber adest elegis, Eratoque, Ceresque, Venusque,
    Et cum purpureâ matre tenellus Amor.
Talibus inde licent convivia larga poetis,
    Sæpiùs et veteri commaduisse mero.
At qui bella refert, et adulto sub Jove cælum,
    Heroasque pios, semideosque duces,
Et nunc sancta canit superûm consulta deorum,
    Nunc latrata fero regna profunda cane,
Ille quidem parcè, Samii pro more magistri,
    Vivat, et innocuos præbeat herba cibos ;
Stet prope fagineo pellucida lympha catillo,
    Sobriaque e puro pocula fonte bibat.
Additur huic scelerisque vacans et casta juventus,
    Et rigidi mores, et sine labe manus ;
Qualis veste nitens sacrâ, et lustralibus undis,
    Surgis ad infensos augur iture Deos.
Hoc ritu vixisse ferunt post rapta sagacem
    Lumina Tiresian, Ogygiumque Linon,
Et lare devoto profugum Calchanta, senemque
    Orpheon edomitis sola per antra feris ;
Sic dapis exiguus, sic rivi potor Homerus
    Dulichium vexit per freta longa virum,
Et per monstrificam Perseiæ Phœbados aulam,
    Et vada fœmineis insidiosa sonis,
Perque tuas, rex ime, domos, ubi sanguine nigro
    Dicitur umbrarum detinuisse greges :
Diis etenim sacer est vates, divûmque sacerdos,
    Spirat et occultum pectus et ora Jovem.
At tu si quid agam scitabere (si modò saltem
    Esse putas tanti noscere siquid agam).
Paciferum canimus cælesti semine regem,
    Faustaque sacratis sæcula pacta libris ;
Vagitumque Dei, et stabulantem paupere tecto
    Qui suprema suo cum patre regna colit ;
Stelliparumque polum, modulantesque æthere turmas,
    Et subitò elisos ad sua fana Deos.
Dona quidem dedimus Christi natalibus illa ;
    Illa sub auroram lux mihi prima tulit.
Te quoque pressa manent patriis meditata cicutis ;
    Tu mihi, cui recitem, judicis instar eris.

ELEGIA SEPTIMA.

Anno ætatis undevigesimo.

Nondum blanda tuas leges, Amathusia, nôram,
    Et Paphio vacuum pectus ab igne fuit.
Sæpe cupidineas, puerilia tela, sagittas,
    Atque tuum sprevi maxime numen, Amor.
"Tu puer imbelles" dixi "transfige columbas ;
    Conveniunt tenero mollia bella duci :

396

LATIN POEMS

Aut de passeribus tumidos age, parve, triumphos ;
    Hæc sunt militiæ digna trophæa tuæ.
In genus humanum quid inania dirigis arma ?
    Non valet in fortes ista pharetra viros."
Non tulit hoc Cyprius (neque enim Deus ullus ad iras
    Promptior), et duplici jam ferus igne calet.
Ver erat, et summæ radians per culmina villæ
    Attulerat primam lux tibi, Maie, diem ;
At mihi adhuc refugam quærebant lumina noctem,
    Nec matutinum sustinuere jubar.
Astat Amor lecto, pictis Amor impiger alis ;
    Prodidit astantem mota pharetra Deum ;
Prodidit et facies, et dulcè minantis ocelli,
    Et quicquid puero dignum et Amore fuit.
Talis in æterno juvenis Sigeius Olympo
    Miscet amatori pocula plena Jovi ;
Aut, qui formosas pellexit ad oscula nymphas,
    Thiodamantæus Naiade raptus Hylas.
Addideratque iras, sed et has decuisse putares ;
    Addideratque truces, nec sine felle, minas.
Et " Miser exemplo sapuisses tutiùs," inquit ;
    " Nunc mea quid possit dextera testis eris.
Inter et expertos vires numerabere nostras,
    Et faciam vero per tua damna fidem.
Ipse ego, si nescis, strato Pythone superbum
    Edomui Phœbum, cessit et ille mihi ;
Et, quoties meminit Penëidos, ipse fatetur
    Certiùs et graviùs tela nocere mea.
Me nequit adductum curvare peritiùs arcum,
    Qui post terga solet vincere, Parthus eques :
Cydoniusque mihi cedit venator, et ille
    Inscius uxori qui necis author erat.
Est etiam nobis ingens quoque victus Orion,
    Herculeæque manus, Herculeusque comes.
Jupiter ipse licet sua fulmina torqueat in me,
    Hærebunt lateri spicula nostra Jovis.
Cætera quæ dubitas meliùs mea tela docebunt,
    Et tua non leviter corda petenda mihi.
Nec te, stulte, tuæ poterunt defendere Musæ ;
    Nec tibi Phœbæus porriget anguis opem."
Dixit, et, aurato quatiens mucrone sagittam,
    Evolat in tepidos Cypridos ille sinus.
At mihi risuro tonuit ferus ore minaci,
    Et mihi de puero non metus ullus erat.
Et modò quà nostri spatiantur in urbe Quirites,
    Et modò villarum proxima rura placent.
Turba frequens, facieque simillima turba dearum,
    Splendida per medias itque reditque vias ;
Auctaque luce dies gemino fulgore coruscat.
    Fallor ? an et radios hinc quoque Phœbus habet ?
Hæc ego non fugi spectacula grata severus,
    Impetus et quò me fert juvenilis agor ;
Lumina luminibus malè providus obvia misi,
    Neve oculos potui continuisse meos.

Unam fortè aliis supereminuisse notabam ;
    Principium nostri lux erat illa mali.
Sic Venus optaret mortalibus ipsa videri,
    Sic regina Deûm conspicienda fuit.
Hanc memor objecit nobis malus ille Cupido,
    Solus et hos nobis texuit antè dolos.
Nec procul ipse vafer latuit, multæque sagittæ,
    Et facis a tergo grande pependit onus.
Nec mora ; nunc ciliis hæsit, nunc virginis ori,
    Insilit hinc labiis, insidet inde genis ;
Et quascunque agilis partes jaculator oberrat,
    Hei mihi ! mille locis pectus inerme ferit.
Protinùs insoliti subierunt corda furores ;
    Uror amans intùs, flammaque totus eram.
Interea misero quæ jam mihi sola placebat
    Ablata est, oculis non reditura meis ;
Ast ego progredior tacitè querebundus, et excors,
    Et dubius volui sæpe referre pedem.
Findor ; et hæc remanet, sequitur pars altera votum ;
    Raptaque tam subitò gaudia flere juvat.
Sic dolet amissum proles Junonia cælum,
    Inter Lemniacos præcipitata focos ;
Talis et abreptum solem respexit ad Orcum
    Vectus ab attonitis Amphiaraus equis.
Quid faciam infelix, et luctu victus ? Amores
    Nec licet inceptos ponere, neve sequi.
O utinam spectare semel mihi detur amatos
    Vultus, et coràm tristia verba loqui !
Forsitan et duro non est adamante creata,
    Fortè nec ad nostras surdeat illa preces !
Crede mihi, nullus sic infeliciter arsit ;
    Ponar in exemplo primus et unus ego.
Parce, precor, teneri cum sis Deus ales amoris ;
    Pugnent officio nec tua facta tuo.
Jam tuus O certè est mihi formidabilis arcus,
    Nate deâ, jaculis nec minus igne potens :
Et tua fumabunt nostris altaria donis,
    Solus et in Superis tu mihi summus eris.
Deme meos tandem, verùm nec deme, furores ;
    Nescio cur, miser est suaviter omnis amans :
Tu modò da facilis, posthæc mea siqua futura est,
    Cuspis amaturos figat ut una duos.

Hæc ego mente olim lævâ, studioque supino,
    Nequitiæ posui vana trophæa meæ.
Scilicet abreptum sic me malus impulit error,
    Indocilisque ætas prava magistra fuit ;
Donec Socraticos umbrosa Academia rivos
    Præbuit, admissum dedocuitque jugum.
Protimùs, extinctis ex illo tempore flammis,
    Cincta rigent multo pectora nostra gelu ;
Unde suis frigus metuit puer ipse sagittis,
    Et Diomedeam vim timet ipsa Venus.

EPIGRAMMATA.

IN PRODITIONEM BOMBARDICAM.

Cum simul in regem nuper satrapasque Britannos
  Ausus es infandum, perfide Fauxe, nefas,
Fallor? an et mitis voluisti ex parte videri,
  Et pensare malâ cum pietate scelus?
Scilicet hos alti missurus ad atria cæli,
  Sulphureo curru flammivolisque rotis;
Qualiter ille, feris caput inviolabile Parcis,
  Liquit Iördanios turbine raptus agros.

IN EANDEM.

Siccine tentâsti cælo donâsse Iäcobum,
  Quæ septemgemino Bellua monte lates?
Ni meliora tuum poterit dare munera numen,
  Parce, precor, donis insidiosa tuis.
Ille quidem sine te consortia serus adivit
  Astra, nec inferni pulveris usus ope.
Sic potiùs fœdos in cælum pelle cucullos,
  Et quot habet brutos Roma profana Deos;
Namque hac aut aliâ nisi quemque adjuveris arte,
  Crede mihi, cæli vix bene scandet iter.

IN EANDEM.

Purgatorem animæ derisit Iäcobus ignem,
  Et sine quo superûm non adeunda domus.
Frenduit hoc trinâ monstrum Latiale coronâ,
  Movit et horrificum cornua dena minax.
Et "Nec inultus" ait "temnes mea sacra, Britanne;
  Supplicium spretâ religione dabis;
Et, si stelligeras unquam penetraveris arces,
  Non nisi per flammas triste patebit iter."
O quàm funesto cecinisti proxima vero,
  Verbaque ponderibus vix caritura suis!
Nam prope Tartareo sublime rotatus ab igni
  Ibat ad æthereas, umbra perusta, plagas.

IN EANDEM.

Quem modò Roma suis devoverat impia diris,
  Et Styge damnârat, Tænarioque sinu,
Hunc, vice mutatâ, jam tollere gestit ad astra,
  Et cupit ad superos evehere usque Deos.

IN INVENTOREM BOMBARDÆ.

Iapetionidem laudavit cæca vetustas,
  Qui tulit ætheream solis ab axe facem;
At mihi major erit qui lurida creditur arma
  Et trifidum fulmen surripuisse Jovi.

AD LEONORAM ROMÆ CANENTEM.

ANGELUS unicuique suus (sic credite, gentes)
    Obtigit æthereis ales ab ordinibus.
Quid mirum, Leonora, tibi si gloria major?
    Nam tua præsentem vox sonat ipsa Deum.
Aut Deus, aut vacui certè mens tertia cæli,
    Per tua secretò guttura serpit agens;
Serpit agens, facilisque docet mortalia corda
    Sensim immortali assuescere posse sono.
Quòd, si cuncta quidem Deus est, per cunctaque fusus,
    In te unâ loquitur, cætera mutus habet.

AD EANDEM.

ALTERA Torquatum cepit Leonora poetam,
    Cujus ab insano cessit amore furens.
Ah miser ille tuo quanto feliciùs ævo
    Perditus, et propter te, Leonora, foret!
Et te Pieriâ sensisset voce canentem
    Aurea maternæ fila movere lyræ!
Quamvis Dircæo torsisset lumina Pentheo
    Sævior, aut totus desipuisset iners,
Tu tamen errantes cæcâ vertigine sensus
    Voce eadem poteras composuisse tuâ;
Et poteras, ægro spirans sub corde quietem,
    Flexanimo cantu restituisse sibi.

AD EANDEM.

CREDULA quid liquidam Sirena, Neapoli, jactas,
    Claraque Parthenopes fana Achelöiados,
Littoreamque tuâ defunctam Naiada ripâ
    Corpore Chalcidico sacra dedisse rogo?
Illa quidem vivitque, et amœnâ Tibridis undâ
    Mutavit rauci murmura Pausilipi.
Illic, Romulidum studiis ornata secundis,
    Atque homines cantu detinet atque Deos.

APOLOGUS DE RUSTICO ET HERO.

RUSTICUS ex malo sapidissima poma quotannis
    Legit, et urbano lecta dedit Domino:
Hic, incredibili fructûs dulcedine captus,
    Malum ipsam in proprias transtulit areolas.
Hactenùs illa ferax, sed longo debilis ævo,
    Mota solo assueto, protinùs aret iners.
Quod tandem ut patuit Domino, spe lusus inani,
    Damnavit celeres in sua damna manus;
Atque ait, "Heu quanto satius fuit illa Coloni
    (Parva licet) grato dona tulisse animo;
Possem ego avaritiam frænare, gulamque voracem:
    Nunc periere mihi et fœtus et ipse parens."

DE MORO.

GALLI ex concubitu gravidam te, Pontia, Mori
    Quis bene moratam morigeramque neget?

400

AD CHRISTINAM, SUECORUM REGINAM, NOMINE CROMWELLI.

BELLIPOTENS Virgo, Septem regina Trionum,
  Christina, Arctoi lucida stella poli!
Cernis quas merui durâ sub casside rugas,
  Utque senex armis impiger ora tero,
Invia fatorum dum per vestigia nitor,
  Exequor et populi fortia jussa manu.
Ast tibi submittit frontem reverentior umbra;
  Nec sunt hi vultus Regibus usque truces.

ELEGIARUM FINIS.

SYLVARUM LIBER.

Anno ætatis 17.

IN OBITUM PROCANCELLARII MEDICI.

PARERE Fati discite legibus,
Manusque Parcæ jam date supplices,
  Qui pendulum telluris orbem
  Iäpeti colitis nepotes.
Vos si relicto Mors vaga Tænaro
Semel vocârit flebilis, heu! moræ
  Tentantur incassùm dolique;
  Per tenebras Stygis ire certum est.
Si destinatam pellere dextera
Mortem valeret, non ferus Hercules
  Nessi venenatus cruore
  Æmathiâ jacuisset Œtâ;
Nec fraude turpi Palladis invidæ
Vidisset occisum Ilion Hectora, aut
  Quem larva Pelidis peremit
  Ense Locro, Jove lacrymante.
Si triste Fatum verba Hecatëia
Fugare possint, Telegoni parens
  Vixisset infamis, potentique
  Ægiali soror usa virgâ.
Numenque trinum fallere si queant
Artes medentûm, ignotaque gramina,
  Non gnarus herbarum Machaon
  Eurypyli cecidisset hastâ;
Læsisset et nec te, Philyreie,
Sagitta Echidnæ perlita sanguine;
  Nec tela te fulmenque avitum,
  Cæse puer genetricis alvo.
Tuque, O alumno major Apolline,
Gentis togatæ cui regimen datum,
  Frondosa quem nunc Cirrha luget,
  Et mediis Helicon in undis,

Jam præfuisses Palladio gregi
  Lætus superstes, nec sine gloriâ ;
    Nec puppe lustrâsses Charontis
      Horribiles barathri recessus.
At fila rupit Persephone tua,
  Irata cum te viderit artibus
    Succoque pollenti tot atris
      Faucibus eripuisse Mortis.
Colende Præses, membra precor tua
  Molli quiescant cespite, et ex tuo
    Crescant rosæ calthæque busto,
      Purpureoque hyacinthus ore.
Sit mite de te judicium Æaci,
  Subrideatque Ætnæa Proserpina,
    Interque felices perennis
      Elysio spatiere campo !

IN QUINTUM NOVEMBRIS.

Anno œtatis 17.

Jam pius extremâ veniens Iäcobus ab arcto
Teucrigenas populos, latèque patentia regna
Albionum tenuit, jamque inviolabile fœdus
Sceptra Caledoniis conjunxerat Anglica Scotis :
Pacificusque novo, felix divesque, sedebat
In solio, occultique doli securus et hostis :
Cum ferus ignifluo regnans Acheronte tyrannus,
Eumenidum pater, æthereo vagus exul Olympo,
Fortè per immensum terrarum erraverat orbem,
Dinumerans sceleris socios, vernasque fideles,
Participes regni post funera mœsta futuros.
Hic tempestates medio ciet aëre diras ;
Illic unanimes odium struit inter amicos :
Armat et invictas in mutua viscera gentes,
Regnaque oliviferâ vertit florentia pace ;
Et quoscunque videt puræ virtutis amantes,
Hos cupit adjicere imperio, fraudumque magister
Tentat inaccessum sceleri corrumpere pectus ;
Insidiasque locat tacitas, cassesque latentes
Tendit, ut incautos rapiat, ceu Caspia tigris
Insequitur trepidam deserta per avia prædam
Nocte sub illuni, et somno nictantibus astris.
Talibus infestat populos Summanus et urbes,
Cinctus cæruleæ fumanti turbine flammæ.
Jamque fluentisonis albentia rupibus arva
Apparent, et terra Deo dilecta marino,
Cui nomen dederat quondam Neptunia proles,
Amphitryoniaden qui non dubitavit atrocem,
Æquore tranato, furiali poscere bello,
Ante expugnatæ crudelia sæcula Trojæ.
  At simul hanc, opibusque et festâ pace beatam,
Aspicit, et pingues donis Cerealibus agros,

Quodque magis doluit, venerantem numina veri
Sancta Dei populum, tandem suspiria rupit
Tartareos ignes et luridum olentia sulphur;
Qualia Trinacriâ trux ab Jove clausus in Ætnâ
Efflat tabifico monstrosus ab ore Typhœus.
Ignescunt oculi, stridetque adamantinus ordo
Dentis, ut armorum fragor, ictaque cuspide cuspis;
Atque " Pererrato solum hoc lacrymabile mundo
Inveni" dixit; "gens hæc mihi sola rebellis,
Contemtrixque jugi, nostrâque potentior arte.
Illa tamen, mea si quicquam tentamina possunt,
Non feret hoc impune diu, non ibit inulta."
Hactenus; et piceis liquido natat aëre pennis:
Quâ volat, adversi præcursant agmine venti,
Densantur nubes, et crebra tonitrua fulgent.
   Jamque pruinosas velox superaverat Alpes,
Et tenet Ausoniæ fines.   A parte sinistrâ
Nimbifer Apenninus erat, priscique Sabini;
Dextra veneficiis infamis Hetruria; nec non
Te furtiva, Tibris, Thetidi videt oscula dantem:
Hinc Mavortigenæ consistit in arce Quirini.
Reddiderant dubiam jam sera crepuscula lucem,
Cum circumgreditur totam Tricoronifer urbem,
Panificosque Deos portat, scapulisque virorum
Evehitur; præeunt submisso poplite reges,
Et mendicantûm series longissima fratrum;
Cereaque in manibus gestant funalia cæci,
Cimmeriis nati in tenebris vitamque trahentes.
Templa dein multis subeunt lucentia tædis
(Vesper erat sacer iste Petro), fremitusque canentûm
Sæpe tholos implet vacuos, et inane locorum:
Qualiter exululat Bromius, Bromiique caterva,
Orgia cantantes in Echionio Aracyntho,
Dum tremit attonitus vitreis Asopus in undis,
Et procul ipse cavâ responsat rupe Cithæron.
   His igitur tandem solenni more peractis,
Nox senis amplexus Erebi taciturna reliquit,
Præcipitesque impellit equos stimulante flagello,
Captum oculis Typhlonta, Melanchætemque ferocem,
Atque Acherontæo prognatam patre Siopen
Torpidam, et hirsutis horrentem Phrica capillis.
   Interea regum domitor, Phlegetontius hæres,
Ingreditur thalamos (neque enim secretus adulter
Producit steriles molli sine pellice noctes);
At vix compositos somnus claudebat ocellos
Cum niger umbrarum dominus, rectorque silentûm,
Prædatorque hominum, falsâ sub imagine tectus
Astitit.   Assumptis micuerunt tempora canis;
Barba sinus promissa tegit; cineracea longo
Syrmate verrit humum vestis; pendetque cucullus
Vertice de raso; et, ne quicquam desit ad artes,
Cannabeo lumbos constrinxit fune salaces,
Tarda fenestratis figens vestigia calceis.
Talis, uti fama est, vastâ Franciscus eremo

403

Tetra vagabatur solus per lustra ferarum,
Sylvestrique tulit genti pia verba salutis
Impius, atque lupos domuit, Libycosque leones.
  Subdolus at tali Serpens velatus amictu
Solvit in has fallax ora execrantia voces :
" Dormis, nate ? Etiamne tuos sopor opprimit artus ?
Immemor O fidei, pecorumque oblite tuorum !
Dum cathedram, venerande, tuam diademaque triplex
Ridet Hyperboreo gens barbara nata sub axe,
Dumque pharetrati spernunt tua jura Britanni :
Surge, age ! surge piger, Latius quem Cæsar adorat
Cui reserata patet convexi janua cæli ;
Turgentes animos et fastus frange procaces,
Sacrilegique sciant tua quid meledictio possit,
Et quid Apostolicæ possit custodia clavis ;
Et memor Hesperiæ disjectam ulciscere classem,
Mersaque Iberorum lato vexilla profundo,
Sanctorumque cruci tot corpora fixa probrosæ,
Thermodoonteâ nuper regnante puellâ.
At tu si tenero mavis torpescere lecto,
Crescentesque negas hosti contundere vires,
Tyrrhenum implebit numeroso milite pontum,
Signaque Aventino ponet fulgentia colle ;
Relliquias veterum franget, flammisque cremabit,
Sacraque calcabit pedibus tua colla profanis,
Cujus gaudebant soleis dare basia reges.
Nec tamen hunc bellis et aperto Marte lacesses ;
Irritus ille labor ; tu callidus utere fraude :
Quælibet hæreticis disponere retia fas est.
Jamque ad consilium extremis rex magnus ab oris
Patricios vocat, et procerum de stirpe creatos,
Grandævosque patres trabeâ canisque verendos :
Hos tu membratim poteris conspergere in auras,
Atque dare in cineres, nitrati pulveris igne
Ædibus injecto, quà convenere, sub imis.
Protinùs ipse igitur quoscunque habet Anglia fidos
Propositi factique mone : quisquamne tuorum
Audebit summi non jussa facessere Papæ ?
Perculsosque metu subito, casuque stupentes,
Invadat vel Gallus atrox, vel sævus Iberus.
Sæcula sic illic tandem Mariana redibunt,
Tuque in belligeros iterum dominaberis Anglos.
Et, nequid timeas, divos divasque secundas
Accipe, quotque tuis celebrantur numina fastis."
Dixit, et adscitos ponens malefidus amictus
Fugit ad infandam, regnum illætabile, Lethen.
  Jam rosea Eoas pandens Tithonia portas
Vestit inauratas redeunti lumine terras ;
Mœstaque adhuc nigri deplorans funera nati
Irrigat ambrosiis montana cacumina guttis ;
Cum sumnos pepulit stellatæ janitor aulæ,
Nocturnos visus et somnia grata revolvens.
  Est locus æternâ septus caligine noctis,
Vasta ruinosi quondam fundamina tecti,

Nunc torvi spelunca Phoni, Prodotæque bilinguis,
Effera quos uno peperit Discordia partu.
Hic inter cæmenta jacent præruptaque saxa
Ossa inhumata virûm, et trajecta cadavera ferro ;
Hic Dolus intortis semper sedet ater ocellis,
Jurgiaque, et stimulis armata Calumnia fauces ;
Et Furor, atque viæ moriendi mille, videntur,
Et Timor ; exanguisque locum circumvolat Horror ;
Perpetuòque leves per muta silentia Manes
Exululant ; tellus et sanguine conscia stagnat.
Ipsi etiam pavidi latitant penetralibus antri
Et Phonos et Prodotes ; nulloque sequente per antrum,
Antrum horrens, scopulosum, atrum feralibus umbris,
Diffugiunt sontes, et retrò lumina vortunt.
Hos pugiles Romæ per sæcula longa fideles
Evocat antistes Babylonius, atque ita fatur :
"Finibus occiduis circumfusum incolit æquor
Gens exosa mihi ; prudens Natura negavit
Indignam penitùs nostro conjungere mundo.
Illuc, sic jubeo, celeri contendite gressu,
Tartareoque leves difflentur pulvere in auras
Et rex et pariter satrapæ, scelerata propago ;
Et quotquot fidei caluere cupidine veræ
Consilii socios adhibete, operisque ministros."
Finierat : rigidi cupidè paruere gemelli.
    Interea longo flectens curvamine cælos
Despicit æthereâ Dominus qui fulgurat arce,
Vanaque perversæ ridet conamina turbæ,
Atque sui causam populi volet ipse tueri.
    Esse ferunt spatium, quà distat ab Aside terrâ
Fertilis Europe, et spectat Mareotidas undas ;
Hic turris posita est Titanidos ardua Famæ
Ærea, lata, sonans, rutilis vicinior astris
Quàm superimpositum vel Athos vel Pelion Ossæ.
Mille fores aditusque patent, totidemque fenestræ,
Amplaque per tenues translucent atria muros.
Excitat hic varios plebs agglomerata susurros ;
Qualiter instrepitant circum mulctralia bombis
Agmina muscarum, aut texto per ovilia junco,
Dum Canis æstivum cæli petit ardua culmen.
Ipsa quidem summâ sedet ultrix matris in arce :
Auribus innumeris cinctum caput eminet olli,
Queis sonitum exiguum trahit, atque levissima captat
Murmura, ab extremis patuli confinibus orbis ;
Nec tot, Aristoride, servator inique juvencæ
Isidos, immiti volvebas lumina vultu,
Lumina non unquam tacito nutantia somno,
Lumina subjectas latè spectantia terras.
Istis illa solet loca luce carentia sæpe
Perlustrare, etiam radianti impervia soli ;
Millenisque loquax auditaque visaque linguis
Cuilibet effundit temeraria ; veraque mendax
Nunc minuit, modò confictis sermonibus auget.
Sed tamen a nostro meruisti carmine laudes,

Fama, bonum quo non aliud veracius ullum,
Nobis digna cani, nec te memorâsse pigebit
Carmine tam longo ; servati scilicet Angli
Officiis, vaga diva, tuis tibi reddimus æqua.
Te Deus, æternos motu qui temperat ignes,
Fulmine præmisso, alloquitur, terrâque tremente :
"Fama, siles ? an te latet impia Papistarum
Conjurata cohors in meque meosque Britannos,
Et nova sceptrigero cædes meditata Iäcobo ?"
Nec plura : illa statim sensit mandata Tonantis,
Et, satis antè fugax, stridentes induit alas,
Induit et variis exilia corpora plumis ;
Dextra tubam gestat Temesæo ex ære sonoram.
Nec mora ; jam pennis cedentes remigat auras,
Atque parum est cursu celeres prævertere nubes ;
Jam ventos, jam solis equos, post terga reliquit :
Et primò Angliacas, solito de more, per urbes
Ambiguas voces incertaque murmura spargit ;
Mox arguta dolos et detestabile vulgat
Proditionis opus, nec non facta horrida dictu,
Authoresque addit sceleris, nec garrula cæcis
Insidiis loca structa silet.   Stupuere relatis,
Et pariter juvenes, pariter tremuere puellæ.
Effœtique senes pariter, tantæque ruinæ
Sensus ad ætatem subitò penetraverat omnem.
Attamen interea populi miserescit ab alto
Æthereus Pater, et crudelibus obstitit ausis
Papicolûm.   Capti pœnas raptantur ad acres :
At pia thura Deo et grati solvuntur honores ;
Compita læta focis genialibus omnia fumant ;
Turba choros juvenilis agit ; Quintoque Novembris
Nulla dies toto occurrit celebratior anno.

Anno ætatis 17.

IN OBITUM PRÆSULIS ELIENSIS.

ADHUC madentes rore squalebant genæ,
  Et sicca nondum lumina
Adhuc liquentis imbre turgebant salis
  Quem nuper effudi pius
Dum mœsta charo justa persolvi rogo
  Wintoniensis Præsulis,
Cum centilinguis Fama (proh ! semper mali
  Cladisque vera nuntia)
Spargit per urbes divitis Britanniæ,
  Populosque Neptuno satos,
Cessisse Morti et ferreis Sororibus,
  Te, generis humani decus,
Qui rex sacrorum illâ fuisti in insulâ
  Quæ nomen Anguillæ tenet.
Tunc inquietum pectus irâ protinùs
  Ebulliebat fervidâ,

Tumulis potentem sæpe devovens deam:
  Nec vota Naso in Ibida
Concepit alto diriora pectore;
  Graiusque vates parciùs
Turpem Lycambis execratus est dolum,
  Sponsamque Neobulen suam.
At ecce! diras ipse dùm fundo graves,
  Et imprecor Neci necem,
Audîsse tales videor attonitus sonos
  Leni, sub aurâ, flamine:
"Cæcos furores pone; pone vitream
  Bilemque et irritas minas.
Quid temerè violas non nocenda numina,
  Subitòque ad iras percita?
Non est, ut arbitraris elusus miser,
  Mors atra Noctis filia,
Erebove patre creta, sive Erinnye,
  Vastove nata sub Chao:
Ast illa, cælo missa stellato, Dei
  Messes ubique colligit;
Animasque mole carneâ reconditas
  In lucem et auras evocat,
(Ut cum fugaces excitant Horæ diem,
  Themidos Jovisque filiæ,)
Et sempiterni ducit ad vultus Patris,
  At justa raptat impios
Sub regna furvi luctuosa Tartari
  Sedesque subterraneas.
Hanc ut vocantem lætus audivi, citò
  Fœdum reliqui carcerem,
Volatilesque faustus inter milites
  Ad astra sublimis feror,
Vates ut olim raptus ad cælum senex,
  Auriga currus ignei.
Non me Bootis terruere lucidi
  Sarraca tarda frigore, aut
Formidolosi Scorpionis brachia;
  Non ensis, Orion, tuus.
Prætervolavi fulgidi solis globum;
  Longèque sub pedibus deam
Vidi triformem, dum coërcebat suos
  Frænis dracones aureis.
Erraticorum siderum per ordines,
  Per lacteas vehor plagas,
Velocitatem sæpe miratus novam,
  Donec nitentes ad fores
Ventum est Olympi, et regiam crystallinam, et
  Stratum smaragdis atrium.
Sed hic tacebo, nam quis effari queat
  Oriundus humano patre
Amœnitates illius loci? Mihi
  Sat est in æternum frui."

NATURAM NON PATI SENIUM.

Heu! quàm perpetuis erroribus acta fatiscit
Avia mens hominum, tenebrisque immersa profundis
Œdipodioniam volvit sub pectore noctem!
Quæ vesana suis metiri facta deorum
Audet, et incisas leges adamante perenni
Assimilare suis, nulloque solubile sæclo
Consilium Fati perituris alligat horis.
  Ergone marcescet sulcantibus obsita rugis
Naturæ facies, et rerum publica Mater,
Omniparum contracta uterum, sterilescet ab ævo?
Et, se fassa senem, malè certis passibus ibit
Sidereum tremebunda caput? Num tetra vetustas
Annorumque æterna fames, squalorque situsque,
Sidera vexabunt? An et insatiabile Tempus
Esuriet Cœlum, rapietque in viscera patrem?
Heu! potuitne suas imprudens Jupiter arces
Hoc contra munîsse nefas, et Temporis isto
Exemisse malo, gyrosque dedisse perennes?
Ergo erit ut quandoque, sono dilapsa tremendo,
Convexi tabulata ruant, atque obvius ictu
Stridat uterque polus, superâque ut Olympius aulâ
Decidat, horribilisque retectâ Gorgone Pallas;
Qualis in Ægæam proles Junonia Lemnon
Deturbata sacro cecidit de limine cæli.
Tu quoque, Phœbe, tui casus imitabere nati
Præcipiti curru, subitâque ferere ruinâ
Pronus, et extinctâ fumabit lampade Nereus,
Et dabit attonito feralia sibila ponto.
Tunc etiam aërei divulsis sedibus Hæmi
Dissultabit apex, imóque allisa barathro
Terrebunt Stygium dejecta Ceraunia Ditem,
In superos quibus usus erat, fraternaque bella.
  At Pater Omnipotens, fundatis fortiùs astris,
Colsuluit rerum summæ, certoque peregit
Pondere Fatorum lances, atque ordine summo
Singula perpetuum jussit servare tenorem.
Volvitur hinc lapsu Mundi rota prima diurno,
Raptat et ambitos sociâ vertigine cælos.
Tardior haud solito Saturnus, et acer ut olim
Fulmineùm rutilat cristatâ casside Mavors.
Floridus æternùm Phœbus juvenile coruscat,
Nec fovet effœtas loca per declivia terras
Devexo temone Deus; sed semper, amicâ
Luce potens, eadem currit per signa rotarum.
Surgit odoratis pariter formosus ab Indis
Æthereum pecus albenti qui cogit Olympo,
Manè vocans, et serus agens in pascua cæli;
Temporis et gemino dispertit regna colore.
Fulget, obitque vices alterno Delia cornu,
Cæruleumque ignem paribus complectitur ulnis.
Nec variant elementa fidem, solitoque fragore

Lurida perculsas jaculantur fulmina rupes.
Nec per inane furit leviori murmure Corus;
Stringit et armiferos æquali horrore Gelonos
Trux Aquilo, spiratque hiemem, nimbosque volutat.
Utque solet, Siculi diverberat ima Pelori
Rex maris, et raucâ circumstrepit æquora conchâ
Oceani Tubicen, nec vastâ mole minorem
Ægæona ferunt dorso Balearica cete.
Sed neque, Terra, tibi sæcli vigor ille vetusti
Priscus abest; servatque suum Narcissus odorem;
Et puer ille suum tenet, et puer ille, decorem,
Phœbe, tuusque, et, Cypri, tuus; nec ditior olim
Terra datum sceleri celavit montibus aurum
Conscia, vel sub aquis gemmas. Sic denique in ævum
Ibit cunctarum series justissima rerum;
Donec flamma orbem populabitur ultima, latè
Circumplexa polos et vasti culmina cæli,
Ingentique rogo flagrabit machina Mundi.

DE IDEÂ PLATONICÂ QUEMADMODUM ARISTOTELES INTELLEXIT.

DICITE, sacrorum præsides nemorum deæ,
Tuque O noveni perbeata numinis
Memoria mater, quæque in immenso procul
Antro recumbis otiosa Æternitas,
Monumenta servans, et ratas leges Jovis,
Cælique fastos atque ephemeridas Deûm,
Quis ille primus cujus ex imagine
Natura solers finxit humanum genus,
Æternus, incorruptus, æquævus polo,
Unusque et universus, exemplar Dei?
Haud ille, Palladis gemellus innubæ,
Interna proles insidet menti Jovis;
Sed, quamlibet natura sit communior,
Tamen seorsus extat ad morem unius,
Et, mira! certo stringitur spatio loci:
Seu sempiternus ille siderum comes
Cæli pererrat ordines decemplicis,
Citimumve terris incolit Lunæ globum;
Sive, inter animas corpus adituras sedens,
Obliviosas torpet ad Lethes aquas;
Sive in remotâ fortè terrarum plagâ
Incedit ingens hominis archetypus gigas,
Et diis tremendus erigit celsum caput,
Atlante major portitore siderum.
Non, cui profundum cæcitas lumen dedit,
Dircæus augur vidit hunc alto sinu;
Non hunc silenti nocte Plëiones nepos
Vatum sagaci præpes ostendit choro;
Non hunc sacerdos novit Assyrius, licet
Longos vetusti commemoret atavos Nini,
Priscumque Belon, inclytumque Osiridem;

Non ille trino gloriosus nomine
Ter magnus Hermes (ut sit arcani sciens)
Talem reliquit Isidis cultoribus.
At tu, perenne ruris Academi decus,
(Hæc monstra si tu primus induxti scholis)
Jam jam poetas, urbis exules tuæ,
Revocabis, ipse fabulator maximus;
Aut institutor ipse migrabis foras.

AD PATREM.

Nunc mea Pierios cupiam per pectora fontes
Irriguas torquere vias, totumque per ora
Volvere laxatum gemino de vertice rivum;
Ut, tenues oblita sonos, audacibus alis
Surgat in officium venerandi Musa parentis.
Hoc utcunque tibi gratum, pater optime, carmen
Exiguum meditatur opus; nec novimus ipsi
Aptiùs a nobis quæ possint munera donis
Respondere tuis, quamvis nec maxima possint
Respondere tuis, nedum ut par gratia donis
Esse queat vacuis quæ redditur arida verbis.
Sed tamen hæc nostros ostendit pagina census,
Et quod habemus opum chartâ numeravimus istâ,
Quæ mihi sunt nullæ, nisi quas dedit aurea Clio,
Quas mihi semoto somni peperere sub antro,
Et nemoris laureta sacri, Parnassides umbræ.
  Nec tu, vatis opus, divinum despice carmen,
Quo nihil æthereos ortus et semina cæli,
Nil magis humanam commendat origine mentem,
Sancta Prometheæ retinens vestigia flammæ.
Carmen amant Superi, tremebundaque Tartara carmen
Ima ciere valet, divosque ligare profundos,
Et triplici duros Manes adamante coercet.
Carmine sepositi retegunt arcana futuri
Phœbades, et tremulæ pallentes ora Sibyllæ;
Carmina sacrificus sollennes pangit ad aras,
Aurea seu sternit mactantem cornua taurum,
Seu cum fata sagax fumantibus abdita fibris
Consulit, et tepidis Parcam scrutatur in extis.
Nos etiam, patrium tunc cum repetemus Olympum,
Æternæque moræ stabunt immobilis ævi,
Ibimus auratis per cæli templa coronis,
Dulcia suaviloquo sociantes carmina plectro,
Astra quibus geminique poli convexa sonabunt.
Spiritus et rapidos qui circinat igneus orbes
Nunc quoque sidereis intercinit ipse choreis
Immortale melos et inenarrabile carmen,
Torrida dum rutilus compescit sibila Serpens,
Demissoque ferox gladio mansuescit Orion,
Stellarum nec sentit onus Maurusius Atlas.
Carmina regales epulas ornare solebant,
Cum nondum luxus, vastæque immensa vorago

Nota gulæ, et modico spumabat cœna Lyæo.
Tum de more sedens festa ad convivia vates,
Æsculeâ intonsos redimitus ab arbore crines,
Heroumque actus imitandaque gesta canebat,
Et Chaos, et positi latè fundamina Mundi,
Reptantesque deos, et alentes numina glandes,
Et nondum Ætnæo quæsitum fulmen ab antro.
Denique quid vocis modulamen inane juvabit,
Verborum sensusque vacans, numerique loquacis?
Silvestres decet iste choros, non Orphea, cantus,
Qui tenuit fluvios, et quercubus addidit aures,
Carmine, non cithará, simulacraque functa canendo
Compulit in lacrymas: habet has a carmine laudes.
  Nec tu perge, precor, sacras contemnere Musas,
Nec vanas inopesque puta, quarum ipse peritus
Munere mille sonos numeros componis ad aptos,
Millibus et vocem modulis variare canoram
Doctus Arionii meritò sis nominis hæres.
Nunc tibi quid mirum si me genuisse poëtam
Contigerit, charo si tam propè sanguine juncti
Cognatas artes studiumque affine sequamur?
Ipse volens Phœbus se dispertire duobus,
Altera dona mihi, dedit altera dona parenti;
Dividuumque Deum, genitorque puerque, tenemus.
  Tu tamen ut simules teneras odisse Camœnas,
Non odisse reor. Neque enim, pater, ire jubebas
Quà via lata patet, quà pronior area lucri,
Certaque condendi fulget spes aurea nummi;
Nec rapis ad leges, malè custoditaque gentis
Jura, nec insulsis damnas clamoribus aures.
Sed, magis excultam cupiens ditescere mentem,
Me, procul urbano strepitu, secessibus altis
Abductum, Aoniæ jucunda per otia ripæ,
Phœbæo lateri comitem sinis ire beatum.
Officium chari taceo commune parentis;
Me poscunt majora. Tuo, pater optime, sumptu
Cum mihi Romuleæ patuit facundia linguæ,
Et Latii veneres, et quæ Jovis ora decebant
Grandia magniloquis elata vocabula Graiis,
Addere suasisti quos jactat Gallia flores,
Et quam degeneri novus Italus ore loquelam
Fundit, barbaricos testatus voce tumultus,
Quæque Palæstinus loquitur mysteria vates.
Denique quicquid habet cælum, subjectaque cælo
Terra parens, terræque et cælo interfluus aër,
Quicquid et unda tegit, pontique agitabile marmor,
Per te nôsse licet, per te, si nôsse libebit;
Dimotâque venit spectanda Scientia nube,
Nudaque conspicuos inclinat ad oscula vultus,
Ni fugisse velim, ni sit libâsse molestum.
  I nunc, confer opes, quisquis malesanus avitas
Austriaci gazas Perüanaque regna præoptas,
Quæ potuit majora pater tribuisse, vel ipse
Jupiter, excepto, donâsset ut omnia, cælo?

Non potiora dedit, quamvis et tuta fuissent,
Publica qui juveni commisit lumina nato,
Atque Hyperionios currus, et fræna diei,
Et circum undantem radiatâ luce tiaram.
Ergo ego, jam doctæ pars quamlibet ima catervæ,
Victrices hederas inter laurosque sedebo ;
Jamque nec obscurus populo miscebor inerti,
Vitabuntque oculos vestigia nostra profanos.
Este procul vigiles Curæ, procul este Querelæ,
Invidiæque acies transverso tortilis hirquo ;
Sæva nec anguiferos extende, Calumnia, rictus ;
In me triste nihil, fœdissima turba, potestis,
Nec vestri sum juris ego ; securaque tutus
Pectora vipereo gradiar sublimis ab ictu.
   At tibi, chare pater, postquam non æqua merenti
Posse referre datur, nec dona rependere factis,
Sit memorâsse satis, repetitaque munera grato
Percensere animo, fidæque reponere menti.
   Et vos, O nostri, juvenilia carmina, lusus,
Si modò perpetuos sperare audebitis annos,
Et domini superesse rogo, lucemque tueri,
Nec spisso rapient oblivia nigra sub Orco,
Forsitan has laudes, decantatumque parentis
Nomen, ad exemplum, sero servabitis ævo.

PSALM CXIV.

Ἰσραὴλ ὅτε παῖδες, ὅτ᾽ ἀγλαὰ φῦλ᾽ Ἰακώβου
Αἰγύπτιον λίπε δῆμον, ἀπεχθέα, βαρβαρόφωνον,
Δὴ τότε μοῦνον ἔην ὅσιον γένος υἷες Ἰούδα·
Ἐν δὲ Θεὸς λαοῖσι μέγα κρείων βασίλευεν.
Εἶδε καὶ ἐντροπάδην φύγαδ᾽ ἐῤῥώησε θάλασσα,
Κύματι εἰλυμένη ῥοθίῳ, ὁ δ᾽ ἄρ᾽ ἐστυφελίχθη
Ἱρὸς Ἰορδάνης ποτὶ ἀργυροειδέα πηγήν·
Ἐκ δ᾽ ὄρεα σκαρθμοῖσιν ἀπειρέσια κλονέοντο,
Ὡς κριοὶ σφριγόωντες ἐϋτραφερῷ ἐν ἀλωῇ·
Βαιότεραι δ᾽ ἅμα πᾶσαι ἀνασκίρτησαν ἐρίπναι,
Οἷα παραὶ σύριγγι φίλῃ ὑπὸ μητέρι ἄρνες.
Τίπτε σύγ᾽, αἰνὰ θάλασσα, πέλωρ φύγαδ᾽ ἐῤῥώησας
Κύματι εἰλυμένη ῥοθίῳ; τί δ᾽ ἄρ᾽ ἐστυφελίχθης
Ἱρὸς Ἰορδάνη ποτὶ ἀργυροειδέα πηγήν ;
Τίπτ᾽ ὄρεα σκαρθμοῖσιν ἀπειρέσια κλονέεσθε,
Ὡς κριοὶ σφριγόωντες ἐϋτραφερῷ ἐν ἀλωῇ ;
Βαιότεραι τί δ᾽ ἄρ᾽ ὕμμες ἀνασκιρτήσατ᾽ ἐρίπναι,
Οἷα παραὶ σύριγγι φίλῃ ὑπὸ μητέρι ἄρνες ;
Σείεο γαῖα τρέουσα Θεὸν μεγάλ᾽ ἐκτυπέοντα,
Γαῖα Θεὸν τρείουσ᾽ ὕπατον σέβας Ἰσσακίδαο,
Ὅς τε καὶ ἐκ σπιλάδων ποταμοὺς χέε μορμύροντας,
Κρήνην τ᾽ ἀέναον πέτρης ἀπὸ δακρυοέσσης.

Philosophus ad Regem quendam, qui eum ignotum et insontem inter reos forte captum inscius damnaverat, τήν ἐπὶ θανάτῳ πορευόμενος, *hæc subito misit.*

Ὦ ἄνα, εἰ ὀλέσῃς με τὸν ἔννομον, οὐδέ τιν' ἀνδρῶν
Δεινὸν ὅλως δράσαντα, σοφώτατον ἴσθι κάρηνον
Ῥηϊδίως ἀφέλοιο, τὸ δ' ὕστερον αὖθι νοήσεις,
Μαψιδίως δ' ἄρ' ἔπειτα τεὸν πρὸς θυμὸν ὀδύρῃ,
Τοιόνδ' ἐκ πόλιος περιώνυμον ἄλκαρ ὀλέσσας.

In effigiei ejus sculptorem.

Ἀμαθεῖ γεγράφθαι χειρὶ τήνδε μὲν εἰκόνα
Φαίης τάχ' ἄν, πρὸς εἶδος αὐτοφυὲς βλέπων.
Τὸν δ' ἐκτυπωτὸν οὐκ ἐπιγνόντες, φίλοι,
Γελᾶτε φαύλου δυσμίμημα ζωγράφου.

AD SALSILLUM, POETAM ROMANUM, ÆGROTANTEM.
SCAZONTES.

O Musa gressum quæ volens trahis claudum,
Vulcanioque tarda gaudes incessu,
Nec sentis illud in loco minus gratum
Quam cum decentes flava Dëiope suras
Alternat aureum ante Junonis lectum,
Adesdum, et hæc s'is verba pauca Salsillo
Refer, Camœna nostra cui tantum est cordi,
Quamque ille magnis prætulit immeritò divis.
Hæc ergo alumnus ille Londini Milto,
Diebus hisce qui suum linquens nidum
Polique tractum (pessimus ubi ventorum,
Insanientis impotensque pulmonis,
Pernix anhela sub Jove exercet flabra)
Venit feraces Itali soli ad glebas,
Visum superbâ cognitas urbes famâ,
Virosque, doctæque indolem juventutis,
Tibi optat idem hic fausta multa, Salsille,
Habitumque fesso corpori penitùs sanum;
Cui nunc profunda bilis infestat renes,
Præcordiisque fixa damnosùm spirat;
Nec id pepercit impia quòd tu Romano
Tam cultus ore Lesbium condis melos.
O dulce divûm munus, O Salus, Hebes
Germana! Tuque, Phœbe! morborum terror,
Pythone cæso, sive tu magis Pæan
Libenter audis, hic tuus sacerdos est.
Querceta Fauni, vosque rore vinoso
Colles benigni, mitis Evandri sedes,
Siquid salubre vallibus frondet vestris,
Levamen ægro ferte certatim vati.
Sic ille charis redditus rursùm Musis

Vicina dulci prata mulcebit cantu.
Ipse inter atros emirabitur lucos
Numa, ubi beatum degit otium æternum,
Suam reclivis semper Ægeriam spectans;
Tumidusque et ipse Tibris, hinc delinitus,
Spei favebit annuæ colonorum;
Nec in sepulchris ibit obsessum reges,
Nimiùm sinistro laxus irruens loro;
Sed fræna meliùs temperabit undarum,
Adusque curvi salsa regna Portumni.

MANSUS.

Joannes Baptista Mansus, Marchio Villensis, vir ingenii laude, tum literarum studio, nec non et bellicâ virtute, apud Italos clarus in primis est. Ad quem Torquati Tassi Dialogus extat de Amicitiâ scriptus; erat enim Tassi amicissimus: ab quo etiam inter Campaniæ principes celebratur, in illo poemate cui titulus GERUSALEMME CONQUISTATA, lib. 20.

> Fra cavalier magnanimi e cortesi
> Risplende il Manso . . . .

Is authorem, Neapoli commorantem, summâ benevolentiâ prosecutus est, multaque ei detulit humanitatis officia. Ad hunc itaque hospes ille, antequam ab eâ urbe discederet, ut ne ingratum se ostenderet, hoc carmen misit.

HÆC quoque, Manse, tuæ meditantur carmina laudi
Pierides; tibi, Manse, choro notissime Phœbi,
Quandoquidem ille alium haud æquo est dignatus honore,
Post Galli cineres, et Mecœnatis Hetrusci.
Tu quoque, si nostræ tantum valet aura Camœnæ,
Victrices hederas inter laurosque sedebis.
Te pridem magno felix concordia Tasso
Junxit, et æternis inscripsit nomina chartis.
Mox tibi dulciloquum non inscia Musa Marinum
Tradidit; ille tuum dici se gaudet alumnum,
Dum canit Assyrios divûm prolixus amores,
Mollis et Ausonias stupefecit carmine nymphas.
Ille itidem moriens tibi soli debita vates
Ossa, tibi soli, supremaque vota reliquit:
Nec Manes pietas tua chara fefellit amici;
Vidimus arridentem operoso ex ære poetam.
Nec satis hoc visum est in utrumque, et nec pia cessant
Officia in tumulo; cupis integros rapere Orco,
Quà potes, atque avidas Parcarum eludere leges:
Amborum genus, et variâ sub sorte peractam
Describis vitam, moresque, et dona Minervæ;
Æmulus illius Mycalen qui natus ad altam
Rettulit Æolii vitam facundus Homeri.
Ergo ego te, Cliûs et magni nomine Phœbi,
Manse pater, jubeo longum salvere per ævum,
Missus Hyperboreo juvenis peregrinus ab axe.
Nec tu longinquam bonus aspernabere Musam,
Quæ nuper, gelidâ vix enutrita sub Arcto,

Imprudens Italas ausa est volitare per urbes.
Nos etiam in nostro modulantes flumine cygnos
Credimus obscuras noctis sensisse per umbras,
Quà Thamesis latè puris argenteus urnis
Oceani glaucos perfundit gurgite crines ;
Quin et in has quondam pervenit Tityrus oras.
    Sed neque nos genus incultum, nec inutile Phœbo,
Quà plaga septeno mundi sulcata Trione
Brumalem patitur longâ sub nocte Boöten.
Nos etiam colimus Phœbum, nos munera Phœbo,
Flaventes spicas, et lutea mala canistris,
Halantemque crocum (perhibet nisi vana vetustas)
Misimus, et lectas Druidum de gente choreas.
(Gens Druides antiqua, sacris operata deorum,
Heroum laudes imitandaque gesta canebant.)
Hinc quoties festo cingunt altaria cantu
Delo in herbosâ Graiæ de more puellæ,
Carminibus lætis memorant Corinëida Loxo,
Fatidicamque Upin, cum flavicomâ Hecaërge,
Nuda Caledonio variatas pectora fuco.
    Fortunate senex ! ergo quacunque per orbem
Torquati decus et nomen celebrabitur ingens,
Claraque perpetui succrescet fama Marini,
Tu quoque in ora frequens venies plausumque virorum,
Et parili carpes iter immortale volatu.
Dicetur tum sponte tuos habitâsse penates
Cynthius, et famulas venisse ad limina Musas.
At non sponte dumom tamen idem et regis adivit
Rura Pheretiadæ cælo fugitivus Apollo,
Ille licet magnum Alciden susceperat hospes ;
Tantùm, ubi clamosos placuit vitare bubulcos,
Nobile mansueti cessit Chironis in antrum,
Irriguos inter saltus frondosaque tecta,
Peneium prope rivum : ibi sæpe sub ilice nigrâ,
Ad citharæ strepitum, blandâ prece victus amici,
Exilii duros lenibat voce labores.
Tum neque ripa suo, barathro nec fixa sub imo
Saxa stetere loco ; nutat Trachinia rupes,
Nec sentit solitas, immania pondera, silvas ;
Emotæque suis properant de collibus orni,
Mulcenturque novo maculosi carmine lynces.
    Diis dilecte senex ! te Jupiter æquus oportet
Nascentem et miti lustrârit lumine Phœbus,
Atlantisque nepos ; neque enim nisi charus ab ortu
Diis superis poterit magno favisse poetæ.
Hinc longæva tibi lento sub flore senectus
Vernat, et Æsonios lucratur vivida fusos,
Nondum deciduos servans tibi frontis honores,
Ingeniumque vigens, et adultum mentis acumen.
O mihi si mea sors talem concedat amicum,
Phœbæos decorâsse viros qui tam bene nôrit,
Siquando indigenas revocabo in carmina reges,
Arturumque etiam sub terris bella moventem
Aut dicam invictæ sociali fœdere mensæ

Magnanimos Heroas, et (O modò spiritus adsit)
Frangam Saxonicas Britonum sub Marte phalanges!
Tandem, ubi, non tacitæ permensus tempora vitæ,
Annorumque satur, cineri sua jura relinquam,
Ille mihi lecto madidis astaret ocellis;
Astanti sat erit si dicam, 'Sim tibi curæ';
Ille meos artus, liventi morte solutos,
Curaret parvâ componi molliter urnâ:
Forsitan et nostros ducat de marmore vultus,
Nectens aut Paphiâ myrti aut Parnasside lauri
Fronde comas; et ego securâ pace quiescam.
Tum quoque, si qua fides, si præmia certa bonorum,
Ipse ego, cælicolûm semotus in æthera divûm,
Quò labor et mens pura vehunt atque ignea virtus,
Secreti hæc aliquâ mundi de parte videbo
(Quantum fata sinunt), et totâ mente serenûm
Ridens purpureo suffundar lumine vultus,
Et simul æthereo plaudam mihi lætus Olympo.

EPITAPHIUM DAMONIS.

ARGUMENTUM.

THYRSIS et DAMON, ejusdem viciniæ pastores, eadem studia sequuti, a
pueritiâ amici erant, ut qui plurimum. THYRSIS, animi causâ profectus,
peregrè de obitu DAMONIS nuncium accepit. Domum postea reversus, et
rem ita esse comperto, se suamque solitudinem hoc carmine deplorat.
DAMONIS autem sub personâ hîc intelligitur CAROLUS DEODATUS, ex
urbe Hetruriæ Lucâ paterno genere oriundus, cætera Anglus; ingenio,
doctrinâ, clarissimisque cæteris virtutibus, dum viveret, juvenis egregius.

HIMERIDES Nymphæ (nam vos et Daphnin et Hylan,
Et plorata diu meminisis fata Bionis),
Dicite Sicelicum Thamesina per oppida carmen:
Quas miser effudit voces, quæ murmura Thyrsis,
Et quibus assiduis exercuit antra querelis,
Fluminaque, fontesque vagos, nemorumque recessus,
Dum sibi præreptum queritur Damona, neque altam
Luctibus exemit noctem, loca sola pererrans.
Et jam bis viridi surgebat culmus aristâ,
Et totidem flavas numerabant horrea messes,
Ex quo summa dies tulerat Damona sub umbras,
Nec dum aderat Thyrsis; pastorem scilicet illum
Dulcis amor Musæ Thuscâ retinebat in urbe.
Ast ubi mens expleta domum pecorisque relicti
Cura vocat, simul assuetâ seditque sub ulmo,
Tum verò amissum, tum denique, sentit amicum,
Cœpit et immensum sic exonerare dolorem:—
"Ite domum impasti; domino jam non vacat, agni.
Hei mihi! quæ terris, quæ dicam numina cælo,
Postquam te immiti rapuerunt funere, Damon?
Siccine nos linquis? tua sic sine nomine virtus
Ibit, et obscuris numero sociabitur umbris?
At non ille animas virgâ qui dividit aureâ

Ista velit, dignumque tui te ducat in agmen,
Ignavumque procul pecus arceat omne silentûm.
  "Ite domum impasti; domino jam non vacat, agni.
Quicquid erit, certè, nisi me lupus antè videbit,
Indeplorato non comminuere sepulchro,
Constabitque tuus tibi honos, longùmque vigebit
Inter pastores.   Illi tibi vota secundo
Solvere post Daphnin, post Daphnin dicere laudes,
Guadebunt, dum rura Pales, dum Faunus amabit;
Si quid id est, priscamque fidem coluisse, piumque,
Palladiasque artes, sociumque habuisse canorum.
  "Ite domum impasti; domino jam non vacat, agni.
Hæc tibi certa manent, tibi erunt hæc præmia, Damon.
At mihi quid tandem fiet modò? quis mihi fidus
Hærebit lateri comes, ut tu sæpe solebas,
Frigoribus duris, et per loca fœta pruinis,
Aut rapido sub sole, siti morientibus herbis,
Sive opus in magnos fuit eminùs ire leones,
Aut avidos terrere lupos præsepibus altis?
Quis fando sopire diem cantuque solebit?
  "Ite domum impasti; domino jam non vacat, agni.
Pectora cui credam? quis me lenire docebit
Mordaces curas, quis longam fallere noctem
Dulcibus alloquiis, grato cum sibilat igni
Molle pirum, et nucibus strepitat focus, at malus Auster
Miscet cuncta foris, et desuper intonat ulmo?
  "Ite domum impasti; domino jam non vacat, agni.
Aut æstate, dies medio dum vertitur axe,
Cum Pan æsculeâ somnum capit abditus umbrâ,
Et repetunt sub aquis sibi nota sedilia Nymphæ,
Pastoresque latent, stertit sub sepe colonus,
Quis mihi blanditiasque tuas, quis tum mihi risus,
Cecropiosque sales referet, cultosque lepores?
  "Ite domum impasti; domino jam non vacat, agni.
At jam solus agros, jam pascua solus oberro,
Sicubi ramosæ densantur vallibus umbræ;
Hic serum expecto; supra caput imber et Eurus
Triste sonant, fractæque agitata crepuscula silvæ.
  "Ite domum impasti; domino jam non vacat, agni.
Heu! quam culta mihi priùs arva procacibus herbis
Involvuntur, et ipsa situ seges alta fatiscit!
Innuba neglecto marcescit et uva racemo,
Nec myrteta juvant; ovium quoque tædet, at illæ
Mœrent, inque suum convertunt ora magistrum.
  "Ite domum impasti; domino jam non vacat, agni.
Tityrus ad corylos vocat, Alphesibœus ad ornos,
Ad salices Ægon, ad flumina pulcher Amyntas:
'Hic gelidi fontes, hic illita gramina musco,
Hic Zephyri, hic placidas interstrepit arbutus undas.'
Ista canunt surdo; frutices ego nactus abibam.
  "Ite domum impasti; domino jam non vacat, agni.
Mopsus ad hæc, nam me redeuntem fortè notârat
(Et callebat avium linguas et sidera Mopsus),
'Thyrsi, quid hoc?' dixit; 'quæ te coquit improbabilis?

Aut te perdit amor, aut te malè fascinat astrum ;
Saturni grave sæpe fuit pastoribus astrum,
Intimaque obliquo figit præcordia plumbo.'
    "Ite domum impasti ; domino jam non vacat, agni.
Mirantur nymphæ, et 'Quid te, Thyrsi, futurum est ?
Quid tibi vis?' aiunt : 'non hæc solet esse juventæ
Nubila frons, oculique truces, vultusque severi :
Illa choros, lususque leves, et semper amorem
Jure petit ; bis ille miser qui serus amavit.'
    "Ite domum impasti ; domino jam non vacat, agni.
Venit Hyas, Dryopeque, et filia Baucidis Ægle,
Docta modos, citharæque sciens, sed perdita fastu ;
Venit Idumanii Chloris vicina fluenti :
Nil me blanditiæ, nil me solantia verba,
Nil me si quid adest movet, aut spes ulla futuri.
    "Ite domum impasti ; domino jam non vacat, agni.
Hei mihi ! quam similes ludunt per prata juvenci,
Omnes unanimi secum sibi lege sodales !
Nec magis hunc alio quisquam secernit amicum
De grege ; sic densi veniunt ad pabula thoes,
Inque vicem hirsuti paribus junguntur onagri :
Lex eadem pelagi ; deserto in littore Proteus
Agmina phocarum numerat : vilisque volucrum
Passer habet semper quicum sit, et omnia circum
Farra libens volitet, serò sua tecta revisens ;
Quem si sors letho objecit, seu milvus adunco
Fata tulit rostro, seu stravit arundine fossor,
Protinùs ille alium socio petit inde volatu.
Nos durum genus, et diris exercita fatis
Gens, homines, aliena animis, et pectore discors ;
Vix sibi quisque parem de millibus invenit unum ;
Aut, si sors dederit tandem non aspera votis,
Illum inopina dies, quâ non speraveris horâ,
Surripit, æternum linquens in sæcula damnum.
    "Ite domum impasti ; domino jam non vacat, agni.
Heu ! quis me ignotas traxit vagus error in oras
Ire per aëreas rupes, Alpemque nivosam ?
Ecquid erat tanti Romam vidisse sepultam
(Quamvis illa foret, qualem dum viseret olim
Tityrus ipse suas et oves et rura reliquit),
Ut te tam dulci possem caruisse sodale,
Possem tot maria alta, tot interponere montes,
Tot silvas, tot saxa tibi, fluviosque sonantes ?
Ah ! certè extremùm licuisset tangere dextram,
Et bene compositos placidè morientis ocellos,
Et dixisse 'Vale ! nostri memor ibis ad astra.'
    "Ite domum impasti ; domino jam non vacat, agni.
Quamquam etiam vestri nunquam meminisse pigebit,
Pastores Thusci, Musis operata juventus,
Hic Charis, atque Lepos ; et Thuscus tu quoque Damon,
Antiquâ genus unde petis Lucumonis ab urbe.
O ego quantus eram, gelidi cum stratus ad Arni
Murmura, populeumque nemus, quâ mollior herba,
Carpere nunc violas, nunc summas carpere myrtos,

418

Et potui Lycidæ certantem audire Menalcam !
Ipse etiam tentare ausus sum ; nec puto multùm
Displicui ; nam sunt et apud me munera vestra,
Fiscellæ, calathique, et cerea vincla cicutæ :
Quin et nostra suas docuerunt nomina fagos
Et Datis et Francinus ; èrant et vocibus ambo
Et studiis noti, Lydorum sanguinis ambo.
  "Ite domum impasti ; domino jam non vacat, agni.
Hæc mihi tum læto dictabat roscida luna,
Dum solus teneros claudebam cratibus hœdos.
Ah ! quoties dixi, cum te cinis ater habebat,
'Nunc canit, aut lepori nunc tendit retia Damon ;
Vimina nunc texit varios sibi quod sit in usus ;'
Et quæ tum facili sperabam mente futura
Arripui voto levis, et præsentia finxi.
'Heus bone ! numquid agis ? nisi te quid fortè retardat,
Imus, et argutâ paulùm recubamus in umbrâ,
Aut ad aquas Colni, aut ubi jugera Cassibelauni ?
Tu mihi percurres medicos, tua gramina, succos,
Helleborumque, humilesque crocos, foliumque hyacinthi,
Quasque habet ista palus herbas, artesque medentûm.'
Ah ! pereant herbæ, pereant artesque medentûm,
Gramina, postquam ipsi nil profecere magistro !
Ipse etiam—nam nescio quid mihi grande sonabat
Fistula—ab undecimâ jam lux est altera nocte—
Et tum fortè novis admôram labra cicutis :
Dissiluere tamen, ruptâ compage, nec ultra
Ferre graves potuere sonos : dubito quoque ne sim
Turgidulus ; tamen et referam ; vos cedite, sylvæ.
  "Ite domum impasti ; domino jam non vacat, agni.
Ipse ego Dardanias Rutupina per æquora puppes
Dicam, et Pandrasidos regnum vetus Inogeniæ,
Brennumque Arviragumque duces, priscumque Belinum,
Et tandem Armoricos Britonum sub lege colonos ;
Tum gravidam Arturo fatali fraude Iögernen ;
Mendaces vultus, assumptaque Gorlöis arma,
Merlini dolus. O, mihi tum si vita supersit,
Tu procul annosâ pendebis, fistula, pinu
Multùm oblita mihi, aut patriis mutata Camœnis
Brittonicum strides ! Quid enim ? omnia non licet uni,
Non sperâsse uni licet omnia ; mî satis ampla
Merces, et mihi grande decus (sim ignotus in ævum
Tum licet, externo penitùsque inglorius orbi),
Si me flava comas legat Usa, et potor Alauni,
Vorticibusque frequens Abra, et nemus omne Treantæ,
Et Thamesis meus ante omnes, et fusca metallis
Tamara, et extremis me discant Orcades undis.
  "Ite domum impasti ; domino jam non vacat, agni.
Hæc tibi servabam lentâ sub cortice lauri,
Hæc, et plura simul ; tum quæ mihi pocula Mansus,
Mansus, Chalcidicæ non ultima gloria ripæ,
Bina dedit, mirum artis opus, mirandus et ipse,
Et circum gemino cælaverat argumento.
In medio Rubri Maris unda, et odoriferum ver,

419

Littora longa Arabum, et sudantes balsama sylvæ ;
Has inter Phœnix, divina avis, unica terris,
Cæruleùm fulgens diversicoloribus alis,
Auroram vitreis surgentem respicit undis ;
Parte aliâ polus omnipatens, et magnus Olympus :
Quis putet ? hic quoque Amor, pictæque in nube pharetræ,
Arma corusca, faces, et spicula tincta pyropo ;
Nec tenues animas, pectusque ignobile vulgi,
Hinc ferit ; at, circum flammantia lumina torquens,
Semper in erectum spargit sua tela per orbes
Impiger, et pronos nunquam collimat ad ictus :
Hinc mentes ardere sacræ, formæque deorum.
   "Tu quoque in his—nec me fallit spes lubrica, Damon—
Tu quoque in his certè es ; nam quò tua dulcis abiret
Sanctaque simplicitas ? nam quò tua candida virtus ?
Nec te Lethæo fas quæsivisse sub Orco ;
Nec tibi conveniunt lacrymæ, nec flebimus ultra.
Ite procul, lacrymæ ; purum colit æthera Damon,
Æthera purus habet, pluvium pede reppulit arcum ;
Heroumque animas inter, divosque perennes,
Æthereos haurit latices et gaudia potat
Ore sacro. Quin tu, cæli post jura recepta,
Dexter ades, placidusque fave, quicunque vocaris ;
Seu tu noster eris Damon, sive æquior audis
Diodotus, quo te divino nomine cuncti
Cælicolæ nôrint, sylvisque vocabere Damon.
Quòd tibi purpureus pudor, et sine labe juventus
Grata fuit, quòd nulla tori libata voluptas,
En ! etiam tibi virginei servantur honores !
Ipse, caput nitidum cinctus rutilante coronâ,
Lætaque frondentis gestans umbracula palmæ,
Æternùm perages immortales hymenæos,
Cantus ubi, choreisque furit lyra mista beatis,
Festa Sionæo bacchantur et Orgia thyrso."

Jan. 23, 1646.

AD JOANNEM ROUSIUM,

OXONIENSIS ACADEMIÆ BIBLIOTHECARIUM.

De libro Poematum amisso, quem ille sibi denuo mitti postulabat, ut cum aliis nostris in Bibliothecâ Publicâ reponeret, Ode.

Ode tribus constat Strophis, totidemque Antistrophis, unâ demum Epodo clausis ; quas, tametsi omnes nec versuum numero nec certis ubique colis exactè respondeant, ita tamen secuimus, commodè legendi potius quam ad antiquos concinendi modos rationem spectantes. Alioquin hoc genus rectius fortasse dici *monostrophicum* debuerat. Metra partim sunt κατὰ σχέσιν, partim ἀπολελυμένα. Phaleucia quæ sunt spondæum tertio loco bis admittunt, quod idem in secundo loco Catullus ad libitum fecit.

STROPHE 1.

   Gemelle cultu simplici gaudens liber,
     Fronde licet geminâ,

Munditieque nitens non operosâ,
Quam manus attulit
Juvenilis olim
Sedula, tamen haud nimii poetæ ;
Dum vagus Ausonias nunc per umbras,
Nunc Britannica per vireta lusit,
Insons populi, barbitoque devius
Indulsit patrio, mox itidem pectine Daunio
Longinquum intonuit melos
Vicinis, et humum vix tetigit pede :

ANTISTROPHE.

Quis te, parve liber, quis te fratribus
Subduxit reliquis dolo,
Cum tu missus ab urbe,
Docto jugiter obsecrante amico,
Illustre tendebas iter
Thamesis ad incunabula
Cærulei patris,
Fontes ubi limpidi
Aonidum, thyasusque sacer,
Orbi notus per immensos
Temporum lapsus redeunte cælo,
Celeberque futurus in ævum ?

STROPHE 2.

Modò quis deus, aut editus deo,
Pristinam gentis miseratus indolem,
(Si satis noxas luimus priores,
Mollique luxu degener otium)
Tollat nefandos civium tumultus,
Almaque revocet studia sanctus,
Et relegatas sine sede Musas
Jam penè totis finibus Angligenûm,
Immundasque volucres
Unguibus imminentes
Figat Apollineâ pharetrâ,
Phineamque abigat pestem procul amne Pegaseo?

ANTISTROPHE.

Quin tu, libelle, nuntii licet malâ
Fide, vel oscitantiâ,
Semel erraveris agmine fratrum,
Seu quis te teneat specus,
Seu qua te latebra, forsan unde vili
Callo tereris institoris insulsi,
Lætare felix ; en ! iterum tibi
Spes nova fulget posse profundam
Fugere Lethen, vehique superam
In Jovis aulam remige pennâ :

STROPHE 3.

Nam te Roüsius sui
Optat peculî, numeroque justo
Sibi pollicitum queritur abesse,
Rogatque venias ille, cujus inclyta
Sunt data virûm monumenta curæ;
Teque adytis etiam sacris
Voluit reponi, quibus et ipse præsidet
Æternorum operum custos fidelis,
Quæstorque gazæ nobilioris
Quam cui præfuit Ion,
Clarus Erechtheides,
Opulenta dei per templa parentis,
Fulvosque tripodas, donaque Delphica,
Ion Actæâ genitus Creusâ.

ANTISTROPHE.

Ergo tu visere lucos
Musarum ibis amœnos;
Diamque Phœbi rursus ibis in domum
Oxoniâ quam valle colit,
Delo posthabitâ,
Bifidoque Parnassi jugo;
Ibis honestus,
Postquam egregiam tu quoque sortem
Nactus abis, dextri prece sollicitatus amici.
Illic legeris inter alta nomina
Authorum, Graiæ simul et Latinæ
Antiqua gentis lumina et verum decus.

EPODOS.

Vos tandem haud vacui mei labores,
Quicquid hoc sterile fudit ingenium,
Jam serò placidam sperare jubeo
Perfunctam invidiâ requiem, sedesque beatas
Quas bonus Hermes
Et tutela dabit solers Roüsî,
Quò neque lingua procax vulgi penetrabit, atque longè
Turba legentûm prava facesset;
At ultimi nepotes
Et cordatior ætas
Judicia rebus æquiora forsitan
Adhibebit integro sinu.
Tum, livore sepulto,
Si quid meremur sana posteritas sciet,
Roüsio favente.

IN SALMASII HUNDREDAM.

QUIS expedivit Salmasio suam *Hundredam*,
Picamque docuit verba nostra conari ?
Magister artis venter, et Jacobæi
Centum, exulantis viscera marsupii regis.
Quòd, si dolosi spes refulserit nummi,
Ipse, Antichristi qui modò primatum Papæ
Minatus uno est dissipare sufflatu,
Cantabit ultrò Cardinalitium melos.

IN SALMASIUM.

GAUDETE, scombri, et quicquid est piscium salo,
Qui frigidâ hieme incolitis algentes freta !
Vestrum misertus ille Salmasius Eques
Bonus amicire nuditatem cogitat ;
Chartæque largus apparat papyrinos
Vobis cucullos, præferentes Claudii
Insignia, nomenque et decus, Salmasii ;
Gestetis ut per omne cetarium forum
Equitis clientes, scriniis mungentium
Cubito virorum, et capsulis, gratissimos.

THE END.

PLYMOUTH:
WILLIAM BRENDON AND SON,
PRINTERS.

BOOK LOVERS' CLASSICS.

PRESS OPINIONS
On "*THE VICAR OF WAKEFIELD.*"

MANCHESTER GUARDIAN.—"A beautifully printed and wonderfully cheap facsimile."

GLOBE.—"A very attractive edition."

CHURCH TIMES.—"Beautifully printed, tastefully bound . . . . it would be difficult to conceive a more worthy representative of Goldsmith's immortal work."

On "*GULLIVER'S TRAVELS.*"

MANCHESTER GUARDIAN.—"A marvellously cheap and taking reprint."

TIMES.—"The book is handy in shape, and the print is excellent."

PALL MALL.—"A verbatim reprint . . . exceedingly well bound."

THE VICAR OF WAKEFIELD. *By* OLIVER GOLDSMITH, with careful reproductions of the whole of the Illustrations by WILLIAM MULREADY, R.A. A facsimile and verbatim reprint of the First Mulready Edition. 320 pages, large crown 8vo.

GULLIVER'S TRAVELS. *By* JONATHAN SWIFT, with reproductions of the original plates. A verbatim reprint of the First Edition. 320 pages. Uniform with the VICAR OF WAKEFIELD.

CRANFORD. *By* Mrs. GASKELL, WITH SIXTEEN FULL-PAGE ILLUSTRATIONS, specially drawn for this edition by T. H. ROBINSON, and separately printed on the finest-surfaced plate paper, and inserted in the volume. 320 pages. Uniform with the VICAR OF WAKEFIELD.

** *The above works are all re-set from new type, with title-pages in red and black, designed by* J. WALTER WEST, *and are printed on choice paper, and bound in two styles:*

  (*a*) Cloth extra, gilt lettered on back, gilt top, and gilt panel on front, *price* **2/6.**

  (*b*) Cloth extra, gilt lettered on back and front, gilt edges, and profusely decorated with gold on front and back, *price* **3/6.**

THE CHEAPEST BOOKS IN THE WORLD.

⁎ *The above works are all re-set from new type, with title-pages in red and black, and are printed on choice antique laid paper, and bound in two styles:*

(*a*) Cloth extra, gilt lettered on back, *price* **2/-**.

(*b*) Cloth extra, gilt lettered on back, gilt edges, and profusely decorated with gold on front and back, *price* **3/6**.

THE BURLEIGH LIBRARY.

Each work is re-set from new type.

Title-page designed by RICHARD MATHER, and printed
in red and black.

SIZE: *Extra Large Crown 8vo.*
PAPER: *White high-class Antique Laid.*
PRICE: 1*s.* 6*d. per vol.*
BINDING: *Scarlet cloth extra, gilt lettered,
cut or uncut.*

VOLUMES ALREADY PUBLISHED:

IVANHOE.	Sir Walter Scott.
JANE EYRE.	Charlotte Brontë.
THE CAXTONS.	Bulwer Lytton.
ERNEST MALTRAVERS.	Bulwer Lytton.
LAYS OF THE SCOTTISH CAVALIERS.	W. E. Aytoun.
VANITY FAIR.	W. M. Thackeray.
THE SCARLET LETTER.	N. Hawthorne.

NEW VOLUMES:

ALICE; OR, THE MYSTERIES.	Bulwer Lytton.
MARY BARTON.	Mrs. Gaskell.

The Cheapest Shakespeare ever issued.

THE MOST ACCURATE TEXT.

THE
COMPLETE WORKS
OF
WILLIAM SHAKESPEARE.
THE FALSTAFF EDITION.

Contents.

In this, the "FALSTAFF" EDITION of Shakespeare's works, the order in which the plays are presented is that of the first folio Edition of 1623, "Pericles," which was not included in that Edition, and the Poems, being added at the end of the volume. No new reading of the text is attempted; and only those variations from the text of the early Editions are included which have been accepted by the best Shaksperian critics. The task of the present editor has consisted solely in the choice between the readings of these critics where they disagree. For the most part the text of Delius has been followed.

In one large, handsome, and well-designed Volume.

SIZE:—Large Super Royal 8vo, 10¼ by 7¼ inches.

TYPE:—Re-set from NEW BOURGEOIS TYPE of the same fount as this line is printed from, and printed with large margins.

PAPER:—Choice Antique laid.

TITLE-PAGE designed by RICHARD MATHER, and printed in red and black.

BOUND in dark scarlet cloth of the best quality, with label in red and black.

1104 PAGES. PRICE **3/6.** OFFERING ABSOLUTELY UNIQUE VALUE.

PRESS AND OTHER OPINIONS

ON THE

FALSTAFF SHAKESPEARE.

(For Advertisement, see preceding page.)

Mr. GLADSTONE says of the "Falstaff Shakespeare," in a note dated November 13th, 1896:

" Accept my thanks for your courtesy in sending me your new and remarkable edition of Shakespeare, which, in itself, gives a startling proof of the great results that British enterprise is able to achieve at the most moderate prices.

" Yours very faithfully,

(Signed) "**W. E. GLADSTONE.**"

PRESS OPINIONS.

Newcastle Daily Chronicle.—". . . The cheapest book ever sold for money. A book as big as a family Bible. In all the populous world of books there is nothing like this impressive reprint."

Pall Mall Gazette.—". . . . A marvel of cheapness . . . good paper, clean-cut type, and stout binding."

Star.—"This remarkable work. There is nothing about it—paper, printing, binding, or arrangement—to suggest why the edition should be published at so low a figure."

Glasgow Herald.—". . . Wonderful value. . . . Will be found a blessing to the eyes when compared to cheap editions in smaller type."

Scotsman —". . . One wonders how such a 'bulk of wit and wisdom' as this Falstaff Edition can be put out at the price."

Sheffield Daily Telegraph.—"No more remarkable book has been published within our time."

Guardian.—"It is handsome, well printed, and everything that a single volume can be."

Methodist Recorder.—". . . The cheapest book ever issued. . . . Worthy of any man's bookshelves."

Methodist Times.—". . . The cheapest book in the world. It is literally the most marvellous three-and-sixpence worth we have ever seen."

Dundee Advertiser.—". . . A marvel of cheapness."

Bookseller.—" . . . Most astoundingly cheap. . . . Good clear type, thick toned paper, title-page in red and black, and tastefully bound."

Newsagent.—". . . The most marvellous three-and-sixpenny book ever issued."

Perthshire Advertiser.—"This is the best edition that has yet appeared—it is a marvel of cheapness. The type is beautiful and distinct."

Globe.—". . . Altogether desirable."

New Saturday.—". . . Amazingly cheap."

Gentlewoman.—"The price is simply absurd."

Christian Commonwealth.—". . . In every sense admirable."

Queen.—"About the most wonderful three-and-sixpence worth that was ever published."

British Weekly.—". . . I do not know that there has ever been anything like the Falstaff Shakespeare."

Liverpool Mercury.—". . . A marvel of excellence and cheapness combined."

Black and White.—". . . Worthy a place in any library."

Vanity Fair.—". . . Cheap, yet *exceedingly well done*. . . . It is altogether complete and adequate."

Press Opinions on " The Cheapest Books in the World " Series.

(Vide page 12.)

Times.—"Should be welcome to many readers."

Daily Telegraph.—"Astonishingly cheap."

Athenæum.—" A marvellous florin's worth."

Birmingham Daily Post.—"May stand unashamed on any library shelf. . . . It is the most wonderfully cheap book we ever saw."

National Observer.—"A marvellous two-shillings' worth."

Methodist Times.—"Splendid reprints . . . their magnificence fairly dazzles me . . . beautifully printed on excellent paper . . . they are the cheapest books in the world."

Of BLISS, SANDS, & CO.'S reprints in general, the '**PALL MALL GAZETTE**' says:—"They have annihilated the hitherto indissoluble alliance between cheap and nasty."

FICTION.

S. R. Crockett. LADS' LOVE. An Idyll of the Land of Heather. A Novel. By S. R. Crockett, Author of "Bog-Myrtle and Peat," etc. Illustrated by Warwick Goble. *Large Crown 8vo, cloth, gilt top, price 6s.*

S. R. Crockett. BOG-MYRTLE AND PEAT : Tales chiefly of Galloway, gathered from the years 1889 to 1895. By S. R. Crockett, Author of "The Stickit Minister," "The Raiders," etc. Third Edition, *Large Crown 8vo, cloth, gilt top, 6s.*

Walter Raymond. CHARITY CHANCE. A Novel. By Walter Raymond, Author of "Tryphena in Love," etc. With a Frontispiece by T. H. Robinson. *Large Crown 8vo, cloth, gilt top, price 6s.*

Oliphant Smeaton. OUR LADDIE. A Novel. By Oliphant Smeaton. Illustrated by Anthony Fox. *Large Crown 8vo, cloth, gilt top, price 6s.*

Frederic Carrel. THE ADVENTURES OF JOHN JOHNS. A Novel. By Frederic Carrel, Author of "The City." *Large Crown 8vo, cloth, gilt top, price 6s.*

Riccardo Stephens. MR. PETERS. A Novel. By Riccardo Stephens, Author of "The Cruciform Mark." *Large Crown 8vo, cloth, gilt top, price 6s.*

Arabella Kenealy. BELINDA'S BEAUX, and other Stories. By Arabella Kenealy, Author of "Dr. Janet of Harley Street," etc. *Large Crown 8vo, cloth, gilt top, price 6s.*

H. D. Lowry. A MAN OF MOODS. A Novel. By H. D. Lowry, Author of "Wreckers and Methodists," etc. *Large Crown 8vo, cloth, gilt top, price 6s.*

J. Ashby-Sterry. A TALE OF THE THAMES. A Novel. By J. Ashby-Sterry, Author of "A Naughty Girl," "The Lazy Minstrel," etc. etc. With Illustrations in verse by the Author, and fifteen Illustrations in black and white by W. Hatherell, R.I. *Large Crown 8vo, cloth, gilt top, price 6s.*

Emeric Hulme-Beaman. OZMAR THE MYSTIC. A Novel. By Emeric Hulme-Beaman. Illustrated. *Large Crown 8vo, cloth, gilt top, price 6s.*

Gabriel Setoun. ROBERT URQUHART. By Gabriel Setoun, Author of "Sunshine and Haar," and "Barncraig." Third Edition. *Large Crown 8vo, deckle edge, cloth, gilt top, 6s.*

L. T. Meade. STORIES FROM THE DIARY OF A DOCTOR. Second Series. By L. T. Meade and Clifford Halifax. *Large crown 8vo, cloth, 6s.*

Hon. Mrs. Henry Chetwynd and W. H. Wilkins. JOHN ELLICOMBE'S TEMPTATION. By the Hon. Mrs. Henry Chetwynd and W. H. Wilkins (part Author of "The Green Bay Tree"). *Crown 8vo, price 6s.*

Charles T. C. James. ON TURNHAM GREEN : being The Adventures of a Gentleman of the Road. *By* CHARLES T. C. JAMES, Author of "Miss Precocity," "Holy Wedlock," etc. Third Edition. *Crown 8vo, cloth,* 6s.

Mona Caird. THE DAUGHTERS OF DANAUS. *By* Mrs. MONA CAIRD. Third Edition. *Crown 8vo, cloth,* 6s.

May Crommelin. DUST BEFORE THE WIND. *By* MAY CROMMELIN. Second Edition. *Crown 8vo, cloth,* 6s.; *also in picture boards, price* 2s.

Helen P. Redden. M'CLELLAN OF M'CLELLAN. *By* HELEN P. REDDEN. *Crown 8vo, cloth,* 6s.

Charles Dixon. 1500 MILES AN HOUR. *By* CHARLES DIXON. A Book of Adventure for Boys. With Illustrations by CAPTAIN ARTHUR LAYARD, *late* R.E. *Crown 8vo, cloth, gilt edges, price* 5s.

E. W. Hornung. THE BOSS OF TAROOMBA. *By* E. W. HORNUNG, Author of "A Bride from the Bush," etc. etc. New and Cheaper Edition. *Cloth, price* 3s. 6d.; *also in picture boards, price* 2s.

Esmè Stuart. INSCRUTABLE. By ESMÈ STUART. *Crown 8vo, cloth,* 3s. 6d.; *also in picture boards, price* 2s.

C. Craigie Halkett. SCANDERBEG : A Romance of Conquest. *By* CONSTANCE CRAIGIE HALKETT. *Large Crown 8vo, cloth, price* 3s. 6d.

Clementina Black. AN AGITATOR : The Story of a Strike Leader. *By* CLEMENTINA BLACK. A Novel Dealing with Social Questions. *Crown 8vo, cloth,* 2s. 6d.

Charlotte Rosalys Jones. THE HYPNOTIC EXPERIMENT OF DR. REEVES, and other Stories. *By* CHARLOTTE ROSALYS JONES. *Fcap. 8vo, cloth,* 2s.

F. W. Maude. VICTIMS. *By* F. W. MAUDE. New and Cheaper Edition. *Crown 8vo, cloth,* 2s.

William Bullock-Barker. LAME DOGS : An Impressionist Study. *By* WILLIAM BULLOCK-BARKER. *Small Crown 8vo, cloth,* 1s. 6d.

Gertrude Atherton. HIS FORTUNATE GRACE. A Novel. *By* GERTRUDE ATHERTON. *Crown 8vo, paper covers,* 1s.

Eden Phillpotts. A DEAL WITH THE DEVIL. *By* EDEN PHILLPOTTS, Author of "In Sugar Cane Land," etc. *Crown 8vo, paper covers,* 1s.

V. Schallenberger. A VILLAGE DRAMA. *By* V. SCHALLENBERGER, Author of "Green Tea." *In paper covers, uniform with "A Deal with the Devil."*